NETWORKS AS CONNECTED CONTRACTS

Business networks consist of several independent businesses that enter into interrelated contracts, conferring on the parties many of the benefits of co-ordination achieved through vertical integration in a single firm, without creating a single integrated business such as a corporation or partnership. Retail franchises are one such example of a network, but the most common instance is a credit card transaction between a customer, retailer, and the issuer of the card. How should the law analyse this hybrid economic phenomenon? It is neither exactly a market relationship – because that overlooks the co-ordination, relational qualities and inter-dependence of the contracts – nor is it a type of business association or company, since it lacks a centralised co-ordinating authority that receives the residual profits.

This book is a translation of Gunther Teubner's classic work on networks, setting out his novel legal concept of 'connected contracts'. In it he explains how this concept addresses the problems posed by networks, such as the question whether the network as a whole can be held legally responsible for damage that it causes to third parties such as customers. A substantial introduction by Hugh Collins explains the analysis of networks in the context of German law and the systems theory from which Teubner approaches the topic. The introduction also explores how far the concept of connected contracts might assist in the common law world, including the UK and the USA, to address the same problems that arise in cases involving networks. As well as making a contribution to comparative law and legal theory, the book will be of interest to scholars interested in contract law, commercial law and the law of business associations.

International Studies in the Theory of Private Law: Vol 7

International Studies in the Theory of Private Law

This series of books edited by a distinguished international team of legal scholars aims to investigate the normative and theoretical foundations of the law governing relations between citizens. The context for such investigations of private law systems is set by important modern tendencies in systems of governance. The advent of the regulatory state marks the withdrawal of the state from direct control and management of social and economic activity, and the adoption instead of procedural regulation and co-regulatory strategies that promote the use of private law techniques of ordering and self-regulation in social and economic interactions between citizens. The tendency known as globalisation and the corresponding increases in cross-border trade produce the responses of transnational regulation of commerce and private governance regimes, and these new systems of governance challenge the hegemony of traditional national private law systems. Furthermore, these tendencies towards transnational governance regimes compel an interaction between different national legal traditions, with their differences in culture and philosophy as well as their differences based upon variations in market systems, which provokes questions not only about competing policy frameworks but also about the nature and adequacy of different kinds of legal reasoning.

The series encompasses a diverse range of theoretical approaches in the examination of these issues including approaches using socio-legal methods, economics, critical theory, systems theory, regulation theory, and moral and political theory. With the aim of stimulating an international discussion of these issues, volumes will be published in Germany, France, and the United Kingdom in one of the three languages.

Volumes published with Hart Publishing, Oxford

1. David Campbell, Hugh Collins und John Wightman (eds), *Implicit Dimensions of Contract: Discrete, Relational and Network Contracts* (2003).
2. Christian Joerges, Inger-Johanne Sand and Gunther Teubner (eds), *Transnational Governance and Constitutionalism* (2004).
3. Oren Perez, *Ecological Sensitivity and Global Legal Pluralism: Rethinking the Trade and Environment Debate* (2004).
4. Harm Schepel, *The Constitution of Private Governance* (2004).
5. Nili Cohen and Ewan McKendrick, *Comparative Remedies for Breach of Contract* (2005).

6. Marc Amstutz and Gunther Teubner (eds), *Networks: Legal Issues of Multilateral Co-operation* (2010).
7. Gunther Teubner (edited and with an Introduction by Hugh Collins), *Networks as Connected Contracts* (2011).
8. Christian Joerges and Josef Falke (eds) *Karl Polanyi, Globalisation and the Potential of Law in Transnational Markets* (2011).

Volumes published in German by Nomos Verlagsgesellschaft, Baden-Baden

1. Peer Zumbansen, *Ordnungsmuster im modern Wohlfahrtsstaat: Lernerfahrungen zwischen Staat, Gesellschaft und Vertrag* (2000).
2. Dan Wielsch, *Freiheit und Funktion: Zur Struktur- und Theoriegeschichte des Rechts der Wirtschaftsgesellschaft* (2001).
3. Marc Amstutz, *Evolutorisches Wirtschaftsrecht: Vorstudien zum Recht und seiner Methode in den Diskurskollisionen der Marktgesellschaft* (2001).
4. Christian Joerges and Gunther Teubner (eds), *Rechtsverfassungsrecht: Recht-Fertigungen zwischen Sozialtheorie und Privatrechtsdogmatik* (2003).
5. Gunther Teubner, *Netzwerk als Vertragsverbund: Virtuelle Unternehmen, Franchising, Just in Time in sozialwissenschaftlicher und juristischer Sicht* (2004).
6. Daniel Dédeyan, *Macht durch Zeichen: Rechtsprobleme der Kennzeichnung und Zertifikation* (2004)
7. Dietrich Claus Becker, *Von Namen und Nummern: Kollisionen unverträglicher Rechtsmassen im Internet* (2005).
8. Vagias Karavas, *Digitale Grundrechte: Elemente einer Verfassung des Informationsflusses im Internet* (2007).
9. Cordula Heldt, *Baukooperation und Franchising als multilaterale Sonderverbindung: Vertragsnetzwerke – Parallelschuldverhältnisse – Personengesellschaften* (2010).
10. Peter Korth, Dritthaftung von Ratingagenturen (2009).
11. Jan Lüsing, *Die Pflichten aus culpa in contrahendo und positiver Vertragsverletzung (§ 241 II BGB): Über den hybriden Charakter der Schutzpflichten und zur Selbstbindung ohne Vertrag* (2010).
12. Moritz Renner, *Zwingendes transnationales Recht: Elemente einer Wirtschaftsverfassung jenseits des Staates* (2010).

Networks as Connected Contracts

Gunther Teubner
(translated by Michelle Everson)

Edited with an Introduction by
Hugh Collins

·HART·
PUBLISHING

OXFORD AND PORTLAND, OREGON
2011

Published in the United Kingdom by Hart Publishing Ltd
16C Worcester Place, Oxford, OX1 2JW
Telephone: +44 (0)1865 517530
Fax: +44 (0)1865 510710
E-mail: mail@hartpub.co.uk
Website: http://www.hartpub.co.uk

Published in North America (US and Canada) by
Hart Publishing
c/o International Specialized Book Services
920 NE 58th Avenue, Suite 300
Portland, OR 97213–3786
USA
Tel: +1 503 287 3093 or toll-free: (1) 800 944 6190
Fax: +1 503 280 8832
E-mail: orders@isbs.com
Website: http://www.isbs.com

British Library Cataloguing in Publication Data

Data Available

ISBN: 978-1-84946-174-0

Typeset by Columns Design XML Ltd, Reading
Printed and bound in Great Britain by
Lightning Source UK Ltd

Acknowledgement

The translation and publication of this work were made possible by a grant from *The Modern Law Review* and financial support from Hart Publishing.

Contents

Introduction to Networks as Connected Contracts

HUGH COLLINS

DOES THE COMMON law need a new legal concept? The common law usually evolves gradually through refinements, differentiations, generalisations and reclassifications. Even bold innovations endeavour to trace their provenance to ancient texts. Whatever novel problem may confront the law, calls for the creation of new legal tools must therefore encounter scepticism, perhaps even hostility. A heavy burden of proof lies on those suggesting any radical changes in basic concepts of the legal system. Daunted but undeterred, the central thesis of this book claims that an innovative business phenomenon has recently emerged, the business network which necessitates the reorientation of legal reasoning around a new legal concept.

What is this novel market phenomenon that is called a business network? In its essentials, a contractual network consists of a number of independent firms that enter a pattern of interrelated contracts, which are designed to confer on the parties many of the benefits of co-ordination achieved through vertical integration in a single firm, without in fact ever creating a single integrated business entity such as a corporation or a partnership. This phenomenon is not vertical disintegration through which a large company outsources many of its activities to separate businesses, but its exact opposite: the creation of many of the features and dynamics of vertical integration through contracts, without ever relinquishing the independence of the businesses concerned. The problem that confronts the law is that neither the law of business associations (company law and partnerships) nor the law of contract fits this economic phenomenon of contractual networks comfortably. As a result the law fails to address adequately some of the conflicts and problems that are generated by networks.

The main text of this book comprises a translation of a work by Gunther Teubner published in German in 2004.[1] That work presents a synthesis and development of many of his earlier essays discussing

[1] G Teubner, *Netzwerk als Vertragsverbund: Virtuelle Unternehmen, Franchising, Just-in-Time in socialwissenschaftlicher und juristischer Sicht* (Baden-Baden, Nomos, 2004).

networks, which were published in both German and English.[2] This English text follows the German original closely, except that some further detail about German law is added in the footnotes to aid the understanding of readers unfamiliar with pertinent details of the law under discussion. This introduction serves to help the reader approaching this material for the first time. For English-speaking lawyers trained in the traditions of the common law, the main text presents at least three unfamiliar and challenging features.

The first of these features is, of course, the concept of contractual networks itself. Although the phenomenon of networks of independent businesses combining together in a loose coalition for productive activities has been recognised in sociological, economic and business studies for a couple of decades,[3] it has rarely surfaced in legal discussions in the common law world.[4] This absence of reference to contractual networks

[2] The key articles in English are: G Teubner, 'Unitas Multiplex: Corporate Governance in Group Enterprises' in D Sugarman and G Teubner (eds), *Regulating Corporate Groups in Europe* (Baden-Baden: Nomos, 1990) 67; G Teubner, 'Beyond Contract and Organisation? The External Liability of Franchise Systems in German Law' in C Joerges (ed), *Franchising and the Law: Theoretical and Comparative Approaches in Europe and the United States* (Baden-Baden, Nomos, 1991) 105; G Teubner, 'Piercing the Contractual Veil? The Social Responsibility of Contractual Networks' in T Wilhelmsson (ed), *Perspectives of Critical Contract Law* (Aldershot, Dartmouth Publishing, 1993) 211; G Teubner, 'The Many-Headed Hydra: Networks as Higher-Order Collective Actors' in J McCahery, S Picciotto and C Scott (eds), *Corporate Control and Accountability* (Oxford, Clarendon Press, 1993) 41; M Hutter and G Teubner, 'The Parasitic Role of Hybrids' (1993) 149/4 *Journal of Institutional and Theoretical Economics* 706; G Teubner, 'Hybrid Laws: Constitutionalising Private Governance Networks' in RA Kagan, M Krygier and K Winston (eds), *Legality and Community: On the Intellectual Legacy of Philip Selznick* (Berkeley, Berkeley Public Policy Press, 2002) 311; G Teubner, 'Expertise as Social Institution: Internalising Third Parties into the Contract' in D Campbell, H Collins and J Wightman (eds), *Implicit Dimensions of Contract: Discrete, Relational and Network Contracts* (Oxford, Hart Publishing, 2003) 333; G Teubner, '*Coincidentia Oppositorum*: Hybrid Networks Beyond Contract and Organisation' in M Amstutz and G Teubner (eds), *Networks: Legal Issues of Multilateral Co-operation* (Oxford, Hart Publishing, 2009) 3; G Teubner, '"And if I by Beelzebub Cast out Devils, …": An Essay on the Diabolics of Network Failure' (2009) 10 *German Law Journal* 115; G Teubner 'Sociological Jurisprudence – Impossible but Necessary: The Case of Contractual Networks' in R Gordon and M Horwitz (eds), *Law, Society and History* (Cambridge, Cambridge University Press, 2011 forthcoming).

[3] Eg EH Lorenz, 'Neither Friends nor Strangers: Informal Networks of Subcontracting in French Industry' in D Gambetta (ed), *Trust: Making and Breaking Co-operative Relations* (Oxford, Blackwell, 1988) 194; WW Powell, 'Neither Market nor Hierarchy: Network Forms of Organisation' (1990) 12 *Research in Organisational Behaviour* 295; G Thompson, J Frances, R Levacic and J Mitchell, *Markets, Hierarchies & Networks: The Coordination of Social Life* (London, Sage, 1991); A Grandori and G Soda, 'Inter-firm Networks: Antecedents, Mechanisms and Forms' (1995) 16(2) *Organization Studies* 183.

[4] There are a few exceptions where a contractual network concept is discussed in connection with the common law relating to inter-firm business relations, eg: JN Adams and R Brownsword, 'Privity and the Concept of a Network Contract' (1990) 10 *Legal Studies* 12; H Collins, 'Ascription of Legal Responsibility to Groups in Complex Patters of Economic Integration' (1990) 53 *MLR* 731; H Beale, 'Customers, Chains and Networks', in C Willett (ed), *Aspects of Fairness in Contract* (London, Blackstone, 1996) 137; D Campbell, H Collins and J Wightman (eds), *Implicit Dimensions of Contract: Discrete, Relational and Network*

also applies to positive German law found in the Civil Code, the Commercial Code, statutes, and judicial decisions, but in contrast to the situation in the common law, the concept of a network has been extensively discussed amongst legal scholars in Germany. This book provides a point of access to those debates among legal scholars and a springboard for equivalent investigations in the common law world.

The second challenging feature of this work concerns its method. The approach can be described loosely as 'sociological jurisprudence'. Its ambition is to combine an understanding of the phenomenon of networks drawn from a broad range of social sciences together with a sophisticated appreciation of how the legal system comprehends and regulates social and economic activity. The starting point of Teubner's version of sociological jurisprudence is known as 'systems theory', a general social theory of how societies are constituted and how they evolve, whose leading exponent was Niklas Luhmann.[5] The book does not devote much space to articulating systems theory, but rather gets on with the job of applying it to this particular context. In order to understand this discussion, it is unnecessary to delve deeply into the intricacies of systems theory, but this introduction tries to provide the reader with the necessary basic orientation in concepts and methods to facilitate a full appreciation of the text. Readers interested in investigating systems theory and its application to law in greater depth should consult the key texts in English: Niklas Luhmann, *Law as a Social System*,[6] and Gunther Teubner, *Law as an Autopoietic System*.[7]

The third challenging feature of this work for English readers is that it discusses German law. Not only will most readers be unfamiliar with the basic legal rules, but also the method of legal reasoning in a codified system like that of Germany differs in important respects from the method of legal reasoning practised in the common law world. The contrasts in method prove subtle, elusive, but pervasive. Perhaps the key difference that is pertinent to this particular work arises from the way in which statute, in the form of a Civil Code, is regarded as a source of fundamental principles in German law, so that vast edifices of judicial precedents and doctrinal elaborations can be built on brief, cryptic phrases in the Code. In contrast, in common law jurisdictions, statutes

Contracts (Oxford, Hart Publishing, 2003); R Brownsword, 'Network Contracts Revisited' in M Amstutz and G Teubner (eds), *Networks: Legal Issues of Multilateral Co-operation* (Oxford: Hart Publishing, 2009) 31; H Collins, 'The Weakest Link: Legal Implications of the Network Architecture of Supply Chains' in M Amstutz and G Teubner (eds), *Networks: Legal Issues of Multilateral Co-operation* (Oxford, Hart Publishing, 2009) 187.

5 N Luhmann, *Social Systems* (trans J Bednarz with D Baeker) (Stanford, CA, Stanford University Press, 1995).

6 (Oxford, Oxford University Press, 2004).

7 (Oxford, Blackwell, 1993).

rarely provide a source of principles, but merely apply like rules in an all-or-nothing manner to particular facts. In the common law, the main source of principles is found in judge-made law and judicial and doctrinal interpretations of precedents. This contrast in legal method, together with other significant differences in the substantive content of the law, need to be understood in order to appreciate the approach in this book.

As well as helping the reader to overcome these three challenges presented by the main text, the introduction also ventures an extensive comparison between, on the one hand, the German law on contractual networks and its elaboration through cases and doctrinal discussions, and, on the other hand, how similar problems are addressed in common law jurisdictions. For this comparative purpose, the similarities between common law jurisdictions count for more than the differences in details, so that useful examples are taken from a wide range of countries including the United Kingdom, the USA, Canada, Australia, New Zealand and South Africa. In particular, through this comparative exercise, the introduction seeks to test the potential applicability to the common law of Teubner's own, controversial, theory of how best to address networks in the legal system, which is his theory of 'connected contracts'.

1. BETWEEN MARKET AND ORGANISATION

Economic productive activity is co-ordinated, broadly speaking, either by market mechanisms or by business organisations. The legal categories of contracts and business associations or corporations represent these two paradigms. In the central case of a contractual relation, the parties agree an exchange of property or services through which they both expect to obtain a residual profit or improvement in welfare after their costs have been deducted. In a business association, such as a company or partnership, the residual profits produced by economic activity co-ordinated by administration or management accrue to the organisation itself. In practice, these paradigms intermingle in co-ordinated economic activity: business associations enter inter-organisational contracts; and to create a business association, it is necessary to enter into contracts, such as the employment of workers. Even so, the contrast between economic co-ordination by consensual exchange and economic co-ordination by management of agents (or employees) describes the two core patterns in the relations of economic production.

Intellectual disciplines in the social sciences interpret the contrast between market and organisation according to their own perspectives and lines of enquiry. Economics poses the central question of when is it more efficient to establish an organisation or firm as opposed to relying on market relationships. Theories of the firm identify such matters as economies of scale, intensification of the division of labour, the reduction of transaction costs, problems of governance or management of agents, and the elimination of failures in competitive markets as reasons for choosing to make a product through an organisation rather than buying it from other businesses in the marketplace. In the recent, most influential, approach of economics to theories of the firm, transaction cost economics, the choice between firm or market, or make and buy, is attributed largely to the transaction costs of using contracts to achieve the necessary co-ordination in order to manage adaptations to changing conditions.[8]

More sociologically oriented studies are interested in the conditions needed for the intense social co-ordination involved in productive activities. This approach points to the way that organisations may serve to create trust between individuals, so that they can establish with greater confidence long-term projects that require a complex combination of the accumulation of capital, research and development, investment in machinery, and effective marketing.[9] But all systems of economic co-ordination, whether through markets or business associations, are also understood to be embedded in broader social structures, such as the character of the state, the institutional organisations of capital and labour, the operations of financial markets, and the customs and symbolic values of a society.[10] Through such mechanisms the necessary trust can be established to enable a social order to develop sophisticated co-operative productive enterprises, to move from taking to trading, and from trading to partnership and organisation.

From a legal perspective, which is concerned mostly with allocations of risk and responsibility between the economic actors, especially when things go wrong and trust breaks down, there are two crucial distinguishing features of markets and organisations as the two main institutional patterns of economic co-ordination. In contracts, each party to the exchange is legally responsible for its own actions, but not those of the other party, and risk is normally allocated between the parties themselves by the terms of the contract or, in the absence of explicit contractual arrangements, by default rules supplied by the law. Within a business organisation, the corporate legal entity bears responsibility for the actions of its agents such as managers and employees and it assumes responsibility for all the risks of the enterprise, both internal and external

[8] O Williamson, 'The Economics of Governance' (2005) 95(2) *American Economic Review* (papers and proceedings) 1.

[9] Eg Gambetta, above n 3; F Fukuyama, 'Differing Disciplinary Perspectives on the Origins of Trust' (2001) 81(3) *Boston University Law Review* 479.

[10] M Granovetter, 'Economic Action and Social Structure: The Problem of Embeddedness' (1985) 91 *American Journal of Sociology* 481; J Rogers, Hollingsworth and R Boyer (eds), *Contemporary Capitalism: The Embeddedness of Institutions* (Cambridge, Cambridge University Press, 1997).

liabilities. In line with these allocations of risk and responsibility, in contractual relationships parties are expected to act exclusively in their own best interests, whereas members or agents of a business organisation owe a legal duty of loyalty to the purposes of the organisation, and the law reflects these expectations in the applicable norms. In short, in law, business organisations differ from contractual methods of co-ordination by the consolidation of risk in a single entity and by the duty of loyalty owed by all the participants to the aims of the organisation.

Hybrids and Relational Contracts

Not every method of economic co-ordination fits comfortably into the binary slots of market or organisation. In a commercial agency, for instance, where the agent markets the product of the principal in return for a commission on sales, we discover a hybrid arrangement: as in a contractual arrangement the agent acts in his own interests by maximising his commissions on sales, but at the same time the agent owes a duty of loyalty to the principal and the sales secured by the agent create contracts between the principal and customers, so that the principal bears the risk and responsibility for defects in the goods or services. Commercial agency is a hybrid, because for some purposes, such as payment by commission on sales, the relation between principal and agent is a market transaction fitting easily within the legal paradigm of contract, and for other purposes, such as the allocation of risk and a duty of loyalty, the business relation functions like an organisation. The law regulates hybrids by classifying them as contracts with special features, such as duties of loyalty and distinctive allocations of risk.[11]

Indeed, given the variety of types of economic co-ordination through market transactions, the simple paradigm of a contract of sale in which goods are purchased for a price only represents one end of a spectrum, with hybrid contracts that closely resemble business organisations at the other. In between the two ends of the spectrum of discrete or spot contracts and hybrids, many types of intermediate inter-organisational arrangements can be discovered. Long-term contracts often possess some hybrid qualities because of the economic interdependence of the parties and the need to adapt to changing circumstances. Such contracts are likely to contain governance mechanisms that permit the parties to manage changes in their arrangement and to resolve disputes whilst preserving the business relationship in pursuit of their long-term goals. In structure, such intermediate contractual relations are often analogous

[11] Eg European Directive 86/653 of 18 December 1986 on the co-ordination of the laws of the Member States relating to self-employed commercial agents.

to contracts of employment within the firm, where the employer holds the right to direct labour as a form of governance structure to ensure adaptation to changing conditions. In a long-term requirements contract, under which one party agrees to meet all the orders for supplies of a specified product or commodity from another party, the ordering of goods resembles the periodic instructions of managers to workers within the organisation to produce a quantity of a product, except that the order is directed to a separate business. Such a requirements contract may construct extremely close co-operation between the parties, so that the deliveries of goods must arrive 'just in time', in order to avoid the need to hold expensive inventories. To ensure zero defects and absence of disruption to production schedules, the purchaser often requires the supplier to adopt management processes of 'total quality management', so that, though remaining formally separate businesses, the purchaser effectively instructs the supplier on how the supplier's business must be managed. This kind of supply arrangement between two businesses, which is sometimes even called a 'supplier partnership', shares features of a business organisation as a result of the intensive co-operation achieved through governance mechanisms, yet it remains at bottom a contractual relation between independent businesses with opposing interests. On the spectrum of types of contracts that are used for economic co-operation, this kind of just-in-time requirements contract is towards the hybrid end.

Many other examples of contracts that construct some features of an organisation can be found. These features may include governance or management systems, the sharing of profits, information, technology, and a variety of other devices including shared computer systems to co-ordinate economic activity. For instance, a temporary agency worker agrees in return for payment by the agency to go to work for a client of the agency, performing a job as if he or she were an employee of the client, with duties to obey instructions and loyalty to the purposes of the client. In this example, the worker is subject to the hierarchical relations of an organisation, but is neither a member of the firm, because his or her contract is with the agency, nor is an employee of the agency, because the contract with the agency specifies that the worker is an independent contractor for whom the agency searches for work. In another example of a contract with hybrid qualities, a joint venture between two or more separate business organisations requires investment, research and development, and long-term commitments to co-operation. A joint venture resembles a partnership, because the parties contribute their resources and skills towards a common purpose, but there is no common business entity that receives the residual profits. Looser kinds of producer coalitions in a locality, where businesses constantly combine and recombine for different projects, are also likely to require similar levels of sharing information, expertise, and skills, though without a formal long-term partnership agreement.

These intermediate contracts, lying within the spectrum of contract types ranging from discrete contracts to hybrids, but toward the hybrid end, are frequently labelled 'relational contracts', though this terminology is not used in any precise and consistent way.[12] In such relational contracts, one will find some or all of the following features: governance mechanisms to manage adaptations, dispute resolution mechanisms, heightened duties of co-operation such as duties to perform in good faith, ongoing duties of disclosure of information, including technical and confidential knowledge, ongoing monitoring of performance including frequent meetings to assess progress, complex allocations of risk between the parties, and incentive systems that redistribute the residual profit between the parties. These phenomena reveal that, in addition to the split in forms of economic co-ordination between markets and firms, within markets we should expect to find a spectrum of business relations from the simple contract paradigm, a discrete contract to purchase a small item in a shop, through various types of intermediate or relational contracts, to hybrid contracts that possess many, but not all, of the features of integrated business organisations.

Multilateral Associations

The sharp contrast in paradigms between market and firm, between contract and corporation, also normally involves a distinction with regard to the number of parties to the legal relation and the co-ordinated activity. The contract paradigm involves two parties to the bilateral exchange. Apart from very simple partnerships between two persons, a business association usually involves numerous participants, such as employees, directors, and investors including banks and shareholders. At the hub of the business association resides the corporate entity, which enters into contracts with the various participants such as employees and directors. Indeed, a typical corporation can be described as a network of contracts in the sense that contractual spokes surround the hub of the

[12] Eg I Macneil, 'Contracts: Adjustment of Long-term Economic Relations under Classical, Neoclassical, and Relational Contract Law (1978) 72 *Northwestern Law Review* 854; IR Macneil, *The New Social Contract: An Inquiry into Modern Contractual Relations* (New Haven, Yale University Press, 1980); D Campbell, 'The Social Theory of Relational Contracts: Macneil as the Modern Proudhon' (1990) 18 *International Journal of the Sociology of Law* 75; D Campbell, 'Ian Macneil and the Relational Theory of Contract' in IR Macneil, *The Relational Theory of Contract: Selected Works of Ian Macneil* (London, Sweet & Maxwell, 2001) 3.

corporate entity,[13] though, for the reasons explained above, the ideas of enterprise risk and responsibility and duties of loyalty distinguish these contracts inside a business association from ordinary market transactions.

There are many types of economic co-ordination involving multiple parties that do not fit the model of a business association, though they share some analogous features. Like an organisation, some inter-organisational market transactions comprise a constellation of bilateral contracts, which are co-ordinated to serve a common purpose. Some of these constellations assume a similar 'hub and spokes' or star pattern to that of a business organisation. Others have the pattern of a chain of contracts, such as a supply chain for food from the farmer through wholesalers and distributors to the retailer. Still others combine a hub with lengthy spokes consisting of chains of contracts.

As an example of the model of hub and spokes, consider a business format franchise, such as those used commonly for fast-food restaurants and take-aways. The franchisor owns the intellectual property rights to the business format. Franchisees acquire a licence to use the format and its logos, together with know-how regarding the exploitation of the brand, in return for payment to the franchisor of a fee and a share of profits. Although this business could be organised within a business association or single organisation, with managers employed by the company operating the different outlets, instead it uses the franchise construct, which makes each operator or franchisee an independent business. Each of these independent franchisees enters into a contract with the franchisor on similar terms. This formal separation of businesses, linked only with the franchisor as the hub, distinguishes the model from a single business organisation. Each franchisee retains the residual profits, having paid costs and fees due to the franchisor. Nevertheless, it is clear that for the franchise to function as a profitable business, all the parties must behave to some extent as if the franchise was a single entity with a purpose, to which each party should be loyal. Harm caused to the brand name by one franchisee not only damages the franchisor, but also threatens the profits of the other franchisees. Failure by the franchisor to promote the brand name effectively through advertising reduces the profitability of all the participants. In many respects the franchise functions as if it were a single business organisation, but at the same time its structure remains one of market contracts, without a single legal entity that represents the organisations as a whole, and with residual profits being earned by both franchisor and franchisee.

[13] M Jensen and W Meckling, 'Theory of the Firm: Managerial Behavior, Agency Costs, and Capital Structure' (1976) 3 *Journal of Financial Economics* 305.

As an example of the model of a hub combined with spokes consisting of chains of contract, consider a construction project. An employer (or owner of the planned building) engages the services of a main contractor, an architect, and other professionals such as a project manager, and these parties work with numerous sub-contractors and sub-sub-contractors to complete the project. A construction project of this kind is constituted by numerous bilateral contracts, which allocate risk and responsibility. But there is necessarily close economic co-operation between the participants, often directed by architects and project managers through governance mechanisms that resemble closely the hierarchical organisation of a firm. Notice, however, that the bilateral contracts only achieve an incomplete coverage of the full extent of the project. Along the chains of contracts that constitute the spokes, the parties at either end of a chain will not be linked directly by a contract: the sub-sub-contractor doing the carpentry work will not have a bilateral contract with the main contractor or the owner of the building. Similarly, members of different spokes of the chains of contracts will not have direct contractual relations with each other: the carpenter will not have a contract with the architect or the project manager. Co-ordination between these parties is therefore not achieved solely by market transactions, but depends in part on administration or governance structures authorised ultimately by the employer, as in a business association.

In these examples, the productive activity is co-ordinated through bilateral contracts, not a single business association or firm. Nevertheless, the level of co-operation achieved between several participants resembles that of a business organisation. This co-operation between multiple parties is achieved through techniques that closely resemble those employed within a firm.

Networks

As a first approximation to an understanding of the concept of networks, they can be described as a combination of relational contracts close to the hybrid end of the spectrum together with co-operative elements found in multilateral associations linked through bilateral contracts. Though closely similar, these forms of economic co-ordination never quite become a business association or a single firm, because they lack a unifying business entity such as a corporation, a partnership, or some kind of 'special purpose vehicle'. As a result, no single entity exists through which to consolidate risk, to channel responsibility, and to which every participant owes its loyalty. Nevertheless, this many-headed hydra, this multilateral construction of bilateral contracts, which obliges the parties to co-operate intensively whilst remaining individually responsible for their actions, functions in many respects like a single business association.

To summarise the features of these networks that render them phenomena that resist simple classification as either market transactions or business organisations:

(1) Network features that resemble an organisation:
   (a) multi-party arrangements, though without a comprehensive network of bilateral contracts between all the parties;
   (b) intensive co-operation between the parties, which is often achieved by hierarchical administrative or governance systems authorised in bilateral contracts and facilitated by computerised sharing of information and monitoring;
   (c) economic interdependence and mutual learning between the businesses, even those not connected to each other through explicit bilateral contracts;
   (d) a long-term stable relationship between the parties;
   (e) economic efficiency and productive success requires intensive co-operation, flexible adaptation to changing conditions, and relies upon higher levels of trust than is characteristic of ordinary market transactions;
   (f) the independent businesses share a common purpose in the success of the overall co-ordinated activity, not just in maximising their own separate residual profits, because in the long term the value of each business depends on and will be maximised by the success of the production operation as a whole.

(2) Network features that resemble a market transaction:
   (a) each business has a separate legal identity, with no single joint identity;
   (b) residual profits go to each business involved, not to a separate corporate entity, so that interests diverge;
   (c) each business enjoys the autonomy to select its partners and contribution to the co-operative enterprise;
   (d) risks are allocated to individual parties, not to a collective entity.

From a legal perspective, however, there is no doubt that these forms of economic co-ordination between multiple parties must be understood as collections of bilateral contracts rather than business associations. In none of these examples have the parties created an independent legal entity, a juristic person, to which the parties owe duties of loyalty and which will be the repository of legal responsibility. Nevertheless, from an economic and sociological viewpoint, these forms of economic co-ordination share many features with organisations. The intense, long-term co-operation, using a variety of governance structures to ensure co-operation, produces a degree of economic interdependence that resembles the features of a single organisation. Functionally, these arrangements can be viewed as closely analogous to business associations or firms, even though from a traditional legal perspective they must be understood as falling within the broad category of contracts. These inter-organisational associations could be labelled in all sorts of ways: quasi-organisations or quasi-firms, virtual enterprises, multi-party hybrid business arrangements, or complex economic organisations.[14] This book chooses to call them networks.

The principal disadvantage of our adoption of the term 'networks' arises from its promiscuous use in a variety of contexts. The appeal of the word (in both German and English) no doubt derives from its association with telecommunications networks, not least the linkage with the most astounding and exciting modern invention of the Internet – the ultimate network of networks. Many scholars of the social sciences have adopted the term to describe other modern phenomena. In political science, especially in the study of international relations, any loose associations that seem to influence events outside the structures of formal organisations may be described as networks. In management science, a discipline particularly prone to catchy phrases, the term 'network' has been used to refer to all sorts of informal patterns of trading between businesses or the potential advantages of specialised industrial districts such as 'Silicon Valley' in California. In sociology, the terms 'network' and 'networking' focus on a person's contacts, demonstrating, amongst other things, the advantages, both material and more generally for well-being, of possessing an extensive address book. The fashion in some approaches to social theory is to think of ourselves as a network society.[15] In economics, there is an appreciation of 'network effects' which arise when a particular technology such as a telephone or pattern (such as the 'qwerty' keyboard on a typewriter) occupies a dominant and exclusionary position in the marketplace.[16] In such cases, a network effect exists when purchasers find a good more valuable as additional purchasers buy the same good or a good compatible with the network, as in the case where the value of a telephone increases as others join the telephone network or where possession of a credit card becomes more useful as the number of retailers who accept the card in payment increases. These broader usages,

[14] H Collins, 'Ascription of Legal Responsibility to Groups in Complex Patterns of Economic Interaction' (1990) 53 *MLR* 731.

[15] M Castells, *The Rise of the Network Society* (Oxford, Blackwell, 2000).

[16] MA Lemley and D McGowan, 'Legal Implications of Network Economic Effects' (1998) 86 *California Law Review* 479.

though suggestive in their detection of amorphous collective entities in what nevertheless remains resolutely a collection of autonomous independent actors, are not ultimately helpful for the task in hand.[17] This work is solely concerned with economic co-operation between businesses, and within that category with multilateral long-term business relationships constructed, at least in part, through contracts, though without an overarching formal business association that binds the parties together.

2. THE INADEQUACY OF LEGAL CONCEPTIONS OF NETWORKS

A central, controversial claim of this book is that ordinary legal conceptions of networks prove inadequate on occasion. Further, it is claimed that this adequacy can be discovered in a common source, which is the failure of the legal system to appreciate the distinctive properties of networks.

This difficulty is obscured because a legal system can understand and regulate networks by classifying them as comprising a number of bilateral contracts. Networks are not so different from other forms of economic co-ordination that they cannot be subsumed within the capacious framework of the general principles of the law of contract. In a supply chain, for instance, the legal analysis suggests that between each business in the chain, from the farmer through wholesalers and distributors to the retailer, there is a contract for the sale of goods in which property is transferred in return for a price. Whilst accurate as far as it goes with respect to the individual transactions, the problem that arises with this conventional understanding is that it cannot represent as part of the legal analysis the business relations between remote parties in the chain and how the relationships along the supply chain are managed. For instance, the retailer may operate a computerised inventory control, which it makes available to its regular suppliers and their suppliers upstream. With this technology, it becomes possible for the participants in the supply chain to deliver replenishment of stock, when and where it is needed, just in time before the shelves are emptied by customers of the retailer. In the absence of direct contractual arrangements between the retailer and all the participants in the supply chain, however, the legal analysis omits reference to the governance of these trading relations between remote parties achieved through computerised stock ordering, management processes, and other mechanisms for supply chain management.

[17] Below, Chapter 1, III.

In most instances, this absence of reference to the dimensions of the network that function outside formal market contracts may not prove significant. If the retailer runs short of a particular item, it can claim damages for breach of contract against its direct supplier, and the liability claims can run up the chain until they reach the point at which responsibility stops on the grounds of causation or excuse. The parties can also use contracts for the benefit of third parties in order to permit direct claims between remote actors, though private law in its doctrine of third party beneficiaries usually requires a contract explicitly to confer a precise benefit on the third party, such as the benefit of an annuity. But, it is contended, these familiar legal techniques of the private law of contract prove inadequate to address disputes that arise in connection with networks in three principal types of case.[18] We can illustrate briefly, in a preliminary manner, the character of these problems by reference to the example of a business format franchise in retailing, such as a fast food outlet.

Loyalty to the Network

The first type of problem arises in claims brought by either the franchisor or the franchisee that the conduct of the other party, though not a breach of the express terms of the agreement, undermines the common purpose of the inter-organisational contract. In other words, the claim amounts to an allegation of disloyalty to the purpose of the franchise. An example of such a claim might be an assertion of the failure of the franchisor to try sufficiently hard to develop more franchise outlets by tempting more franchisees to join the system. Existing franchisees will be damaged by such behaviour, because they rely on the visibility of the brand to increase their customers, and an increase in the number of franchisees is likely to produce economies of scale in advertising and purchasing of supplies.

In some jurisdictions, such a claim might be presented as a breach of an implied duty to perform the contract in good faith or a similar implied term. But invariably the main obstacle to advancing such claims is to

[18] Other legal issues may, of course, arise in connection with networks, such as the protection of the network against interference by third parties (eg the tort of interference with business by unlawful means) and breaches of unfair competition law by the network, which will be omitted from this introduction, though they are considered to some extent in the main text. See further: M Wolf, 'The Protection of Contractual Networks Against Interference by Third Parties', in M Amstutz and G Teubner (eds), *Networks: Legal Issues of Multilateral Co-operation* (Oxford, Hart Publishing, 2009) 225; H Collins, 'Ascription of Legal Responsibility to Groups in Complex Patters of Economic Integration' (1990) 53 *MLR* 731, 742–3; Lemley and McGowin, above n 16.

avoid the conclusion that self-interested action that does not breach the terms of the contract should not count as a breach of contract or implied duty such as good faith, but must be regarded as normal market behaviour designed to maximise residual profits. If the franchisor decides that the cost of finding additional franchisees exceeds the potential benefits to itself, it is rational behaviour not to seek further franchised outlets, even though this will reduce the profitability of the existing franchisees' operations and may diminish the profits of the franchise network, viewed as a single business entity. Certainly, it would be wrong to impute to the parties the intention to adopt any kind of fiduciary relationship, under which one or both parties puts the interests of the other before its own. The parties are not acting as agents for each other in the technical sense.

Nevertheless, the franchisor's conduct might be described as disloyal to the interests of the franchise operation as a whole. In such a case, the law could attribute meaning to a good faith requirement, not by requiring the franchisor to put the interests of franchisees before its own, but rather by placing the interests of the franchise operation as a whole before its own or on a par with its own interests. In other words, though the legal analysis still accepts that the franchise operation should be understood primarily as a collection of bilateral contracts, it might also accept that the network, like a business association, is owed a duty of loyalty by its participants, with the effect that self-interested contractual behaviour may amount to a breach of this duty of loyalty or good faith that is owed to other participants in the network.

Internal Non-contractual Liability in Networks

A second situation where the traditional legal analysis falls short concerns the business relations between those parties to the network who do not have direct bilateral contractual relations. In the example of business format franchises, this situation normally arises between the franchisees. Under the hub and spokes model of networks, though each franchisee is bound by contract to the franchisor, the franchisees lack direct contractual arrangements between themselves, though it is quite likely that they will meet regularly at events organised by the franchisor to address matters of general concern for the franchise operation. It is evident that one franchisee can damage the interests of all of the franchisees and the franchisor. If one franchised restaurant is closed temporarily by public health inspectors because it is infested with vermin, or a customer at a restaurant is injured by a negligently caused explosion from a pizza oven, the damage to the reputation of the brand is likely to affect adversely the profits of all the franchised restaurant outlets.

In such a case, the franchisee that is responsible for the damage to the reputation to the franchise may well be in breach of contract with the franchisor. The express terms of that bilateral contract will almost certainly require the franchisee to conform to a detailed operations manual, which will specify health and safety requirements applicable to the business format. Yet the franchisor may not be in a hurry to enforce its contractual rights for a number of reasons. Its contracts may secure fixed fees, so that it is personally unaffected by a downturn in profits of the franchisees. Alternatively, franchisees that take short-cuts on matters of health and safety may earn greater profits, so that under a profit-sharing arrangement the franchisor may have a strong economic incentive to turn a blind eye to occasional lapses in performance by the franchisees. Even if the franchisor does enforce its contractual rights and perhaps obtains damages from the delinquent franchisee, those damages may not include a sum representing the losses to the third party franchisees, since the franchisor may not be obligated to compensate the other franchisees for their losses caused by damage to the franchise brand name. And finally, even if the franchisor obtains a broad basis for compensation that includes a general sum representing damage to the goodwill of the franchise brand, it may prove difficult for the other franchisees to obtain their fair share of the compensation paid to the franchisor.

Technically, in this situation, franchisees are third parties to a contract between franchisor and the delinquent franchisee, who are seeking to recover compensation for pure economic loss. Whether brought in contract, by means of an exception to the doctrine of privity of contract, or in tort, such claims by third parties are normally blocked on the ground that they create potential indeterminate amounts of liability to an indeterminate number of plaintiffs. But is there a case for making an exception to the general rule against recovery for pure economic loss by third parties for these horizontal relations between the spokes in the franchise operation? Is there some kind of special relationship or assumption of responsibility, to use the terms favoured by the English courts in cases of claims for recovery of pure economic loss, which would justify the creation of a legal duty owed directly between the franchisees? Does the concept of a network help us to understand the character and limits of such an exception to the general ban on recovery for pure economic loss by third parties?

External Network Liability

The third type of problem where traditional legal analysis appears to fall short concerns the external liability of the franchise operation. Suppose that a customer in one of the restaurants claims to have suffered personal injury and psychological shock as a result of having realised that she had probably consumed half of a decomposed snail, the remainder of which she discovered in her hamburger. The customer can certainly claim compensation against the particular franchisee retailer from whom she purchased the food. But suppose that route to compensation is blocked by, for instance, the insolvency of the franchisee or the absence of adequate liability insurance held by that franchisee. Can the customer bring a claim for compensation for personal injury against the franchisor or the franchise operation as a whole?

If the restaurant were a managed outlet of a unified business association, the claim could be brought against the whole organisation, for each restaurant outlet would be acting as an agent for the entire enterprise. But vicarious liability in tort does not generally pierce through contracts between independent businesses, so that normally the franchisor will not be held responsible for the negligence of its franchisees towards their customers. Some specific exceptions to this general rule apply in some instances of other kinds of networks. For instance, product liability creates the possibility of direct actions imposing strict liability for the consumer up a supply chain against the manufacturer of a defective product that causes personal injury or damage to property.[19] Alternatively, if a franchisor maintains constant managerial supervision over its franchisees, it is possible that the law might infer that this degree of control brings with it vicarious legal responsibility. Again, specific statutory exceptions may apply to some other kinds of networks. For instance, the organiser of a package holiday is held directly responsible to the customer for defective services, even if it is another member of the network, such as the provider of the hotel, who was entirely responsible for the disappointing holiday.[20] But in general, particularly in the realm of services, the independence of the franchisees provides sufficient shelter for the franchisor against vicarious liability for a claim in tort.

Even if the customer were permitted to bring a direct action against the franchisor, it seems not entirely satisfactory that the franchisor should carry the entire burden of the liability. The other members of the network, the franchisees, all share the benefits of the enterprise, so should they not also bear some of the costs of external liability? In the absence of explicit contractual allocations of risk, however, the franchisor will not be able to pass on the costs of liability around the whole franchise operation.

[19] European Directive 85/374 of 25 July 1985 on the approximation of the laws, regulation and administrative provisions of the Member States concerning liability for defective products, implemented in the UK by Consumer Protection Act 1987.

[20] Package Travel, Package Holidays and Package Tours Regulations 1992, SI 1992/3288, Regulation 15, implementing European Directive 90/314 of 13 June 1990 on package travel, package holidays and package holidays, Article 5.

Should not a franchise operation, like a business association, shoulder this risk and distribute it across the whole enterprise, so that the costs of external liability will be internalised across the whole enterprise? In the absence of a single entity like a company that gathers together profits and losses, such a mechanism for internalising the costs throughout the whole organisation will be unavailable. It is here that the idea of a network may prove useful in the sense that it could provide a framework both for justifying a direct claim by a consumer against the franchisor and an explanation of why the costs of a successful claim should be shared throughout the operation onto the shoulders of franchisees as well as franchisors.

In this book, in Chapters 4, 5, and 6 Gunther Teubner provides a detailed analysis of the many dimensions of these three principal issues and how they have been and might be addressed in German law. Later in this introduction, we will explore how these problems have been addressed in common law jurisdictions. Before proceeding any further with the legal analysis, however, we need to consider some important methodological considerations that lie at the heart of this book.

3. SOCIOLOGICAL JURISPRUDENCE

'Network is not a legal concept'.[21] With this opening phrase, Gunther Teubner acknowledges the central problem to be addressed in this work. Even if it is accepted that the idea of a network aptly describes a distinctive type of multilateral inter-organisational business arrangement, it is neither helpful nor realistic simply to assert that the law should adopt a new legal concept of network or something like it. Legal categories and concepts do not automatically reflect social practices and norms. The process of constructing legal norms will be influenced by social practice, but the legal system also has a degree of autonomy or independence. Developing an adequate response of the legal system to networks poses instead a significant challenge to legal reasoning and scholarship.

The methodology employed in this work may be described as 'sociological jurisprudence'. Its general ambition is to combine a study of society with legal doctrinal reasoning. It rejects the idea that legal reasoning should proceed completely autonomously, developing rules on the basis of principles and standards that already have been posited within the law. Instead, the method of legal scholarship should include systematic observations of society by using those observations to inform

[21] RM Buxbaum, 'Is "Network" a Legal Concept?' (1993) 149 *Journal of Institutional and Theoretical Economics* 698, 704.

the development of legal rules. Law must evolve in ways that respond to and are compatible with its context or environment. At the same time, however, the legal scholar should recognise that the legal system has its own functional demands of coherence and integrity. In order to preserve the authority of the legal system and for it to remain faithful to its organising principles, such as treating like cases alike, legal rules must fit within an intelligible and justifiable normative scheme of principles. Sociological jurisprudence combines the close observation of social practices with a deep understanding of the integrity of legal doctrine with a view to proposing developments in the law that provide an appropriate response to the social field being regulated.

The method of sociological jurisprudence is, as Teubner confesses, an 'impossible necessity'.[22] It is not possible, he insists, for the law both to preserve its own integrity and at the same time to understand and regulate society entirely appropriately in ways that are fully sensitive to the variety of contexts. From his theoretical perspective of systems theory, different parts of society function according to their own communication systems, following their own schemes for understanding and regulation. Events and relationships can be understood and responded to within one of these communication systems, but each system is likely to produce its own understanding and response. Consider, for instance, the event of an employer dismissing a worker from her job. From the perspective of the employer, the decision can be understood from a perspective of business efficiency: the costs of employing the worker exceed the benefits to the business, so that in order to maximise profits, which is the principal aim of the business, the right thing to do is to dismiss the worker. From a legal perspective, however, questions arise about whether the dismissal was in breach of contract or contrary to statutory job protection laws. According to such rules, the dismissal might be wrongful, requiring its reversal or the payment of compensation. In this simple example, the communication system of management that understands and measures every event or action against a goal of maximising efficiency is opposed to the communication of the legal system that requires promises to be kept or demands compliance with job security regulations. The same event of a dismissal can therefore be understood as good (efficient) from a business perspective and bad (unlawful breach of contract) from a legal perspective. The terms 'good', 'bad', 'right', 'unlawful', 'efficient', 'appropriate', or 'inevitable' make sense within a particular communication system. But each

[22] G Teubner, '*Coincidentia oppositorum*: Hybrid Networks Beyond Contract and Organization', above n 2.

differentiated communication system has its own perspective, criteria of evaluation, and measures of appropriateness and success.

Given this functional differentiation between social subsystems, the ideal of sociological jurisprudence becomes impossible. In contrast to the teaching of legal economics, Teubner insists that the law cannot (and should not try to) arrange its rules and principles (its communication system) so that it mirrors exactly those of other social systems such as markets and business associations. In order to retain its legitimacy and integrity, the law must remain faithful to its own methods and doctrines. Nevertheless, the law has a job to do. As an embodiment of state power, it needs to create a defensible and justifiable mechanism for regulating society and resolving disputes. Whilst remaining faithful to its own principles, the law should try to understand the social relations it governs and to appreciate the different perspectives on events and relationships presented by different social subsystems. The law can be more or less sensitive to its environment, to the diversity of communication systems, without ever collapsing its reasoning into the analysis of a different social system.

A legal system can appreciate, for instance, that a breach of contract was efficient, without ever relinquishing hold of its principle that breach of contract is an illegal action. In such a case, where the logic of business clashes with the logic of the law, a court might seek a partial reconciliation between the systems by holding that the appropriate remedy in the event of an efficient breach of contract is not an order to perform the contract, such as reinstatement of the employee in the case of breach of a contract of employment, but rather compensatory damages payable to the employee, so that the economic benefits of breach are shared by the parties rather than appropriated only by one of them. More generally, Teubner analyses law as a governance system for reconciling the competing and colliding demands and norms of the variety of social systems though without every fully dissipating the contradictions.[23]

Networks present a major challenge for the method of sociological jurisprudence. Both sides of the equation of society and law look fraught with difficulty. Looking at networks as they are understood within economics, sociology and business studies generally, it becomes apparent that they are puzzling methods of economic co-operation, because they do not fit easily into established categories such as market and hierarchy. Equally, since 'network' is not an established legal concept and these inter-business arrangements do not fit easily into the existing legal

[23] G Teubner, '*Altera Pars Audiatur*: Law in the Collision of Discourses' in R Rawlings (ed), *Law, Society and Economy* (Oxford, Clarendon Press, 1997) 149.

categories of contract or business associations, the law experiences difficulty in understanding and regulating their practices. The best that one can do, Teubner argues convincingly, is to do the best one can to understand networks from the perspectives of a variety of social subsystems, such as economics and sociology, and then use these understandings to suggest ways in which the law might evolve within its own rules and logic to regulate networks more appropriately. This is the method of sociological jurisprudence, though, it must be confessed, it is more an ideal to which one should strive than a prescription for completion of a certain task.

4. THE DISTINCTIVE PROPERTIES OF NETWORKS

The method of sociological jurisprudence therefore requires a detailed examination of the distinctive properties of networks, taking into account the variety of perspectives drawn from economics, sociology, and business studies. The ultimate aim of these interdisciplinary studies is not to acquire a perfect empirical understanding of the social practice of networks, even assuming such an understanding were to be possible. It is rather to construct a legal concept, one which will enable the law to grasp the essential characteristics of networks as understood from these different perspectives. The legal construction is a normative project, to shape legal categories and principles that address adequately and successfully the task of regulating networks. The search for a legal concept goes beyond merely creating *ad hoc* some exceptional rules of liability, some particular statutory fixes for difficulties that emerge in the practice of networks. The ambitious goal is to create a basic legal concept composed of categories and norms that provide a coherent, principled basis for regulating all the foreseeable and unforeseen problems that arise in the form of economic co-ordination described as network. To construct such a legal concept requires a deep understanding of the essential features of networks, an understanding that requires familiarity with the variety of interdisciplinary perspectives. The search for those distinctive properties of networks, however, leads to a series of paradoxical conclusions.

One site where inter-organisational business networks may be discovered is in the science parks that have grown up around major universities. The network involves the university and its researchers who associate with local businesses, both large and small. Those businesses are also likely to be linked to each other informally in a variety of ways. These science parks combine organisations that have the purpose of pure scientific research with others that are driven primarily by the profit motive. For the purposes of fruitful innovation, clearly both of these elements are necessary. The network combines both the logics of doing fundamental research and engineering products that are marketable, even though they will often be in tension. It is possible, perhaps likely, that the network framework is superior to that of either a single organisation or arm's-length market relation in finding productive ways of combining these logics. How does a network do so? The answer seems to be that it never actually combines the logics, but rather leaves them in tension, subject to constant renegotiation, so that the pure researchers have to accommodate market considerations, and the venture capitalists have to create the space in their operations for scientific research and discovery. Networks help to manage the tensions, but never fix them into a settled form of economic co-ordination, so that fluid adaptation between the imperatives of 'do science' and 'make money' is always possible.

Networks of producers of similar products in industrial districts clearly remain independent businesses in competition with each other. Yet, co-operation between these businesses also assists their production and marketing. They may share financial risks, exchange personnel, form temporary ventures to bring together technical skills and innovative design. Marketing of products may be achieved through a co-operative website, sometimes known as a virtual enterprise. Again we find two logics in tension: compete with other businesses for staff, innovation, design, and market share, but co-operate with other businesses for staff, innovation, design, and market share. Act in one's own self-interest to maximise profits, but also trust others in the sense of preserving friendly co-operative relationships. Again it seems possible that a network is superior either to arm's-length market relations or a single business association in achieving the required innovation, quality, and adaptability to constantly shifting consumer markets. Members of the network are neither friends nor strangers,[24] but both at the same time.

As a third and final example of these paradoxical conclusions regarding the distinctive properties of networks, consider again the operation of a business format franchise. Why operate a successful chain of fast-food restaurants as a franchise rather than a single business? A single business, managed closely from the centre, should ensure better consistency in the brand and secure all the residual profits to the investors in the corporation. It is true that franchising may facilitate the acquisition of the capital necessary for rapid expansion, but given that the franchisor may often have to supply a large portion of the capital such as the purchase or lease of suitable premises, this advantage may often prove marginal. It is also true that a franchise operation externalises a substantial part of the risk of failure of particular restaurants onto franchisees, an arrangement

[24] Lorenz, above n 3.

which may also facilitate rapid expansion into unexplored and uncertain markets. Such advantages of franchises may be appealing to small businesses with limited access to capital, but it is striking that many large businesses such as petroleum companies and automobile manufacturers, which could easily acquire the necessary capital and bear the risks of occasional failure, also use the franchise system for marketing. Why, then, do franchises flourish in distribution and retailing?

At the core of the franchise relation between franchisor and franchisee there is another paradox. On the one hand, the franchisor insists that franchisees should do what it says: follow the detailed operational handbook, use the computerised account system, and obey all instructions loyally. On the other hand, the franchisor tells the franchisee to use its autonomous business judgment, innovate at the margins, expand market share with sales promotions, and take advantage of opportunities for good staff in the local labour market. Erich Schanze captures this tension elegantly with the idea of symbiotic contracts,[25] invoking by this metaphor, for example, the perilous relationship of the birds that feed from the teeth of crocodiles, an activity which incidentally cleans and preserves their sharp incisors. In a non-legal sense, there is a double agency relation in franchises: the franchisee acts as agent for the franchisor by complying with its instructions, but at the same time using its initiative to maximise its profits, like a commercial agent on sales by commission; at the same time, the franchisor acts like an agent of the franchisee, by promoting and expanding the franchise operation, learning from the operation about improvements and innovations, and spreading this knowledge back to franchisees, whilst, of course, at the same time ensuring that it maximises its own profits from the franchise operation. The economic logic on both sides tells the parties to act in their own best interests to secure the maximum share of the surplus, but also to work to the benefit of the other party at the same time. It is a double, cross-over principal and agent relationship. Here the paradox produced by the analysis of marketing and distribution networks such as franchises is the simultaneous logic for all the parties both to compete and to co-operate.

Yet this model of symbiotic contracts still does not quite capture all the perplexing features of networks. It omits those dimensions of the association that almost seem to create a collective entity, which is separate from its constituent parts. As well as each party having its own ends or

[25] E Schanze, 'Symbiotic Contracts: Exploring Long-Term Agency Structures Between Contract and Corporation' in C Joerges (ed), *Franchising and the Law: Theoretical and Comparative Approaches in Europe and the United States* (Baden-Baden, Nomos, 1991) 67; E Schanze, 'Symbiotic Arrangements' (1993) 149 *Journal of Institutional and Theoretical Economics* 691.

purposes, the franchise network as a whole has its own purpose or objective. Maximising the profits or benefits to the franchise is likely to benefit both parties to the transaction in most instances, but this outcome of a 'win-win' situation is not invariably true. The franchisor and a particular franchisee may construct a contractual arrangement that suits their interests, but which in the long term damages the reputation of the franchise network, to the detriment of other franchisees in particular, or to the disadvantage of parties who are outside the network. So the complete instruction within a franchise network amounts to the paradoxical demand to act in one's own interest, whilst also acting in the interest of the other party to the commercial contract, and at the same time act in the best interests of the franchise operation as a whole.

Examination of these examples with the aim of finding the essential characteristics of networks produces what seems to be an inevitable conclusion: the essential characteristic of networks is that they are founded on paradox.[26] In this context a paradox means that there is a simultaneous presence of contradictory, even mutually exclusive, elements or logics of behaviour. In the regrettable habit of German legal scholarship, Teubner relishes the expression of this conclusion in snappy Latin oxymorons: *unitas multiplex* (a single entity, which is a collection of independent parts), and *coincidentia oppositorum* (a united purpose, whilst comprised of parts with opposing purposes). A hallmark of networks is their combination of the imperatives of both co-operation and competition with their partner businesses. Perhaps this conclusion about the paradoxical quality of networks should not surprise us, because our starting point was the observation that networks function at the same time both like organisations and like market transactions. But even if the conclusion is not surprising, it is certainly perplexing, because we still must address the question of how the law should conceptualise the phenomenon of networks.

Western law, which prides itself on its rationality, consistency, and coherence, shuns paradox. Contradictions in legal doctrine are remorselessly removed by doctrinal engineers. The favoured technique of hoeing these weeds is to create doctrinal distinctions. The rules of public and private law, or of tort and contract law, for instance, do not contradict each other only because legal doctrine insists that they are separate categories with different fields of application, even though in practice, in social life, which is not organised by reference to these legal categories, these rival normative systems constantly compete with each other. The

[26] The paradoxical qualities of successful business organisations has been an important theme in management studies and organisational theory: eg RE Quinn and KS Cameron, *Paradox and Transformation: Toward a Theory of Change in Organization and Management* (Cambridge, MA, Ballinger Publishing, 1988).

law manages its own contradictions by the evolution of normative sub-systems such as contract and tort.[27]

Networks present a nice problem of a contradiction between normative subsystems. As they function, they behave in part like market transactions, suitable for the law of contract, and in part like business organisations, which might appropriately be regulated by the law of business associations. The contradictory logics at the heart of networks, which we identified above, seem to be replicated, perhaps unsurprisingly, in the contradictory responses of the competing legal subsystems of contract and corporate law.

In a sense, though, the discovery and acknowledgement of paradox at the heart of networks provides the key to the construction of an appropriate legal concept and normative framework. Somehow, despite the tendencies of the legal system to iron out contradictions and inconsistencies, the legal concept must conserve a potential to display both sides of the coin at once, both the market and the organisational qualities of networks. The first step of recognising a separate legal concept of a network, a distinctive legal entity between markets and organisations, a hybrid with special qualities, serves to diminish the apparent contradictions by isolating networks from other normative frameworks in the legal system. But it is also necessary to take a second step of constructing a legal concept of a network which preserves in its essential characteristics its paradoxical qualities which combine the competing economic logics of co-operation and competition.

5. THE CHALLENGE OF COMPARATIVE SOCIOLOGICAL JURISPRUDENCE

In pursuing this project of constructing an adequate legal concept of networks, Gunther Teubner can enjoy a lively conversation with other German legal scholars, who each propose their different legal constructs that might serve to regulate networks intelligently and constructively. His distinctive contribution derives from his commitment to engage fully in sociological jurisprudence within the analytical framework of systems theory. Other German scholars have participated in these interdisciplinary discussions of the most appropriate legal conceptualisation of networks, drawing on the management sciences, institutional and transaction cost economics, and sociological perspectives. This methodology requires intensive scrutiny of actual social practice and the dynamics and logic of social action. It brings the insights of sociology, business studies,

[27] H Collins, 'Legal Classifications as the Production of Knowledge Systems' in P Birks (ed), *The Classification of Obligations* (Oxford, Clarendon Press, 1997) 57.

and economics to bear on the assessment of the adequacy of proposed legal solutions to disputes that may arise within networks or with parties external to networks. Teubner differs from these approaches by his use of systems theory, which, in turn, enables him to countenance and even to celebrate, unlike other German legal scholars, the preservation of paradox and contradiction at the heart of his conceptualisation of networks. Whereas other German legal scholars feel compelled to construct a legal concept of networks that fits into a recognised compartment of legal doctrine, such as 'contracts with protective effects for a third party' and 'multilateral agency', Teubner is more willing to embrace the novelty of a paradoxical legal concept, which is simultaneously both a contract and an organisation.

Even so, Teubner, along with the other German legal scholars, must explain how their concepts of networks fit into the established legal categories. The proposals have to be located within the dense framework of the Articles of the German Civil Code and other national legislation and legal doctrine. Whereas socio-economic studies are not limited to or strongly affected by national idiosyncrasies in production regimes, the legal analysis is resolutely national in its orientation.

For the foreign observer, such as a lawyer trained in the common law, this national orientation of the legal analysis presents obvious problems. Not only are the intricacies of the debates between the German legal scholars about the appropriate legal conceptualisation of networks hard to follow, but also it is difficult to evaluate the plausibility of the proposed solutions in the sense of their fit and coherence within their national legal system. A solution that might make sense within the common law may be roundly rejected by German legal scholars, and vice versa.

Sometimes a difference in legal method creates a further obstacle to the creation of a shared multi-jurisdictional concept of a network. In codified systems of law, it is always important to tie legal analysis and conclusions to particular articles of positive law, though elaborate constructs can be created on slender foundations in the Code. The common law lacks this discipline of the need to find a root in a particular text, and the statutory texts themselves are not perceived generally as a source of principle that can be developed. Instead, novel legal concepts usually have to be presented as variations on already existing concepts and principles, a more refined differentiation of legal doctrine rather than a genuine novelty.

The most obvious source of divergences and communication problems between legal systems stems from differences in the substantive law. For instance, whereas a German legal scholar can manipulate such doctrines as good faith in contracts, contracts with protective effects for a third party, and '*culpa in contrahendo*' to solve the problems of risk and liability that may arise in network contracts, these handy tools are not readily available to the common lawyer. The existence of a duty to perform a contract in good faith, for instance, is much contested in most common law jurisdictions, whereas, in contrast, in German law it is accepted as a general principle, albeit one whose application to particular circumstances can prove controversial. It is true that, whilst not employing legal rules with the same words and concepts, it may be possible for lawyers to achieve a similar result in a particular case. What a German lawyer might describe as a breach of the requirement of good faith, an English lawyer might be able to characterise as a breach of an implied term in the contract based on the unexpressed intentions of the parties. Nevertheless, it is almost certainly too much to hope that one day we may find a set of legal concepts that provide adequate regulatory tools for networks for legal systems that differ significantly.

This obstacle to the discovery of a legal concept of a network suitable for a variety of legal systems has been obscured by the apparent similarities between national private law systems, all of which recognise the two basic categories of contract and corporation, as we might expect from co-evolutionary processes between law and the rise of a market capitalist economy. But the endeavour to try to construct a third model suitable for networks exposes the differences between the details of the national private law systems. A sophisticated doctrinal model that might seem plausible for networks in one legal system may make little sense within the doctrinal framework of another.

Consider, for instance, the problem of constructing a legal principle that expresses the idea that the parties to a network should be loyal to the aims of the network. The objective of this legal concept is to provide a method for rejecting the dominant private law norm that the parties to contracts should be permitted to act in a self-interested way and for constructing a standard that requires loyalty to the network without requiring the parties to put the interests of the network always ahead of their own, as would be the case in a formal business organisation such as a company. In pursuing such an endeavour, it is clearly helpful if the legal system already possesses a variety of legal concepts of loyalty, not simply a binary opposition between permitting self-interest and imposing a fiduciary duty to put the interests of the other foremost. If the legal system has a doctrine that requires good faith or fair dealing in the performance of contract, for instance, this doctrine could provide the stepping stone to the construction of a duty of loyalty towards the aims of the network as a whole. In the context of a network, performance in good faith could be understood as requiring performance that supports the aims of the network or at least does not subvert them for self-interested purposes. If the relevant legal system lacks the requirement in its rules that contracts should be performed in good faith, however, as in many jurisdictions of the common law, this stepping stone towards an adequate legal framework will be missing, thereby making the endeavour much harder, and perhaps impossible.

From a systems theory perspective, as we have observed already, sociological jurisprudence within a single legal system is, strictly speaking, impossible, because it requires undistorted communication between the normatively closed ('autopoietic') communication systems of sociology and law. Nevertheless we press forward with the endeavour, since the alternative of purely doctrinal exegesis seems unlikely to result in productive legal concepts in tune with the complexities of a market economy. The insertion of a comparative law dimension, such as finding a productive legal solution that makes sense both in the common law and in German law, makes the task even harder. The project of comparative sociological jurisprudence is doubly impossible, because it adds to the existing problem of finding adequate modes of communication between law and socio-economics the further problem of establishing communications (or transplants) between autonomous national legal systems.

Even so, it is certainly time to commence a consideration of that comparative law dimension of sociological jurisprudence in relation to networks. In Europe, the pressure is to find routes towards the harmonisation of commercial law in order to reduce obstacles to the creation of the internal market. If it is correct that networks represent a new paradigm in productive business organisation, the new European private law needs to be able to accommodate these arrangements and to regulate them in an intelligent way that promotes their economic success whilst safeguarding both participants and outsiders against such problems as opportunism, free-riding, and the irresponsible externalisation of risk.[28]

The Draft Common Frame of Reference (DCFR), a synthesis of European private law systems commissioned by the European Union, takes some hesitant steps in this direction.[29] It does not embrace a concept of a network (or for that matter hybrids and relational contracts). But it does adopt some principles that could provide suitable tools for regulating networks. Issues of loyalty are addressed to some extent by the use of a duty not to exercise contractual rights in a way that does not conform to a standard of good faith and fair dealing.[30] Similarly, the parties to a contract are obliged to co-operate with each other when and to the extent that this can reasonably be expected.[31] With regard to the problem of

[28] F Cafaggi, 'Contractual Networks and the Small Business Act: Towards European Principles?' (2008) 4(4) *European Review of Contract Law* 493.

[29] C Von Bar and E Clive (eds), *Principles, Definition and Model Rules of European Private Law: Draft Common Frame of Reference* (DCFR) (Oxford, Oxford University Press, 2010).

[30] DCFR III.-1:103.

[31] DCFR III.-1:104.

special relationships between parties not bound formally by contracts, the DCFR permits third parties to enforce benefits explicitly provided in contracts between others.[32] But this rule for protection of third parties would not be applicable simply on the ground of mutual reliance and interdependence, without the presence of an explicit contractual provision that confers a benefit intended to be legally enforceable. The general part of the DCFR does not address the issue of external liability of networks as an economic unit or quasi-organisation.

A more innovative aspect of the DCFR of relevance to networks is found in its distinctive treatment of the group of marketing arrangements described as commercial agencies, franchises, and distributorships. Although there are specific rules proposed for each of these types of economic co-ordination, the DCFR proposes some general rules for all three forms of marketing, which are for the most part default rules applicable in the absence of contrary agreement. There is a pre-contractual duty to supply sufficient information for the other party to decide on a reasonably informed basis whether or not to enter into a contract of this type.[33] As is likely to be appropriate in these relational contracts, there is a strengthened duty of co-operation, which requires the parties to collaborate actively and loyally and co-ordinate their respective efforts in order to achieve the objectives of the contract.[34] The comment makes clear that this duty of loyalty does not amount to a fiduciary duty. It does, however, require a principal, franchisor, or supplier to treat its agents, franchisees or distributors equally.[35]

The idea of a network appears explicitly in the DCFR in connection with a franchise. There is an implied obligation that the franchisor must make reasonable efforts to promote and maintain the reputation of the 'franchise network'.[36] The franchisee is placed under a mandatory obligation to take reasonable care not to harm the franchise network.[37] But these specific references to the economic value of the network do not appear to have led to proposals for obligations that might arise as between parties outside bilateral contracts, as between franchisees themselves, or with regard to external liability. There is no similar reference to networks in the context of distribution, though in the DCFR distribution is regarded as a broad category of types of inter-organisational relationship, which fills a spectrum between commercial

[32] DCFR II.-9:301.
[33] DCFR IV.E.-2:101.
[34] DCFR IV.E.-2:201.
[35] DCFR p 2291.
[36] DCFR IV.E.-4:207
[37] DCFR IV.E.-4:303.

agency and franchises, so it is not always appropriate to apply the network idea to a distribution agreement so defined.

6. THE CONCEPT OF CONNECTED CONTRACTS

What kind of legal regulation is needed for networks? The first point to make is that, given the hybrid and paradoxical character of networks, the traditional strategies of conceptualising all forms of business co-operation as either contract or business association will not prove satisfactory. To think of networks as just a new species of business association will place an institutional framework on them that will damage the inherent flexibility achieved in networks through their shifting patterns of bilateral contracts. Equally, simply to regard networks as constellations of unconnected bilateral contracts will fail to grasp the elements of organisation that function like the pull of gravity to bind the network together.

A second point about the appropriate style of legal regulation is that it should not be limited to the prohibition of the kinds of conduct that can be regarded as a betrayal of network contracts. In North America, for instance, legislation has been enacted at federal and state level, which addresses what have been perceived as abuses occurring in certain market sectors, such as petroleum distribution through outlets which are controlled and franchised by the major oil companies, or similar arrangements for distribution of new automobiles.[38] The legislation differs between these diverse jurisdictions, but there are some recurrent themes. The legislation may require full disclosure of material information prior to conclusion of a distributorship or franchise; it is likely to place a limit on peremptory termination of the contract by requiring cause for termination or reasonable notice (in order to protect sunk investments on the part of the franchisee or distributor); and it often imposes a more general duty of fair dealing and performance in good faith. The political popularity of this legislation feeds off a widespread perception of inequality of bargaining power and oppression by the big company, such as the oil producer or the automobile manufacturer, over the small business that operates a franchise or distributorship. No doubt, in some instances, the

[38] Eg US Federal Trade Commission Rule: Disclosure Requirements and Prohibitions Concerning Franchising and Business Opportunity Ventures 16 CFR pt 436; California Franchise Investment Law (1971); Delaware Franchise Security Law (1970); New Jersey Franchise Practices Act (1971); Ontario, Canada: Arthur Wishart Act (Franchise Disclosure) 2000; US Petroleum Marketing Practices Act 15 USC ss 2801–2806; US Automobile Dealers Day in Court Act 15 USC ss 1221–1225. For a detailed survey of US legislation: ABA Section of Antitrust Law, *The Franchise and Dealership Termination Handbook* (Chicago, American Bar Association, 2004).

big companies have used their market power to ride roughshod over their small franchisees in order to transfer economic risks wholly onto the weaker party.[39] But this image of the business relation can also prove misleading, as where the franchisee is itself a large company, with multiple outlets across many states, which specialises in distribution and marketing.[40] This kind of 'command and control' regulation is, in our view, unlikely to prove satisfactory on its own.

For a start, the legislation approaches the subject of networks from the narrow perspective of particular interest groups. In the North American legislation, for instance, the small business lobby has clearly been effective in presenting the case for the protection of the small independent franchisee against the oppression of the multi-national automobile and oil companies. This is an important perspective in the legal regulation of networks, because certainly large companies can take opportunistic advantage of the economic dependence of franchisees once they have made substantial investments. But the economic dependence exists on both sides: a franchisor's reputation can be seriously damaged by a negligent franchisee. Unlike the political process, legal doctrine needs to construct a more balanced perspective, which appreciates fully the economic logic of networks.

A further general problem encountered by business regulation of this kind is that it provokes avoidance, circumvention, or conduct designed to comply in the most minimal way. To some extent legislation can be designed to address these problems of effectiveness by prohibiting avoidance techniques, but that creates the further danger that the need to comply with the legislative straightjacket will undermine the efficiencies that may be obtained through inter-organisational networks.[41]

Furthermore, the demands placed on the parties by such legislation typically remain indeterminate and contested. What information is 'material', so that it must be disclosed? What amounts to a 'good cause' or 'reasonable notice' for termination? What kind of conduct breaches the duty to perform in good faith? To answer these kinds of question, the law needs to possess a firmer conceptualisation of the paradoxical qualities of networks. The law needs to support stable network expectations by articulating and reconciling through a systematic vision these paradoxical demands. The law also needs to understand the economic risks posed

[39] P Steinberg and G Lescatre, 'Beguiling Heresy: Regulating the Franchise Relationship (2004) 109 *Penn State Law Review* 105.

[40] WL Killion, 'The Modern Myth of the Vulnerable Franchisee: The Case for a More Balanced View of the Franchisor–Franchisee Relationship (2008–2009) 28 *Franchise Law Journal* 23.

[41] Teubner has elaborated on these problems of the 'regulatory trilemma': G Teubner, 'After Legal Instrumentalism? Strategic Models of Post-regulatory Law' in G Teubner (ed), *Dilemmas of Law in the Welfare State* (New York/Berlin, Walter de Gruyter, 1988) 298, 309.

by networks, both internal and external, and how those risks can be managed without subverting the functional efficiency of networks.

A major part of Teubner's endeavour in this book is to provide the kind of conceptualisation of networks that can provide the foundations for the necessary and appropriate regulation of economic risks presented by networks. He argues that it may be possible to use section 358 of the German Civil Code (BGB) as the legal basis or, more precisely, the original legal concept on which to construct a legal model that more adequately handles networks. We should therefore examine these German legal provisions and the kernel of the idea that they present. This examination also serves the purpose of the further elucidation of the concept of networks. A subsequent comparison with the analogous rules in UK law, however, illustrates the principal obstacle faced by comparative sociological jurisprudence, which is that national legal systems differ substantially, with the effect that concepts developed in one legal system cannot easily be transplanted into another. We should also note a typical contrast in method between codified systems and the common law: whereas Teubner is compelled by German legal method to find an article of the Civil Code to which he can attach a legal conceptualisation of networks, in the common law, in the absence of a detailed statutory framework, lawyers must rely on general principles of private law.

Section 358 BGB

Section 358 BGB introduces the idea of connected or linked contracts. The central idea is that two contracts, which the law normally analyses as entirely distinct, in fact will be regarded as interdependent for certain purposes. Section 358(3) explains that the idea of connected contracts can include multi-party relations between a supplier, a consumer, and a creditor financing the consumer's purchase:

> (3) A contract for the supply of goods or for the provision of some other performance and a consumer loan contract are linked, if the loan fully or partially serves to finance the other contract and both contracts constitute an economic unit. An economic unit is to be assumed in particular if the entrepreneur himself finances the consideration of the consumer or, in the case of financing by a third party, if the lender in preparation for or for entering into the consumer loan contract uses the services of the entrepreneur.[42]

[42] Translations of the German civil code benefit considerably from, but do not always follow exactly, the translation provided by the Federal Ministry of Justice in co-operation with juris GmbH, Saarbrucken, available at http://www.gesetze-im-internet.de/englisch_bgb/.

In a purchase by a consumer using a credit card, the potential interdependent contracts identified by section 358 are, first, the contract of sale between the retailer and the consumer and, second, the credit card arrangement between the consumer and the bank lender.

This provision is undoubtedly attractive to advocates for the legal recognition of a concept of networks. Notice in particular that the subsection creates the idea of an 'economic unit', which is distinct from the individual contracts involved, but somehow embraces them all. An economic unit is formed where the lender or creditor, such as a bank, uses the services of the retailer or entrepreneur in order to create the credit arrangement. For the purchase of a car, for instance, a common arrangement is that the lender uses the services of the retailer of the car to establish the loan to the consumer for the purpose of purchasing the car.

Where there are connected contracts under section 358, if a consumer has a statutory right to revoke or withdraw from the transaction with the retailer, the consumer is also deemed to be able to cancel the credit arrangement. Such a right to withdraw or revoke a contract applies, for instance, to consumer purchases made through distance selling, such as through the Internet. Thus, under section 358(1), if the consumer exercises a statutory right to cancel the purchase of goods, the loan from a lender used to acquire the goods is also cancelled automatically, with the effect that the consumer is deemed not to have borrowed money at all. The interdependent contracts stand or fall together: if the consumer exercises the statutory right to cancel the contract to purchase goods or services, the connected contract of loan from the lender is also automatically cancelled as well. Normally, under the general principles of private law, the rescission of one contract should not affect the validity of another in the absence of a specific term making the existence of one conditional on the existence of the other. But section 358 recognises the functional interdependence of the contracts by treating the existence of the contracts in some respects as mutually supportive.

The implications of section 358 can be illustrated by a case considered by the European Court of Justice, which had to assess the compatibility of earlier German legislation on connected contracts with the European consumer protection Directives that provide for a consumer's right to revoke a contract under certain conditions. In *Schulte v Deutsche Bausparkasse Badenia AG*,[43] the consumers had entered into a 'buy to let' investment scheme. Under the scheme, the consumers purchased a renovated flat from a builder. The property was to be occupied by third parties and, for tax reasons, the purchase needed to be financed entirely

[43] C–350/03, [2005] ECR I–9215. To the same effect: C–229/04, *Crailsheimer Volksbank eG v Conrads* [2005] ECR I–9273.

by a loan from a bank. Under the scheme, the rents from the entire apartment building would be pooled, and then the income would be distributed by the bank to meet the interest repayments on the loans. The loan was secured on the property, but also the consumers agreed to personal liability and a charge on all their assets. An intermediary company, specialising in property and financial services, handled the marketing of this scheme to consumers. The marketing method involved a representative of the intermediary contacting consumers at home, and visiting them on several occasions to explain the tax advantages of the scheme. The loan and charges were signed in their home. In none of this documentation was there any mention of the consumer's right to cancel the contract. The risks of such transactions include both an overvaluation of the apartment and the chance that rental receipts will be less than anticipated. The consumers failed to meet their monthly repayment obligations under the loan, presumably because the rental income proved inadequate, so the bank terminated the agreement, demanded immediate repayment of the loan, and then sought to enforce the charge over the property. Ten years after the original transaction, the consumers purported to cancel the secured credit contract on the ground that it had been a doorstep-selling situation. This cancellation was permitted, because in *Heininger*[44] the Court had earlier decided that when a consumer had not received any notice of the right to cancel the contract, there would be no time limit on the exercise of the right. The problem now facing the consumers was that, having cancelled the credit agreement, the bank could invoke an entitlement under German law to repayment of the loan in full. The European Directive provides explicitly that the consequences of cancellation of a contract are to be determined by national law. The consumers were unable to revoke the purchase agreement for the flat, because the right of cancellation does not apply to the purchase of immovable property. What the consumers sought was to extricate themselves from the whole series of transactions, because merely cancelling the secured credit agreement still left them with ownership of the apartment, which was not worth enough to pay off the loan, and liable immediately to the bank for the full repayment of the outstanding loan and interest. Apparently, under German law, the consumers would have been better off if they had not cancelled the credit agreement, because they would then have had the time to pay off the loan under that agreement. The German court referred the case to the European Court of Justice, asking whether this outcome was consistent with the requirements of the Directive.

[44] C–481/99 *Heininger v Bayerische Hypo- und Vereinsbank AG* [2001] ECR I–9945.

The European Court of Justice held that in the normal case, where the bank or its intermediary had notified the consumers of their right to cancel within seven days, and that right had been invoked, it would be appropriate for national law to require the consumers to repay the loan and rescind any sale agreement. It was common ground that if that had happened in this case, the whole network of contracts, including the purchase of property, would have been cancelled. But since notice of the right to cancel had not been given in this case, the aim of consumer protection by providing an effective right of revocation of doorstep transactions would be defeated by the national law's requirements. According to the Court, the Directive requires national law in such a case to protect consumers who have been unable to avoid exposure to the risks inherent in such investments by adopting suitable measures to save them from bearing the consequences of the materialisation of such risks. In effect, the Court is telling the national court that, to implement the Directive correctly, it must permit the consumer to be able to unravel all the transactions, including the purchase of the property, so that the parties are put back into the position as it was before the transactions took place. This case provides an example of connected contracts. The credit agreement and the purchase of the flat, though technically completely separate contracts, are linked into an 'economic unit'. The consumer's right to cancel one of the contracts will not be effective unless both can be cancelled.

Although this idea of connected contracts in the German Civil Code is directed towards the particular problem of consumers' withdrawal from contracts entered into using a credit agreement with the retailer or a third party, the method of legal reasoning in codified legal systems permits legal scholars to argue that the core idea of connected contracts might be generalised as a principle. As a principle, it could be applied to networks of independent businesses. The way in which the provision on connected contracts both understands that the contracts are simultaneously separate but interdependent, both market transactions and at the same time also part of a loose kind of business association or 'economic unit', certainly captures one of the central paradoxical features of networks.

Cancellation of Connected Contracts under English Law

The directly comparable law in the United Kingdom, however, does not embrace the identical idea of connected contracts becoming an economic unit. English law is organised in a different way, and expressed in detailed legislation and regulations. The legislation on distance selling[45] and doorstep sales[46] spells out in detail the consequences of cancellation of contracts by consumers. For instance, Regulation 15 of the Consumer Protection (Distance Selling) Regulations 2000 states that the notice of cancellation shall also have the effect of cancelling any related credit agreement. The same rule applies to doorstep sales.[47] A related credit agreement is defined as an agreement under which credit for a fixed amount which fully or partly covers the price is granted by the supplier or by another person under an arrangement with the supplier. The Regulation also provides that any security provided under the credit agreement shall be treated as never having had effect and any property given as security to the creditor must be returned to the consumer immediately. When the right to cancel has been exercised, the supplier or retailer becomes under an obligation to inform and repay the creditor.[48] Unlike the German law, there is no automatic invalidation of the credit agreement between consumer and creditor bank; on the contrary, that agreement remains applicable and the consumer is liable for interest on the loan until the loan and interest has been repaid. German law may be based upon a logic of trilateral synallagmatic contracts, under which, if one of the performance obligations is invalid or has not accrued in the first place, then simultaneously, following the Latin tag *do ut des ut det*, the same invalidity or unenforceability applies to the remaining entwined bilateral contractual relationships.[49] In function, however, these UK Regulations achieve pragmatically the same effect as the German law in relation to the cancellation of connected contracts, but characteristically the UK rules do not create the concept of the economic unit of the network of contracts, but merely require the credit agreement to be related and then articulate the consequences of cancellation for each of the bilateral contracts in the triangular business relationship.

Entry into a credit card agreement is itself a type of contract from which a consumer can withdraw during a cooling-off period, provided the contract is entered into away from the business premises of the card issuer.[50] Section 69 of the Consumer Credit Act 1974 provides that cancellation of the credit card agreement operates to cancel any linked transaction. Following cancellation of the credit card agreement, express

[45] Consumer Protection (Distance Selling) Regulations 2000, SI 2000/2334.

[46] Cancellation of Contracts made in a Consumer's Home or Place of Work etc Regulations 2008, SI 2008/1816.

[47] *Ibid*, Regulation 11.

[48] *Ibid*, and Distance Selling Regulations 2000/2334, Regulation 14.

[49] PW Heerman, 'Multilateral Synallagmas in the Law of Connected Contracts', in M Amstutz and G Teubner (eds), *Networks: Legal Issues of Multilateral Co-operation* (Oxford, Hart Publishing, 2009) 103, 106.

[50] Consumer Credit Act 1974, s 67 *et seq*.

legal duties are placed on the parties to refund any payments to the consumer and for the consumer to permit the supplier to retrieve the goods. This provision is perhaps the closest analogy to that found in German law, with its use of a device of automatic cancellation, but it does so without reference to any kind of network idea.

Connected Lender Liability under English Law

Although the UK rules on cancellation of consumer contracts do not replicate the German approach in its reference to an economic unit, in a closely related part of the law it does reveal closer analogies to the idea of connected contracts. Section 75(1) of the Consumer Credit Act 1974 creates an analogous exception to the normal principles of private law to that described in the German doctrine of connected contracts. It makes a creditor under a debtor-creditor-supplier agreement jointly and severally liable with the supplier in respect of any misrepresentation or breach of contract by the supplier in relation to a transaction financed by the agreement. In order to include credit card transactions, a debtor-creditor-supplier agreement is defined in section 12 to include an unrestricted-use credit agreement which is made by the creditor under pre-existing arrangements between himself and a person (the 'supplier') other than the debtor in the knowledge that the credit is to be used to finance a transaction between the debtor and the supplier. The scope is limited to transactions for any single item to which the supplier has attached a cash price that exceeds £100 and is less than £30,000. In this slightly cumbersome manner, the law establishes connected lender liability for consumer purchases of expensive items or services where payment is made by a loan or a credit card. In a sale of goods, for instance, where the retailer has misrepresented a material feature of the goods or where the goods fall below the mandatory standard of satisfactory quality, the consumer may not only claim a remedy against the retailer, but also the issuer of the credit card or lender. The creditor is entitled to seek an indemnity against the supplier for any loss incurred in satisfying this connected liability, including reasonable costs incurred in defending legal proceedings. This right to an indemnity would probably arise on general principles of private law, but in order to avoid any doubt it is also expressly stated in section 75(2).

Although there are some analogies between this scheme for awarding a consumer a right of redress against the lender as well as the retailer and the German doctrine of connected contracts, significant differences remain. The German linkage between two legally separate but functionally interdependent contracts is not restricted to a consumer's statutory right to withdraw from a contract, but is extended by article 359 of the civil code to include the application of defences available to the consumer against the retailer also by way of defences against the lender. Nevertheless, this extension of defences may not go as far as the ability of the consumer under English law to assert a broad range of legal rights against the creditor. One consumer right that cannot be asserted against the creditor bank in English law, however, is the right to withdraw from the contract during the cooling off period, since this right of revocation is a special statutory right, based upon EU directives, and does not fit into the categories of 'misrepresentation' or 'breach of contract'. More generally, unlike German law, there is no suggestion in the UK legislation that these functionally linked, but separate contracts should be regarded as creating an economic entity. Nevertheless, in order to support the goal of consumer protection, judicial interpretations of section 75 do implicitly recognise the unity of the triangular relation between retailer, creditor and consumer.

In *Office of Fair Trading v Lloyds TSB Bank plc and others*,[51] the relevant regulatory agency sought to establish two points regarding the applicability of section 75. The first question was whether the right applied when the consumer purchased goods abroad: it would obviously be more convenient for consumers to claim compensation for defective goods against a local bank in the consumer's home state than to seek redress against a foreign trader in that trader's jurisdiction. The banks who issue credit cards resisted liability on the ground that UK legislation does not normally have extra-territorial effect. But the House of Lords held the banks liable under section 75 even for foreign purchases by consumers. Lord Hope explained that the Act's policy of consumer protection

> applies to debtors and creditors within the territorial reach of the Act generally. Transactions of that kind are to the commercial advantage of the supplier and the creditor. The creditor is in a better position than the debtor, in a question with a foreign supplier, to obtain redress. It is not to be assumed that the creditor will always get his money back. He is in a better position, if redress is not readily obtainable, to spread the cost. He is in a better position to argue for sanctions against a supplier who is not reliable. For his part, the debtor is entitled to assume that he can trust suppliers who are authorised to accept his credit card.[52]

These remarks demonstrate an awareness of the functional integration of the credit card transaction with the sale. Lord Hope makes the further suggestive point about the functional integration of the tripartite

[51] [2007] UKHL 48, [2008] 1 AC 316.
[52] *Ibid*, para 13.

arrangement that the creditor has authorised the retailer to accept payments by card, with the implied representation by the creditor towards consumers that such merchants have a certain degree of trustworthiness.

The second contentious issue before the court concerned the application of section 75 to more elaborate networks. Since the enactment of the legislation, business practice had altered. Lord Mance describes the new business arrangements in terms of networks:

> Large-scale consolidation has led to card issuers becoming members of one of the two main international credit card networks, VISA and MasterCard. Under the rules of these networks, certain card issuers are authorised to act as 'merchant acquirers', in practice only within their home jurisdictions. They contract with suppliers ('merchants') to process all such suppliers' supply transactions made with cards of the relevant network, by paying to such suppliers the price involved, less a 'Merchant Service Charge'. Suppliers do not become members of the network, but contract with merchant acquirers to honour the cards of the network (ie to accept them in payment of supplies). Where the merchant acquirer is itself the issuer of the card used in a particular transaction, the transaction is tripartite and the merchant acquirer locks directly to its card holder (debtor) for reimbursement of the price. But in the more common (and in the case of a foreign transaction inevitable) case of use of a card issued by a card issuer other than the merchant acquirer who acquired the particular supplier, the network operates as a clearing system, through which the merchant acquirer is reimbursed by the card issuer, less an 'Interchange fee'. This is a fee less than the Merchant Service Charge, so that both the merchant acquirer and the card issuer receive a commission on the transaction.[53]

Under this four-party network, therefore, the supplier of the goods to the consumer will not be in a contractual relationship with the issuer of the card, but rather with a domestic merchant acquirer (in practice normally a local bank), which itself has a contract with the credit card network, and through that, to the issuer of the card. In this situation, the banks argued that section 75(1) could not apply to this four-party network, because there were no 'arrangements', pre-existing or in contemplation, between the card issuer and the retailer, as required by s12(b) of the 1974 Act. The House of Lords rejected that contention, insisting that the word 'arrangements' was broad enough to include the credit card network that provided indirect links between the retailer and the card issuer. The policy argument in favour of this result was that it preserved the consumer-protection aim of section 75 in the case of the proportion of transactions (about 10 per cent) where credit cards issued by merchant acquirers in the United Kingdom were used abroad. Members of the

[53] *Ibid*, para 23.

credit card network could ensure that their internal contractual arrangements provided a system of indemnities for card issuers.

Conclusion

From this brief comparison, it is evident that English law lacks, either in common law principle or in detailed regulation, any concept that is directly comparable to the idea of the economic unit of connected contracts in German law. Instead, the English legislation analyses the problem from the perspective of a series of bilateral contracts, and, though recognising the interdependence of the transactions, regulates the consequences of this interdependence for each separate bilateral contractual relationship. In particular, unlike the German notion of the triangular credit arrangement crashing down like a pile of cards on cancellation of the consumer's contract of sale because it forms an economic entity, English law in fact preserves the credit contract unless and until the credit has been repaid.

In return, however, the consumer is granted a direct claim against the lender of financial credit for defects and non-conformity of the goods or service. This connected lender liability, without stating the idea expressly at any point, seems to embrace the German idea of an economic unit by attributing responsibility for the quality of the goods and services jointly to the two other parties to the network, both the retailer and the supplier of credit. But English lawyers would not regard connected lender liability under section 75 of the Consumer Credit Act 1974 as establishing a principle of law, let alone a new concept in the legal system. It is rather regarded as an exceptional rule, motivated by consumer policy, which is confined to the particular situations where it applies by virtue of the statutory rules. It is true that those rules can be interpreted purposively so that they apply in very similar situations of consumer credit arrangements, but they could never, it is suggested, be applied to inter-organisational relations between businesses.

The absence of a direct comparison in English law with the German Civil Code's idea of a connected contract does not lead to the conclusion that the comparison is unfruitful or that transplants from one system to the other are impossible. But this result does suggest that Teubner's precise proposal of a doctrine of connected contracts as the source of an adequate legal conceptualisation of networks looks a relatively unpromising route for scholars in the common law systems to take. Even so, German law has only comparatively recently evolved the idea of connected contracts from an earlier position that more closely resembled English law, and it is possible the common law, in its search for more satisfactory solutions to some of the puzzles posed by networks to the legal system, will borrow or develop an analogous concept. We now turn to the three standard types of puzzles that networks pose for legal systems, as described above, in order to compare in more detail the German and common law solutions.

7. NETWORK EFFECTS ON INTERPRETATION OF BILATERAL CONTRACTS

The first family of such problems concerns the conflicts of interest between two parties to a bilateral contract within a network. These bilateral contracts might comprise, for instance, a requirements contract between a just-in-time supplier of components with a manufacturer of a finished product, or a distribution agreement between a manufacturer of a product and a distributor, or a business format franchise between a franchisor and franchisee. These contractual arrangements are likely to possess hybrid or relational qualities, because they seek to create a long-term co-operative relationship. When disputes regarding the respective obligations arise in such a business relationship, it is likely to be appropriate for a court to interpret the contract in such a way as to imply more diffuse obligations of co-operation and loyalty than would be appropriate in a discrete transaction conducted at arm's length. As a matter of legal technique, in German law such obligations can readily be derived from the general requirement to perform a contract in good faith, though this requirement may not supply an appropriate level of an obligation of loyalty for some of these relational contracts.

In the absence of such a principle in the English common law, the courts might rely on an implied term based on 'business necessity' or argue that the implied term is standard to this type of transaction. Although pertinent to the subject of networks, the development of such obligations of co-operation and loyalty in relational contracts does not address the particular complexity of the additional element of the multilateral contractual inter-organisational relationships found in networks.

The central idea of the theory of connected contracts is that the quasi-organisational qualities of networks make it possible to envision that the entity as a whole has a purpose or aim. This purpose is not identical either to the particular and divergent interests of the parties to a bilateral contract, such as manufacturer and distributor, or to the purpose of the bilateral contract itself. As regards the bilateral relation between manufacturer and distributor, evidently they can have divergent interests over such matters as the price at which products are supplied, the range of products, and the quantity of products available for delivery or held in stock by the distributor for immediate sales to customers. In such a business relationship, it is possible also to develop a view about the purpose of the contract, such as the efficient distribution of the manufacturer's products to distributors, so that they may retail them to customers efficiently whilst maximising sales and profits for both distributor and manufacturer. On the basis of such a view of the purpose of the contract, it is possible to give more concrete expression to a general principle of good faith or to imply a term requiring co-operation on the basis of business necessity. For instance, if the manufacturer deprives a distributor of a popular product, with the effect of depressing the distributor's turnover, in the absence of a good business reason for the bottleneck in the supply of the product, the manufacturer might be held to be acting in bad faith or to be in breach of an implied term to provide adequate supplies to the distributor. How far one should develop such implied duties in such relational contracts remains a matter of legal controversy in most legal systems.

The task here, however, is to add a further complexity to that controversy by insisting that a further source of implied obligations should be recognised as arising from the economic entity of the network itself. In other words, the network as a whole, the multilateral collection of networked contracts in its totality, should be regarded as having a purpose or aim. This network purpose provides a further criterion for determining the application of general principles such as good faith or the precise scope of implied terms based on business necessity.

Consider, for instance, the example of the manufacturer failing to supply a distributor with an adequate amount of a product to meet the demand from customers. If the manufacturer has a good business reason for the shortage of supply, such as an interruption in the deliveries of a component owing to strike action, a court is unlikely to hold the manufacturer to be in breach of an implied term or a principle of good faith (though the manufacturer may be in breach of an express promise to supply a minimum quantity of the product, if the obligation is one of strict liability). If the situation is different, so that the manufacturer possesses some supplies of the product, but chooses not to deliver any of them to this particular distributor for a capricious reason, this conduct might amount to a breach of the good faith principle or an implied term, because the manufacturer is defeating the aim of the contract with this particular distributor for no good business reason. Finally, there is a third situation, where the manufacturer has some supplies of the product, but not sufficient to meet the needs of all its distribution outlets, and again the manufacturer decides to favour some outlets over others, but this time for a good business reason, such as the fact that some distributors receive lower rates of commission or some distributors are wholly owned subsidiaries of the manufacturer. In this last example, the manufacturer's decision is not capricious at all: it meets the normal standards of self-interested action in market relations. Therefore, it may not amount to a breach of the principle of good faith or an implied term based on business necessity.

Yet, in the light of the theory of networks, in such a case it may be possible to argue nevertheless that the manufacturer is in breach of an implied obligation. This obligation requires the manufacturer to treat its distributors equally, without discrimination, in order to protect the long-term value of the distribution network as a whole. This objective would only arise in a tightly controlled distribution network, where the manufacturer insists upon standardisation of such matters as the space and appearance of the retail outlet, opening hours, and range of products on sale in all outlets. In view of the purpose of such a tightly organised network, the manufacturer should try to keep all its distributors in business, so that they can maintain as far as possible the general standards of the network. The manufacturer should supply each distributor with equal amounts of the product or at least some fair proportion based on their normal turnover. Discrimination against a particular distributor, even if based on a rational business judgment designed to maximise profits, might in these circumstances be regarded as a breach of the principle of good faith or another implied obligation, because the manufacturer's conduct is contrary to the interests of the network, viewed as an independent entity.

It is important to appreciate that the addition of the recognition of the purpose of the network entity does not change the legal analysis fundamentally. The presence of a network does not transform the contractual arrangements into a business association in which all the participants owe strict duties of loyalty to the organisation as whole. Instead, the legal duty of loyalty and fair dealing, however it may be expressed, tolerates a tension between the differing interests of the parties: the paradoxical qualities of networks are represented in the legal discourse. But in the context of networks, as opposed to other kinds of bilateral relational contracts, the correct interpretation of the legal duty of loyalty and fair dealing must also take into account the purpose of the network as a whole, not simply the purpose of the bilateral relational contract.

A case drawn from South Africa, based on the common law, provides a concrete illustration of how the recognition of the network entity might influence the interpretation of contracts and the allocation of the risks and benefits between the parties. In *Seven Eleven Corporation of SA (PTY) Ltd v Cancun Trading No 150 CC*,[54] the Supreme Court of Appeal of South Africa had to consider the application of an alleged duty of loyalty and fair dealing within a franchise chain for convenience stores. The dispute

[54] Case No 108/2004, 24 March 2005.

concerned the allocation of the benefit of various kinds of rebates obtained by the franchisor. Under this franchise system, the franchisee was required to purchase all stock either from the franchisor or from its nominated suppliers. All negotiations with suppliers about prices and discounts were conducted by the franchisor. Like a large retail chain owned by a single business association, by virtue of its size a franchisor can obtain various trade discounts and rebates when ordering supplies from third parties. These price reductions for supplies confer a competitive advantage on franchised outlets over independent stores, but only if the franchisees receive at least some proportion of the benefit. In this particular case, the first contract between franchisor and franchisee made no mention of any discounts at all, though the promotional literature that was used to persuade the franchisee to join the network highlighted the point that discounts were passed on to the franchisee. In a second, replacement contract between the parties, agreed when the franchisee changed its premises, the contract stated that 'the franchisor shall in its sole and absolute discretion afford the franchise the benefit of trade discounts received by it as a result of bulk purchases for goods and merchandise purchased on the franchisee's behalf'. The dispute in this test case concerned whether the franchisees should be entitled to the benefit of some or all of the discounts obtained by the franchisor from its suppliers.

This dispute illustrates the problem of loyalty in network contracts. From one perspective, there is a market transaction between the franchisor and franchisee, which allocates the risks and benefits between these competing organisations. How the pie of discounts should be distributed between them was a matter for negotiation. Passing on the discounts to franchisees would dent the franchisor's profits, and vice-versa. Indeed, the franchisee in this case claimed that given the other charges payable to the franchisor under the contract, it was not possible to make a profit without the benefit of these discounts. Viewed as a bilateral, relational contract, it could be argued that the franchisor, by not passing on the benefits of discounts and rebates, had not acted in good faith. But this argument about a breach of an implied obligation would clearly stand in tension with the term in the second contract that the franchisor reserved complete discretion whether or not to pass on discounts and rebates. If this discretionary power in the contract were exercised arbitrarily, capriciously, or for no good business reason, the franchisees would have a strong chance of success in claiming a breach of an implied obligation.[55] But if the franchisor merely exercised the power

[55] H Collins, 'Discretionary Powers in Contracts' in D Campbell, H Collins and J Wightman (eds), *Implicit Dimensions of Contract: Discrete, Relational, and Network Contracts* (Oxford, Hart Publishing, 2003) 219.

in a rational manner designed to maximise its profits under the contract, it would be much harder, perhaps impossible, to succeed in an allegation of breach of an implied obligation.

From a different perspective, however, one that views the franchise operation as a network entity, it could be argued that the discounts belonged in a sense to the operation as a whole, and that they should be distributed in a way that served the retailing network as a whole, which in this case would probably involve sharing them between franchisor and franchisees. At least in part, the purpose of the network is to achieve the economies of scale from which large integrated businesses benefit, though without the strong organisational form. One of the reasons that franchisees join a network is to benefit from market power of a larger organisation, whilst at the same time remaining a small independent business, entitled to residual profits. In *Dymocks Franchise Systems (NSW) Pty Ltd v Todd*,[56] a central issue was whether or not the franchisee had repudiated the franchise contract. The franchisee had become dissatisfied with this book store franchise, arguing that the failure of the franchisor, Dymocks, to secure a critical mass of franchised stores in New Zealand led to the consequence that the franchisees did not benefit from any better discounts than independent retailers, even though they had to pay substantial franchise fees. The franchisee sent a letter to the other franchisees in New Zealand saying that he did not intend to participate in the activities of the franchise operation, a statement which would be understood to include group purchases at discounts. On appeal from the New Zealand Court of Appeal, the Privy Council held that the communication with the other franchisees, which the trial judge had analogised to a call for strike action, amounted to a repudiatory breach of contract. The Privy Council insisted that, whatever the position with regard to an alleged implied term of good faith, the conduct of the franchisee amounted to a fundamental breach of the basic principles underlying the contract. In adopting this view, the Privy Council appreciated the vital importance of bulk purchasing to the comparative success of a network and how, even if the contract reserves some discretion to franchisees in the extent to which they participate in bulk purchases, a complete refusal to participate strikes at a fundamental purpose of the network entity.

In the *Seven Eleven* stores case itself, in the absence of clear guidance from the contract, the dispute about the proper allocation of the rebates and discounts was resolved in the end by the court approving the actual practice of the franchisor. The franchisor had passed on to franchisees the benefit of price discounts awarded by suppliers for bulk purchases. But

[56] [2002] UKPC 50 (7 October 2002).

the franchisor had not passed on the benefit of other kinds of retrospective price rebates awarded by the suppliers. These rebates might be obtained by early payment for stock or for reaching a target for growth in orders. With the court's approval, the franchisor regarded these rebates as its own reward for running the franchise efficiently and achieving growth, not as benefit obtained by the franchise operation as a whole. The court rejected an interpretation of the contract or an implied term that would require the franchisor to pass on the benefit of all such rebates to the franchisees, arguing that, on the business model concerned, the rebates constituted a significant proportion of the franchisor's profits and served to motivate the franchisor to run it efficiently and to extend its operation. This judgment therefore implicitly recognises the significance of the network entity in calibrating the implied duty of loyalty when the network itself has been necessary to achieve the benefit of bulk ordering at a discount. The court tries to draw a distinction between the benefit of discounts, which should be used to the benefit of the network as a whole, and the franchisor's actions that had primarily functioned to reduce its own costs. Although this distinction is far from clear in practice, the court develops an intelligible strategy of dividing up the benefits or 'profit-sharing', so that the network both protects the incentives for the franchisor by letting him retain the rebates, but at the same time forces a distribution of other benefits from discounts throughout the network on the ground that those benefits can only be secured by the co-operation of all the participants in the network.

The *Seven Eleven* case illustrates how the law can recognise the presence of a network in its interpretation of bilateral contracts within the network. The discretion of the franchisor provided in the contract must be exercised in such a way that not only must it be rational in the interests of the franchisor, but at the same time, paradoxically, it must be rational in the interests of the network as a whole. Perhaps wisely, when viewing this contradictory economic logic, the court decided that the franchisor had in fact in its actual practice reached a reasonable way to accommodate these conflicting demands. In the main text, Teubner discusses a similar German case concerning the allocation of discounts in a retail franchise called 'Optik'.[57] The legal problem there differed in important respects, because the contract expressly provided that the franchisor would pass on to franchisees 'advantages, ideas and improvement' that would enable the optimisation of business success. This term was interpreted to mean that the franchisor should pass on the whole benefit of discounts and rebates, not just a portion of them, to franchisees.

[57] Below, Chapter 4, I. See also: R Bohner, 'Asset-sharing in Franchise Networks: The Obligation to Pass On Network Benefits' in M Amstutz and G Teubner (eds), *Networks: Legal Issues of Multilateral Co-operation* (Oxford, Hart Publishing, 2009) 153.

Teubner criticises this reasoning and result precisely because, unlike in the *Seven Eleven* case, the German Federal High Court failed to appreciate that franchisors and franchisees must both compete for a share of the profits and also co-operate to maximise profits. On this view, the clause in the contract about passing on advantages should not be interpreted to mean that the franchisor would necessarily pass on all discounts and rebates. Instead, to reflect the attributes of the network, the interpretation of the term 'advantages' and the application of the implied duty to perform the contract in good faith, should have adopted a more nuanced approach, neither permitting the franchisor to retain all the benefits of discounts, as would occur in a single business organisation, nor requiring the franchisor to pass on all the benefits, as might be required by the application of a duty to perform in good faith in a bilateral contract.

A similar criticism might be ventured against the decisions of some courts in the United States of America when they apply an implied obligation to perform in good faith to distribution and franchise contracts. The general pattern in such cases is that the implied duties of good faith and fair dealing will not override express terms of the contract, such as terms that permit termination at will,[58] unless there is evidence of extreme dishonesty or unfairness and the franchisee stands to lose a significant investment.[59] Viewing franchises as long-term relational contracts, Gillian Hadfield argues that the courts have interpreted a good faith requirement unduly narrowly, as merely requiring the franchisor to have an objective business reason for the decision, acting in its own best interests, not taking into account the interests of the franchisee against opportunism.[60] In the American example of *Burger King*,[61] the contract required a franchisee to open 10 outlets in a period of 10 years in this fledgling, untested, franchise. The franchisor terminated the contract when the franchisee had only managed to open nine outlets. The franchisor could then sell these franchises at a much higher rate than in the deal with this franchisee, since in the meantime the franchise concept had proven successful. Acting in accordance with the express terms of the contract, the franchisor was not regarded as having acted in bad faith. The decision can be criticised on the ground that by opening nine outlets in a new franchise operation, the franchisee had invested substantially in the success of the franchise, and its efforts should have

[58] *Taylor Equip Co v John Deere Co* 98 F 3d 1028 (8th Cir 1996).

[59] *Bak-a-Lum Corp of America v Alcoa Building Products* 351 A 2dn 349 (New Jersey, 1976).

[60] GK Hadfield, 'Problematic Relations: Franchising and the Law of Incomplete Contracts' (1990) 42 *Stanford Law Review* 927, 984.

[61] *Burger King Corp v Family Dining*, 426 F Supp 485 (ED Pa), aff'd, 556 F 2d 1168 (3d Cir 1977).

been better rewarded since these sunk investments could not be recovered after termination. This criticism emphasises the relational and hybrid character of franchises, in which to some extent the parties share the risks and should benefit from the success of their endeavours. Adding to this point, the theory of connected contracts suggests, however, that one should not expect the franchisor to act in a fiduciary manner, to put the interests of the franchisee before its own, but it is appropriate to demand that the franchisor should also recognise the need to act in the best interests of the franchise network as a whole as well as in its own best interest. As Teubner puts it, the network purpose becomes a yardstick for loyalty duties.[62] Such an approach might lead to an interpretation of the good faith standard that would require the franchisor not to terminate franchises on a technicality when the franchisee has performed successfully and has helped the franchise network to grow.

Roger Brownsword suggests another occasion when courts should take into account the presence of a network when addressing issues of loyalty and performance in bilateral contracts between members of a network.[63] Under English law, the validity of exclusion clauses in standard form contracts will be assessed according a statutory test in the Unfair Contract Terms Act 1977 that requires such terms to be fair and reasonable in the circumstances in the contemplation of the parties at the time of the formation of the contract. In making such judgments, courts must take into account a broad range of circumstances including any inequality of bargaining power between the parties. When a court assesses a term that excludes all liability, it may appear harsh and unreasonable when it is viewed solely in the context of the particular bilateral contract between A and B, raising perhaps the suspicion of one party having taken advantage of its superior bargaining power. In a network of contracts, such as a supply chain, the exclusion clause may be drafted to protect other members of the network, C, D, and E, upstream of the supply chain. The question then arises whether any inequality of bargaining power between A and B is relevant to the fairness of the term when the dispute arises from either C, D, or E's attempt to rely on the exclusion clause to provide immunity from liability. Brownsword asks: should the court restrict its assessment to the facts relevant to the relationship between A and B? Or should the court look also or alternatively at the relation between A and C, D, or E? Or, finally, should the court assess the fairness of the exclusion clause from the perspective of the network or chain of contracts as a whole? When a court appreciates

[62] Below, Chapter 4, III.
[63] R Brownsword, 'Network Contracts Revisited', in M Amstutz and G Teubner (eds), *Networks: Legal Issues of Multilateral Co-operation* (Oxford, Hart Publishing, 2009) 31.

how risks have been allocated throughout a contractual network, this exclusion clause lodged in only one of the chain of contracts may appear more reasonable. Indeed, taking into account the context of the whole network of contracts and its purpose, a term that might be regarded as reasonable, as between A and B, might be regarded as unfair in its application between A and C, and vice versa. The best approach for the courts when assessing the validity of exclusion clauses should be, according to Teubner's theory of connected contracts, to consider the question of unfairness in both these contexts, that is both in the relationship between A and B and that of A and C, but also, to resolve any contradictions arising from these assessments, to take into account the purpose of the network as a whole as a vital relevant circumstance.

In the context of exclusion clauses, Teubner points to a problem that may arise under German law in just-in-time supply contracts along a chain.[64] Systems of sales law often place some kind of duty or incentive on a buyer to inspect the goods properly on taking possession of them. If the buyer fails to carry out such an inspection and the goods subsequently prove defective and the defect could have been discovered by an inspection, sales law may relieve the seller of liability on the ground that the buyer has been careless, or has assumed the risk of loss, or has simply left it too late to complain. Although this approach may achieve an equitable result in commercial sales in general, it fits uncomfortably into just-in-time supply systems. The purpose of these systems, with their combination of computerised inventory control and total quality management, is to remove the need for the buyer to inspect incoming goods and for the need to make a judgment about their quality. Accordingly, in some German contracts governing just-in-time systems of supply, the terms have purported to exclude the seller's legal duty under the Commercial Law Code to inspect the goods for apparent defects. According to German legal doctrine, however, because such clauses in contracts deviate from the normal standards that allocate risks equitably between sellers and buyers, the terms should be regarded as void for unfairness. Teubner criticises this approach, because when viewed from the perspective of the network purpose as a whole, it should be the seller's responsibility to ensure quality inspection controls in a just-in-time system. A term in the contract that relieves the buyer of any duty to inspect the goods should be upheld as fair in view of the network context. On the other hand, Teubner suggests that the buyer should not necessarily be relieved entirely from responsibility for the defects, because that would also subvert the co-operative purpose of the network,

[64] Below, Chapter 4, VI.

since the supply system and the seller's methods of production may have been determined by the buyer according to the principles of total quality management.

Similar problems for just-in-time systems are unlikely to arise in the UK. English sales law does not impose a duty on the buyer to inspect the goods for apparent defects, but states that if the buyer examines the goods before the contract is made, the buyer assumes the risk of defects that the examination ought to have revealed.[65] This rule fits just-in-time supply systems exactly, because the buyer's failure to carry out any inspection at all does not shift the risk from the seller. It is only when the buyer carries out a cursory, negligent inspection that the risk of defective quality may shift to the buyer.[66] Closer to the German position is the rule that in the case of a contract for sale by sample, the buyer cannot complain of defects that a reasonable examination of the sample should have revealed.[67] Under English law, these statutory rules could be reversed by a suitably worded exclusion clause, provided that it passed the test of reasonableness. Since English courts usually grant wide latitude to commercial parties to exclude default rules, the problem of invalidity of a term requiring or eliminating the need for inspections arising in connection with just-in-time systems in Germany is unlikely to arise. Nevertheless, following the spirit of Teubner's argument, were such a clause to be challenged, it would be appropriate for an English court to assess the reasonableness of the exclusion clause in the light of the just-in-time system with a view to permitting a removal of the buyer's obligation to examine the sample for apparent defects.

Many other examples might be given of when reference to the purpose of the network should influence the interpretation of the express and implicit obligations in a contract. If a contract can be terminated on giving reasonable notice, the appropriate period of notice might be extended in order to take into account potential deleterious effects on other members of the network.[68] In this vein, Marina Wellenhofer supports the decision of the German Federal Court of Justice relating to the termination of a McDonald's franchise on the ground that the operator did not conform to the exact temperature required by the franchisor for grilling hamburgers. At first sight, the decision to terminate the franchise looks harsh in view of the relatively trivial breach of the contractually

[65] Sale of Goods Act 1979, s 14(2C)(b).

[66] *Thornet & Fehr v Beers & Son* [1919] 1 KB 486; MG Bridge, *The Sale of Goods*, 2nd edn (Oxford, Oxford University Press, 2009) pp 448–9.

[67] Sale of Goods Act 1979, s 14(2C)(c).

[68] See also: G-P Calliess, 'Fitness Clubs: Consumer Protection between Contract and Association', in M Amstutz and G Teubner (eds), *Networks: Legal Issues of Multilateral Co-operation* (Oxford, Hart Publishing, 2009) 241, using a network analysis to justify lengthy notice periods for termination of membership of clubs.

required operating procedures. But if reference is made to the purpose of the network and the need to preserve the reputation of the brand name, the termination might appear more of a fair reaction to a franchisee who displays symptoms of trying to be a free rider.[69] Given that the bilateral contracts comprising a network will usually exhibit relational qualities, the courts already encounter considerable difficulty in fine tuning their interpretations of express and implied duties of co-operation and loyalty. The context of the network surrounding a particular bilateral contract may provide a court with reasons either to augment obligations, such as a duty to give longer notice of termination, or to permit reliance on the express terms of the contract, as in the McDonald's case. Recognition of the network concept in this context does not require a major reconceptualisation of the law, but merely subtle tweaks to the interpretation of the parties' obligations in the light of the purpose of the network.

8. INTERNAL NETWORK LIABILITY

Most private law systems share some general legal principles that apply to the business relations between parties to a network. In the absence of an express bilateral contract between two parties in a network, the law is unlikely to explain their relationship as contractual, but will analyse it under the general principles of tort law, as a relation between strangers. As we noted earlier, usually franchisees will not have direct contracts with each other, only with the franchisor; similarly, remote parties in a supply chain will lack direct contractual relations. As a result, any liability that may arise between franchisees or remote parties in a chain is likely to be categorised in law as a claim in tort. As a general rule, however, claims in tort for pure economic loss such as loss of profits caused by the delinquent behaviour of a particular franchisee are not recoverable. The likely result of the legal analysis in European legal systems is therefore that parties to a network will not be able to bring economic claims against each other unless they have taken the precaution of entering an explicit bilateral contract.

Private law systems usually acknowledge some exceptions to this basic legal framework. A contractual claim may be constructed in some instances on such grounds as agency or a contract for the benefit of third parties, and a contract can occasionally be implied between two parties on the basis of necessity. A tort claim for pure economic loss, as opposed to one for personal injury or property damage, is sometimes recognised

[69] M Wellenhofer, 'Third Party Effects of Bilateral Contracts within the Network', in M Amstutz and G Teubner (eds), *Networks: Legal Issues of Multilateral Co-operation* (Oxford, Hart Publishing, 2009) 119, 124–25.

within certain types of special relationships, where the business relationship is akin to a contractual one. The scope and limits of such exceptions can be controversial, particularly in circumstances where reasonable reliance has been placed on another, but none of the exceptions appear to be so broad as to apply routinely to a claim for a loss incurred through misplaced reliance upon another member of a network.

The central question to be considered here is whether, in the absence of an explicit contract, business relations between members of a network should be interpreted as falling within one of these exceptions, and if so, which exception might be most appropriately applied. To put the matter more concretely: if by his conduct one franchisee damages the economic interests of other franchisees, should these franchisees, in the absence of an explicit contract with the delinquent franchisee, be generally permitted to bring a claim for their loss, and if so, should such a claim be generally understood as based on an exception to the general principles found in either contract or tort? A similar question might be posed about the non-contractual relations between remote links in a network chain.

The case for applying one of the exceptions in this context arises from the qualities of networks. If the network had been created as a vertically integrated business, the absence of direct contractual links between the spokes of the organisation would not matter because the central organisation would determine responsibility and how best to react to the problem. Since the organisation receives all the residual profits, it has a strong incentive to construct an efficient solution that minimises internal costs. In contrast, in a network of independent businesses, the incentives are not necessarily aligned in a way that maximises the profit of the whole network. At the hub of the network, the franchisor may decide not to act against the delinquent franchisee; at the end of the supply chain, the retailer may decide to change its whole supply chain, thus punishing those in the chain who are innocent of any default. As Teubner points out,[70] this is a central paradoxical quality of networks: the parties are motivated simultaneously by the contradictory economic logics of the competitive market and the co-operative organisation. In networks, the element of organisational co-operation can be achieved without direct bilateral contracts. Franchisees can be organised through regular meetings, newsletters, and computer links through the franchisor. In a supply chain, again computer links establish co-operation based on disclosure of detailed information without the necessity for formal contracts. The case for recognising claims between parties within a network, whether or not they have entered bilateral contracts, rests on this insight that the multilateral collection of relational contracts creates a similar degree of

[70] Below, Chapter 5, II.

co-ordinated mutual economic interdependence to that found within a vertically integrated firm, but without the organisational entity of a business association to allocate responsibility and risk efficiently and equitably.

Once it is accepted that there may be a case for developing economic liability between all parties to a network, whether or not they are bound by an explicit contract, two issues have to be addressed. The first comprises an attempt to specify the conditions under which this internal network liability should arise. The second concerns the question of which of the various possible legal claims in contract and tort should be permitted.

Conditions for Internal Network Liability

With respect to the first issue, it will no doubt prove difficult to identify the tipping point at which a constellation of connected contracts has a sufficiently close organisational relation that a general inter-party liability could be presumed to arise. Consider, for instance, the example of construction contracts. For a big project, there will certainly be a constellation of connected contracts involving the employer, the main contractor, sub-contractors, as well as professionals such as architects, quantity surveyors, and project managers. The economic activity is also certainly co-ordinated overall, because there is a general, shared aim, to complete the building project; and the principal role of the professionals is to co-ordinate activity towards that aim. On the other hand, the various sub-contractors may have little contact with each other, especially if they work sequentially on the project, or they may even be competing with each other for different segments of the work. Does this constellation of connected contracts amount to a network for the purposes of establishing internal network liability?

Teubner argues that more than a constellation of connected contracts is needed. There must be (1) mutual referencing of these contracts to one another in the sense that the contracts need to refer to the activities governed by the other contracts in the network; (2) there must be a network purpose, which is understood as separate from the purpose of the particular bilateral contracts; and (3) there must be intensive factual co-operation between all the different parties in the network, not merely between those bound by explicit bilateral contracts. With regard to this last criterion, Teubner adds that the network must be 'overlain by an overarching private order'.[71] Such a 'private order' can be informal in the

[71] Below, Chapter 5, IV.

sense that it need not be contained in a framework contract, but there must be intense co-ordination that requires the parties actively to co-operate with each other, usually under the direction of another party such as the architect or project manager. This proposal suggests that in a normal construction project, the conditions for internal network liability should not be presumed to exist. Although conditions (1) and (2) are likely to be satisfied in a construction project, the third condition is not a necessary feature of construction projects. But some projects or parts of them may satisfy the additional condition of more intense co-ordination through informal ordering.

It may be possible to detect the English courts struggling towards a result that matches that theoretical proposal. In *Norwich City Council v Harvey*,[72] the claimant council had entered into a contract with a main contractor to build an extension to a swimming pool complex. The contract provided that the council would assume the risk of fire damage and it undertook to maintain adequate insurance against that risk. A sub-contractor doing roofing work managed to set fire to the whole complex. The council claimed compensation for damage to its property against the sub-contractor. In the absence of a direct bilateral contract between them, the claim was brought in the tort of negligence for damage to property. Normally, if negligence on the part of the sub-contractor were established, such a claim for damage to property would be successful, but the sub-contractor proposed a defence that its liability had been excluded by the term in the main contract regarding fire insurance. In principle, this defence was not available because the sub-contractor was not a party to the main contract, and nor did any of the exceptions, such as protection for intended third party beneficiaries, apply in this case. Nevertheless, the defence was accepted by the English Court of Appeal on the ground that the term in the main contract had qualified the sub-contractor's normal duty of care under the law of tort in order to exclude fire damage. The court emphasised the point that there were direct communications between the council and this sub-contractor and other sub-contractors on the project, with a view to ensuring that they all contracted on a like basis, which included the council's assumption of the risk of fire. Strictly speaking, this case does not involve internal network liability, but rather the exclusion of liability. Yet, in order to permit the defence, the court directed its attention to those elements that might be described as informal private ordering through direct communications between the council and the sub-contractors. It was because of those direct communications that the court felt able to argue that the sub-contractors could rely on the understanding of the exclusion

[72] [1989] 1 All ER 1180, CA.

of liability for fire damage, even though there was no express contractual agreement to that effect between the council and the sub-contractors. The reason why it was not 'fair, just and reasonable' to impose liability for the fire on the sub-contractors was that they had participated in a network, in which, with a view to reducing costs for the project overall, the risk of fire had been assumed by one participant in the network, no doubt because the council needed to have fire insurance in any event, and the project had been informally and non-contractually organised on that basis.

A case where network liability was imposed was *Junior Books Ltd v Veitchi Co Ltd*,[73] though the decision has subsequently been doubted and distinguished. In this construction project for a factory, the owners used a standard form contract with the main contractors that permitted the owners to nominate preferred sub-contractors for parts of the work. The owners nominated this particular sub-contractor for the job of laying a special concrete floor, but there was no direct contract between the owners and the sub-contractor. When the floor later developed cracks, it was decided that it would be cheaper in the long run to replace the floor. The owners brought an action against the sub-contractor in the tort of negligence for the cost of replacing the floor. The sub-contractor replied that in the absence of a contract, there could be no liability for the cost of replacing the floor, relying on the normal exclusion of liability for pure economic loss in tort. In the House of Lords, the owners were successful in establishing their right to bring a claim. The Judicial Committee placed great emphasis on the fact that the sub-contractors had been nominated by the owner, not chosen by the main contractor, which demonstrated that the owner had relied on the sub-contractor's skill and experience. It was said that the relationship between the owner and the sub-contractor was akin to contract. With these phrases, the court is pointing to additional features of this constellation of contracts that provide the kind of informal private ordering, which, according to Teubner's argument, should provide the basis for internal network liability. It is true that subsequent cases have not found the argument based upon owner's nomination of sub-contractors sufficiently persuasive to justify the imposition of liability for pure economic loss. It may well be correct that the special kind of private ordering required for general internal network liability will not be created by the owner of the building nominating a sub-contractor, since this practice is commonplace in many construction projects. The position might be different, for instance, if the work was highly specialist, requiring great skill and experience, and the owner had

[73] [1983] 1 AC 520, HL.

had direct communications with the potential sub-contractors and had selected only one of them as the nominated sub-contractor for this particular project.

These examples illustrate how Teubner's proposed three conditions for internal network liability might be applied to familiar examples drawn from English law. To some extent the judges in these cases seem to be feeling their way towards similar principles for determining the incidence of liability. These examples therefore suggest that Teubner's proposal might be suitable for transplant into English law.

Legal Classification of Claim

If these three factual conditions for the construction of internal network liability can be established and it is accepted that they justify the imposition of internal network liability, the next question is how this form of liability might be constructed within a legal system. Teubner considers and rejects two exceptional instances of contractual liability: agency and contracts with protective effects for third parties.

The agency construction is familiar in the common law. The legal model is that one party, such as the franchisor, enters into contracts personally with franchisees, but also, simultaneously, as agent for all the other existing and future franchisees. If the franchise agreement were to explicitly state this agency relationship, there is little doubt that it would succeed in creating direct bilateral contracts between franchisees, so that each could sue the other. More troublesome would be the question of what obligations might be created between the franchisees, since the obligations in a franchise contract are focused on the bilateral duties owed between franchisor and this particular franchisee. In English law, where the agency technique has been used, as in carriage of goods by sea,[74] its main purpose has been a narrow one: to allocate risks efficiently by exclusion clauses throughout the chain of contracts between the seller of goods, the carrier, intermediaries such as stevedores, and the ultimate buyer. In these instances, the agency technique has been successful in conferring the benefit of an exclusion clause on third parties, though there remains some doubt over the question whether the agency technique can work in connection with parties whose identity was unknown at the time of the formation of main contract. But it is important to note that the agency argument only appears to be successful where there is an

[74] *New Zealand Shipping Co Ltd v Satterthwaite & Co Ltd (The Eurymedon)* [1974] 1 All ER 1015, PC; *Port Jackson Stevedoring Pty Ltd v Salmond & Spraggon Pty (Australia) Ltd, The New York Star* [1980] 3 All ER 257; *The Pioneer Container* [1994] 2 All ER 250, PC; *The Mahkutai* [1996] 3 All ER 502, PC.

explicit declaration of agency in the contract.[75] An agency cannot simply be implied from the circumstances. Even if that were possible, the point about networks as distinctive forms of business co-ordination is that the businesses remain distinct, not acting as agents for each other or in partnership, so that factually it would be inappropriate to infer an implied agency relationship. Following the method of sociological jurisprudence, where the aim is to try to find legal concepts that best articulate the reality and logic of business relationships, the agency construct is inappropriate because it imagines links and duties such as fiduciary duties that are plainly not expected within a network.

The second legal model considered by Teubner is the German doctrine that contracts may establish rights that entitle a third party to some level of protection against adverse effects stemming from a breach of contract. The leading German case demonstrates that a third party may claim recovery for pure economic loss caused by negligence where there is a special link of proximity. The case concerned a negligent delay by a lawyer in having a will notarised, with the consequence that when the client died intestate, his daughter received only half of the estate rather than her expectation of nearly all of the estate. She succeeded in a claim in contract law to obtain financial compensation from the lawyer for the reduced sum of her inheritance.[76] The proximity of her claim was established because the lawyer must have appreciated that she was the only person likely to suffer loss as a result of the lawyer's failure to act promptly. This German case has direct parallels with decisions in the common law. In *White v Jones*, the House of Lords awarded compensation on the basis of the tort of negligence on the ground that a special relationship justifying a duty of care to prevent pure economic loss had arisen by virtue of the lawyer's assumption of responsibility to provide the legal service. In the Supreme Court of California, the leading case of *Lucas v Hamm* permitted the action in principle (though not on the facts of the case) in both tort and contract.[77]

Although the results of these decisions are remarkably similar, there is an important difference in legal technique. German legal doctrine regards the protection of the third party as an extension of the principle that a contract may expressly confer enforceable benefits on a third party, though the nature of the claim differs because the third party is not demanding proper performance of the contract but rather compensation for losses caused by foreseeable reliance upon performance by the promisor. In contrast, in English law, owing to the stronger doctrine of privity of contract, the claim must be grounded in tort and it must be

[75] *Scruttons Ltd v Midland Silicones Ltd* [1962] AC 446, HL.
[76] Bundesgerichtshof 6 July 1965, NJW 1965, 1955.
[77] *Lucas v Hamm*, 15 Cal Rptr 821 (1961).

fitted rather uneasily into the recognised narrow exceptions for the construction of liability for pure economic loss. The scope of the exception is much narrower than that provided by German law, with decisions such as *White v Jones* being regarded as anomalous examples.

The German doctrine of contracts with protective effects for third parties could evidently be used to establish appropriate liabilities within networks. For instance, one franchisee might claim the protective effect of a contract between the franchisor and another franchisee as a device for establishing a direct claim against the franchisee for defective performance of its obligations to maintain the quality standards of the franchise. But Teubner regards this legal analysis as ultimately inadequate, because it does not reflect the way in which a network has a common project, the network purpose, and mutual co-operative relationships.[78] The doctrine of contracts with protective effects for a third party addresses selected adverse external effects of bilateral contracts, but does not adequately reflect the associational and co-operative aspects of networks through which the participants contribute to a common goal. Teubner suggests that the doctrine will be especially problematic in a case where the network contains a diversity of contracts, as in a supply chain. Here a participant in the chain may find itself in the difficult position of having conflicting demands placed on it by the upstream and downstream contracts to which it is party, such that its performance of one contract may have adverse effects on performance of the other. The doctrine of contracts with protective effects for a third party might enable the party suffering adverse effects to bring a claim, even though the decision to favour one contractual performance over the other may have better served the general purpose of the network as a whole. For this reason, Teubner argues that his favoured doctrinal construction of connected contracts will better help the courts to allocate risks and liabilities within networks in tune with their economic purposes.

Furthermore, the doctrine of contracts with protective effects for third parties, like a tort claim, merely grants a claim for reliance losses, whereas the more appropriate level of liability in some claims might be for the protection of an expectation of a share of the benefits or profits of a network. For instance, if one party to a network misuses confidential information it has received through participation in the network in order to make a profit for itself, the appropriate remedy for other parties in the network might not be recovery for their losses, which may in fact be nil, but rather a share of the profits achieved through misuse of confidential information. In English law, this particular objection to the use of a tort

[78] Below, Chapter 5, V, 3.

claim may not prove applicable in every instance. In the case of confidential information, a court may order in equity that the party who has misused the confidential information should account for its profits to the owners of the information.[79] The difficulty in devising such a claim would be to identify the owners of the confidential information. There is a risk that in the absence of the notion of connected contracts, the confidential information would be regarded as the sole property of one member of the network, the originator of the information, which will often be the hub of the network or the party that exercises most hierarchical controls.

What is the outcome of these deliberations regarding the best legal classification of internal network claims between parties who are not connected by an explicit bilateral contract? In some instances, it must be acknowledged that tort claims for pure economic loss or the similar German claim regarding contracts with protective effects for a third party may be appropriate techniques for protection against reliance losses. But these legal claims do not respond adequately to claims that are founded essentially on duties of loyalty owed to the network as a whole. Teubner concludes that to create an adequate legal framework to handle all the various types of internal network claim, it is necessary to use his theory of connected contracts. Under this theory, if the three conditions for internal network liability can be satisfied, direct claims should be available, even in the absence of an explicit bilateral contract between claimant and defendant. Furthermore, these claims should be regarded as contractual in character, not merely tortious, so that the claimant can sue for the expected benefits of participation in the network and support for its purpose, not merely for recovery of the costs of misplaced reliance on other members of the network.

Temporary Agency Workers

A useful example drawn from English law illustrates the superiority of Teubner's approach through the concept of connected contracts. Temporary agency work has become very common in Britain, with perhaps in excess of 1 million workers earning their living by this contractual mechanism. The contracts create a small network between a client, an agency, and a worker. In the contract between the agency and the worker, it is determined that the worker is an independent contractor offering his or her services, a legal position that is sometimes reinforced by a requirement that the worker should form a company that makes the contract with the agency. The agency makes a contract with the client to

[79] *Attorney-General v Blake* [2001] AC 268, HL.

provide the services of the worker in return for a fee. Part of the fee is then paid to the worker as payment for services, leaving the residual as profit for the agency. Under the terms of the contract between agency and worker, the worker agrees to comply with the instructions of the management of the client, as if the worker were directly employed by the client. There is no direct contract, however, between the worker and the client. The worker's claim for payment lies against the agency. Agency work is often substituted for regular employment by the client dismissing its direct labour force and then requiring former employees to seek re-engagement through an agency. This method enables the client to make savings on labour costs by, for instance, avoiding the rates of pay mandated by a collective agreement with a trade union or eliminating expensive fringe benefits such as occupational pensions and sick pay.

But what is the legal position if the client decides to terminate this particular agency worker, perhaps as a result of false or unproven allegations of misconduct? In the absence of an explicit bilateral contract between worker and client, no contractual claim for wrongful dismissal is available. Under the statutory protection against unfair dismissal, the worker also has no claim owing to the absence of a contract of employment with either the client or the agency. Even if there were a contract of employment with the agency, it would be hard to attribute the unfair conduct of the client to the agency. The agency is not responsible for the conduct of its clients, which are separate businesses and over which it has no control. The result must be that the dismissed worker has no claim against the wrongfulness or unfairness of the dismissal against anyone, neither the client nor the agency.[80]

The claim of the worker against the client for unfair termination of work displays the features of a problem of internal network liability. It satisfies the conditions proposed by Teubner for the construction of internal network liability: (1) mutual referencing of the two bilateral contracts to one another; (2) a network purpose understood as separate from the purpose of the particular contracts (providing the services of this particular worker to the client); and (3) intensive factual co-operation between all the different parties in the network, not merely between those bound by explicit bilateral contracts (the worker obeys the instructions of the client). But how can the worker construct a legal claim against unfair termination of his paid work in the absence of any explicit contract between the client and the worker?

Is it possible to find a solution to this problem under the ordinary principles of the common law? Could the worker claim as a third party the benefit of the contract between the agency and the client? The main

[80] *James v London Borough of Greenwich* [2008] EWCA Civ 35; [2008] ICR 545.

problem here is that the client is likely to have conformed to the terms of its contract with the agency, because those provisions are unlikely to place any burden on the client of fair treatment of workers supplied by the agency. So the client will not have breached the contract, and a third party worker cannot claim beneficial rights that are not even mentioned in the contract. As for a claim in tort against the client, in a particularly egregious case there is a remote possibility of an action for deliberate infliction of emotional shock or psychiatric illness, but otherwise the worker's claim for unfair dismissal would be one for pure economic loss. Although such a claim in tort is not completely excluded by private law, the existence of contractual allocations of risk in the network of contracts between client, agency and worker, would almost certainly deprive the worker of the possibility of asserting a duty of care. Finally, it is worth noting that English courts considered, but ultimately rejected, the idea of inventing a direct bilateral contract between the client and the worker. The proposal was untenable because it had to pass a legal test of necessity. English courts will not imply a contract unless it is necessary to explain the economic relationship between the parties.[81] In the case of temporary agency work, such an additional implied contract was unnecessary to explain how the network could function effectively. The ordinary principles of the common law therefore appear to present the worker with no prospects of success of any claim for unfair dismissal.

In response to this problem, it has been suggested that the client and the agency should be regarded as the joint employers of the worker.[82] This suggestion is unsatisfactory because in effect it tries to invent a business association or firm like a partnership when the business reality is rather a heterarchical network between autonomous businesses. The invention of a quasi-partnership between the client and the agency fails to follow the method of sociological jurisprudence, which requires an approximation of the legal analysis as closely as possible to the economic logic under which the actors operate. In a temporary agency arrangement, the client and the agency are linked by a market co-ordination mechanism of contract, not an organisational one. There is an intensified division of labour through which the agency performs some of the functions of human resources management that were once done in-house by the client. The network has the purpose of providing this function of personnel management efficiently, but it is performed through contracts in which the parties deal at arm's length with a view to maximising their own interests, not the interest of a jointly owned business entity. What the legal analysis requires is a conceptual scheme that both recognises the

[81] *The Aramis* [1989] 1 Lloyd's Rep 213, CA.

[82] G Davidov, 'Joint Employer Status in Triangular Employment Relationships' (2004) 42 *British Journal of Industrial Relations* 727.

fundamental contractual character of the market ordering in the relation between the parties, whilst at the same time adding the dimension of the multilateral associational qualities of the network.

The theory of connected contracts would suggest that within the network of contracts comprising the temporary agency relationship, the worker should have a claim against the client that is fundamentally contractual in character. But would the worker have the same claim for compensation for dismissal as if the worker had been an ordinary employee of the client? In answering this question in the negative, Teubner first draws a distinction based in German law between, on the one hand, a primary action for fulfilment of the contractual obligation or specific performance of an obligation, and, on the other hand, a mere claim for compensatory damages. The theory of connected contracts only justifies a claim for damages, not for specific performance. In the example of temporary agency work, this limitation would rule out any claim for reinstatement of the worker.

Yet in this example, there is a further problem. What exactly is the content of the obligation that the client is supposed to have breached? On the plausible assumption that the client has not breached its contract with the agency by terminating the worker, what additional obligation may be owed to the worker in the connected contract? Loyalty to the purpose of the network and damage to its purpose provides the source of this obligation. The question is whether the client has opportunistically or collusively taken advantage of the network structure to achieve cost savings to the detriment of the network as a whole and to the worker in particular. A cynical response to this question might insist that, far from subverting the purpose of the network of temporary agency work, the client has used and revealed its primary purpose, which is to shield a business from the normal consequences of employment law and social regulation. If, however, we rule out avoidance or evasion of legal regulation as an appropriate purpose to attribute to a network, the answer should lie in an intensification of the division of labour with regard to the recruitment and management of workers by means of outsourcing aspects of those tasks. In the absence of an explicit arrangement between the client and the agency over the outsourcing of the responsibility for dealing with workers fairly, maintaining 'trust and confidence' or performing in good faith, the client retains that responsibility and other duties such as health and safety that arise in the workplace. On this interpretation of the contractual network, the obligation owed by the client to the worker, in fidelity to the purpose of the network, is the basic obligation of fair treatment owed by every employer to its workers.

Multilateral Hierarchical Networks

The above example of a temporary agency worker presents a relatively simple instance of a proposal for 'piercing liability', through which a claim characterised as a breach of contract is created between two parties, even in the absence of a direct contract between them, but when they are linked together in a closely co-ordinated network. Owing to the fictional character of this contractual claim, Teubner limits the remedy to one of compensatory damages. But such a remedy will not always be sufficient in the light of the purpose of the network. In some instances, the protection of the purpose of the network may require a court not only to permit a claim for compensation by piercing the veil of connected contracts, but rather to compel the correct performance of the network of contracts.

Consider, for instance, the problem of the franchisee who behaves like a free-rider. In such a case, the franchisee benefits from the brand name in marketing its products or services, but fails to conform to the required standards, thereby potentially inflicting losses on other franchisees in the form of reduced sales. If the franchisor fails to insist upon conformity to the required standards, what remedy might the other franchisees possess? Under the theory of connected contracts, provided that the three conditions regarding close co-operation are satisfied, the franchisees should be entitled to bring a claim for compensatory damages. But such a remedy would not prevent the recurring damage to the brand name of the franchise operation.

In assessing this type of claim, Teubner suggests that a useful analogy might be drawn with the use of a derivative action in company law. The derivative action permits a member of the company, such as a shareholder, to bring a legal claim on behalf of the company when the organs of the company that normally act on its behalf, such as the board of directors, are failing to take action. The occasions when a derivative action can be useful in companies, such as when the board of directors are misusing corporate funds themselves, may be replicated in franchises, as in the case where the franchisor colludes with the delinquent franchisee. In such a case that may arise in a multilateral hierarchical network, such as a franchise, it seems appropriate that one of the other franchisees should be permitted to bring an action on behalf of the franchise operation as a whole, in order to maintain the purpose of the franchise and its brand name. To be effective, such a claim would need to be more than a claim for damages for losses to the franchisees. In order to protect the brand name, this kind of derivative action brought by a franchisee would require an effective remedy, such as an injunction against a continuing breach of the required standards.

9. EXTERNAL NETWORK LIABILITY

Turning finally to the third group of legal problems posed by networks, here we consider the liability of the network to persons outside the network. As the network lacks a formal collective legal identity as a legal person such as a corporation, the network cannot straightforwardly be held liable for the risks it creates. On the contrary, according to the general principles of private law, only the member of the network that has directly caused the damage to the outsider will generally be liable for breach of contract or a tortious wrong. As independent businesses, other members of the network will not be held responsible on grounds of agency or vicarious responsibility. The outsider will therefore be restricted to a claim against the member of the network who is directly responsible for causing the loss.

This delimitation of liability to outsiders may prove inadequate and unsatisfactory in many instances, such as where the particular member of the network who is liable for the damage lacks the resources to meet the claim. From a policy point of view, this restriction may also be vulnerable to the criticism that it allocates responsibility in the wrong place. Where, for instance, the member of the network is merely following the business procedures dictated by the central hub of the network, the placement of the risk of liability on the individual member rather than on the hub or the network as a whole fails to provide the appropriate incentive for the central hub to improve its business procedures. Teubner illustrates this latter problem with the example of the sale of defective financial products within a network of financial services brokers, in which the products are developed at the level of the network and merely marketed by the individual brokers in the network.[83]

Boundaries of Networks

Before examining any further the possibility of external network liability, however, it should be stressed that the division between internal and external network liability is far from clear in practice. In the absence of a formal business association or a corporate entity, the boundaries of a network may often seem unclear and may indeed shift rapidly in some kinds of network with frequent entry and exit of the participants. For instance, was it correct to describe the worker in the temporary agency

[83] Below, Chapter 6, I.

network as an insider to the network, or should the worker be regarded as an outsider, a victim of the risks created by the temporary agency system for provision of work?

In another example, at the very end of the retail supply chain lies the consumer purchasing goods from a retailer; is the consumer an outsider or effectively merely the final link in the chain, bound to the network through loyalty cards, discounts for frequent purchases, and computerised records and predictions of the consumer's purchasing patterns?[84]

By defining networks as comprising independent businesses, Teubner excludes a consumer from membership of the network, so the rights of a consumer will always be analysed in his framework as those of an outsider. But the example of the temporary agency reveals the fragility of this analysis, because that contractual network insists that the worker enters the contract with the agency as an independent business, not an employee of the agency, with the effect that the worker becomes a member of the network, not an outsider. Similarly, in a purchase of goods by using a credit card, if the purchaser uses a card supplied by his or her employer, on Teubner's definition of a contractual network, the purchaser becomes part of the network with the retailer and the issuer of the card, but if the purchaser is a consumer, he or she seems to be categorised as external to the network. With some justification, Peter Heerman observes that results such as these seem 'confusing' and 'strange'.[85] Even so, the differentiation of consumer transactions for some purposes is commonplace in the law, and in the particular example of credit card transactions it is worth recalling the presence of connected lender liability for defective goods and services. This unusual extension of responsibility for defects to the provider of finance might be interpreted as symbolically placing the consumer outside the network for some purposes, even though the consumer must participate in the network in order to make a legally effective acquisition.

Even granted the exclusion of consumers from networks, once one takes into account all the different forms of alliances between businesses, the precise reach of any particular network steadfastly resists precise analysis. Consider the example of Starbucks coffee franchise: as well as managing and expanding its familiar retail format franchises, it arranges for concessions in other franchises such as bookstores, secures exclusive supply arrangements for its coffee in hotel and hospitality chains and

[84] H Collins, 'The Weakest Link: Legal Implications of the Network Architecture of Supply Chains', in M Amstutz and G Teubner (eds), *Networks: Legal Issues of Multilateral Co-operation* (Oxford: Hart Publishing, 2009) 187.

[85] PW Heerman, 'Multilateral Synallagmas in the Law of Connected Contracts', in M Amstutz and G Teubner (eds), *Networks: Legal Issues of Multilateral Co-operation* (Oxford, Hart Publishing, 2009) 103, 110.

franchises, and enters into alliances with established foreign competitor companies to expand the brand into distant markets.[86] Where should the limits of this franchise operation be determined? Damage to the value of the brand would adversely affect all these parties, so in that sense they are bound together with a common purpose, a coalition of separate firms that competes with other brands globally for market share and profitability.

This difficulty of determining the scope of networks must be viewed as another of their paradoxical characteristics. It is the very indeterminacy of the ambit of the network that facilitates its adaptation to changing circumstances, its ability to combine resources and knowledge rapidly and to combine diverse expertise by mutual learning,[87] and its fast response to business opportunities. The response of a network strategy to the question whether to make or buy a product is simply to do both, simultaneously, but co-operatively with others, according to what contributions they might bring to the overall project. Under this business strategy, the precise boundaries of a network will seldom prove transparent and indeed there may be good business and legal reasons to confuse the boundaries between separate organisations. To speak therefore of the external liability of networks should not be understood as involving an implicit claim regarding the certainty of the scope of a network. On the contrary, many of the puzzles considered under the heading of external liability concern precisely those inter-organisational relations where their boundaries remain fuzzy.

Responsibility in Groups of Companies

Owing to the indeterminacy of the scope of networks, the problem of external network liability shares some features with the ascription of responsibility in groups of companies. A holding or parent company, which controls its subsidiaries and receives the residual profits, is, in the absence of special legal provisions, formally not responsible for the actions of its subsidiaries, because they are independent legal entities. Most legal systems have appreciated the need to 'pierce the corporate veil' in appropriate cases, so that the parent company is held legally responsible for the actions of its wholly controlled subsidiary. For example, the parent company may decide to close its subsidiary on grounds of

[86] PWL Vlaar, *Contracts and Trust in Alliances: Discovering, Creating and Appropriating Value* (Cheltenham, Edward Elgar, 2008) p 4, citing D Ernst, 'Envisioning collaboration', in HD Bamford, B Gomes-Casseres and MS Robinson (eds), *Mastering Alliance Strategy* (San Francisco, Jossey-Bass, 2003) 19.

[87] B Nooteboom, *Inter-firm Collaboration, Learning and Networks* (London, Routledge, 2004).

insolvency, causing economic dismissals of its workforce. The social costs of these dismissals will not be the responsibility of the parent company, as a separate legal entity, and the workers may not be fully compensated for any lost wages and benefits claimed against the insolvent subsidiary company. Furthermore, it should be remembered that the insolvency of the subsidiary company is itself produced by a decision of the parent company not to provide additional capital. In these circumstances, the law might permit a direct claim by the workers for their wages against the parent company. In several contexts in English labour law, workers of one employer are deemed to have legal relations with an 'associated employer', in order to ensure that the protective effects of the legislation are not subverted by formal corporate distinctions within a centrally owned as managed group of companies.[88] By permitting a claim against an associated employer, the law in effect 'pierces the corporate veil'. By analogy, Teubner sometimes speaks of 'piercing the contractual veil' in networks, by which he means that the law permits an action against the hub of the network or the network as a whole, even though under the normal principles of private law only the node in direct contact with the outsider would be legally responsible. But this analogy between corporate groups and networks cannot be drawn precisely owing to the paradoxical features of networks.

A network that is closely controlled by a dominant business hub, as in franchising, acts like the parent company in a group of companies by issuing instructions to the nodes of the network. Like subsidiary companies, members of the network are expected to comply with these instructions. Yet, at the same time, the members of the network are expected to act in their own interests, to be autonomous, and to accept sole responsibility for their own actions. Depending on the challenges it faces, a network can function alternatively either like a centralised organisation or as a constellation of independent businesses. This flexible method of co-ordination probably enjoys efficiency advantages in terms of adaptation and innovation, but at the same time it creates the space for opportunism. When it suits the network, as in the case of bulk purchases, it acts as if it were a single business organisation in order to obtain market power, but when it is sued by an external party, such as the workers dismissed by an insolvent franchisee, the network insists that it comprises autonomous business entities, none of which are legally responsible for the actions of the others.

[88] Trade Union and Labour Relations (Consolidation) Act 1992, s 297; Employment Rights Act 1996, s 231; H Collins, 'Ascription of Legal Responsibility to Groups in Complex Patters of Economic Integration' (1990) 53 *MLR* 731, 739.

Organised Irresponsibility

Unless the law responds appropriately to these particular qualities of networks, this type of business co-ordination creates the risk of 'organised irresponsibility'. In other words, the network achieves the level of organisation that it requires for efficient co-ordination of productive relations, but simultaneously minimises the risk of external liability for the network as a whole.

In response to this problem, Teubner suggests that in some examples of highly co-ordinated networks controlled by a central business hub, as in many instances of franchising, external liability should be attributed to the hub in the same instances as where the corporate veil would be pierced in order to establish the responsibility of a parent company. He justifies this measure as an appropriate response to a 'misuse of the legal form'.[89] For example, if the operating handbook for a restaurant franchise requires franchisees to prepare food in a particular way and it is shown that this method creates a risk of a health problem for consumers which has materialised in this particular claim, the presence of a tightly co-ordinated network would justify, according to Teubner's proposal, holding the whole network responsible for the liability for personal injury, not solely the particular franchisee from whom the customer purchased the unhealthy food.

But in other, less centralised networks, Teubner proposes that other members of the network should be held liable to external parties to the extent and in the proportion that they were involved in the particular transaction with the external party.[90] Because the network is not itself a legal entity, the function of the network concept in this context is to explain the transfer in whole or part of legal responsibility to other members of the network. For example, in a case where a customer of a bank instructs its bank to transfer funds to the account of the customer of another receiving bank, in the event of loss, delay, or misapplication of the funds, the transferor bank should be permitted to shift responsibility onto the bank directly responsible for the loss or misapplication of the funds, whether it be an intermediary bank or the receiving bank. But does this shift of responsibility suggest that the customer should enjoy a direct cause of action against the intermediary or receiving bank that failed to comply with its instructions correctly? The rules of privity of contract would normally prevent a direct claim for breach of contract by the customer against a remote bank for failure to comply with instructions. Similarly, English courts have rejected claims in tort for pure

[89] Below, Chapter 6, III, 1.
[90] Below, Chapter 6, III, 2.

economic loss, holding that a bank does not owe a duty of care to non-customers, arguing instead that recourse should be made via the existing contractual relationships.[91]

Marc Amstutz discusses a case of this kind that arose within the Swiss Interbank Clearing system, a giro network between the banks.[92] The federal court permitted a direct contractual claim against the receiving bank, which had misapplied the funds.[93] Surprisingly, the court did not justify its decision on orthodox grounds such as agency, a contract in favour of a third party, or a contract with protective effects for third parties. Instead the court insisted more straightforwardly, but without any clear doctrinal foundation, that customers of banks need to be protected from mistakes by all the banks co-operating together in the giro system and that the appropriate way to achieve that goal was to permit a direct contractual claim of the customer against the bank that had misapplied the funds. The court seems to take the view that a bank giro network should not be analysed as a collection of bilateral contracts but rather as a multilateral co-operative system, which, for the purposes of identifying responsibility for external liability, should be regarded simultaneously both as an entire, autonomous system, in order to 'pierce the contractual veil', and as comprised of separate businesses to identify which banks should be held directly liable to the customer for the loss.

Such a radical departure from the ordinary principles of contractual responsibility seems unlikely to be imitated in the common law. In the absence of fraud, the customer would normally be limited to its contractual remedy against the transferor bank, which in turn could seek an indemnity down the contractual chain. It is possible that if the customer could prove negligence on the part of an intermediate or receiving bank, it could bring a claim for pure economic loss, but it would probably have to be shown that the negligent bank had assumed responsibility towards the customer for the correct application of the instructions rather than simply receiving the instruction from another bank.[94] Assuming that the chain of contracts between the banks holds and is not disrupted by

[91] *Wells v First National Commercial Bank* [1998] EWCA Civ 112; special rules apply to cheques, which pass through the network of the clearing system, such that any bank that misapplies a cheque may be liable to the true owner of the cheque in the tort of conversion, but a bank benefits from a special statutory defence of contributory negligence on the part of the issuer of the cheque: Cheques Act 1957, s 4; see R Goode, *Commercial Law* 3rd edn (London, Penguin, 2004) 549.

[92] M Amstutz, 'The Constitution of Contractual Networks' in M Amstutz and G Teubner (eds), *Networks: Legal Issues of Multilateral Co-operation* (Oxford, Hart Publishing, 2009) 309, 329; see also PW Heerman, 'Multilateral Synallagmas in the Law of Connected Contracts', in M Amstutz and G Teubner (eds), *Networks: Legal Issues of Multilateral Co-operation* (Oxford, Hart Publishing, 2009) 103, 110–11.

[93] BGE 121 III 310.

[94] *Customs and Excise Commissioners v Barclays Bank* [2006] UKHL 28; [2006] 1 WLR 1.

disclaimers or insolvency, ultimately the bank responsible for the misappropriation would be held liable to indemnify the others back up the chain. Thus the outcome would be the same as in the Swiss decision, in the sense that the customer would receive compensation and the negligent bank would foot the bill, but the legal reasoning in the common law would differ because the customer could not sue directly the bank at fault. The legal position in the EU has now been harmonised by the Payment Systems Directive.[95] Articles 75–77 establish the basic position that the customer should claim compensation or a refund against its own bank, and grants that bank a right of recourse against any other bank or intermediary in the payment network that has misapplied the funds.

In some cases of external network liability, however, it will prove impossible to determine which of the various members of the network had actually caused the problem. Indeed, it will be the failure to co-ordinate activity between several independent businesses that may be at the root of the problem. An example may arise in connection with a franchised transport system: the responsibility for a train derailment may be difficult to determine in the circumstances where the production of the service requires the successful co-ordination of a network of companies, such as the franchise operator, the track operator, the contractors responsible for maintenance and repair, and the contractors responsible for supervision of operations. In such a case, only the franchise operator has a contract with an injured passenger, but the cause of the accident may lie in a combination of failures to disclose information and to process it efficiently between the various members of the network. Where clear causal explanations for individual responsibility for the accident are not available, Teubner suggests that there should be joint and several liability of all the network members who appear to have been involved.[96] In such a case, the existence of the network justifies this unusual response to the difficulties of causally attributing a wrong to a particular business. But the network is not liable itself; its existence rather justifies the relaxation of the normal rules of responsibility that require the ascertainment of the individual that caused the wrong. In English law, an analogy might be drawn with cases where it is impossible scientifically to determine the correct attribution of responsibility among a small group of defendants. In such cases, the courts have permitted the claimant to succeed, holding all the defendants jointly and severally liable for the tort.[97] The presence

[95] Directive 2007/64.

[96] Below, Chapter 6, VI, 2.

[97] *Fairchild v Glenhaven Funeral Services Ltd* [2002] UKHL 22; [2003] 1 AC 32. In *Barker v Corus* [2006] UKHL 20; [2006] 2 WLR 1027, the liability was apportioned according to the relative degree of contribution to the risk, but this was reversed in Compensation Act 2006, s 3, to re-establish joint and severable liability, with the possibility of contribution from others for contributory negligence.

of a network of connected contracts might similarly justify the extension of liability to other members of the network where they have contributed to the creation of the risk of harm.

This discussion of the external liability of networks examines their darker side. Although many business-oriented discussions justly celebrate the competitiveness and virtues of networks in certain kinds of productive activities, the issue of external legal liability raises the question of whether these novel forms of business organisation achieve part of their advantage over other mechanisms of economic co-ordination by externalising and evading the risks of their activities. The mission of sociological jurisprudence is to try to identify when such unjustified externalisation of risk may be occurring and to propose techniques by which the law may reconstitute the legal issues to prevent that from happening. Under the theory of connected contracts, the external liability of networks does not require the law to view networks as the same as corporations or business associations. The members of the network will be held individually responsible for their actions to the extent that they have contributed to the causation of loss to an outsider. The network as a whole is not held responsible in itself. But the concept of a network of connected contracts explains and justifies why it may not be appropriate to restrict liability to or focus liability entirely on the member of the network who had a direct contractual relation with the injured party.

10. CONCLUSION

The sceptical reaction of common lawyers to the vigorous German debate about networks is perhaps nicely summed up by Terence Daintith in his observation:

> If ... 'network' is not a legal concept, the decision to describe any given cluster of contracts as a network is essentially one of intellectual taste and not worth extended argument.[98]

The main objective of this introduction has been to persuade a reader schooled in the common law that arguments about networks matter, not just at the level of conceptual architecture and theoretical purity in law, but also in helping to resolve recurrent commercial disputes.

The theory of networks addresses a business phenomenon that sometimes puzzles and confuses private law. Some kinds of inter-firm co-operation exhibit a degree of co-ordination and organisation that,

[98] T Daintith, 'Mixed Public-Private Networks as Vehicles for Regulatory Policy', in M Amstutz and G Teubner (eds), *Networks: Legal Issues of Multilateral Co-operation* (Oxford, Hart Publishing, 2009) 291, 298–99.

despite their constitution in a collection of bilateral contracts rather than in a formal association with a legal personality, seems to warrant regarding them for some purposes as having elements of a collective identity. In the common law, the unease when confronted with networks has been experienced perhaps most keenly in connection with construction projects, where the traditional legal analysis in the form of a web of bilateral contracts seems to ignore unjustifiably the organisational aspects of the project. The symptom of that unease can been seen in the pressure to create exceptions to the doctrine of privity by manipulating the rules of tort, either by expanding or confining duties of care between parties that lack direct contractual links between them. As has been appreciated in German legal doctrine, however, the challenge presented by networks to traditional private law principles and rules should be understood more broadly to encompass a wide range of inter-organisational co-operative arrangements.

Whilst the study of the debates in German law and other legal systems in the civil law family should heighten the awareness of common lawyers to the difficulties presented by networks, it is more troublesome to view the solutions proposed, such as Teubner's theory of connected contracts, as ready candidates for transplant into the common law. What the German doctrinal debates may teach common lawyers instead is that existing traditional solutions to the problems posed by networks will probably not work satisfactorily in the end. In some cases it may be possible to manipulate the law of agency, stretch the law of tort, invent on grounds of business necessity a collateral contract, or imply an obligation of greater loyalty than one normally discovers in commercial contracts. Similarly, legislation may be able to address particular problems, such as to award franchisees mandatory rights against the controllers of the network or to deem some businesses to be associated and jointly liable for the purposes of a particular instance of external liability. But none of these solutions addresses the underlying problem that networks present us with this Janus-faced practice of economic co-ordination, not simply a cluster of bilateral contracts, but not quite a single business association either. Whilst common lawyers may prefer to use pragmatic regulatory fixes to solve identifiable narrow problems, German lawyers have sought a more fundamental, systematic solution, one in which 'network' would become a legal concept.

Introduction

The Aims of Legal Analysis of Networks

'NETWORK IS NOT a legal concept' – the argument pursued by this book begins where Richard Buxbaum's article ends.[1] The discussion focuses on the appropriate legal regulation of business networks, virtual enterprises, just-in-time systems and franchise chains that are normally concluded in the form of bilateral contracts, but at the same time give rise to multilateral (legal) effects. Such networks are extraordinarily confusing phenomena of private co-ordination, since they fit neither within the market category nor within the concept of organisation. After much hesitation, sociologists and economists have responded with theories that conceive of networks as 'independent institutions', differing starkly from traditional forms of economic co-ordination.[2] But how should the law react when networks exhibit traits of 'organised irresponsibility', when they give rise to conflicts about internal responsibility, or when they produce negative externalities that impact on outsiders? The concept of 'network' itself is clearly inappropriate as a technical legal term since networks cut across the conceptual framework of private law doctrine. In legal terms, networks can take the form either of partnerships, corporate groups, relational contracts or of special tort/contractual relationships. For this reason alone, the autonomy of legal doctrine precludes the immediate adoption of the social science concept of 'network' as a legal category.

But this is only the start of the difficulties. Legal doctrine must develop its categories with sensitivity to its social environment. Legal categories must be carefully adapted to the productive possibilities and potential risks of new social phenomena. 'Socially adequate' legal concepts are a 'corollary of the autonomy of legal doctrine'.[3] Law is therefore obliged to

[1] Richard M Buxbaum (1993), 'Is "Network" a Legal Concept?', *Journal of Institutional and Theoretical Economics* 149, 698*ff*, 704.

[2] For an informative discussion on these theories, see Johannes Weyer (ed) (2000), *Soziale Netzwerke: Konzepte und Methoden der sozialwissenschaftlichen Netzwerkforschung*. Munich: Oldenbourg; Arnold Windeler (2001), *Unternehmungsnetzwerke: Konstitution und Strukturation*. Wiesbaden: Westdeutscher.

[3] On the autonomy of legal doctrine and its contemporaneous social dependency, see Niklas Luhmann (1974), *Rechtssystem und Rechtsdogmatik*. Stuttgart: Kohlhammer, 49*ff*; (2004), *Law as a Social System*. Oxford: Oxford University Press, 423*ff*.

develop an independent and, at the same time, 'network appropriate' categorisation, which is responsive to the network's logic of action. Whilst legislation and the judiciary may be satisfied with isolated instances of regulation of networks, legal doctrine needs to develop a fully fledged 'social model' of networks, which highlights their considerable social risks and presents us with a normative perspective within which they may be combated.[4]

By reference to these standards, does the concept of 'connected contracts' provide an adequate legal categorisation of networks? This is the central question tackled by this book. Connected contracts were first given form in a variety of contexts within a lengthy chain of cases. They were then adopted within special consumer legislation and were recently given a legal definition within the German Civil Code (*Bürgerliches Gesetzbuch* (BGB)).[5] The category of connected contracts needs to be tested to ascertain whether it is sensitive to logic of networks and suitable for coping with the risks generated by networks. 'Generalised reciprocity' is the shorthand formula used to identify the normative content of connected contracts; the concept denotes the temporal, material and social generalisation of synallagmatic obligations within the bilateral contract.

At the same time, however, 'generalised reciprocity' is the central characteristic of social networks.[6] It is the normative response to the specific contradiction to which networks and connected contracts, in their paradoxical *unitas multiplex*, are exposed. This contradiction, however, possesses its own potential. The concept of connected contracts was of course originally developed to tackle the very specific problems of purchases obtained on credit supplied by a financial institution (financed purchasing), and was later, only very cautiously, applied to other forms of financed property transactions. Within the current context, however, the category is bound excessively to the narrowly specific problems of purchases supported by financial credit and must now be generalised before we can attempt to re-specify it for networks.

[4] On legal social reality models, Dan Wielsch (2000), *Freiheit und Funktion: Zur Struktur- und Theoriegeschichte des Rechts der Wirtschaftsgesellschaft*. Baden-Baden: Nomos, 166*ff*, with further references.

[5] § 358 (III) BGB. Legal doctrine on connected contracts has been developed by Joachim Gernhuber (1973), 'Austausch und Kredit im rechtsgeschäftlichen Verbund: Zur Lehre von den Vertragsverbindungen' in Gotthard Paulus (ed), *Festschrift für Karl Larenz zum 70. Geburtstag*. Munich: Beck, 455*ff*; (1989) *Das Schuldverhältnis: Begründung und Änderung, Pflichten und Strukturen, Drittwirkungen*. Tübingen: Mohr Siebeck, 710*ff*.

[6] Klaus Semlinger (1993), 'Effizienz und Autonomie in Zulieferungsnetzwerken: Zum strategischen Gehalt von Kooperation' in Wolfgang H Staehle and Jörg Sydow (eds), *Managementforschung 3*. Berlin: de Gruyter, 309*ff*, 333*f*, with further references; Walter Powell (1990), 'Neither Market nor Hierarchy: Network Forms of Organization', *Research in Organizational Behavior* 12, 295*ff*.

In methodological terms, an 'institutional analysis' of networks must be interdisciplinary in nature. Contract law doctrine as well as the relevant case law and existing legislation must be analysed, in order to determine to what degree 'connected contracts' possess the 'conceptual readiness' to react appropriately to the 'opportunity structure' presented by the social phenomena of networks as it has been identified in numerous economic and sociological studies.[7] However, in its efforts to give appropriate form to the opportunities and risks posed by networks, private law must also take care to maintain an adequate distance from its neighbouring disciplines. At no time should the efficiency principle used by economists to characterise networks as a market/hierarchy hybrid be permitted to serve as a legal norm for networks.[8] Similar care should be exercised in relation to the principle of the 'social embeddedness' of economic transactions, which sociologists recognise as being characteristic of networks.[9] In stark contrast, legal doctrine should insist on an interdisciplinary division of labour within which each discipline furnishes an autonomous contribution from its own perspective. In other words: social science analyses should explore the logic of action within networks, should reveal the opportunities and risks posed by operations of networks, and should reveal perspectives on alternative solutions beyond our traditional categories of market and hierarchy. Legal doctrine should take note of such analyses as 'irritations', but evolve concepts, norms and principles out of its own conceptual tradition, which might then be appropriate as grounded legal solutions to novel problems of co-ordination and liability.[10]

[7] Institutional analysis as a methodologically demanding research programme in the form proposed by Philip Selznick (1969), *Law, Society and Industrial Justice*. New York: Russell Sage, 35*ff*; (1992), *The Moral Commonwealth: Social Theory and the Promise of Community*. Berkeley: University of California, 229*ff*.

[8] See the most prominent proponent of economic network analysis, Oliver Williamson (1985), *The Economic Institutions of Capitalism: Firms, Markets, Relational Contracting*. New York: Free Press; (1991a), 'Comparative Economic Organization: The Analysis of Discrete Structural Alternatives' *Administrative Science Quarterly* 36, 269*ff*; (1996), *The Mechanisms of Governance*. Oxford: Oxford University Press.

[9] See the most prominent proponent of sociological network analysis, Powell (1990).

[10] On the effort to create an autonomous but contemporaneously interdisciplinary private legal doctrine, see Christian Joerges and Gunther Teubner (eds) (2003), *Rechtsverfassungsrecht: Recht-Fertigungen zwischen Sozialtheorie und Privatrechtsdogmatik*. Baden-Baden: Nomos; Marc Amstutz (2001), *Evolutorisches Wirtschaftsrecht: Vorstudien zum Recht und seiner Methode in den Diskurskollisionen der Marktgesellschaft*. Baden-Baden: Nomos, 303*ff*; Hugh Collins (1999), *Regulating Contracts*. Oxford: Oxford University Press, 3*ff*; Thomas Raiser (1999), *Das lebende Recht: Recht in Deutschland*. 3rd edn, Baden-Baden: Nomos, 33*ff*, 44*f*; Gunther Teubner (1993a), *Law as an Autopoietic System*. London: Blackwells, chap. 6 and 7; Rainer Walz (ed) (1983), *Sozialwissenschaften im Zivilrecht*. Neuwied: Luchterhand, 6*ff*. On the perspectives for a social science oriented jurisprudence, which studies networks as an exemplary case of application, see Dorothea Jansen (2003), 'Soziologie, Rechtssoziologie und Rechtswissenschaft' in Stefan Machura (ed), *Recht, Gesellschaft, Kommunikation: Festschrift für Klaus Röhl*. Baden-Baden: Nomos, 24*ff*, 31*ff*.

Accordingly, the book has the following structure. The first Chapter deploys social science research on networks and concentrates on the new risks that they pose, in order to identify the regulatory problems to which law should respond with norms apportioning responsibility and liability. The second Chapter attempts to use social science analyses, in order to determine which legal categories are best suited to dealing with the very particular operational logics, structural conditions, potentialities, hazards and conflicts associated with networks. In particular, legal categories will be examined in order to ascertain whether they are able to take account of those contradictory expectations that social scientists have identified in networks. In the third and defining Chapter, the legal category of 'connected contracts' will be more closely tested, in order to ascertain whether it has sufficient normative potential to permit the elaboration of legal principles upon which appropriate norms governing responsibility in networks might be built. Sociological analyses of the phenomena of 'double attribution' within networks prove to be relevant here.

The subsequent chapters will elaborate the specifics of the general model developed here. Each seeks to confront the social science analyses of a typical constellation of conflicts in networks with some potential solutions in legal doctrine. The fourth Chapter concerns the internal constitution of networks. The focus is on the structural contradiction between bilateral exchange and multilateral connectivity. What impact do network effects have upon the manifold bilateral exchange relationships within the network? The legal question here is one of whether the concept of the 'network purpose' – in contrast to the contractual purpose or the corporate purpose – furnishes adequate standards for network-specific obligations within the bilateral contract and for the judicial review of standard form contracts. The fifth Chapter tackles a further contradiction that arises typically in networks. Since the social sciences have identified an unusual tension between co-operation and competition in networks, what consequences does this have for the regulation of internal legal relationships? In practice, one of the most relevant questions is whether members of the network are directly liable to each other; that is, the question of whether the legal characterisation of such relations as connected contracts permits the construction of quasi-contractual duties between those members of the network who do not stand in a bilateral contractual relationship with one another. The sixth Chapter tackles questions of external liability in the light of the contradiction between the collective and the individual orientation that is manifested in the paradoxical demand for a *unitas muliplex*. The focus is on the question of whether third parties external to the network can only bring legal claims against individual contractual parties, or whether a 'collective' liability might arise with respect to the network centre or other members of the network under certain conditions.

1

The Network Revolution

New Risks – Unsolved Legal Issues

I. TWO 'IRRITATING' LEGAL CASES

IN A COURAGEOUS decision, the Stuttgart Court of Appeals (*Oberlandesgericht*) established 'piercing liability' between members of a distribution system who did not stand in a contractual relationship with one another. The grounds for the judgment, however, are highly unconvincing.[1]

The automobile firm, Fiat, had established a two-tier distribution system.[2] In a first tier Fiat concluded direct distribution contracts with so-called A-dealers. In their turn, A-dealers concluded independent contracts with B-dealers in a second distribution tier. Whilst Fiat was not a contractual partner within second-tier contracts, they were able to exert influence on the second tier of distribution since A-tier contracts imposed the obligation on A-dealers to include clauses within B-tier contracts making the validity of such contracts reliant upon Fiat's agreement. In addition, Fiat was able to demand that A-dealers should ensure that their contracts with B-dealers could be terminated under certain conditions. Following pressure from Fiat, an A-dealer, who had no wish to do so, terminated his contract with a B-dealer, ending the distributorship at very short notice. In response to the B-dealer's claim against both the A-dealer and Fiat, the Court of Appeals imposed liability upon Fiat by means of 'piercing liability'.

[1] OLG Stuttgart NJW-RR 1990, 491.

[2] This two-tier organisational network structure is typical for car manufacturers. See, generally, Peter Florenz (1992), *Das Konzept des vertikalen Marketing: Entwicklung und Darstellung am Beispiel der deutschen Automobilwirtschaft*. Bergisch Gladbach: Eul, 181*f*; Carsten-Thomas Ebenroth and Marc Strittmatter (1993), 'Fremdbestimmte Investitionen in der Umstrukturierung von Absatzmittlungsverhältnissen auf dem Automobilsektor', *Betriebs Berater* 48, 1521*ff*, 1530; Rainer Kulms (2000), *Schuldrechtliche Organisationsverträge in der Unternehmenskooperation*. Baden-Baden: Nomos, 107*ff*.

Without even touching upon the difficult questions of liability arising from the incitement to terminate the contract,[3] the Court found that the Fiat distribution centre, which had no direct contractual relationship with the B-dealer, was liable under 'contractual provisions'. However, the Court stumbled across so many difficulties in its endeavour to construct a 'quasi-contract' that, in order to make contractual liability at all plausible, it was forced to identify factual hooks within the social context. First, it sought out elements of trust and, in a daring analogy to existing case law on duties of disclosure of information between banks (!), established a relationship of trust between the Fiat distribution centre and the B-dealer, in order to justify the existence between them of a 'continuing business relation'.[4] In addition, the Court of Appeals distinguished an element of 'incorporation' of the B-dealer within the business organisation and, deploying labour and company law principles – without, though, specifying their exact legal provenance – found in favour of contractual liability on the basis that the B-dealer formed a part of the distribution system controlled by Fiat.[5] Then the Court implicitly referred back to the law of corporate groups: the dual influence that the centre of the distribution system exercises on B-dealer contracts makes B-dealers 'dependent' and gives the centre a 'controlling position'. The question of whether this entails an analogy to the law of corporate groups nonetheless remains open. In a final analysis, the demand made of A-dealers by Fiat at the centre of the distribution system that they should terminate contracts with B-dealers and discontinue distribution is defined as a direct breach of contractual obligations owed by Fiat to the B-dealer. *Ex facto jus oritur*?

The second 'irritating' case concerns the external relationship of a distribution system with clients. The Karlsruhe Court of Appeals (*Oberlandesgericht*) confirmed that a client who had been the victim of misinformation on the part of a direct dealer within a contractual distribution

[3] See Thomas in *Palandt* (2003), *Bürgerliches Gesetzbuch*. 62nd edn, Munich: Beck, § 826, 52.

[4] Comprehensively on this legal institution and critical of its potential status as an autonomous legal obligation, see Joachim Gernhuber (1989), *Das Schuldverhältnis: Begründung und Änderung, Pflichten und Strukturen, Drittwirkungen*. Tübingen: Mohr Siebeck, 409*ff*. Also critical of the Court's construction, Mathias Rohe (1998), *Netzverträge: Rechtsprobleme komplexer Vertragsverbindungen*. Tübingen: Mohr Siebeck, 465, who seeks to support the plausible result with a notion of 'liability arising out of a network contract'.

[5] The Court seems to be wholly unaware of the difficulties associated with applying the principle of 'incorporation' to 'total institutions'; see, here, however, two early references to incorporation, Wolfgang Siebert (1935), *Das Arbeitsverhältnis in der Ordnung der nationalen Arbeit*. Hamburg: Hanseatische Verlagsanstalt; and to the concept of the 'total institution', Erving Goffman (1961), *Asylums: Essays on the Social Situation of Mental Patients and Other Inmates*. Garden City: Anchor Books.

system might enforce a piercing liability claim against the central distribution node. Here too, however, the Court was unable to identify a satisfactory doctrinal basis for piercing liability.[6]

A Japanese car importer had built up a dealer distribution system in Germany. The importer had only succeeded in gaining German market entry relatively late in the day and consequently had difficulties in finding responsible dealers. Accordingly, the importer was reliant upon dealers whose business credentials and solvency were not immediately apparent. The distribution contract with dealers stipulated that vehicles would remain the property of the importer until full payment of the sales price had been made. A customer took possession of a vehicle from a dealer, paying an initial instalment on the sale price. The customer was given the vehicle, keys and road licence, but not ownership papers since, according to the importer's distribution contract, these remained in trust until full payment of the sales price had been made. Under pressure from the dealer and their incorrect claim that full payment was necessary for the internal process of completion of the sale, the customer paid the remainder of the price, without, however, receiving the vehicle's ownership papers. On the insolvency of the dealer, the importer demanded the return of the vehicle from the customer. The customer then claimed that the importer, as the central node within the distribution system, was liable for the failure of the dealer to fulfil its legal obligations.

The court first confirmed the importers' demand for the return of property under § 985 of the German Civil Code (BGB) and rejected the customer's defence of receipt of property in good faith on the basis that the customer's naiveté constituted gross negligence under § 932(II) BGB and § 366 of the Commercial Code (HGB). However, the court then permitted the customer to advance a claim for liability in damages against the importer, which it then limited on the basis of contributory negligence. The court thus imposed piercing liability on the central distribution node, whereby the dealer's breach of contractual obligations was ascribed to the importer.

The grounds for the decision are adventurous.[7] The Court creates an explosive mix of three different ingredients of tort law: organisational culpability, breach of director's liability, and liability for the acts of assistants. The quality of the judgment is not improved, however, even if we make a clear distinction between the various grounds for liability. The court should either have explicitly extended at least one of these principles of liability, clearly distinguishing it from previous precedent, or it should have rejected piercing liability. The finding of organisational

[6] OLG Karlsruhe NZV 1989, 434.
[7] OLG Karlsruhe NZV 1989, 435.

culpability under § 31 BGB,[8] which the Court of Appeals held was present by virtue of the inclusion of less than trustworthy dealers within the distribution system, would fail under current precedents for two reasons. First, notwithstanding the recent expansion within this form of liability, a contractual dealer acting in his own name and at his own cost still cannot be recognised as a 'functional representative' of the distribution centre, since a vital precondition remains one of action within a unitary enterprise.[9] Second, organisational liability is still in principle restricted to authentic legal persons and has no application to multiple contractual relationships.[10] By the same token, the finding of liability in tort under § 823(I) BGB[11] is precluded by the intrusion of independent contractual dealers into the business network. Equally, the escape hatch of vicarious liability under § 831 BGB[12] is closed since independent enterprises simply do not qualify as agents for each other.[13] Further, even were one to impute this latter categorisation of agents to independent enterprises,[14] one would still be confronted with the notorious difficulties posed by § 831, which for the most part preclude vicarious liability.

Are these two judgments best summed up by the cruel phrase 'the soundest judgment with the dullest opinion'? Certainly, the result is plausible and the justification weak. Nonetheless, we cannot simply say that the reasoning is wrong. Rather, both cases concerned a phenomenon that cannot currently be addressed within the concepts of contract and tort – the network phenomenon. The legal system has been confronted with an evolutionary trend, which it cannot decode entirely using its own analytical tools: independent businesses commit themselves to closely

[8] S. 31 BGB: The association is liable for the damage to a third party that the board, a member of the board or another constitutionally appointed representative causes through an act committed by it or him in carrying out the business with which it or he is entrusted, where the act gives rise to liability in
damages.

[9] See Heinrichs in *Palandt* (2003) § 31, 3.

[10] Herbert Roth (1989), 'Anmerkung zu OLG Karlsruhe', *Neue Zeitschrift für Verkehrsrecht* 2, 435*ff*, 436.

[11] § 823(1) BGB: A person who, intentionally or negligently, unlawfully injures the life, body, health, freedom, property or another right of another person is liable to make compensation to the other party for the damage arising from this.

[12] § 831(1) BGB: A person who uses another person to perform a task is liable to make compensation for the damage that the other unlawfully inflicts on a third party when carrying out the task. Liability in damages does not apply if the principal exercises reasonable care when selecting the person deployed and, to the extent that he is to procure devices or equipment or to manage the business activity, in the procurement or management, or if the damage would have occurred even if this care had been exercised.

[13] See Thomas in *Palandt* (2003) § 831, 8.

[14] Thus, Roth (1989), 436; Peter Bräutigam (1994), *Deliktische Außenhaftung im Franchising: Eine Untersuchung zur außervertraglichen Schadensersatzhaftung der Mitglieder von Franchisesystemen*. Baden-Baden: Nomos, 130*ff*; Edgar Pasderski (1998), *Die Außenhaftung des Franchisegebers*. Aachen: Mainz, 174.

inter-connected co-operative networks that cut through the distinction made between market and hierarchy and that made between contract and corporation.

If distribution systems were organised as unitary enterprises under company and labour law, we would still be confronted by the problem of determining liability, but this would no longer be an issue of piercing liability, neither would it violate the rules on privity of contract. In both cases, standard private law claims would as a matter of course result in the contractual liability of the corporation. In the Fiat case, a direct contractual relationship would be established between the corporation and the branch manager, within the terms of which the legality of the termination of the contract and any consequent liability might be judged. In the Japanese car importer case, the client would have enjoyed contractual claims against the unitary enterprise.

If, in contrast, the distribution relations were wholly constituted by the market (in line with the traditional model of independent stratified market processes: manufacturers – wholesale distributors – retail distributors), the problem of piercing liability would similarly not arise. In neither of these cases would the correct application of tort or contractual norms permit the establishment of liability. In the case of Fiat, the termination of the contract with B could only be judged with regard to an internal relationship, so that no liability claim could successfully be made against the manufacturer as a third party to the contract. The fraudulent behaviour of the dealer in the Japanese car importer case could not be laid at the door of the manufacturer/large-scale distributor. Where the distribution of goods takes place by means of independent stratified processes, which are competitively organised within markets, the piercing of the distribution system is precluded in both constellations: neither is it possible with regard to internal relationships, nor can it be established in the case of external relationships.

In conclusion, the networking of independent economic organisations causes judicial irritation. The construction of an integrated distribution system, which, on the one hand, entails more than simple market relationships, but, on the other, does not create any true organisational relationships, forces the judges to establish piercing liability, but at the same time, causes them huge difficulties when they attempt to justify this decision.

'Judicial irritation' – the concept has a double significance: judges are irritated by network phenomena and are provoked to respond to these anomalies with piercing liability. In turn, these precedents on piercing liability irritate legal doctrine, which regards such seemingly equity-oriented or *ad hoc* exceptions to privity of contract as a challenge to the workability of doctrinal concepts.[15] Is traditional doctrine able to characterise network phenomena such that simple equitable exceptions can be transformed into conceptually precise rules that both do justice to reality and are founded in principle?

II. APPROPRIATE DOCTRINAL RESPONSES?

Even the most detailed of doctrinal understandings are of little use in any further analysis of the case law. The limited perspectives of the courtroom preclude proper appreciation of the historical impact of economic networks within distribution systems, delivery systems, and other multilateral co-operative relationships. Their construction of reality, grounded in 'two-party proceedings', necessarily dissects the complex relationships that multilateral networks establish into bilateral claims and counterclaims. Working from the viewpoint of the claimant or defendant, this approach to understanding the phenomenon can only take limited note of the overarching conflicts and risks that the networking of market relationships entails. In this respect, any doctrinal approach seeking to characterise network phenomena within general legal concepts must reproduce the classical claim and counter-claim culture and inevitably conclude by balancing up the interests of the two parties.

However, courtroom proceedings gain significance in their guise as smoke alarms for social conflicts. Where ingenious judges intervene via piercing liability into contractual distribution systems on only the flimsiest of legal grounds, this is a clear signal that doctrinal reasoning must be comprehensively reviewed.[16] Further, even those weak justifications that are offered supply us with indicators of where the real problems are to be found. It is no accident that the court in the Fiat case referred to 'incorporation' within the network', to 'dependence' and to 'control', and

[15] For comprehensive discussion of the relationship between piercing liability and doctrine, see Eckhard Rehbinder (1969), *Konzernaußenrecht und allgemeines Privatrecht: Eine rechtsvergleichende Untersuchung nach deutschem und amerikanischem Recht*. Bad Homburg: Gehlen, 69*ff*; (1997), 'Neues zum Durchgriff unter besonderer Berücksichtigung der höchstrichterlichen Rechtsprechung' in Heinz-Dieter Assmann (ed), *Wirtschafts- und Medienrecht in der offenen Demokratie: Freundesgabe für Friedrich Kübler*. Heidelberg: Müller, 493*ff*, 496*ff*.

[16] This viewpoint, emphasising the two facets of case law irritation, is characteristic of case law analyses by Joerges, who has productively applied the notion to network phenomena in order to identify new doctrinal orientations in the law of unjust enrichment, consumer law and franchising law. See Christian Joerges (1977), *Bereicherungsrecht als Wirtschaftsrecht: Eine Untersuchung zur Entwicklung von Leistungs- und Eingriffskondiktion*. Cologne: Otto Schmidt, 61*ff*; (1981), *Verbraucherschutz als Rechtsproblem: Eine Untersuchung zum Stand der Theorie und zu den Entwicklungsperspektiven des Verbraucherrechts*. Heidelberg: Recht and Wirtschaft, 58*ff*; (1991), 'Status and Contract in Franchising Law' in C Joerges (ed), *Franchising and the Law: Theoretical and Comparative Approaches in Europe and the United States*. Baden-Baden: Nomos 11*ff*, 21*ff*.

alluded to parallel problems within corporations. Similarly, it is no accident that the court in the Japanese car importer case imposed new 'organisational' obligations and responsibilities upon the distribution centre, impacting far beyond the formal limits of the firm, and thus revealed the acute organisational co-ordination difficulties that are present within contractual networks. This is the path that doctrine must follow – far beyond the simple incorporation of new contractual forms within existing legal relationships – in its endeavours to capture the problems arising from economic networking within more generalisable legal categories.

Consequently, doctrine should free itself decisively from limited judicial models of social reality that can only react to the irritations of networks with particularistic equitable corrections. 'Their description of reality only entails two contrasting spheres of influence, represented either by the plaintiff or by the defendant. In this manner, courtroom proceedings are projected into the social order such that points of [legal] decisional reference can in turn be identified within the social order'.[17] Such proceedings are fatal with regard to network phenomena precisely because the latter are distinguished by their multi-polar structure.

Similarly, it is not enough to adopt a 'legislative policies' perspective, because this only reproduces the reality constructs of participating economic interest groups, political parties, and national and European political institutions.[18] Legal doctrine, as opposed to case law and legislation, will only make a genuine contribution to the emerging law of networks if and when it establishes a 'third way' of approaching the changes in the organisation of economic relations. This third way can now only be achieved through the 'structural coupling' of law with other social science disciplines, which, though founded in intensive co-operation, ensures both the autonomy of law and of social science.[19]

It is noteworthy that legal scholarship has now developed a heightened sensitivity for the social sciences in relation to franchising and other marketing systems, as well as just-in-time contracts, virtual enterprises, and other co-operative business relationships that display such new characteristics. These legal forays across the borders of the social sciences have proven successful, since they have discovered the opportunities and risks posed by networking and have allowed this material to guide novel legal solutions. Martinek's pioneering analyses of franchising made

[17] Niklas Luhmann (1965), *Grundrechte als Institution: Ein Beitrag zur politischen Soziologie*. Berlin: Duncker & Humblot, 206.

[18] In such a case, one is drawn into the dilemma of the dogmatisation of 'legislative policies'. See Ernst Steindorff (1973), 'Politik des Gesetzes als Auslegungsmasstab im Wirtschaftsrecht' in Gotthard Paulus (ed), *Festschrift für Karl Larenz*. Munich: Beck, 217*ff*.

[19] See, on the structural coupling of legal and social sciences, Luhmann (2004), 543*f*.

detailed reference to business management studies and distinguished new legal categories in close proximity to the organisational demands of franchising systems.[20] In an influential typology, he identified different types of franchising systems (subordination, co-ordination, coalition, and federation), subjecting each to its own regulatory regime. Nagel based his risk analysis of new forms of 'systemic' dependence within 'just-in-time' systems upon detailed organisational science studies, which have unveiled the importance of computer-based integration as opposed to contractual or corporate forms of dependence, and, by analogy to corporation law, he drew legal consequences in the form of 'business constitutions'.[21] It is now *de rigeur* for new books upon networks – Rohe, Lange Bayreuther, Wellenhofer-Klein, Schimansky – to include management science studies about the motivations of individual network actors within their detailed legal analyses of interest conflicts.[22] Lange's book on the law of virtual enterprises similarly makes repeated recourse to existing management science studies in order to explicate the specificities of co-ordination and liability within networks.[23]

It is certainly true that interdisciplinary contact with management science has been fruitful, especially where conflicts arise within networks owing to the motivations of those involved. Nonetheless, if the task is to reconstruct in legal doctrine the network revolution in a manner that is relevant for the economy and for society as a whole, then the management science perspective is far too narrow, because it focuses only upon the economic networking of individual firms. Its normative viewpoint is

[20] Michael Martinek (1987), *Franchising: Grundlagen der zivil- und wettbewerbsrechtichen Behandlung der vertraglichen Gruppenkooperation beim Absatz von Waren und Dienstleistungen.* Heidelberg: Decker and Schenck, 231*ff.* After taking an initially hostile position towards competing social sciences influences (see, for example, the Book Review by Christian Joerges (1993a), 'Buchbesprechung: Franchising and the Law' *Rabels Zeitschrift* 57, 577*ff*, especially 581), Martinek has recently developed an open attitude towards interdisciplinary perspectives that do not rely wholly upon empirical analyses of business management, but instead also draw strength from sociological and economic theory, for example, in *Staudinger* (1995) § 675, A 155*ff.*

[21] Bernhard Nagel, Birgit Riess and Gisela Theis (1989), 'Der faktische Just-in-Time-Konzern: Unternehmensübergreifende Rationalisierungskonzepte und Konzernrecht am Beispiel der Automobilindustrie', *Der Betrieb* 42, 1505*ff*, 1506*ff*; (1990), *Just-in-Time-Strategien: Arbeitsbeziehungen, Gestaltungspotentiale, Mitbestimmung*. Düsseldorf: Hans-Böckler-Stiftung.

[22] Rohe (1998), 384*ff*, 412*ff*; Knut Werner Lange (1998), *Das Recht der Netzwerke*. Heidelberg: Recht und Wirtschaft, 41*ff*; Marina Wellenhofer-Klein (1999), *Zulieferverträge im Privat- und Wirtschaftsrecht*. Munich: Beck, 5*ff*; Frank Bayreuther (2001), *Wirtschaftlich-existentiell abhängige Unternehmen im Konzern-, Kartell- und Arbeitsrecht*. Berlin: Duncker & Humblot, 366*ff*, 534*ff*; Schimansky (2003), 26*ff.*

[23] Knut Werner Lange (2001a), *Virtuelle Unternehmen. Neue Unternehmenskoordinationen in Recht und Praxis*. Heidelberg: Recht und Wirtschaft, 27*ff*; similarly Markus Ackermann (1998), 'Rechtliche Aspekte von virtuellen Unternehmen', *Handbuch der modernen Datenverarbeitung* 200, 40*ff.*

similarly limited, since it concentrates upon the efficiency, the effectiveness and (occasionally) the legitimacy of individual firms that form part of a network. This is far too restricted a basis for a legal appraisal of the opportunities and risks posed by networks. Legal doctrine needs to establish contact with economic theory, specifically, transaction-cost theory, property rights theory, and institutional economics. Adopting this viewpoint, Möschel and Rohe deploy theoretical studies in economics on banking gironets and other networks for the analysis of new conflicts of interest and for their solution through the highly controversial category of the 'network contract'.[24] Schanze's study of symbiotic contracts and Kirchner's analysis of business networks, which both pay homage to institutional economics, put strong emphasis on the efficiency advantages of networking and further demand that it be subject to its own form of legal institutionalisation.[25] Kulms is particularly successful in using various economic approaches in order to analyse the changes in organisational contracts to which intensified co-operation has given rise and to develop parallel duties to co-operate.[26] Studies by Lemley on the effects of networks and their legal consequences in various areas are similarly productive.[27]

In order to contextualise business networks within their political and social environment, however, a juridical reconstruction of sociological network theory is also necessary.[28] If law seeks to develop 'socially appropriate' concepts, the relationship between market and networks established by economic theories must be widened to encompass broader social and political environments. Joerges' suggestions, inspired by social

[24] Wernhard Möschel (1986), 'Dogmatische Strukturen des bargeldlosen Zahlungsverkehrs', *Archiv für die civilistische Praxis* 186, 211*ff*; Rohe (1998), 66*ff*, 81*ff* and passim.

[25] Erich Schanze (1991), 'Symbiotic Contracts: Exploring Long-Term Agency Structures Between Contract and Corporation' in Christian Joerges (ed), *Franchising and the Law: Theoretical and Comparative Approaches in Europe and the United States*. Baden-Baden: Nomos, 67*ff*, 89*ff*; (1993), 'Symbiotic Arrangements', *Journal of Institutional and Theoretical Economics* 149, 691*ff*; Christian Kirchner (1993), 'Unternehmensorganisation und Vertragsnetz: Überlegungen zu den rechtlichen Bedingungen zwischen Unternehmensorganisation und Vertragsnetz' in Claus Ott and Hans-Bernd Schäfer (eds), *Ökonomische Analyse des Unternehmensrechts*. Heidelberg: Physica, 196*ff*, 202*ff*; (1996), 'Symbiotic Arrangements as a Challenge to Antitrust', *Journal of Institutional and Theoretical Economics* 152, 226*ff*; (2000), 'Horizontale japanische Unternehmensgruppen (keiretsu) im deutschen Konzernrecht' in Theodor Baums, Klaus J Hopt and Norbert Horn (eds), *Corporations, Capital Markets and Business in the Law: Liber Amicorum Richard M Buxbaum*. London: Kluwer, 339*ff*, 351*ff*.

[26] Kulms (2000), 55*ff*, 240*ff*.

[27] Mark A Lemley and David McGowan (1998), 'Legal Implications of Network Economic Effects', *California Law Review* 86, 479*ff*.

[28] This social contextualisation of economic operations is a working programme within economic sociology, and as such shares far more in common with preferred legal doctrine perspectives than do purely economically oriented analyses; representative, Neil J Smelser and Richard Swedberg (eds) (1994), *The Handbook of Economic Sociology*. Princeton: Princeton University Press.

theory, are noteworthy here since they individualise the semi-autonomous status of network actors and seek to institutionalise them legally.[29] Schimansky explicates the legal concept of the network in the light of sociological studies which focus on the risks of the paradoxical constitution of franchising.[30] Casper's study on standard contracts used in just-in-time systems investigates the role that case law might play in supporting productive networks and in limiting institutional misuse of law.[31] The studies by Collins, Buxbaum and John Esser on the juridical relevance of networking are sociologically informed.[32] Similarly, lawyers with a background in systems theory seek to deploy its analytical potential, responding to the risks of networking with constructions allocating legal responsibility.[33]

[29] Joerges (1991), 17*ff*.

[30] Schimansky (2003), 104*ff*, 112*ff*.

[31] Steve Casper (1995), 'How Public Law Influences Decentralised Supplier Network Organization: The Case of BMW and Audi', *WZB-Discussion Paper FS I 95–314*; (2001), 'The Legal Framework for Corporate Governance: Explaining the Development of Contract Law in Germany and the United States' in Peter A Hall and David Soskice (eds), *Varieties of Capitalism: The Institutional Foundations of Comparative Advantage*. Oxford: Oxford University Press, 387*ff*, 397*ff*.

[32] Hugh Collins (1990a), 'Ascription of Legal Responsibility to Groups in Complex Patterns of Economic Interaction', *MLR* 53, 731*ff*, 732*ff*; (1990b), 'Independent Contractors and the Challenge of Vertical Disintegration to Employment Protection Laws', *OJLS* 10, 353*ff*, 356*ff*; (1999), 248*ff*; Buxbaum (1993), 700*ff*; John P Esser (1996), 'Institutionalizing Industry: The Changing Forms of Contract', *Law and Social Inquiry* 21, 593*ff*, 620*ff*.

[33] For systemic analyses of network society, see Karl-Heinz Ladeur (1992), *Postmoderne Rechtstheorie: Selbstreferenz – Selbstorganisation – Prozeduralisierung*. Berlin: Duncker & Humblot, 176*ff*; (2000), *Negative Freiheitsrechte und gesellschaftliche Selbstorganisation*. Tübingen: Mohr Siebeck, 204*ff*; (2001), 'Die Regulierung von Selbstregulierung und die Herausbildung einer "Logik der Netzwerke"', *Die Verwaltung. Beiheft* 4, 59*ff*, 64*ff*. On the difficulties of apportioning responsibility from the viewpoint of systems theory, see Gunther Teubner (1991), 'Beyond Contract and Organization? External Liability of Franchising Systems in German Law' in Christian Joerges (ed), *Franchising and the Law: Theoretical and Comparative Approaches in Europe and the United States*. Baden-Baden: Nomos, 105*ff*, 119*ff*; (1993b), 'The Many-Headed Hydra: Networks as Higher-Order Collective Actors' in Joseph McCahery, Sol Picciotto and Colin Scott (eds), *Corporate Control and Accountability: Changing Structures and the Dynamics of Regulation*. Oxford: Oxford University Press, 41*ff*, 54*ff*; (1992), 'Piercing the Contractual Veil? The Social Responsibility of Contractual Networks' in Thomas Wilhelmsson (ed), *Perspectives of Critical Contract Law*, London: Dartsmouth, 211*ff*, 213*f*, 218*f*, 226*ff*; (2002a), 'Hybrid Laws: Constitutionalizing Private Governance Networks' in Robert Kagan and Kenneth Winston (eds) *Legality and Community: On the Intellectual Legacy of Philip Selznick*, Berkeley: Berkeley Public Policy Press, 311*ff*, 324*ff*; Rodrigo Mendes (2002), *'In medio stat virtus': Außenhaftung von virtuellen Unternehmen. Magisterthesis*. Frankfurt: Fachbereich Rechtswissenschaft; Marc Amstutz (2003), 'Vertragskollisionen: Fragmente für eine Lehre von der Vertragsverbindung' in Heinrich Honsell (ed) *Aktuelle Aspekte des Schuld- und Sachenrechts: Festschrift für Heinz Rey*. Zürich: Schulthess, 161*ff*, especially 167*ff*.

III. LEGALLY RELEVANT NETWORKS

Clearly, any effort to identify network risks and potentials can only proceed on the basis of a drastic conceptual limitation of the numerous network phenomena addressed. Networks seem today to be omnipresent and the current inflationary usage of the term 'network' is such that the networks addressed by this study must be carefully distinguished from other networking phenomena. This study is limited to instances of contractual business co-operation since this offers the best chance of establishing sufficient commonalities,[34] and has the advantage of a median level of abstraction.[35] A multitude of network phenomena will be excluded from the study; nonetheless, care will be taken to retain relevant experiences derived from such excluded networks for appropriate application within the narrower analysis.

If used in its widest compass to denote the multiple relations of a single social unit with a variety of other units, the term 'network' is not useful for the purposes of this study: for example, studies of the recursive networking of operations with other operations, or the multilateral relationships that are associated with particular positions in diverse social contexts, fall outside the scope of interest. This 'relational' network concept, as it is deployed in sociological analyses of networks, is too broad, too formal, and too lacking in material content for our purposes.[36] It encompasses network phenomena of every form within groups, families, organisations, markets, and even international relations, and is thus so lacking in specificity that it offers little or no potential for the identification of typical risks and conflicts of interest. Nonetheless, one lesson that we should take from this sociological concept is its refusal to conceive of networks as collective entities. Network theory is decisively individualistic in its orientation: all collectivisation tendencies apart,

[34] This is also the focus of Sydow's organisational investigations; see Jörg Sydow (1992), *Strategische Netzwerke: Evolution und Organisation*. Wiesbaden: Gabler, 15*ff*; Günther Ortmann and Jörg Sydow (1999), 'Grenzmanagement in Unternehmensnetzwerken: Theoretische Zugänge', *Academy of Management Review* 59, 205*ff*, 207*f*.

[35] Similarly, Lange's delimitation (1998), 5; but see also Rohe (1998) 2*ff*, whose emphasis upon secondary transactions leads to an expansion in his category to include other networking forms that are excluded here as 'technical networks'. Martinek (1993a), 353*ff*, seeks a higher level of abstraction through his endeavour to identify general principles for modern contractual forms.

[36] On structural network theories, Harrison C White (1993), 'Markets, Networks and Control' in Siegwart M Lindenberg and Hein Schreuder (eds), *Interdisciplinary Perspectives on Organization Studies*. Oxford: Pergamon, 223*ff*; Peter Kappelhoff (2000a), 'Komplexitätstheorie und Steuerung von Netzwerken' in Jörg Sydow and Arnold Windeler (eds), *Steuerung von Netzwerken*. Opladen: Westdeutscher, 347*ff*; (2000b), 'Der Netzwerkansatz als konzeptueller Rahmen für eine Theorie interorganisationaler Netzwerke' in *ibid*, 25*ff*; Stephan Fuchs (2001), 'Networks', *Soziale Systeme* 7, 125*ff*, 129*ff*. On the application of this theory to business networks, see Arnold Windeler (2001), *Unternehmungsnetzwerke: Konstitution und Strukturation*. Wiesbaden: Westdeutscher, 117*ff*.

networks are at core based upon the autonomous behavioural, decisional, and reflexive potential of individual actors.[37]

The same is true of certain sociological conceptions of a network as a simple 'address book'. In this sense, a 'network' determines the communicative potential of a single position across systems boundaries:[38] it is too abstract a concept to be of aid within a specific risk analysis. Once again, however, a particular feature is worthy of retention within this study. This use of the term 'network' counteracts prevailing trends that simply deploy it to denote differentiation processes and the creation of autonomous systems consisting of homogeneous elements. Networks are instead 'highly unlikely reproductive correlations of heterogeneous elements'.[39] They fulfil the function of fostering relationships between autonomous functional systems[40] or between formal organisations.[41] They promote the cross-boundary integration of autonomous operational logics, which also determine the potentialities and risks associated with the organisational forms that we are addressing.[42]

Likewise, the broad cultural trend encapsulated within the term 'network society' is not informative within our terms of reference.[43] It encompasses far too many networking phenomena to be captured here within institutional considerations. The term describes secular transformation processes from hierarchical to heterarchical co-ordination in a

[37] 'Non-individualistic' systems theory insists that social networks are usually not fully fledged social systems but mere structures for the individual actions of persons and organisations. Only under certain conditions will networks constitute themselves as autonomous social systems, as formal organisations or even as collective actors. See Teubner (1993b), 54*ff*; (1992), 226*ff*; (2002a), 324*ff*; Niklas Luhmann (2000), *Organisation und Entscheidung*. Opladen: Westdeutscher, 407*ff*; Fuchs (2001), 138*ff*.

[38] Veronika Tacke (2000), 'Netzwerk und Adresse', *Soziale Systeme* 6, 291*ff*; see also Rudolf Stichweh (2000), 'Adresse und Lokalisierung in einem globalen Kommunikationssystem' in R Stichweh, *Die Weltgesellschaft: Soziologische Analysen*. Frankfurt: Suhrkamp, 220*ff*.

[39] Dirk Baecker (2002), *Organisation und Gesellschaft*. Witten-Herdecke: Universität, 14.

[40] Helmut Willke (1992), *Ironie des Staates: Grundlinien einer Staatstheorie polyzentrischer Gesellschaften*. Frankfurt: Suhrkamp, 183*f*; Niklas Luhmann (1997), *Die Gesellschaft der Gesellschaft*. Frankfurt: Suhrkamp, 788; André Brodocz (1996), 'Strukturelle Kopplung durch Verbände', *Soziale Systeme* 2, 361*ff*, 366*ff*.

[41] Eckard Kämper and Johannes FK Schmidt (2000), 'Netzwerke als strukturelle Kopplung: Systemtheoretische Überlegungen zum Netzwerkbegriff' in Johannes Weyer (ed), *Soziale Netzwerke: Konzepte und Methoden der sozialwissenschaftlichen Netzwerkforschung*. Munich: Oldenbourg, 211*ff*, 227*ff*.

[42] See, on the concept of 'fractional integration' through 'the control of differences', Michael Hardt and Antonio Negri (2000), *Empire*. Cambridge, MA: Harvard University Press, 325*ff*.

[43] Renate Mayntz (1993), 'Modernization and the Logic of Interorganizational Networks', in John Child, Michel Crozier and Renate Mayntz (eds), *Societal Change Between Market and Organization*, Aldershot: Ashgate, 3*ff*; Dirk Messner (1997b), *The Network Society: Economic Development and International Competitiveness as Problems of Social Governance*. London: Frank Cass.; Manuel Castells (2000), *The Rise of the Network Society*. Oxford: Basil Blackwell, 77*ff*; Ladeur (2000), 204*ff*; (2001), 62*ff*.

most diverse collection of social spheres. In a sphere of governmental behaviour, encompassing both internal actions and external relations, the dominant trend is the transformation of hierarchies into heterarchies.[44] Networks play a particularly significant role within globalisation processes in their guise as transnational forms of co-operation.[45] Trends that weaken both the corporatist-pluralist mode of mediating between state and business and the chances of creating an enduring 'common interest' between the two have made themselves felt within private transnational associations. Instead, context-bound decisions are now commonly subject to direct discussions between the state and individual firms, or between the state and a network of firms.[46] Inter-organisational networks have sprung up amongst firms to which the most fundamental business-political decisions are delegated. Similarly, decentralising and heterarchical trends are also apparent within firms, and further form the basis for the evolution of business internal networks.[47]

Once again, however, these various networking trends are subjugated to a 'network logic' that also impacts upon the network phenomena tackled here. The evolution of heterarchical co-ordination determines that the organising principle is no longer one that is directed to a higher 'goal'. Rather, organisation is instead a strategic and contextual matter that no longer distinguishes between general public and particularistic private interests.[48]

'Technical networks' similarly play a peripheral role in this study.[49] Such networks concern the closer degree of co-operation necessitated by technical factors that determine that certain goods and services can no longer be produced within the market, but only within a technically

[44] See comprehensively Fritz W Scharpf (1991), 'Die Handlungsfähigkeit des Staates am Ende des Zwanzigsten Jahrhunderts', *Politische Vierteljahresschrift* 32, 621*ff*; Helmut Willke (1997), *Supervision des Staates*. Frankfurt: Suhrkamp, 136*ff*; Hauke Brunkhorst (1999), 'Heterarchie und Demokratie' in H Brunkhorst and Peter Niesen (eds), *Das Recht der Republik*. Frankfurt: Suhrkamp, 373*ff*, 384*ff*.

[45] See contributions to Elmar Altvater, Achim Brunnengräber, Markus Haake and Heike Walk (eds) (1997), *Vernetzt und Verstrickt: Nicht-Regierungs-Organisationen als gesellschaftliche Produktivkraft*. Münster: Westfälisches Dampfboot.

[46] Ladeur (2001), 64; for a new interpretation of associations, Brodocz (1996).

[47] On the interpretation of both trends in the creation of internal and external business networks, see Castells (2000), 163*ff*.

[48] Network logic will be more closely investigated in Chapter 2.

[49] See Uli Kowol and Wolfgang Krohn (1995), 'Innovationsnetzwerke: Ein Modell der Technikgenese' in Jost Halfman (ed), *Theoriebausteine der Techniksoziologie: Jahrbuch 'Technik und Gesellschaft'*. Frankfurt: Campus, 749*ff*; Daniel Bieber (1997), 'Probleme unternehmensübergreifender Organisation von Innovationsprozessen' in D Bieber (ed), *Technikentwicklung und Industriearbeit: Industrielle Produktionstechnik zwischen Eigendynamik und Nutzerinteressen*. Frankfurt: Campus, 111*ff*; Jost Halfmann (1997), 'Die Implementation von Innovationen als Prozess sozialer Einbettung' in *ibid*, 87*ff*; Philipp Hessinger, Friedhelm Eichhorn, Jürgen Feldhoff and Gert Schmidt (2000), *Fokus und Balance. Aufbau und Wachstum industrieller Netzwerke*. Opladen: Westdeutscher.

intertwined infrastructure. Transport, energy-provision and telecommunications networks are the organisational end result. The traditional solution to technical networking in transport, energy and communication spheres was that of the 'natural' monopoly of an integrated enterprise. Although these monopolies have been dissolved, they have not been replaced with market structures, but have instead developed as networks whose operations are largely governed by external regulation. Consequently, specific forms of market organisation are defined by so-called network effects. A commodity's value increases in direct proportion to the number of its users who can be reached through the network (telephone, fax, Internet, software).[50] Such forms of market networks have myriad impacts upon the law: competition law, intellectual property law, company law and contract law.[51] Importantly, however, these particular network effects are not a structural characteristic of the operations of a business network directed to one common project – although of course such effects might also appear, albeit in a transformed form, in association with such a network. Rather, technical networks are so operationally distinct from contractual instances of business co-operation that it makes little or no sense to deal with them in common. Notwithstanding all the parallels that may be drawn, the determinative distinction between the two is provided by the fact that technologically determined networks give rise to very different potentialities and risks from those that are posed by their socio-economically inspired counterparts.

The same is true of 'information networks', now ubiquitous by virtue of individual computer networking. The Internet is only the most prominent amongst a multitude of information networks. It is beyond doubt that the potential offered by the Internet, the Intranet and the Extranet has had an extraordinarily dynamic impact upon business co-operation; indeed, certain forms of co-operation, such as virtual enterprises, would simply not exist without the Internet.[52] However, the particular

[50] On general network effects, see Michael Katz and Carl Shapiro (1985), 'Network Externalities, Competition, and Compatibility', *American Economic Review* 75, 424*ff*, and, in particular on the distinction between positive and negative network effects, Stan J Liebowitz and Stephen E Margolis (1994), 'Network Externality: An Uncommon Tragedy', *Journal of Economic Perspectives* 8, 133*ff*, 135.

[51] On the legal relevance of such network effects in various legal areas, see Lemley and McGowan (1998), 31*ff*.

[52] Ackermann (1998), 41; Dieter Specht and Joachim Kahlmann (2000), 'Regelung kooperativer Tätigkeit im virtuellen Unternehmen', *Zeitschrift für Betriebswirtschaft* 70 *Ergänzungsheft* 2, 55*ff*, 56*f*; Lange (2001a), 29*ff*; (2001b), 'Virtuelle Unternehmen' in Ulrich Noack and Gerald Spindler (eds), *Unternehmensrecht und Internet: Neue Medien im Aktien-, Börsen-, Steuer- und Arbeitsrecht*. Munich: Beck, 169*ff*; (2001c), 'Virtuelle Unternehmen für Finanzdienstleistungen', *Betriebs Berater* 56, 1801*ff*.

co-ordination prerequisites for the Internet (Internet Architecture – Internet Code), as well as the highly diverse social relationships that result from them,[53] are so distinct from the generalised reciprocity found within business networks that common legal principles will be also inappropriate in this case. Contractual business networks form themselves into something resembling an independent collective operational unit, which must be addressed from a legal liability and co-ordination perspective according to its own constitutive principles; this is not an approach suited to the gigantic and diffuse market of the Internet and its multiple contact forms.

This study nonetheless focuses particularly on the peculiar market entry rules that apply in technical and information networks. Network entry is not dependent upon a centralised decision, a common act, or a declaration of entry made to the collective, but rather simply flows from a local connection to one of very many network nodes.[54] The simple connection to an existing node results in incorporation within the entire net. The typical network structure of 'and so forth' is also a feature of business networks and leads amongst others to the question of whether a specific legal concept of a 'network contract' is appropriate.[55] A similarly relevant question is: how should the law treat particular network effects – in other words, how should the law, at least to the degree that the phenomenon is also present in cases of business co-operation, address the issue of incremental networking value?[56]

'Trust networks' are far more relevant to our purposes.[57] Here, the term 'network' denotes a typical social relationship, within which structured

[53] See, for the legal and constitutional problems that arise, Lawrence Lessig (1999), *Code and Other Laws of Cyberspace*. New York: Basic Books, 30*ff*, 111*ff*.

[54] On network structure of the 'and-so-forth', see the sociological analyses of Stichweh (2000), 220*ff*.

[55] Möschel (1986), 211*ff*; Rohe (1998), 66*ff*, 81*ff* and passim. For a detailed treatment, see Chapter 2 (VI).

[56] The question is particularly relevant in relation to duties of care of network actors and the distribution of profits arising out of network effects between network centre and network nodes; see Chapters 4 (III) and 5 (III).

[57] On trust networks, see in particular Powell (1990); see also, however, Simon Deakin, Christel Lane and Frank Wilkinson (1994), '"Trust" or Law? Towards an Integrated Theory of Contractual Relations Between Firms', *Rechtstheorie* 21, 329*ff*; Birgit Mahnkopf (1994), 'Markt, Hierarchie und soziale Beziehungen: Zur Bedeutung reziproker Marktgesellschaften' in Niels Beckenbach and Werner van Treeck (eds), *Umbrüche gesellschaftlicher Arbeit: Soziale Welt. Sonderband* 9. Göttingen: Schwartz, 65*ff*, 71*ff*; Michael de Vries (1998), 'Das virtuelle Unternehmen: Formentheoretische Überlegungen zu Grenzen eines grenzenlosen Konzepts' in Andreas Brill and Michael de Vries (eds), *Virtuelle Wirtschaft*. Opladen: Westdeutscher, 54*ff*, 71; Christel Lane and Reinhard Bachmann (1996), 'The Social Construction of Trust: Supplier Relations in Britain and Germany', *Organization Studies* 17, 365*ff*; Niklas Luhmann (2000), *Organisation und Entscheidung*. Opladen: Westdeutscher, 25, 407*ff*; Reinhard Bachmann (ed), (2000) *Die Koordination und Steuerung interorganisationaler Netzwerkbeziehungen über Vertrauen und Macht*. Opladen: Westdeutscher; Teubner (2002a) 315*ff*; Günther Ortmann (2003), *Organisation und Welterschließung*. Opladen: Westdeutscher, 216.

trust forms the basis for co-operation. In this sense, networking is distinguished both from formal organisational membership and from reciprocal exchange relations since it entails a particular form of trust relationship that is constituted by visible interests, repeat interactions, and third party observation. Trust networks are mostly very fluid structures, but can also exist in the form of an institutionalised social system. Such network expectations evolve from a variety of sources that are located outside formally constituted relationships: they derive from personal relationships, family ties, kinship, friendship, neighbourly feelings, solidarity, profession, power, influence and other forms of social interdependence. The variety within such networks is thus so diverse as to require further delimitation. Trust networks extend from traditional forms of patronage, to client relationships, to *amici degli amici degli amici* (friends of friends of friends), to quasi-feudal allegiances, to old boy networks, to mafia-type structures, though charitable networks, traditional business relationships and 'amicably' bound firms to encompass even the most modern forms of co-operation within the economy.

Amongst this enormous variety of trust networks, this study is particularly concerned with 'business networks' that have recently established themselves as an extraordinarily successful, if hazardous, form of business organisation.[58] Business networks are defined as:

> modes of organising economic activities that bind formally independent firms who are more or less economically dependent upon one another through stable relationships and a complex reciprocity that is more co-operative than competitive in form.[59]

Particular attention is paid here to three types of business network: virtual enterprises, just-in-time contracting, and franchising chains. In a preliminary characterisation: business networks pursue common projects making use of co-operation between autonomous firms. They are founded upon trust relationships, but at the same time – and this distinguishes them from the simple trust networks described above – constitute a unique mix of organisational and contractual features, with

On the general phenomenon of trust within organised contexts, see Roderick M Kramer (1999), 'Trust and Distrust in Organizations: Emerging Perspectives, Enduring Questions', *Annual Review of Psychology* 50, 569*ff*.

[58] Important social science studies on the particular phenomenon of business networks, Sydow (1992); J Carlos Jarillo (1993), *Strategic Networks: Creating the Borderless Organization*. Oxford: Oxford University Press; Hartmut Hirsch-Kreinsen (1995), 'Dezentralisierung: Unternehmen zwischen Stabilität und Desintegration', *Zeitschrift für Soziologie* 24, 422*ff*; (2002), 'Unternehmensnetzwerke – revisited' *Zeitschrift für Soziologie* 31, 106*ff*; Peter Littmann and Stephan A Jansen (2000), *Oszillodox: Virtualisierung – die permanente Neuerfindung der Organisation*. Stuttgart: Klett; Windeler (2001).

[59] Thus, Sydow's influential definition (1992), 82*ff*.

all of their co-operative advantages. They are intersystemic networks; that is, they link autonomous units from different social systems with one another.[60]

IV. THE NEW ECONOMIC RELEVANCE OF PRE-MODERN NETWORKS

Why should the most efficient forms of business co-operation, together with their law, have reason to take note of trust relationships? Mixing economic operations with personal, familial, friendship-based, ethnic and local forms of co-operation and anchoring them within social, political and religious communities lends them the flavour of typically traditional networks;[61] that is, pre-modern obligation systems, whose significance within modernity has long been waning in the face of the increasing dominance of an institutionally secured instrumental rationality.[62] Contemporary law has long had difficulty affording such personal network relationships an institutional value of their own.[63] In view of the dominance of contract and organisation, modernity's pre-eminent rationality institutions, it has been difficult for some time to conceive of them as institutions in their own right; indeed, where they have been perceived as such, they have often tended to be denounced as pre-modern institutions that have sabotaged or even corrupted the new instrumental rationality. Consequently, modern private law's reaction to such personal network relationships has veered between an explicit judgment of illegality, a cold indifference, and a cautious recognition.[64] To the extent that such networks appear to have threatened modern institutional integrity, law has sought to suppress them as illegal instances of corruption, sabotage of hierarchy, market collusion, cartel building and other anti-competitive practices. Other network phenomena, such as the informal building of groups within hierarchical organisations, have not attracted negative legal sanctions, but have been obscured behind the handy veil of legal ignorance. Only very few networks have received a cautious degree of legal recognition. They were not, however, recognised as independent social institutions, but were

[60] Their specific characteristics will be detailed in the following chapters, each in their relation to doctrinal concepts and individual legal problems; see, on their social structure, Chapter 2 (III) and on their legal structure, Chapter 3 (IV).

[61] See, Jeremy Boissevain (1974), *Friends of Friends: Networks, Manipulators and Coalitions*. Oxford: Oxford University Press; Charles Perrow (1986), *Complex Organizations*. 3rd edn, New York: Random House, Chapter 1, 4.11.

[62] Helmut Dubiel (1990), 'Die Ökologie der gesellschaftlichen Moral' in Stefan Müller-Doohm (ed), *Jenseits der Utopie*. Frankfurt: Suhrkamp, 123*ff*, 126*f*; see for an early opinion Max Weber (1978), *Economy and Society*, Berkeley: University of California Press, chap. 1 § 9.

[63] See Luhmann (2000), 385*ff*.

[64] See the distinction between legal/illegal networking in Luhmann (2000), 385*ff*.

rather given only guarded legal acknowledgment in the form of formulas such as 'reliance upon (pre-) contractual expectations', 'socially binding obligations' or 'tort-law-based obligations'. Although private law was prepared to give concrete form to some network expectations, and even to sanction their disregard, sanctions were mostly inadequate and inappropriately addressed.[65] Commonly, sanctions were extrapolated from general clauses and principles in contract law, such as, 'good faith' (*Treu und Glauben*), the obligations arising out of a relational contract, quasi-contractual duties of care and duties of care owed in 'special relationships', or alternatively from tort-based duties of care and corporate obligations. Nonetheless, such doctrinal constructions were barely able to hide the fact that such obligations had not been constituted through voluntary – contractual or corporate – agreement, but had instead, and crucially so, been formed in the course of non-consensual social relations.[66] By the same token, signifying such relations as 'legislative' obligations or as jurisprudentially created duties of care would also belie their true origin within the spontaneous process of institutional building by private actors.[67] Overall the situation remained and remains one of careful and uncertain legal recognition. Such networks are to be found in a grey zone, forever subject to the suspicion that they constitute illegitimate practices.

In the meantime, however, we have witnessed a 'network revolution' that has dramatically altered the strategic position of networks within the economy and that is now forcing law to recognise them in their own right. Empirical studies from many industrial sectors have provided comprehensive proof of the exponential expansion in business networking over the last 20 years:

> Network relationships [exist] between dealers, manufacturers, systems' and components' producers, not only within the automobile and electronics industry, but also within McDonald's, within financial services networks that encompass, for example, insurers, agents and clients, within transport and logistics networks, such as the Trans European Alliance Network (TEAM), Thyssen-Haniel logistics or NDX International, and within manufacturing networks, such as Adidas, or within networks of dealers, such as Marks & Spencer,

[65] Similarly critical of doctrinal answers to increasing networking in goods and services markets, see Eduard Picker (1999), 'Gutachterhaftung: Außervertragliche Einstandspflichten als innergesetzliche Rechtsfortbildung' in Volker Beuthien (ed), *Festschrift für Dieter Medicus*. Cologne: Heymanns, 397*ff*, 428*ff*. Theoretically ambitious and doctrinally detailed analyses of contract law without contracts can be found in Johannes Köndgen (1981), *Selbstbindung ohne Vertrag: Zur Haftung aus geschäftsbezogenem Handeln*. Tübingen: Mohr Siebeck, 97*ff*, 283*ff*.

[66] See Gunther Teubner (1980), 'Die Generalklausel von "Treu und Glauben"' in *Alternativkommentar*. Neuwied: Luchterhand, 32*ff*. See also Chapter 3 (IV).

[67] On the relation between networks and spontaneous orders, see Chapter 3 (IV).

> Benetton or Ikea, as well as within 'regional networks' in industrial regions such as 'the third Italy', or, indeed, within virtual enterprises.[68]

Supposedly pre-modern, irrational and quasi-corrupt network relations have suddenly established themselves as the decisive motor within hypermodern economic arrangements.[69] By the same token, network relations that were once treated with suspicion are no longer perceived to be instances of a dangerous pre-modern recidivism, but are rather greeted in the form of a productive 'social capital' that modern rational institutions might deploy in order to open up new channels to their social environments.[70] In the following scheme of trends that have emerged in the face of a crisis in traditional business organisation, the social capital generated within networks plays the decisive role:

1 Flexible production: specialisation, customised production
2 Reinvigoration of small and medium-sized business, more precisely: networking and incorporation of small businesses within restructured large-scale businesses
3 Toyotism: management-worker co-operation, comprehensive quality control
4 Business networks
   a Co-operation amongst medium-sized businesses
   b Satellites of large business
   c Strategic alliances
5 Horizontal corporations and global business networks.[71]

'Networks are the fundamental stuff of which new organizations are and will be made.'[72] One decisive reason for their renaissance within the post-modern world is the expanding basis of knowledge that is apparently necessary for production and the inability of traditional transactional forms of material production to supply this capacity. Likewise, networks have benefited from a fundamental reorganisation in wealth creation chains. Non-tangible goods, such as:

> intellectual capital (knowledge base) and social capital (image and trust), as well as relational capital (personal networks) have a paradoxical character. On

[68] Windeler (2001), 13, giving a systematic overview of the most significant empirical studies on networks in various industrial branches.

[69] Bo Hedberg, Göran Dahlgren, Jörgen Hansson and Nils-Göran Olve (1992), *Virtual Organizations and Beyond: Discover Imaginary Systems*. Chichester: Wiley; Nitin Nohria and Robert Eccles (1992), *Networks and Organizations: Structure, Form, and Action*. Boston: Harvard Business School.

[70] Littmann and Jansen (2000), 110*ff*.

[71] These transformation trends 'from industrialism to informationalism' are analysed by Castells (2000), 163*ff*.

[72] Castells (2000), 180.

the one hand, they lack substance, on the other hand they are deeply rooted within social systems (embedded knowledge).[73]

The communication of non-marketable knowledge is more deeply anchored within long-term inter-personal co-operative relations and is less dependent on individual acts of impersonal exchange (the latter being characteristic for the production and distribution of material or tangible goods). As a direct consequence, businesses have been forced to restructure themselves as network-type arrangements, within which trust-based co-operation forms the basis for enduring informational relations, recursive reinterpretation of events, and for the collective construction of knowledge. At first glance, a formal organisation might appear more appropriate to meet these aims. However, an entrenched organisation is simply not in a long-term position to develop and cultivate the necessary knowledge that is dispersed afar throughout the market. Accordingly, the current demand is for flexible, decentralised structures – beyond both market and organisation – that can comb the market for sources of information and bind such sources together within co-operative relationships.[74] In addition, new information technologies have lowered outsourced data processing costs, so that the re-emergence of hierarchical structures has become ever more unlikely.[75]

The reorganisation of wealth creation chains is the second decisive factor behind the renewed significance of social networks.[76] Here, a remarkable dual trend may be observed: although decentralisation and outsourcing processes have disaggregated vertically integrated organisations into individual firms, the subsequent relationships maintained between those firms are not market-based in nature. The new distribution and production techniques based on close co-operation that have sprung up in reaction to dysfunctionality within formal organisations – caused either by the demand for larger market actors, or by the failure of hierarchy to supply efficient direction – are themselves dysfunctional both in terms of market transactions and of an integrated organisation. The crisis within the traditional hierarchically centralised organisation has not led to the true externalisation of activities within the market. Instead, it has given rise to the 'quasi-externalisation' of activities within

[73] Stephan Jansen (2000), 'Konkurrenz der Konkurrenz: Co-opetition als Form der Konkurrenz-Typen, Funktionen und Voraussetzungen von paradoxen Koordinationsformen' in S Jansen and Stephan Schleissing (eds), *Konkurrenz und Kooperation*. Marburg: Metropolis, 13*ff*; Joseph L Badaracco (1991), *The Knowledge Link: How Firms Compete Through Strategic Alliances*. Boston: Harvard Business School.

[74] See Powell (1990); Ladeur (1992), 176*ff*; (2000), 204*ff*.

[75] Kirchner (1993), 199*ff*; (1996), 227*ff*.

[76] Uli Kowol and Wolfgang Krohn (1997), 'Modernisierungsdynamik und Innovationslethargie' in Birgit Blättel-Mink and Ortwin Renn (eds), *Zwischen Akteur und System: Die Organisierung von Innovation*. Opladen: Westdeutscher, 39*ff*.

networks of manufacturers, co-producers and distributors that also include customers and consumers within their wealth-creating chains.[77]

By the same token, the process also sees formerly independent market firms integrated ever more closely within the wealth-creating network without, however, ending in the establishment of integrated firms. Instead, increasing numbers of independent businesses have joined together within networks. In other words, there is no true internalisation within formal organisational terms, but rather a process of 'quasi-internalisation'.[78] The trend is one of fragmentation into small business units and the emergence of common network usage. Just-in-time distribution systems, virtual enterprises and franchising chains are the most commonly known network types.

The new network enterprise thus stems from disintegration tendencies within the traditional firm on the one hand, and from quasi-integration tendencies within markets on the other. Globalisation processes and the dynamics of technological change have not inevitably resulted in the establishment of vast multinational corporations, but have instead given rise to external and internal networking:

> While market size was supposed to induce the formation of the vertical, multi-unit corporation, the globalization of competition dissolves the large corporation in a web of multi-directional networks which become the actual operating unit.[79]

Strange as it may appear, such networks are also grounded within a structured trust relationship, albeit that this relationship is starkly distinguished from the form of trust found within personal relations. Although 'personal trust' is absent from large anonymous networks, 'systemic trust' – or the belief in the depersonalised reliability of normal technical operations – is certainly observable.[80] Such networked wealth creation chains not only continually create technical standards, but also contemporaneously manufacture – either through informal co-ordination or through formal decision-making – standardised social expectations that lead to novel types of constellations of trust. Intimate knowledge of context or personal character is not required, but rather an overview of technologically induced operational consequences. This is the reason why both traditional free market competition and simple exchange relations have often proved to be so inadequate that a different form of

[77] Castells (2000), 163*ff*.

[78] Charles Sabel (1991), 'Moebius-Strip Organizations and Open Labor Markets: Some Consequences of the Reintegration of Conception and Execution in a Volatile Economy' in Pierre Bourdieu and James Coleman (eds), *Social Theory for a Changing Society*. Boulder: Westview, 23*ff*; Sydow (1992), 78*ff*.

[79] Castells (2000), 209.

[80] On these categories, see Niklas Luhmann (1982), *Trust and Power*, New York: Wiley.

co-operation has evolved. As a consequence, decentralisation trends have not found their end within a competitive free market, but have instead seen integrated, if stratified, organisations replaced with co-operative/hierarchical networks, whose operations are largely anchored within systemic trust. Overall, the trend still justifies a stronger networking of organisations with their environment: the complexity of technical products, savings in the cost of warehousing, integration of consumer preferences within production processes, the negation of information asymmetries and improved co-operation with a variety of clients within necessarily co-operative projects.[81] These are the reasons for the extraordinary return to the use of trust networks within hypermodern institutions.

V. FORMS OF NETWORK AND THEIR REGULATORY PROBLEMS

The extraordinary variety of existing forms of business co-operation is highly confusing. Various network typologies have now been developed.[82] The following typology of business networks offers a systematic perspective on the evolution within wealth creation chains of tendencies towards concentration that are mediated through trends towards decentralisation.[83] Networks are distinguished according to their position within the wealth creation chain and the typology further highlights the extraordinary halfway house position of networks between autonomous production strata on the one hand and vertical integration within formal organisations on the other. The following typology includes at the same time an identification of the particular economic and legal problems that networks pose within wealth creation chains.[84]

1. Innovation networks aim to create design and production technologies and to facilitate common research and development. A common characteristic of these networks is that they are not confined to a process of business co-operation, but rather, in addition to fulfilling normal economic functions, are also subject to political priorities, undertake long-term scientific research without regard for immediate economic

[81] Luhmann (2000), 70. For details, see the contributions to Bachmann (ed) (2000).

[82] Jerald Hage and Catherine Alter (1997), 'A Typology of Interorganizational Relationships and Networks' in Rogers Hollingsworth and Robert Boyer (eds), *Contemporary Capitalism*. Cambridge: Cambridge University Press, 94*ff*; Windeler (2001), 39*ff*.

[83] Dieter Ernst (1994), *Inter-firms Networks and Market Structure: Driving Forces, Barriers and Patterns of Control*. Berkeley: University of California Press, 5*f*; Castells (2000), 207.

[84] See, Halfmann (1997), 98*ff*; Bieber (1997), 114*ff*; Ingo Schulz-Schaeffer, Michael Jonas and Thomas Malsch (1997), 'Innovation reziprok', *Jahrbuch Technik und Gesellschaft* 9, 91*ff*; Dieter Sauer and Christa Lang (eds) (1999), *Paradoxien der Innovation: Perspektiven sozialwissenschaftlicher Innovationsforschung*. Frankfurt: Campus; Abel (2000), 163*ff*.

advantages, and must also be able to secure their own social acceptance. As a consequence, political bodies, scientific institutions and other social network actors bring their non-market perspectives to bear within the network, which is a process that gives rise to novel types of co-ordination problems within such inter-systemic networks.[85] The law is thus confronted with the need for new forms of regulation (heterarchical regulation) and with new collisions problems (the profit motive versus unprejudiced knowledge creation versus social usage).

2. Supply networks: OEM (original equipment manufacturing) and ODM (original design manufacturing) are vertical relationships between focal firms (network centres) and the suppliers of components. They are typically organised as hierarchical networks encompassing a central business and its satellites. Just-in-time production is a particularly challenging form of supply network that has dramatically reduced the costs of inventories, created a demand for particularly close agreements between producers and suppliers, and given rise to strong dependency on information systems.

3. Producer networks encompass horizontal co-production processes within which competing producers combine their production capacity (finances, labour force) in order to maximise their product range and geographical coverage. Virtual enterprises are the primary players within such networks, having sprung free from the economic and legal boundaries of unitary corporate groups and then created a demand for the evolution of forms of horizontal co-operation beyond simple social co-operation.[86]

4. Distribution networks concern vertical relations between manufacturers, distributors, marketing channels, distribution outlets and end users. Franchising in particular has established itself as an efficient distribution mechanism, which has proved to be remarkably successful in contrast with traditional distribution systems. However, its precarious network structure also gives rise to a whole host of legal problems, especially with regard to the internal relationship between franchisor and franchisees, but also in terms of the relationship established with external creditors.

[85] See the first public law efforts to react to networks, Udo Di Fabio (1997), 'Verwaltung und Verwaltungsrecht zwischen gesellschaftlicher Selbstregulierung und staatlicher Steuerung', *Veröffentlichungen der Vereinigung der deutschen Staatsrechtslehrer* 56, 235*ff*, 252*ff*; Ladeur (2000), 229*ff*; (2001), 64*ff*. In view of connected contracts, Amstutz argues for the development of a contract law of collisions in (2003), 170*ff*.

[86] William H Davidow and Michael S Malone (1992), *The Virtual Corporation: Structuring and Revitalizing the Corporation for the 21st Century*. New York: Harper; Stephan Duschek (1998), 'Kooperative Kernkompetenzen: Zum Management einzigartiger Netzwerkressourcen', *Zeitschrift Führung und Organisation* 67, 230*ff*; Gordon Geiser (2001), 'Virtuelle Unternehmen und reale Unternehmensträger', *Multimedia und Recht* 4, 715*ff*.

5. Client networks are designed to incorporate clients within production and manufacturing processes. We are confronted here with the traditional problem of consumer protection.

6. Wealth creation networks are overarching concentrations that bind various production stages together into a quasi-integrated firm through contractual co-operation. A particular example is furnished by standardisation networks that seek, by means of the creation of global standards, to bind as many firms as possible to their own products or to cross-cutting standards.[87]

VI. SPECIFIC RISKS OF NETWORKS

1. Euphoria and Sobriety

Both in practice and in academic analysis, the greatest advantage of networking forms within wealth creation chains is identified as being their ability to facilitate the bundling of the resources and capacities of networked enterprises in order to broaden their product/service range and to allow them to operate in a far more flexible manner than would have been the case within a vertically integrated and hierarchically co-ordinated organisation.[88] In particular, much excitement has greeted positive 'network effects' in this area as multi-directional relationships amongst all members of the network have generated a positive surplus.[89] This advantage would alone justify juridical support for the social institutionalisation of networks. In addition to their business-related advantages in efficiency, however, networks are also perceived as undertaking far broader social functions. As polycentric systems, networks are assumed to promote decentralised social decision-making structures, the dissipation of power, and the democratisation of the economy.[90] Networks, it is said, have a network-typical integrative effect in that they

[87] See Ernst (1994), 5*f*; Castells (2000), 207.

[88] Hirsch-Kreinsen (2002), 107*f*; in detail, Sydow (1992), 80*ff*; 242*ff*; (1999), 'Management von Netzwerkorganisationen: Zum Stand der Forschung' in Sydow (ed), *Management von Netzwerkorganisationen*. Wiesbaden: Westdeutscher, 293*ff*; Semlinger (1993), 337*ff*; Windeler (2001), 14*ff*. On empirical measurement and its efficiency, see Keith G Provan and H Brinton Milward (1995), 'A Preliminary Theory of Interorganizational Network Effectiveness', *Administrative Science Quarterly* 40, 1*ff*; Jörg Sydow and Arnold Windeler (1998), 'Organizing and Evaluating Interfirm Networks', *Organization Science. Special Issue: Managing Partnership and Strategic Alliances* 9, 265*ff*; Keith G Provan (2001), *Conceptualizing and Assessing Network Effectiveness: The Evaluation Perspective.* Lyon: European Group for Organizational Studies.

[89] Katz and Shapiro (1985); Liebowitz and Margolis (1994), 135; Lemley and McGowan (1998), 31*ff*.

[90] Rudolf Stichweh (2001), 'Strukturen der Weltgesellschaft', *Frankfurter Rundschau* 13 March 2000, 22; see also Charles Perrow (1992), 'Small-firm Networks' in Nitin Nohria and

counter trends in social differentiation.[91] In particular, networks are categorised as appropriate organisational forms for the utilisation of decentralised social knowledge.[92] In this analysis, private law should no longer place its complete trust in the bilateral contract as a mechanism to ensure the adequate balancing of interests and appropriate protection against risks. Bilateral contracts can no longer properly capture the manifold conflicts of interest and the intermeshed risks present within contemporary social organisation. The networking phenomenon is a prime example of the fact that multi-polar and organisational legal relationships can no longer be adequately addressed through individualised perspectives.[93] Rather, law should now 'invent' reality constructions that give adequate voice and corporeal form to the variety and magnitude of networking impacts. In the final analysis, the search is on for a legal semantic of autonomy that not only gives voice to other interests, and in particular, to the public interest, but that also contemporaneously operationalises networking through distributive rights.[94]

In a sobering trend, however, recent years have also witnessed a marked reappraisal of the original euphoric judgments about networks. Although there had been some early voices of dissent that were sceptical of notions of 'organised irresponsibility' within networks, and which, amongst other things, argued for their legal correction,[95] enduring doubts have only now arisen in the light of recent empirical findings that

Robert G Eccles (eds), *Networks and Organizations: Structure, Form and Action*. Boston: Harvard Business School, 445*ff*. Sceptical by contrast, Bennett Harrison (1994), *Lean and Mean: The Changing Landscape of Corporate Power in an Age of Flexibility*. New York: Basic Books. Networks ('lean and mean') are forms of economic concentration without decentralisation.

91 Tacke (2000), 296*ff*, 311*ff*; from a socio-legal perspective, Amstutz (2003), 164*ff*.

92 Ladeur (2000), 204*ff*.

93 Peer Zumbansen (2000), *Ordnungsmuster im modernen Wohlfahrtsstaat: Lernerfahrungen zwischen Staat, Gesellschaft und Vertrag*. Baden-Baden: Nomos, 269, with further references.

94 Rudolf Wiethölter (1988), 'Zum Fortbildungsrecht der (richterlichen) Rechtsfortbildung: Fragen eines lesenden Recht-Fertigungslehrers', *Kritische Vierteljahreszeitschrift für Gesetzgebung und Rechtswissenschaft* 3, 1*ff*, 21*ff*.

95 Collins (1990a), 732*ff*; (1990b), 346*ff*; (1999), 248*ff*; Teubner (1991), 107*ff*; (1993b), 57*ff*; (1992), 215*ff*; Alan Felstead (1991), 'The Social Organization of the Franchise: A Case of "Control-led Self-Employment"', *Work, Employment and Society* 5, 37*ff*; Joerges (1991), 17*ff*; Stewart Macaulay (1991), 'Long-Term Continuing Relations: The American Experience Regulating Dealerships and Franchises' in Christian Joerges (ed), *Franchising and the Law: Theoretical and Comparative Approaches in Europe and the United States*. Baden Baden: Nomos, 179*ff*, 215*ff*; Silvana Sciarra (1991), 'Franchising and Contract of Employment: Notes on a Still Impossible Assimilation' in *ibid*, 239*ff*, 251*ff*; Claus Ott (1995), 'Contract Network in Distribution Systems', *Journal of Institutional and Theoretical Economics* 151, 212*ff*, 214*f*. The reprimand that this was an 'unfair' lack of trust in the face of efficient networks was not long in coming: Rohe (1998), 418; Bayreuther (2001), 399. Whether the new sobriety will also have an impact upon those lawyers who, fascinated by networks, sceptical about doctrinal renewal and mindful of private autonomy, have to date preached a strict non-interventionist doctrine, remains to be seen. Will they begin to argue for strengthened liability provisions? More on this point, see Chapter 6.

have systematically uncovered, in addition to the multitude of networking advantages, a series of networking disfunctionalities such as blockages within network co-ordination and extreme negative externalities.[96] The conflicts arising out of contradictions between the asymmetrical powers and formal autonomy of network nodes, the enduring tensions between notions of co-operation, competition and conflict, network-induced boundary confusion between individual firms, the institutional externalities of network creation and structural conservatism within networking – these unintended consequences have now accumulated within a general formula of 'network failure'.[97] In other words, networking is subject to a unique developmental logic. Network phenomena that developed precisely in response to 'market failure' and organisational failure are now suddenly themselves confronted with their own grave and socially significant consequences.

> This is a result of their contradictory relationship with economic aims: on the one hand, business networks seek increased expansion and intensified economic efficiency within business activities; on the other hand, this very action endangers their own functionality and existence, being especially challenging for the primary pre-condition for relations between network actors, for stability.[98]

[96] Gernot Grabher (1993), 'The Weakness of Strong Ties: The Lock-in of Regional Development in the Ruhr Area' in G Grabher (ed), *The Embedded Firm: On the Socio-Economics of Industrial Networks*. London: Routledge; (1994), *Lob der Verschwendung*. Berlin: Sigma; Dirk Messner (1994), 'Fallstricke und Grenzen der Netzwerksteuerung', *Zeitschrift für kritische Sozialwissenschaft* 24, 563*ff*; (1997a), 'Netzwerktheorien: Die Suche nach Ursachen und Auswegen aus der Krise staatlicher Steuerungsfähigkeit' in Elmar Altvater, Achim Brunnengräber, Markus Haake and Heike Walk (eds), *Vernetzt und Verstrickt: Nicht-Regierungs-Organisationen als gesellschaftliche Produktivkraft*. Münster: Westfälisches Dampfboot, 26*ff*; (1997b); Horst Kern (1996), 'Vertrauensverlust und blindes Vertrauen: Integrationsprobleme im ökonomischen Handeln' in Stefan Hradil (ed), *Differenz und Integration: Die Zukunft moderner Gesellschaften – Verhandlungen des 28. Kongresses der Deutschen Gesellschaft für Soziologie in Dresden 1996*. Frankfurt: Campus 1997, 171*ff*; Hartmut Hirsch-Kreinsen (1997), 'Innovationsschwächen der deutschen Industrie: Wandel und Probleme von Innovationsprozessen' in Gotthard Bechmann (ed), *Technik und Gesellschaft. Jahrbuch 9: Innovation – Prozesse, Produkte, Politik*. Frankfurt: Campus, 153*ff*; on the interpretation of this data, see Bieber (1997), 119*ff*; Daniel Rölle and Birgit Blättel-Mink (1998), 'Netzwerke in der Organisationssoziologie: Neuer Schlauch für alten Wein?' *Österreichische Zeitschrift für Soziologie* 23, 66*ff*, 76*ff*; Ortmann and Sydow (1999), 206; Sydow (1999), 305*ff*; Jörg Abel (2000), 'Netzwerke und Leitbilder: Die Bedeutung von Leitbildern für die Funktionsfähigkeit von Forschungs- und Entwicklungsnetzwerken' in Johannes Weyer (ed), *Soziale Netzwerke: Konzepte und Methoden der sozialwissenschaftlichen Netzwerkforschung*. Munich: Oldenbourg, 161*ff*, 166*f*; Martin Heidenreich (2000), 'Regionale Netzwerke in der globalen Wissensgesellschaft' in *ibid*, 87*ff*, 98*ff*; Eckhard Heidling (2000), 'Strategische Netzwerke' in *ibid*, 63*ff*, 76*ff*; Hirsch-Kreinsen (2002), 111*ff*.

[97] Messner (1994), 566*ff*; Johannes Weyer (2000), 'Zum Stand der Netzwerkforschung in den Sozialwissenschaften' in Weyer (ed), *Soziale Netzwerke: Konzepte und Methoden der sozialwissenschaftlichen Netzwerkforschung*. Munich: Oldenbourg, 1*ff*, 25. Hirsch-Kreinsen (2002), 119*f*, even maintains that networks are simply 'transitory phenomena'.

[98] Hirsch-Kreinsen (2002), 118.

Networks that were once feted as 'the organizational form of the future'[99] have now been brought back down to earth. In common with markets and organisations, networks also tend to undermine their own preconditions for stability. This fact lends them the status of being only one of many potential business organisational forms: whilst their undoubted efficiency gains promote them above other business organisations, their dysfunctional consequences nevertheless demand a heightened form of social attention to their activities.[100]

What does all this mean for network law? Law is certainly not in a position simply to defeat the newly identified risks posed by economic networking. Nonetheless, certain regulatory frameworks might impact positively upon certain of these risks, at least to the degree that they can contribute to a re-stabilisation of self-destructive and fragile networks and can compensate for their negative externalities.[101] This demands that we relinquish any optimistic appraisal that law's useful contribution in this area can effectively direct the concrete behaviour of network actors. Comparable policy and property theory approaches that place their regulatory faith in incentives and costs have failed repeatedly in practice.[102] Legal operations must be more subtly constructed: regulation should not be directed at actor behaviour, but should rather support stable networks expectations by giving them symbolic re-statement in cases where concrete network behaviour contradicts them. Likewise, law should not seek to negate network-typical risks, but should instead seek to translate economic risks into legal risks by means of their transformation into a liability regime. In contrast to sanction-based regimes of

[99] Charles C Snow, Raymond E Miles and Henry J Coleman (1992), 'Managing 21st Century Network Organizations', *Organizational Dynamics* 21, 5*ff*; Raymond E Miles, Charles C Snow and Grant Miles (2000), 'The future. org' *Long Range Planning* 33, 300*ff*; similarly, William H Davidow and Michael Malone (1992); Brian Bosworth and Stuart A Rosenfeld (1993), *Significant Others: Exploring the Potential of Manufacturing Networks*. Chapel Hill, NC: Regional Technology Strategies, Inc, 1; Werner Rammert (1997), 'Innovation im Netz: Neue Zeiten für technische Innovationen', *Soziale Welt* 48, 397*ff*.

[100] See, for a sobering appraisal that distances itself from alarmism, Lemley and McGowan (1998), 198; Elmar Gerum, Wieland Achenbach and Frank Opelt (1998), 'Zur Regulierung der Binnenbeziehungen von Unternehmensnetzwerken: Ein Problemaufriss', *Zeitschrift Führung und Organisation* 67, 266*ff*, 267*ff*; Sydow (1999), 299 *ff*; Windeler (2001), 336*ff*.

[101] For a notable perspective from an economist, see Jürgen Noll (2002), 'Who Should Be Liable in a Virtual Enterprise Network', accessible at www.pages.ssrn.com, who argues for an effective legal liability regime in order to stabilise threatened business networks, that should not simply be restricted to internal net relations, but that should also include heightened external liability of the network. An interesting comparison can be made to legal studies that minimise network risks: Rohe (1998), 416*ff*.

[102] This is why regulatory regimes should be more complex, see generally John Paterson and Gunther Teubner (1998), 'Changing Maps: Empirical Legal Autopoiesis', *Social and Legal Studies* 7, 451*ff*.

behavioural control, these legal mechanisms offer the only effective possibility of giving support to the social institutionalisation of networks.

In summary, this argument furnishes a systematic vision of connections between network-typical risks and appropriate approaches to their legal regulation.[103] At the same time, it reveals the particular underlying social risks that were confronted by the judges in our two opening cases, not by means of systematically refined generalisations, but with recourse to a deft construction of piercing liability.[104] In practice, their somewhat metaphysical usage of terms such as 'trust', 'dependence', 'functional representation' and 'organisational responsibility' does indeed speak to the risks posed by networks. However, in contrast to this metaphysical approach, the equitable orientation of current case law will only be replaced with legal concepts that are appropriate for networks upon the successful completion of a systematic endeavour to categorise the causal relationships within novel network structures and their negative consequences, and further to transform social risks into legal consequences through positive legal regulation.

2. Risks Associated with Trust

The legal combating of social risks associated with trust is a particularly well-trodden path of juridification in a wide variety of social spheres.[105] Fundamental reliance upon long-term trust is a defining characteristic of networks. The specific conditions of trust between members of the network facilitate the 'long-term repayment' of the 'preliminary performance' of a partner in the network by the entire network.[106] In this regard, legal sanctions for breach of trust in networks can be constructed, not only to provide compensation for isolated instances of breach, but also to contain structural risks associated with trust, which arise within the whole of the business network,[107] since 'cost minimisation pressures, heightened time pressure and increasing demands for flexibility result in opportunistic behaviour on the part of individual network actors'.[108]

[103] For legal network regulation from the constitutional rights perspective, Ladeur (2000), 204*ff*.

[104] OLG Karlsruhe NZV 1989, 434; OLG Stuttgart NJW-RR 1990, 491.

[105] For a sociological perspective, Luhmann (1968), 43*ff*; for an institutionalist perspective, Christoph Engel (2001), *Vertrauen: Ein Versuch*. Bonn: Max-Planck-Projektgruppe Recht der Gemeinschaftsgüter; for a private law view, Claus-Wilhelm Canaris (1971), *Die Vertrauenshaftung im deutschen Privatrecht*. Munich: Beck.

[106] Powell (1990); Deakin and Wilkinson (1994); Luhmann (2000), 25, 407*ff*; Bachmann (2000); Teubner (2002a), 316*ff*.

[107] From the viewpoint of economics, legal liability is justified by structural threats to trust, Noll (2002), with other references to relevant literature.

[108] Hirsch-Kreinsen (2002), 112.

Supply networks, in particular, exhibit a heightened risk of transformation into simple strategic pricing systems by virtue of an underlying lack of trust in relation to the loss of know-how amongst members of the network.[109] This is an example of the aforementioned mechanism in action: the economic orientation of networks simply erodes their own trust-based components as an instrumental rationality is brought to bear.[110] Since trust is nonetheless a precondition for the operation of networking, a compensatory mechanism, more specifically, legal sanctions, for the breach of trust must be imposed. In addition to judicial control of standard contracts, in order to secure network trust relationships institutionally, potentially one of the most appropriate legal interventions would surely be an evolution through case law of duties of care within the network that are comparable to duties of care that have already been successfully established within contract, company and labour law jurisprudence.[111]

3. Bilateralisation

Networks create large-scale multi-polar relations out of a variety of local bipolar relations. From a legal point of view, however, supply networks, virtual enterprises, and marketing systems are typically construed simply as manifold bilateral contracts without an overarching legal framework. This facilitates their elasticity, flexibility and decentralised nature, but at the same time creates its own dangers in relation to collective behaviour. Collective entities established by mere bilateral contracting do not possess the requisite organisational mechanisms to allow either for the establishment of a common network purpose or for the co-ordination of the common operational context; neither do they possess mechanisms that would provide for the translation of the network purpose into its constituent bilateral contracts.[112] It is therefore unsurprising that a legal debate has repeatedly suggested that this deficit should be compensated for by applying company and corporate law. The judicial metaphor of 'incorporation' refers directly to company law. Alternatively, contract law equivalents are sought for judicially developed duties of care, whilst further legal efforts are concentrated upon new organisational perspectives within contract law. Finally, a third approach is provided by the question of whether the dangers posed by the bilateralisation of group structures can be combated by imposing a

[109] Inge Lippert (1998) *Zwischen Pfadabhängigkeit und radikalem Wandel: Neuordnung von Prozessketten im internationalen Maschinenbau*. Berlin: Sigma; Casper (1995); (2001), 397*ff*.

[110] Hirsch-Kreinsen (2002), 118.

[111] See Chapters 4 and 5 on internal network relations.

[112] See, for a contract theory analysis of bilateralisation, Collins (1999), 17*ff*.

strict non-discrimination duty upon the network centre in relation to its network operations. All three approaches, however, are characterised by their efforts to translate the collective networking dimension into internal bilateral relationships and to subordinate 'remote' network actors, who are not contractually bound to one another in bilateral relationships, to the common network purpose.[113]

4. Asymmetries of Power and Information

Typically within hierarchical networks (especially in the case of franchising and just-in-time systems), the network centre possesses structural advantages over other network actors. Within business networks, and even more so within technologically driven business co-operation amongst independent firms,[114] the individual firm can no longer be identified as the economic centre of power, 'rather, its dominance is usurped by the power of production networks, whose focal companies function as new centres of power and domination'.[115] This results in new conflicts of interest, problems of co-ordination, and power and information asymmetries.[116] As both the Fiat and Japanese car importer cases readily demonstrate, the analogous application of corporate and employment law to such multiple dependency relationships is an immediately tempting step in order to limit the opportunistic behaviour of network centres towards network nodes and to compensate for insufficient internal oversight over the activities of the centre by means of company law mechanisms.[117] In particular, the question is raised as to whether and to what degree the centre's appropriation of network advantages can be legally regulated through the imposition of duties to promote the network, or even to redistribute profit and risk. More generally, the problem

[113] Chapter 5 analyses the special legal relationship between network actors who are not contractually bound to one another.

[114] See, for a summary, Ott (1995), 214*ff*; Wellenhofer-Klein (1999), 61*ff*; Bayreuther (2001), 541*f*.

[115] Dieter Sauer and Volker Döhl (1994), *Kontrolle durch Autonomie*. Opladen: Westdeutscher, 267; (1997), 'Die Auflösung des Unternehmens?', *Jahrbuch sozialwissenschaftliche Technikberichterstattung* 6, 19*ff*; Gerum, Achenbach and Opelt (1998), 266*ff*; Hirsch-Kreinsen (2002), 115; see also Castells (2000), 208*ff*.

[116] This leads various authors to conceive of networks as political *governance structures*, and, in particular, to analyse their power creation and exercise processes: Hakan Hakansson and Jan Johanson (1993), 'The Network as a Governance Structure: Interfirm Cooperation Beyond Market and Hierarchies' in: Gernot Grabher (ed), *The Embedded Firm*. London: Routledge, 35*ff*; Hakan Hakansson (1997), 'Organization Networks' in Arndt Sorge and Malcolm Warner (eds), *The Handbook of Organizational Behaviour*. London: Thomson, 232*ff*.

[117] In particular the careful examination by Bayreuther (2001), 242*ff*, 338*ff*, 541*ff*.

is one of whether the judicial review of standard contracts can counter inappropriate transfers of risks from the network centre to members of the network.[118]

By the same token, however, the peculiar ambivalences present within networks often determine that power and information asymmetries operate in exactly the opposite direction.[119] The typical independence of nodes in the network facilitates opportunistic nodal behaviour towards the centre or towards other nodes. Can free riding be defeated by limiting the autonomy of network actors through the imposition of duties of loyalty to other network actors, the network centre, and the network purpose? Is it conceivable that we might introduce a legal category of 'network purpose', on analogy with the purpose of a company as specified in its articles of association? Could a legal concept of 'network purpose' restrict the conduct of network actors, as for example in the case of abrupt termination of the contract?[120]

5. Externalities of Networks

Problems created by decentralised decision making are not restricted to internal relationships between members of the network. The contractualisation of collective units entails a dramatic transfer of risks to third parties. On the one hand, networks profit from the fact that they can present themselves to their environment as highly organised supply, co-operation or distribution systems, equipped with their own strict internal organisation and highly developed sense of 'corporate identity'.[121] On the other hand, they constitute themselves only in the form of individual bilateral contracts concluded either between various nodes or between nodes and a network centre. This 'self-dissolution' of the formal organisation into a multitude of individual contracts almost automatically results in the further 'dissolution' of the legal liability of the entire organisation into the individual liability of members of the network. In comparison with simple market transactions, the networking phenomenon thus leads to a new form of risk transference: end service users are

[118] For the issue of *profit transfers* from net centre to the nodes, Chapter 4 (I and V). On the question of risk distribution as a problem for judicial control of standard contracts, Chapter 4 (VI).

[119] This is especially true for just-in-time relationships. See the detailed analyses of Lange (1998), 91*ff*; Bayreuther (2001), 555*ff*. See also Bernhard Nagel (1988), 'Der Lieferant On Line: Unternehmensrechtliche Probleme der Just-in-time-Produktion am Beispiel der Automobilindustrie', *Der Betrieb* 41, 2291*ff*; Herbert Zirkel (1990), 'Das Verhältnis zwischen Zulieferer und Assembler: eine Vertragsart sui generis?' *Neue Juristische Wochenschrift* 43, 345*ff*, 346.

[120] Such questions are treated in Chapter 4 (III and IV) and in Chapter 5.

[121] For an evaluation of management science research, see Martinek (1987), 75*ff*.

confronted with an increasingly acute danger of aggregated harmful effects. At they same time, however, the degree of legal protection available to them is reduced. Danger appears in a new guise: new forms of co-operation may be emptied of all legal responsibility.[122]

> Intensified recourse to 'contractless' organization above contractually embedded co-operation results instead in normative incongruence, giving rise in turn to a legal vacuum within a central area of economic life: where new forms of co-operation establish themselves, real-world co-operation patterns are not subject to a matching liability scheme.[123]

Novel organisational entities are established in business practice that have no matching degree of normative responsibility. They have notable room for manoeuvre within which to carry out explicitly 'irresponsible' actions. Networks suffer from all the usual externality problems posed by a formal organisation: internal agreements are reached to the disadvantage of third parties; networking gives rise to collective behaviour without contemporaneous collectivisation of responsibility; collectivisation increases risks and, as a result of failing to take corresponding precautions for their absorption within the network, displaces them externally.[124]

In addition, economic network theory has revealed negative network effects above and beyond the negative effects of simple incorporation. Highly decentralised multi-directional network communication structures not only furnish the best known of positive network effects, but also impact negatively on third parties. To the degree that the market fails to do so, their internalisation will become a job for the law.[125] Taking a closer look at all their negative externalities, negative 'size effects' deriving from organisational growth cumulate with the negative 'collective effects' that arise in relation to risks posed by corporate actor behaviour

[122] Economic plaudits for network liability regimes, such as Noll (2002), confirm that this is not simply a phantasm of legal consciousness.

[123] See for this pointed connection of liability risks with net specific structures, Picker (1999), 431*f*; see also on similar constellations within special relationships, Picker (1983), 'Positive Forderungsverletzungen und culpa in contrahendo: Zur Problematik der Haftungen zwischen Vertrag und Delikt' *Archiv für die civilistische Praxis* 183, 369*ff*, 385*ff*; (1987) 'Vertragliche und deliktische Schadenshaftung: Überlegungen zu einer Neustrukturierung der Haftungssysteme', *Juristenzeitung* 42, 1041*ff*, 1047*ff*. Similarly, Peter Krebs (2000), *Sonderverbindung und außerdeliktische Schutzpflichten*. Munich: Beck, 381*ff*.

[124] On organised (ir)responsibility of networks, Collins (1990a), 732*ff*; (1990b), 346*ff*; (1999), 248*ff*; Teubner (1991), 107*ff*; (1993b), 57*ff*; (1992), 230*ff*; (2002a), 324*ff*. See also Reich (1995), 76; Ackermann (1998), 47; Krebs (2000), 316*f*, 344*ff*, 380*ff*, 421*ff*; Bayreuther (2001), 399*f*; Lange (2001a), 184*ff*; Marc Amstutz and Walter R Schluep (2003), *Innominatverträge: Allgemeine Lehren und Besonderer Teil*. 3rd edn, Basel: Helbing & Lichtenhahn, 888; Walter Schluep (2003), 'Zusammengesetzte Verträge: Vertragsverbindung oder Vertragsverwirrung' in Heinrich Honsell (ed) *Aktuelle Aspekte des Schuld- und Sachenrechts: Festschrift für Heinz Rey*. Zürich: Schulthess, 285*ff*, 290.

[125] Lemley and McGowan (1998), 198.

to combine finally with negative 'network effects' that are of particular interest here and arise out of mutual communicative accessibility.

As the Fiat case demonstrates, networks pose external liability problems which are so acute that legal doctrine handles them only with the greatest degree of caution.[126] In the light of both the network's contributory responsibility and the danger of insolvency of one node, can the process of contractual limitation of liability to one single, directly involved, network actor simply be accepted as naturally predetermined? Alternatively, is legal liability in relation to the network centre, other network actors, or even the network as a whole now required?[127]

6. Boundary Blurring

Networks pose additional risks to their environment to the degree that they also blur boundaries between firms.[128] This improves the position of firms within the market, but also defeats the apportionment of responsibility. One and the same network might make an appearance within one environment as a multitude of actors, but in another present itself as a collective actor, or as an autonomous operational unit with a well-defined identity. 'Either the identity and unity of the network will be more prominent, or the distinctions between the individual organizations will take precedence, depending upon the situational addressees and the contextual dependencies.'[129] The chameleon-like nature of hybrid networks allows them to operate within environments that would be closed to them were they either simple contractual relationships or simple collectives. Viewed from the outside, hybrid networks are a confusing *unitas multiplex*; a form facilitative of opportunistic external appearances in line with changing

[126] The first comprehensive franchising study by Martinek (1987) avoids addressing external liability altogether. Others, for example, Rohe (1998), 416*f*, sidestep the problem by denying the existence of a liability vacuum, recognising its existence only in relation to franchising in the services sector.

[127] From an economic perspective, see Mitu G Gulati, William A Klein and Eric M Zolt (2000), 'Connected Contracts', *University of California Los Angeles Law Review* 47, 887*ff*; Noll (2002). Liability problems will be investigated in Chapter 6.

[128] This addresses the question of whether networks place existing firm boundaries in doubt and so give rise to the need for a new legal definition of the firm: Badaracco (1991); Sabel (1991), 23*ff*; Arnold Picot and Ralf Reichwald (1994), 'Auflösung der Unternehmung? Vom Einfluss der Informations- und Kommunikationstechnik auf Organisationsstrukturen und Kooperationsformen', *Zeitschrift für Betriebswirtschaft* 56, 547ff; (1996), *Die grenzenlose Unternehmung: Information, Organisation und Management*. 4th edn, Wiesbaden: Gabler; Ron Ashkenas, Dave Ulrich, Todd Jick and Steve Kern (1995), *The Boundaryless Organization*. San Francisco: Jossey-Bass; Ulrich Krystek, Wolfgang Redel and Sebastian Reppegather (1997), *Grundzüge virtueller Organisationen: Elemente und Erfolgsfaktoren, Chancen und Risiken*. Wiesbaden: Gabler; Ortmann and Sydow (1999), 207*ff*; Luhmann (2000), 236*f*; Windeler (2001), 262 *ff*; Hirsch-Kreinsen (2002), 114.

[129] Ortmann and Sydow (1999), 214 from an organisational science perspective.

interests. Is decision making centralised or decentralised? This is relevant to the following contract law question: who is the contractual partner? Equally, legal problems arise in relation to apparent agency. This has relevance for the question of liability: can damage be traced back to centralised or decentralised, collective or individual decision making? Further problems arise in relation to the question of who had the relevant knowledge: will liability law be able to respond with similarly flexible forms of liability?

7. Interface Problems

The dissolution of hierarchical organisations into heterarchical networks creates interface problems between working groups, divisions and business branches.[130] Empirical studies demonstrate that decentralised contexts pose new and magnified risks of cross-cutting liability.[131] Who is responsible for network co-ordination and therefore liable? Traditionally, within the unitary organisation, management is held liable in cases of overlapping responsibility between internal departments. Within a pure market, the client is responsible for the co-ordination of partial transactions. Within the network, however, there is a systematic lack of clarity. Knowledge-based production in particular results in an overlap between the spheres of responsibility of the network actors. It is very hard to apportion blame to any one entity.[132] Practice has responded to such problems with the experimental creation of 'overlapping management'. In order to regulate this special form of responsibility, the law will be called upon to evolve new duties for organisations. It must take particular care with regard to contractually determined distribution

[130] On the interface risks in heterarchical organisations Gottfried Kremer (1984), 'Risiken bei Anlagenverträgen aus technischer Sicht' in Fritz Nicklisch (ed), *Bau- und Anlagenverträge: Risiken, Haftung, Streitbeilegung*. Heidelberg: Müller, 7*ff*; Klaus Brockhoff and Jürgen Hauschildt (1993), 'Schnittstellen-Management: Koordination ohne Hierarchie', *Zeitschrift Führung und Organisation* 62, 396*ff*; Günter Specht (1995), 'Schnittstellenmanagement' in Bruno Tietz, Richard Köhler and Joachim Zentes (eds), *Handwörterbuch des Marketing*. Stuttgart: Schaeffer-Poeschel, 2265*ff*.

[131] George Eads and Peter Reuter (1983), *Designing Safer Products: Corporate Responses to Product Liability Law and Regulation*. Santa Monica: Rand, 95; on the risks of a division of labour in supply networks, Endres (1996), 95*ff*.

[132] See for a legal perspective on just-in-time systems, Jürgen Niebling (1995), 'Simultaneous Engineering aus Sicht des beratenden Juristen', *Wirtschaftsrechtliche Beratung* 15, 505*ff*; Friedrich Graf von Westphalen and Carl-Otto Bauer (1993), *Just-in-Time-Lieferungen und Qualitätssicherungsvereinbarungen*. Cologne: Kommunikationsforum Recht, Wirtschaft, Steuern, 60.

and management of risk and risk.[133] It will respond with schemes of apportionment of responsibility that target the network centre in hierarchical networks and each individual firm in heterarchical networks.[134]

[133] Wellenhofer-Klein (1999), 164*f*.

[134] Alain Supiot (2001), *Beyond Employment: Changes in Work and the Future of Labour Law in Europe*. New York: Oxford University Press, 50; Teubner (2002a), 327.

2

Socio-economic Analyses and Legal Characterisation

I. MARKET REGIME: NETWORKS AS CONTRACTS?

AS WE HAVE seen in the previous Chapter, private law has faced problems in categorising networks.[1] In their guise as trust-based relationships, networks are rooted within pre-modern contexts and appear curiously foreign to modern purposive institutions, such as contracts and organisations. Nonetheless, to the degree that law has acknowledged their existence at all, it has subsumed networks within contract and corporate law, by reconstructing their structures as impliedly agreed upon 'duties of care', and by serenely accepting any frictions with the specific institutional rules caused by this translation. Initial legal indifference faded as the economy made ever more explicit use of network organisations in production, supply, distribution and research, and fashioned new contractual forms out of business practices: franchising, just-in-time contracts and virtual enterprises are particularly striking instances. These new institutional arrangements could not be reconciled with the traditional contract law/corporate law dichotomy. And not by accident, these phenomena are not merely trust-based co-operative relationships, but, at the same time, embody hybrid institutions, lying mid-way between 'market and hierarchy', and revolve around the infusion of organisational elements into contracts.[2] With very good reason, economists and organisation theorists are now not only concerned with the social capital generated by trust-based networks, but also pay close attention to their androgynous position between market and hierarchy.[3] Such 'intermediate organisations' have now become so important (particularly in Japan, but also in the USA and Europe) that

[1] Chapter 1 (IV).

[2] The network discussion has circled both these poles of 'trust' and 'hybrid' in many variants. On the institutional separation of the two and their recombination, see Teubner (2002a), 320*ff*. For an interesting attempt to bind the two within the concept of the structural coupling of organisations, see Mendes (2002), 17*f*.

[3] For a representative selection of hybrid networks, see Patrick S Kenis and Volker Schneider (eds) (1996), *Organisation und Netzwerk: Institutionelle Steuerung in Wirtschaft und Politik*. Frankfurt: Campus.

current scholarship emphasises a 'third arena of resource allocation' alongside market and organisation.[4] When first confronted with this economic and social dynamic, all relevant academic disciplines – organisation theory, economics and law – continued somewhat helplessly to apply the traditional dichotomy between market and organisation. Only very recently have efforts been made to develop a more ambitious conceptual framework within which to address these hybrid institutions.

The legal categorisation of networks remained mired in the market/ organisation dichotomy. Legal doctrine attempted simultaneously to break with and retain the dichotomy. This is worthy of closer analysis; particularly with regard to oscillation between the two poles of contract and organisation that seems never to end, even when a decision has been made in favour of one or the other. Dominant legal opinion naturally begins its analysis with unconditional respect for private autonomy. In nominal terms at least, it accepts the contractual construction of networks. Hybrid contracts are deemed to be what the parties to the contract wish them to be: that is, contracts. As a consequence, hybrid networks make their appearance as simple market transactions, and all their organisational characteristics are subsequently blended out. Nonetheless, the organisational elements within such hybrids have always worked to frustrate their smooth doctrinal qualification as simple contracts. According to Karsten Schmidt, who expresses general disquiet about their treatment as contracts, it is impossible to overlook the fact that 'a contractual model that derives in principle from bilateral relationships will be unable to capture and explain multilateral economic operations in the long term'.[5] This is the reason why, in the first half of the 20th century, jurisprudence as well as various legal scholars emphasised obvious organisational elements within distribution systems, qualified dealer networks as 'similar to companies', and analogously applied selected rules of corporate law to them.[6] However, the following years

[4] Ken-ichi Imai and Hiroyuki Itami (1984), 'Interpenetration of Organization and Market: Japan's Firm and Market in Comparison with the US', *International Journal of Industrial Organization* 2, 285*ff*, 285, 296.

[5] Karsten Schmidt (1999) *Handelsrecht*. 5th edn, Cologne: Heymanns, 1019.

[6] For company-like character, see, eg, RGZ 65, 37; 78, 385; 92, 201; 95, 166. See also RGZ 95, 66; RGZ 145, 275; RGZ 142, 212, 214; BGH DB 1959, 733; BGH WM 1962, 108; BGH ZIP 1992, 191, 194; OLG Celle NJW 1965, 339; KG ZIP 1980, 963, 964. BGH NJW 1972, 1128, 1129; BGH WPM 1962, 1086; BGH LM Nr. 6 relating to § 723 BGB; OLG Celle NJW 1965, 339; OLG Cologne JMBl. NRW 1962, 269; Joachim Schulze-Osterloh (1972), *Das Prinzip der gesamthänderischen Bindung*. Munich: Beck, 60; Werner Flume (1977), *Die Personengesellschaft. Allgemeiner Teil des bürgerlichen Rechts. Band 1.1.* Berlin: Springer, 47; Karl Larenz and Claus-Wilhelm Canaris (1994), *Lehrbuch des Schuldrechts. Band II. Besonderer Teil. Halbband 2.* 13th edn, Munich: Beck, 56*f*; Kessler in *Staudinger* (1995) § 705, 64, 73–75c; Thomas in *Palandt* (2003) § 705, 9.

witnessed their 're-contractualisation'; organisational elements were distilled out of commercial distribution systems, out of contractual dealer and commission agent networks, and most recently out of franchising systems.[7] For the most part, this was achieved with the aid of bilateral constructions. Distribution systems were subsumed under the category of fiduciary contracts.[8] This operation secured their contractual character – though paradoxically only by virtue of their strict hierarchical organisation. The legal notion of 'incorporation' of the sales intermediary into the distribution system provided cover for organisational elements.[9] A second criterion was the residual autonomy of individual units, their independent pursuit of profit, which enabled distribution systems to be distinguished from relations governed by either labour law or corporate law.[10]

However, the repressed organisational elements were returning through the back door. Franchising proved particularly troublesome, once again confronting the law with the hybrid nature of distribution systems. This was no surprise. In economic analysis, '[T]he central feature of franchise organizations is the presence of both market-like and firm-like qualities.'[11] Or, in an even more pointed formulation: 'Franchising is more like an integrated business than a set of independent firms'.[12] In contrast to traditional merchandising networks, most franchising systems are highly centralised. Since they present themselves as a unitary

[7] In opposition to the 'company-like character' of the distribution system, see Heinz-Dieter Köhler (1974), *Über die Anwendbarkeit von Gesellschaftsrecht auf die sogenannten gesellschaftsähnlichen Rechtsverhältnisse*. Munich: Universität München, 3*ff*, 81*ff*, 162*f*; Kurt Ballerstedt (1963), 'Der gemeinsame Zweck als Grundbegriff des Rechts der Personengesellschaften', *Juristische Schulung* 3, 253*ff*, 261; Peter Ulmer (1969), *Der Vertragshändler: Tatsachen und Rechtsfragen kaufmännischer Geschäftsbesorgung beim Absatz von Marktwaren*. Munich: Beck, 206, 322; Hadding in *Soergel* (1991), vor § 705, 19; Ulmer in *Münchener Kommentar* (1997), vor § 705, 82, 89*ff*; in supply systems, Saxinger (1993), 143*ff*.

[8] Ulmer (1969), 321*ff*; Carsten-Thomas Ebenroth (1980), *Absatzmittlungsverträge im Spannungsverhältnis von Kartell- und Zivilrecht*. Konstanz: Universitätsverlag, 32*ff*; Herbert Stumpf and Matthias Jaletzke (1997), *Der Vertragshändlervertrag*. 3rd edn, Heidelberg: Recht and Wirtschaft, 25*ff*. Continuing jurisdiction since BGHZ 54, 340.

[9] Ulmer (1969), 206.

[10] Ulmer (1969), 322; Manfred Mack (1975), *Neuere Vertragssysteme in der Bundesrepublik Deutschland: Eine Studie zum Franchising*. Bielefeld: Gieseking, 100; Hansjörg Weber (1983), '"Franchising" – ein neuer Vertragstyp im Handelsrecht', *Juristische Arbeitsblätter* 15, 347*ff*, 351; Rohe (1998), 416, 419*ff*.

[11] Seth W Norton (1988), 'An Empirical Look at Franchising as an Organizational Form', *The Journal of Business* 61, 197*ff*.

[12] Antony W Dnes (1991), 'The Economic Analysis of Franchising and its Regulation' in Christian Joerges (ed), *Franchising and the Law: Theoretical and Comparative Approaches in Europe and the United States*. Baden Baden: Nomos, 133*ff*, 141.

marketing unit with one comprehensive image and one shared competitive goal, it has become ever more inappropriate to qualify them as simple instances of contractual co-operation between autonomous commercial units.[13]

Organisational components have similarly become more apparent within supply contracts. Minutely detailed agreements and, in particular, computer-supported networking so closely bind just-in-time suppliers within producers' operations that legal definitions need to be readjusted.[14] Multi-polar supply relationships, close and mutual decision making of all partners, centralisation on the part of the producer and close relationships between research and development – all these tendencies work to undermine the analysis in terms of a bipolar exchange contract.[15]

II. ORGANISATIONAL REGIME: NETWORKS AS BUSINESS ASSOCIATIONS?

Equally, the greater the organisational pressures posed by complex contracts, the more that networking seems to be dominated by corporate law elements.[16] Nonetheless, rarely is the radical consequence drawn of reclassifying the business network in pure corporate law terms, either as a company or as a partnership under the commercial code.[17] Instead,

[13] Particularly impressive, Martinek (1987), 123*ff*, 214*ff*. For a critique of pure contractual conceptions, see Andreas K Baumgarten (1993), *Das Franchising als Gesellschaftsverhältnis: Eine Studie zur spezifischen zivilrechtlichen Qualität des Rechtsverhältnisses zwischen Franchise-Geber und Franchise-Nehmer*. Göttingen: Universität, 55*ff*.

[14] For a critique of the conceptual qualification of just-in-time systems, see Axel Merz (1992), *Qualitätssicherungsvereinbarungen: Zulieferverträge, Vertragstypologie, Risikoverteilung, AGB-Kontrolle*. Cologne: Heymanns, 22, 70, 229, 261; Jürgen Ensthaler (1994), 'Haftungsrechtliche Bedeutung von Qualitätssicherungsvereinbarungen', *Neue Juristische Wochenschrift* 47, 817*ff*, 819; Wellenhofer-Klein (1999), 146*ff*; Bayreuther (2001), 538*ff*.

[15] Arguments in favour of their designation as company-like, by Helmut Schlotke (1990), 'Vertikale Verknüpfungen von Unternehmen verschiedener Produktionsstufen durch Qualitätssicherungssysteme und Just-in-Time Lieferungen: Komplexe Langzeitverträge besonderer Art?' in Fritz Nicklisch (ed), *Verträge über Computertechnik in Forschung, Verwaltung, Wirtschaft und Technik*. Heidelberg: Müller, 267*ff*, 273*f*; Zirkel (1990), 350*f*; Hans-Peter Gebhardt (1994), *Der Zuliefervertrag*. Cologne: Heymanns, 70; Stefan Bernhard-Eckel (1997), *Der Just-In-Time-Vertrag*. Baden-Baden: Nomos, 100.

[16] Kulms (2000), 32.

[17] Franchising is qualified as a partnership by Baumgarten (1993), 114*ff*; Sibylle Kessal-Wulf (1995), *Die Innenverbände: Am Beispiel Publikumsgesellschaft, Franchising, Mitarbeiterbeteiligung und Betriebsverband*. Frankfurt: Lang, 249*ff*. For distribution systems as partnerships, OLG Hamm *Europäisches Wirtschaftsrecht* 1985, 281; in contrast, BGH *Europäisches Wirtschaftsrecht* 1985, 665. For just-in-time systems, Christoph Engel (1993), 'Rezension: Oliver E Williamson: Die ökonomischen Institutionen des Kapitalismus', *Rabels Zeitschrift für ausländisches und internationals Privatrecht* 57, 556*ff*, 561; Kulms (2000), 248*f* pleads in favour of the direct application of company law norms; within the same trend, Michael Lehmann (1990), 'Just in time: Handels- und AGB-rechtliche Probleme', *Betriebs Berater* 45,

more sophisticated solutions dominate, which seek both to give adequate recognition to organisational elements and to avoid the discounting of contractual elements. The only question is: how? Martinek attempts to identify a suitable legal framework for networks by means of a differentiated, in part corporate and in part contractual, characterisation of franchising systems. According to Martinek, contractual franchising systems might 'tip over' into corporate organisations, when they cross a particular threshold in the density of co-operation. He distinguishes four constellations: subordination, co-ordination, coalition and confederation. A contractual classification suffices in the case of vertical 'subordination franchising', as well as in the case of the horizontal 'co-ordination franchising'. Two further constellations, however, entail such dense co-operation that they can only be characterised as corporate entities: 'coalition franchising', bundling together a number of business associations, and 'confederal franchising', bringing together a centre and various distribution units within one large business association.[18] Martinek even goes so far as to subsume extremely strictly managed franchise systems to the law of corporate groups; that is, cases of 'subordination franchising' are subject to the law governing vertical groups, whilst cases of 'confederal franchising' are subject to that of horizontal groups.[19] This has drastic consequences, particularly for the external liability of franchising systems that are then subject to corporate law.[20]

Although this model is initially tempting, deeper consideration gives rise to doubts. Can such a dichotomous conception – either contract or organisation – truly capture the hybrid nature of distribution networks? Although the notion of 'tip-over' from contract into corporation facilitates the distinguishing of networks according to their organisational intensity, it does not avoid the negation of organisational and contractual

1849*ff*. For virtual business see Horst Mayer, Angelo Kram and Bianca Patkos (1998), *Das virtuelle Unternehmen: Eine neue Rechtsform?* Dresden: Dresdner Forum für Revision und Steuerlehre, 45*ff*; similarly, but only under certain conditions, see Lange (2001a), 77*ff*; (2001b) 169*ff*; (2001c) 1805*ff*.

18 Martinek (1987), 67*ff*, 231*ff*, 378*ff*; (1992), *Moderne Vertragstypen. Band II: Franchising, Know-How-Verträge, Management- und Consultingverträge*. Munich: Beck, 35*ff*; (1997), 92*ff*; (2001), 327*ff*; Martinek in *Staudinger* (1995) § 675 D 15*ff*. Peter-Christian Müller-Graff expresses sympathy for the corporate qualification of franchising systems: (1988), 'Franchising: A Case of Long-Term Contracts', *Journal of Institutional and Theoretical Economics* 144, 122*ff*, 141.

19 Martinek (1987), 633*ff*.

20 See, in particular, Bayreuther (2001), 368*ff*; also Jürgen Oechsler (1997a), 'Die Anwendung des Konzernrechts auf Austauschverträge mit organisationsrechtlichem Bezug', *Zeitschrift für Gesellschafts- und Unternehmensrecht* 26, 464*ff*, 482*ff*.

elements discussed above. In fact, it intensifies it! When Martinek identifies the presence of a corporate entity, he disregards the existence of contractual elements; when he says there is a contract, he ignores the presence of the organisation.

When Martinek characterises loosely co-ordinated franchising systems as contracts, he contradicts his own empirical analyses, as well as his critique of legal doctrine. In this situation, he reproduces exactly the error that he accuses dominant legal opinion of – he disregards the organisational elements.[21] The common purpose of sales maximisation, is, in this case, supposed to be only an 'economic' goal, not a common purpose in the legal sense; in this situation, the law recognises only the individual aims of the contractual partners. No general duty of loyalty toward the whole franchising system is placed upon members.[22] This is especially strange in the case of 'co-ordination franchising' (such as, franchised hotel chains or transport franchises with a centralised infrastructure). The distribution system as such is supposedly not legally relevant; individual system members are not subject to a duty to support the unitary purpose of the system, but rather are subject only to the usual good faith duties arising out of individual exchange contracts.[23]

By the same token, when Martinek 'tips' closely co-ordinated distribution systems into partnerships, he makes the same error, except in a reverse constellation. Now, even though they exhibit close co-operation processes throughout, he suddenly empties the individual aims of contractual partners – the reaping of residual profits – of all legal meaning. Now, the unitary purpose of the system is no longer merely 'economic', but rather becomes relevant for the law as the common purpose of a partnership under § 705 BGB.[24] Now, the individual interests of business partners are no longer of interest for the law, but are to be considered mere 'economic' motives.[25] Thus, in both cases Martinek's construction fails to capture the defining characteristic that economists have identified as distinguishing centralised franchising chains from vertically integrated firms: residual profits and, in particular, the residual risk born by franchisees.[26]

21 On the one hand, Martinek (1987), 196, 214*ff* (a critique of legal opinion oriented to the individual contract), on the other hand, Martinek (1987) 247, 251, 256*ff*, 378*ff* (the common interest is only economically and not legally relevant in relation to both subordination franchising and co-operative franchising).

22 Martinek (1987) 280*ff*.

23 Martinek (1987), 378*ff*, especially 386.

24 By a partnership agreement, the partners mutually put themselves under a duty to promote the achievement of a common purpose in the manner stipulated by the contract, in particular, without limitation, to make the agreed contributions.

25 Martinek (1987), 251f, 391*ff*, 412, 420*ff*.

26 Explicitly opposed to the equation of franchising with companies, Dnes (1991), 136.

In summary, Martinek's solution is not able to address the typical simultaneous pursuit of individual and collective interest in networks. It fails to pay adequate attention to co-operative elements in the contractual arena, whilst also failing, in the corporate arena, to lay sufficient emphasis upon the pursuit of individual interests, relegating them instead to the status of simple economic aims without legal consequences.

The question whether business networks should be characterised as corporations or partnerships is most intensively discussed with regard to franchising, but also comes up in relation to other types of network. Just-in-time networks struggle with similar difficulties. Here, contract law is subject to the same critique that it is unable to capture the organisational elements present within tightly interconnected supply chains. Neither rules on exchange relations nor rules on relational contracts pay adequate regard to tightly integrated business operations.[27] Particular emphasis is placed on the 'systemic' dependence of suppliers created by computerised communications networks, in order to subordinate closely co-ordinated just-in-time systems to corporate law.[28]

Similar arguments are deployed in the case of virtual enterprises, which should, on such a view, be treated as partnerships, at least in cases of close interconnection. In contrast to purely co-operative contractual arrangements,[29] virtual enterprises are to be viewed as corporations or partnerships in nature, since a common purpose is pursued.[30] Sometimes a distinction is drawn between hierarchical and polycentric structures, with the operations of polycentric virtual enterprises being treated as

[27] Zirkel (1990), 350*f*; Martinek (1993c), 'Sind Rügeverzichtsklauseln in Just-in-time-Verträgen AGB-rechtlich wirksam?' in M Martinek (ed), *Festschrift für Günther Jahr*. Tübingen: Mohr Siebeck, 305*ff*, 312*f*; Lange (1998), 422*ff*; Bayreuther (2001), 538*ff*.

[28] For just-in-time systems as partnerships, see Engel (1993), 561; Kulms (2000), 248*f*. Quasi-partnerships: Zirkel (1990), 350; Merz (1992), 260*f*; Christina Steinmann (1992), *Qualitätssicherungsvereinbarungen zwischen Endproduktherstellern und Zulieferern*. Heidelberg: Decker, 27*f*. For the applicability of the law of corporate groups: Wolfgang Däubler (1988), 'Informationstechnische Unternehmensverkettung und Arbeitsrecht', *Computer und Recht* 4, 834*f*; (1993) 'Mitbestimmung und logistische Kette' in Wolfgang H Staehle and Jörg Sydow (eds), *Managementforschung 3*. Berlin: de Gruyter, 1*ff*; Nagel, Riess and Theis (1989), 1508; Joachim Wagner (1992), '"Just-in-Time"-Produktion und betriebsverfassungsrechtliche Mitbestimmmung: Miteinander vereinbar oder "inkompatibel"?', *Demokratie und Recht* 19, 63*ff*, 69*f*; Holger Kessen (1996), *Nachfragemacht der Automobilindustrie: Eine Analyse unter den Gesichtspunkten Kartellrecht, AGB-Recht und Konzernrecht*. Frankfurt: Lang, 185; Marina Wellenhofer-Klein (1997), 'Just-in-time Production und betriebsverfassungsrechtliche Mitbestimmung', *Der Betrieb* 50, 978*ff*, 981; Bayreuther (2001), 538*ff*.

[29] Ackermann (1998), 43.

[30] Thomas J Olbrich (1994), 'Das Modell der "Virtuellen Unternehmen"', *Information Management* 4, 28*ff*; Thomas Müthlein (1995), 'Virtuelle Unternehmen: Unternehmen mit einem rechtssicheren Rückgrat', *HMD – Praxis der Wirtschaftsinformatik* 185, 68*ff*, 73; Mayer, Kram and Patkos (1998), 55*ff*; 60*ff*; Christian Scholz (1994), 'Virtuelle Unternehmen: Faszination mit (rechtlichen) Folgen', *Jur-PC* 6, 2927*ff*; Elisabeth Berwanger (2000), *Der Gesellschaftsvertrag eines virtuellen Unternehmens*. Münster: Universität Münster, 27*ff*; Geiser (2001), 720.

partnerships.[31] Sometimes the decision between contract and the law of business associations is made dependent on the intensity of co-operation.[32] These solutions, however, exhibit the same advantages and disadvantages displayed by Martinek's differentiated characterisation of franchising.

Nonetheless, such characterisations of networks as partnerships or business associations are also subject to a vehement critique that crystallises around the question: do members of the network really pursue a common purpose in the sense of § 705 BGB? Curiously, it is exactly this question that reveals the contradictions in the arguments raised by critics. On the one hand, they cannot simply deny the existence of a common purpose which is binding on all members. On the other hand, they hesitate to subordinate networks effectively to the law of partnerships. The legal consequences applied by the law of business associations neither match the intentions of members of the network, nor suit the real-world structures of co-operation between individual units, which lack formal principal and agency relations, unitary management systems, and common property.[33] The technical legal issue of a 'common purpose' (§ 705 BGB) obscures the real question of whether networking is a distinct co-operative form, differing in all its essentials from a partnership.

Wiedemann and Schulz make clear that collective and individual goals overlap within the network. They seek nonetheless to distinguish between the common interest and the individual interest by asking which interest has priority within the concrete network: exchange or co-operation?[34] If exchange only serves the goal of the common project, then the network must be characterised as 'company-like'. In contrast, if co-operation facilitates exchange, then we are in the realm of contract. In fact, this solution does have the advantage of avoiding the failings of Martinek's 'tip-over' characterisation, since it recognises the overlap of exchange and co-operation and responds with an analogous application of appropriate company law norms. However, this 'purpose–performance test' again fails to prove convincing in the most typical of network constellations. In franchise systems, common advertising and common marketing are an aid to exchange between the franchisor and the franchisee. But, by the same token, the exchange also serves the common distribution organisation. It is the contradictory structure of the

[31] Jürgen Ensthaler and Dagmar Gesmann-Nuissl (2000), 'Virtuelle Unternehmen in der Praxis: Eine Herausforderung für das Zivil-, Gesellschafts- und Kartellrecht', *Betriebs Berater* 55, 2265*ff*, 2266*f*.

[32] Lange (2001a), 77*ff*; 91*ff*; (2001b), 169*ff*; (2001c), 1805*ff*.

[33] Mack (1975), 99; Lange (1998), 449*f*; BGH EWiR § 705 BGB, 1985, 665 with notations.

[34] Herbert Wiedemann and Oliver Schultz (1999), 'Grenzen der Bindung bei langfristigen Kooperationen', *Zeitschrift für Wirtschaftsrecht* 20, 1*ff*, 3.

network that undermines such clear distinctions. In the end, this endeavour rests upon the traditional distinction between exchange purpose and common purpose.[35] It is, however, exactly this distinction that might be doubted in the case of networks since the purpose–performance relationship is circular.

Attempts are frequently made to avoid this dilemma by distinguishing between the so-called 'unitary' network purpose and the 'common' corporate goal.[36] Alternatively, the talk is of 'common interest' of members of the network in contrast to the 'common purpose' specified in § 705 BGB.[37] In this way, one tries to take account of a common goal whilst avoiding a characterisation that demands the application of the law of business associations. However, these efforts end in strained distinctions. Certainly, simple parallel behaviour is easily distinguished from intentional co-ordination.[38] However, where 'common' is taken to mean that the purpose has either been consented to or requires co-operation between participants, then it becomes very difficult to deny that the supposedly simple 'unitary' co-operative purpose is wholly comparable with the purposes of profit maximisation that are 'common' to all participants. The latter derives equally from an agreement and demands the co-ordination of all participants. Reference to the pooling of resources is also of little help here. Even in the absence of common property, the energies of individual participants are bundled such that a purposive association is founded. The parallel constellation of bank consortia, which are recognised as partnerships with a common purpose, makes clear that no meaningful distinction can be made between a 'unitary' and a 'common' purpose.

[35] Peter W Heermann (1998), *Drittfinanzierte Erwerbsgeschäfte: Entwicklung der Rechtsfigur des trilateralen Synallagmas auf der Grundlage deutscher und U.S.-amerikanischer Rechtsentwicklungen*. Tübingen: Mohr Siebeck, 71.

[36] Andreas Saxinger (1993), *Zulieferverträge im deutschen Recht: Zugleich eine Abhandlung zu den Besonderheiten langfristiger Schuldverhältnisse*. Baden-Baden: Nomos, 144; Gebhardt (1994), 69; Bernhardt-Eckel (1997), 98; Ulmer in *Münchener Kommentar* (1997), vor § 705, 99; Rohe (1998), 358*ff*, 407*ff*, 437*ff*; Wellenhofer-Klein (1999), 168*f*; Krebs (2000), 315; Bayreuther (2001), 289; Lange (2001a), 81*ff*; Annika Schimansky (2003), *Der Franchisevertrag nach deutschem und niederländischem Recht unter besonderer Berücksichtigung seines Netzcharakters und der Ansprüche bei Vertragsbeendigung*. Tübingen: Mohr Siebeck, 91*ff*, 114*ff*; see also Wolfgang Fikentscher (1974), 'Zu Begriff und Funktion des "gemeinsamen Zwecks" im Gesellschafts- und Kartellrecht' in Wolfgang Hefermehl (ed), *Festschrift für Harry Westermann*. Karlsruhe: Müller, 87*ff*, 90, 96.

[37] Ulmer (1969), 322; Ebenroth (1980), 35.

[38] Karsten Schmidt (2002), *Gesellschaftsrecht*. 4th edn, Cologne: Heymanns, 57*ff* distinguishes the company purpose from the simple common nature of individual interests.

In fact, all business networks pursue a 'common purpose'.[39] It is nevertheless true that they should still not be characterised as corporations or partnerships.[40] Why should this be? The reason is not a fictional distinction between 'unitary' and 'common' purpose, but the simultaneous presence of the pursuit of individual and common interests. This simultaneous presence is contrary to corporate law by definition, but, strikingly, is also the creative characteristic exhibited by networks.[41] Law must respond to the contradiction as such, not by making the contradiction disappear through artificial distinctions, but by deploying more complex legal characterisations, which furnish internal creative tensions within those networks with a firm institutional backbone.

III. HYBRID REGIMES: NETWORKS AS INSTITUTIONALISED CONTRADICTIONS

But why on earth should the law institutionalise the contradictory pursuit of interests within networks? Why should it be the task of law to secure the contradictory nature of networking rather than to establish logical clarity, normative consistency and social parity? What can possibly justify the legal distinction between networks and exchange contracts on the one side and business associations on the other? Law itself has no answer to this question since it can only respond to the networks' contradictions by reference to the parties' will. However, in private law, any finding that the will of the parties is 'contradictory' is itself undesirable since law has three unpleasant modes of response: (1) an authoritarian approach that 'objectively' interprets the will of the parties to exclude any contradiction; (2) 'contractual perplexity', which makes the contract void on grounds of public policy under § 138 BGB;[42] (3) '*venire contra factum proprium*', or a breach of good faith under § 242 BGB.[43] There is, however, a different response which can be distilled out of sociological and economic analyses of networking paradoxes.[44]

[39] Martinek (1987), 231*ff*; (2001) 337*ff*; Baumgarten (1993), 127*ff*; Kessal-Wulf (1995); similarly for franchising, Zirkel (1990), 350; Engel (1993), 561; Kulms (2000), 248*f*; for just-in-time systems Olbrich (1994), 28*f*; Berwanger (2000), 27*ff*; Ensthaler and Gesmann-Nuissl (2000), 2266*f*; Lange (2001a), 91*ff*; (2001b), 169*ff*; (2001c), 1805*ff*.

[40] Kulms (2000), 34.

[41] In detail under III.

[42] (1) A legal transaction which is contrary to public policy is void.

[43] An obligor has a duty to perform according to the requirements of good faith, taking customary practice into consideration.

[44] Organisational literature is increasingly aware of the destructive/productive effects of paradoxes on organisational construction. The arguments expanded here build on the ideas of Karl E Weick (1985), *Der Prozeß des Organisierens*. Frankfurt: Suhrkamp, 341, 346, on the productive role of ambiguities within the organisation. On its specific application to networks, see Littmann and Jansen (2000), 27*ff*. On the relationship between innovatory

The thesis is as follows: various economic developments expose business units to a double-bind situation, which requires them to respond via contradictory modes of internal organisation. Double-bind situations arise when: (1) the unit is confronted with unavoidable but contradictory and/or paradoxical demands by its environment; (2) such demands are so central to business survival that they cannot be simply ignored, and (3), they can only be explicitly addressed with great difficulty.[45] The institutional answer to these problems is neither contract nor organisation, but a hybrid network, since this configuration transforms external incompatibilities into internally manageable contradictions. In its turn, private law must evolve a double response: on the one hand, normalising and stabilising network contradictions and, on the other, compensating for their unwarranted consequences.

Hybrid networks facilitate escape from the double-bind situation. They are institutional arrangements, in which, in contrast to simple contractual or organisational logic, network logic is made responsive to contradictory environmental demands. More precisely, hybrids respond to paradoxical situations (in their widest sense) that threaten to paralyse the operational capacities of actors. The paralysis is due to their ambivalence (A is or is not A), their contradictory nature (A is not A) or their paradoxical character in the strict sense (A because not-A and not-A because A).[46]

paradoxes and network-type organisation building Sauer and Lang (1999). On different strategies for dealing with paradoxes in economic organisations, see Luhmann (2000), passim; Oswald Neuberger (2000), 'Dilemmata und Paradoxa im Managementprozess' in Georg Schreyögg (ed), *Funktionswandel im Management: Wege jenseits der Ordnung*. Berlin: Duncker & Humblot, 173*ff*, 208*ff*.

[45] On the paradoxical situation of the double bind, see the classic by Gregory Bateson (1987), *Steps to an Ecology of Mind: Collected Essays in Anthropology, Psychiatry, Evolution, and Epistemology*. Northvale, NJ: Aronson; building on that, Paul Watzlawick, Janet H Beavin and Don D Jackson (1967), *Pragmatics of Human Communication: A Study of Interactional Patterns, Pathologies, and Paradoxes*. New York: Norton. On the application of the double-bind to organisations see Fritz B Simon (1997), *Die Kunst, nicht zu lernen: Und andere Paradoxien in Psychotherapie, Management, Politik*. Heidelberg: Carl-Auer-Systeme.

[46] In a strict logical sense, paradoxes describe circular situations in which 'A is, because it is not A and vice versa', eg the Cretan paradox. In a broader rhetorical sense, paradoxes describe ambiguities and contradictions that paralyse thinking within a given framework. For the purposes of paradox usage within social science and legal doctrine, one further conception suggests itself, which is founded on blockage effects and their decongestion. On the distinction between contradictions and paradoxes in a general pragmatic setting, see Hans Ulrich Gumbrecht and Ludwig K Pfeiffer (eds) (1994), *Materialities of Communication (Writing Science)*. Stanford, California: Stanford University; Watzlawick, Beavin and Jackson (1967). On paradoxical situations in economic businesses, Neuberger (2000), 187*ff*. For legal treatment of paradoxes, George P Fletcher (1985), 'Paradoxes in Legal Thought', *Columbia Law Review* 85, 1263*ff*; Peter Suber (1990), *The Paradox of Self-Amendment: A Study of Logic, Law, Omnipotence and Change*. New York: Lang, accessible at: http://www.earlham.edu/~peters/writing/psa/index.htm; and various contributions in the collective volume, Oren Perez and Gunther Teubner (eds) (2005), *Paradoxes and Contradictions in Law*. Oxford: Hart.

Generally speaking, there are two paths out of such an impasse. The one is repressive, suppressing contradictions by admitting only one of the contradictory instructions and dismissing the other. The other is constructive, seeking to make paradoxes fruitful, to the degree that it establishes a more complex representation of the world. This is what is meant by the concept of 'morphogenesis', which Krippendorff has evolved in order to deal with paradox:

> Unless one is able to escape a paradoxical situation which is what Whitehead and Russell achieved with the theory of logical types, paradoxes paralize an observer and may lead either to a collapse of the construction of his or her world, or to a growth in complexity in his or her representation of this world. It is the latter case which could be characterised as morphogenesis.[47]

In hybrid networks, the double-bind derives from external conditions which demand that business units simultaneously ought to obey different and contradictory imperatives.[48] Many of these problematical demands stem directly from contradictory economic pressures. Others result from a collision between economic requirements on the one hand, with scientific, cultural, medical and political demands on the other.

Contradictory demands can be traced to economic trends that have increasingly overburdened individual firms and have forced them to engage in networking: 'trends such as increased technological complexity, increased pressure on productivity and costs, as well as simultaneous market demands for a high degree of flexibility'.[49] Empirical studies in the context of intra-company co-operation have systematically researched the particular contradictions with which we are concerned

[47] Klaus Krippendorff (1984), 'Paradox and Information' in Brenda Dervin and Melvin J Voigt (eds), *Progress in Communication Sciences 5*. Norwood: Ablex, 45*ff*, 51*f*. On morphogenesis in social systems, see Niklas Luhmann (1990), 'Sthenography', *Stanford Law Review* 7, 133*ff*, 135*ff*; (1997), 57*f*. On exemplary reactions to the paradoxical demands of just-in-time systems, Kathleen Eisenhardt and Brian Westcott (1988), 'Paradoxical Demands and the Creation of Excellence: The Case of Just-in-Time Manufacturing' in Robert E Quinn and Kim S Cameron (eds), *Paradox and Transformation: Towards a Theory of Change in Organization and Management*. Cambridge, MA: Ballinger, 169*ff*, 191.

[48] The relationship between network building and contradictory environmental demand forms the basis for different analyses, though each is differently accented: Kim S Cameron and Robert E Quinn (1988), 'Organizational Paradox and Transformation' in *Paradox and Transformation: Towards a Theory of Change in Organization and Management*. Cambridge, MA: Ballinger, 1*ff*; Buxbaum (1993), 701; Messner (1994), 564; Michael Reiß (1998), 'Mythos Netzwerkorganisation', *Zeitschrift Führung und Organisation* 4, 224*ff*; Maria Funder (1999), *Paradoxien der Reorganisation*. Munich: Hampp; Holm-Detlev Köhler (1999), 'Auf dem Weg zum Netzwerkunternehmen? Anmerkungen zu einem problematischen Konzept am Beispiel der deutschen Automobilkonzerne', *Industrielle Beziehungen* 6, 36*ff*; Sauer and Lang (1999); Ortmann (1999), 253*ff*; Luhmann (2000), 407*ff*; Hirsch-Kreinsen (2002), 107.

[49] Hirsch-Kreinsen (2002), 107.

here.[50] Increasingly, the market demands 'flexible specialisation'. Following the demise of standardised mass production, the market buzz word is 'client-specific mass production'. This goal gives rise to a barely surmountable contradiction between the flexibility and the efficiency of business. The trend in production is towards 'systematic rationalisation'. This optimisation standard cloaks a contradiction between complexity and reliability. Similarly, business organisation is required to follow the goal of 'decentralised self-direction', laying itself open to a contradiction between the autonomy of and the simultaneous tight control of decentralised business units. Business organisations are then left with the question of whether they should choose only one organisational structure, or whether they must seek out the far harder path of combination, fusion and trade-offs between these contradictions. The demand is one of squaring of the circle.

> [I]n order to close the functional gap between 'market' and 'hierarchy', business should combine effective market model incentives, the production and communication advantages of transaction specific investments and the reliability of traditional hierarchical transactions, with the flexibility of loosely co-ordinated networks.[51]

Eisenhardt and Westcott have analysed closely the paradoxical demands that participants in just-in-time supply systems are exposed to (error quota: zero; warehouse capacity: zero; costs: zero; demand and supply time lapse: zero) and have suggested various strategies to combat these paradoxes.[52] The solution to paradoxes appears to lie within 'Japanese production strategies', which have supplied the network model for just-in-time systems:

> The principle seems to be as follows: perfection is possible (although it is not possible). Challenges are broken down as narrowly as possible into their individual situational components, such that they provide multiple reflections of a harmonious world, and are then evolved in close communication from situation to situation. In this manner it appears possible to exclude the problems that typically characterise western thinking, and are connected with notions of difference, distinction, linearity and chain evolution etc.[53]

In essence, innovatory networks evolve contextual linkages between the many 'innovation paradoxes' and innovation policies they meet. Such conditions are to be found in a 'regime of innovation', that is, in a

[50] Semlinger (1993), 313*ff*.
[51] Semlinger (1993), 332.
[52] Eisenhardt and Westcott (1988), 191.
[53] Luhmann (2000), 460, fn 31.

'network type investment pool of innovation practice' that facilitates and supports recursive self-organisation.[54]

Buxbaum analyses these tensions within networks from a legal perspective. The simultaneous external demands for 'know-how, trust and speed' are in themselves so contradictory that neither the market nor the organisation can fulfil them. For this reason alone, an ambiguous institutional response to contradictory demands suggests itself when:

> the sector needs inputs that neither markets nor firms can provide in ways that comport with their typical advantage. These inputs may be of a quality that the market may not be able to price well, or of a quality that permits their opportunistic capture under existing rules of contract law, leading over time to underinvestment in them. They may be of a quality that typical styles of hierarchical processing within firms also do not handle well: for example, technological information that only speedy processing, difficult to obtain within the firm hierarchy, can exploit.[55]

The decisive factor in such situations is thus the choice of institutional arrangement. Should the choice be made in favour of the contract, then the logic of the organisation takes a back seat. Here, exchange, pursuit of individual interest, the individual apportionment of rights and duties and the strict privity principle take precedence. In contrast, if an organisational form is chosen, exchange logic is forced into the background. The issue is then exclusively one of co-operation, of the pursuit of collective interest, of the pooling of resources, and of multi-polar relationships. In each case, the conflict between contradictory demands is 'solved' since the choice of institutional form favours one of the two colliding logics of action, which, at the same time, forces the other logic into an informal sphere. The institutional arrangement thus provides actors with sufficiently clear operational directions, but only at the price of failing to reflect ambiguities emanating from external demands. And if the official law intervenes into these institutional arrangements and gives one or the other operational logic official recognition through a clear characterisation of the arrangement either as a contract or a corporation, then it would only reinforce this less-than-productive solution. Even a differentiated legal network characterisation, which is sensitively based upon the factual dominance of this or the other operational logic, would also suppress the residual operational logic.

Under specific conditions, hybrid networks make an institutional arrangement available that does not suppress ambiguous, contradictory or paradoxical communication, but in contrast, tolerates, promotes, institutionally facilitates it, and – in the optimal case – makes productive use

[54] Sauer and Lang (1999), 20*f*; Ortmann (1999), 253, 258.
[55] Buxbaum (1993), 701.

of it. On this view, hybrid networks result from the fragile co-existence of different and contradictory logics of action.[56] However, they can only work as a productive institutional response to incompatible environmental demands, when they succeed in transforming such external contradictions into internal imperatives that can be made situationally compatible with one another. This gives rise to a 'paradoxical structure' of inter-organisational interpenetration, since it is founded on 'contradictory demands' that are simultaneously 'functional'.[57] The neologism of the 'oscillating organisation' was introduced in order to characterise the oscillation of networks between the poles of various contradictions.[58] Hybrid networks are capable of transforming the intractable contradictions that confront businesses into sustainable conflicts between different levels of network nodes, network centre and the entire network.[59]

Thus, the legal characterisation of networks needs to be reformulated. The ambiguities, contradictions, collisions and paradoxes that constantly accompany the question of contract or organisation are not to be considered 'errors of analysis', but are rather to be greeted as mirrors of the productive aspects of networking. They should thus never be sacrificed to a contradiction-free legal construct by means of which law denies the existence of the contradictory expectations in favour of an internally consistent institution. In contrast to the treasured legal ability to furnish turbulent life with sufficient clarity, reliability and precision, legal doctrine in this context needs to produce ambiguous concepts that not only encompass contradiction, but that even cultivate and intensify them. In the case of social networking, law must be ready with concepts that institutionalise contradictory logics of action.[60] And the law of hybrid networks has the difficult task of coping with contradictions between bilateral exchange and multilateral connectivity, between co-operation and competition, between hierarchy and heterarchy, and between varying rationalities within one and the same organisation.

The paradoxical character of hybrids has far-reaching consequences for their regulation in private law, a theme that is constantly addressed in the following Chapters. It appears in various guises, however, varying in the light of each Chapter's major emphasis, with Chapter 3 concentrating upon the constitutive elements of networks, Chapters 4 and 5 dwelling

[56] Bieber's analyses clarify just how precarious this interaction is: Bieber (1997), 16*ff*.

[57] For other network contexts, see Arthur Benz (1996), 'Regionalpolitik zwischen Netzwerkbildung und Institutionalisierung: Zur Funktionalität paradoxer Strukturen', *Staatswissenschaften und Staatspraxis* 1, 23*ff*, 24.

[58] Littmann and Jansen (2000).

[59] Semlinger (1993), 332.

[60] Some legal scholars now argue along similar lines: see, explicitly, Ensthaler and Gesmann-Nuissl (2000), 2268; Lange (2001a), 179*f*; Amstutz (2003), 167*ff*; Amstutz and Schluep (2003), 888.

upon legal consequences with regard to internal relationships and Chapter 6 tackling the issue of the external liability of networks. With regard to our current concern about legal classification or characterisation, this paradoxical character puts the question beyond doubt: networks differ in principle from existing forms provided by the law of business associations.

This leads us back to the issue of 'common purpose' discussed above. It is no accident, but inherent in network structure, that the issue of 'common purpose' can only be responded to with a contradiction. Network participants must adapt to a contradictory double challenge: following their own individual interest and realising the overarching network purpose in one and the same operation. In contrast to this, traditional corporate law entails a strong presumption that operations within the sphere of collective action (such as management, voting rights) must be pursued with sole reference to the 'common purpose'. Members of the network may only pursue their individual interests in non-collective action spheres (such as rights to profits, individual rights of review).[61] *Tertium non datur*. Within corporate law, the functions of management must not be exercised by reference to an individual interest, but only for the benefit of the common purpose. Collective interests do not, to be sure, take absolute precedence; there is room for the pursuit of individual interest, but only to the degree that this does not violate the corporate interest.[62]

Whilst the demands made by the corporation are explicit, networks impose contradictory demands in relation to the pursuit of individual or collective goals. The individual member that diverts the profits from corporate business operations into its own pocket is in breach of its corporate duties. The same action within a network, however, expresses networking virtue! This is the exact scenario captured by the phrase network-typical *profit sharing*.[63] This difference is so fundamental that it must be translated into the institutional distinction between corporate and network-like co-operation. The lack of real meaning in the distinction made between 'common' and 'unitary' purpose notwithstanding, this is the reason why the corporate purpose must be distinguished from the network purpose. At core, then, those authors who starkly distinguish between network purpose and corporate purpose are correct to do so.[64] This, however, is not a function of the supposed distinction between

[61] Ulmer in *Münchener Kommentar* (1997), § 705, 161, 186, 190*ff*.

[62] Ulmer in *Münchener Kommentar* (1997), § 705, 161; BGHZ 37, 381, 384: employee of a firm, self-employed activity only if no significant interests of the firm are affected; KG OLGZ 1969: use of property for personal interests in breach of trust.

[63] See, for more detail, Chapter 4 (I and V).

[64] See, the notations in fn 36.

the 'unity' of the network and the 'community' of the association, but rather a result of the (contradictory) simultaneous presence of individual and collective purposes.

In principle, the oscillation between individual legal and collective legal orientation will never end. Networks have an exchange contract character, but still react like formal organisations. They expect individual members rigorously to pursue their own individual goals, but also to remain true to the contradictory demand for co-operation and the pursuit of the common interest.[65] The double orientation of network participants forces law to recognise the co-existence of collective and individual goal setting in relation to the same sphere of action.

These internal contradictions are not only present in relation to purpose, but also leave their traces in various other characteristics. The unique nature of networks as opposed to corporate bodies is revealed in the following distinctions. Networks do not create a corporate entity in their own right, rather, they are simply formed out of connections made between decentralised decision-making centres. External contacts with the network do not take place as an agreement with a corporate entity, but rather follow out of bilateral connection to decentralised units. Usual management provisions and rules of agency are not appropriate since, in their guise as autonomous firms, members of the network are responsible for the consequences of their own decisions. Common property is not provided for, since network resources are not pooled, but remain within the purview of individual network nodes. Such structural distinctions between networks and corporate entities preclude the characterisation of business networks as partnerships or corporations, regardless of the degree of their centralisation.[66] As a consequence, law must dispense with the traditional characterisations of business associations and find a new way to characterise appropriately the uncontrovertibly collective nature of networks.

IV. COMMUNITARIAN REGIME: NETWORKS AS 'COMMUNITIES'?

The fundamental distinction between networking and corporate action equally explains why the legal characterisation of networks as 'communal relations' or associations necessarily leads us astray. Accordingly, this variant need only be briefly touched upon. Building on the works of

[65] More explicitly, see Kirchner (2000), 351*ff*.

[66] See also the results of comprehensive interest analyses for just-in-time systems: Lange (1998), 422*ff*; for franchising, Schimansky (2003), 90*ff*.

Jhering and Gierke,[67] various authors have designed a variety of collectivity-based legal constructions, with whose aid associations established 'outside' corporate law might yet be subject to special rules that take proper account of their collective elements. Larenz, Wolf and Paschke have engaged in an ambitious attempt to subordinate the participation of a number of persons within a common frame of reference to the norms of collective decision making.[68] Their aim is to develop a special private law of collectives outside the framework of corporate law, which builds upon principles of participation, participatory rights, majority decision making and equal treatment.

Paschke, in particular, has established a notion of extra-contractual relationships that facilitates the legal recognition of groups and organisation building outside the ambit of corporate law.[69] This legal construction aims to characterise organisational relationships outside the ambit of corporate law as 'organised non-contractual' special relationships. If employees within a firm, property owners and neighbours are subject to such non-contractual norms in practice, then networks might also be candidates for inclusion within this category.[70]

However, rules of associations are not adequate to tackle the peculiarities of networking. As noted above, networks neither create autonomous collective spheres, nor do they give rise to legal personality, management structures, agency rules, or, indeed, result in the establishment of common property. Notwithstanding the intense degree of relational positioning of individual participants, networking still rests firmly upon the individual apportionment of business operations, rights, duties and property; a situation that excludes a community-based approach.

V. MIXED REGIME: NETWORKS AS A TYPE OF MIXED CONTRACT?

If networks institutionalise contradictory expectations, it is readily apparent that any legal characterisation of networks as a straightforward

[67] Rudolf von Jhering (1871), 'Die Reflexwirkungen oder die Rückwirkung rechtlicher Thatsachen auf dritte Personen', *Jherings Jahrbücher* 10, 245*ff*; Otto von Gierke (1914), 'Die Wurzeln des Dienstvertrags' in Juristische Fakultät der Friedrich-Wilhelms-Universität Berlin (ed), *Festschrift für Heinrich Brunner*. Munich: Duncker & Humblot, 37*ff*.

[68] Karl Larenz (1933), 'Zur Lehre von der Rechtsgemeinschaft', *Jherings Jahrbücher* 83, 108*ff*, 142*f*; Ernst Wolf (1973), 'Grundlagen des Gemeins', *Archiv für die civilistische Praxis* 173, 97*ff*, 101*f*; Marian Paschke (1987), 'Außervertragliche Sozialbeziehungen: Eine Herausforderung der zivilrechtlichen Dogmatik', *Archiv für die civilistische Praxis* 187, 60*ff*, 63*ff*, 72*ff*.

[69] Paschke (1987), 63*ff*.

[70] As an aside, however, newer network monographs no longer seek to establish links to corporate law: Lange (1998); Rohe (1998).

'contract', 'company' or 'community' will lead us astray. Can networks then simply be designated as 'mixed contracts'?[71]

Certainly, various types of contract are mixed up within franchising, just-in-time systems, and virtual enterprises. To this extent, notions of mixed-type contracts are appropriate.[72] This characterisation is more problematic when it comes to the combination of co-operation with competition and of bipolar with multipolar relationships, since the notion of mixed contracts in its various forms cannot really cope with typical contradictions in networks.[73]

The 'absorption concept', according to which the dominant contract absorbs the other contract,[74] is inappropriate for networks. The most exciting features of networks – their double character of contract and organisation, the contradictions that they pose – would simply and counterintuitively be 'absorbed' within the dominant element. By the same token, a 'combination concept' that seeks to distinguish differing functional areas, and subjects each to its own type of legal regime, also fails.[75] Such an approach would demand a strict internal distinction within the network between areas governed by contract and those governed by corporate law. However, although a vague distinction can be drawn in franchising between individual activities (purchasing) and collective activities (advertising, strategy building, logistics and common rules), such an endeavour would once again undermine the unique nature of franchising, which seeks to fashion individual activities in line with the interest of the network and to relate collective activities to the individual interests of franchisees. Even if the distinction is made, both activities would be subject to the dual pressures of individual interests and collectivisation.[76] This becomes even clearer in relation to virtual enterprises and just-in-time relationships, where each individual action on the part of participants in the network must be tailored to the strict demands of the overall context of production.[77] The narrow intertwining

[71] See also Amstutz (2003), 162*f*.

[72] On just-in-time, Zirkel (1990), 350*f*; Martinek (1993c), 312*ff*; Saxinger (1993), 159; Gebhardt (1994), 51, 63, 70; Wellenhofer-Klein (1999), 190*ff*; Bayreuther (2001), 539; on franchising Martinek (1987), 294*ff*; Baumgarten (1993), 53*f*; Schimansky (2003), 85*ff*; Weidenkaff in *Palandt* (2003), vor § 581, 22.

[73] See comprehensively, Zirkel (1990), 350*f*. Sceptical, Teubner (1992), 231*f*; Oechsler (1997a), 464; Lange (1998), 111*f*.

[74] See Gernhuber (1989), 157*ff*, 162*f*.

[75] See Gernhuber (1989), 162*f*.

[76] See comprehensively Baumgarten (1993), 170*ff*.

[77] For virtual business, Davidow and Malone (1992); Stephan Duschek (1998), 'Kooperative Kernkompetenzen: Zum Management einzigartiger Netzwerkressourcen', *Zeitschrift Führung und Organisation* 67, 230*ff*; Geiser (2001), 715*ff*; Lange (2001a), 163*ff*; (2001b), 169*ff*; (2001c), 1805*ff*; for just-in-time systems, Martinek (1993c), 312*ff*; Lange (1998), 211*ff*.

of network elements precludes the effort by the combination theory to establish a strict separation between functional areas.

A more attractive concept is that of 'overlapping', which is predicated upon the comprehensive interpenetration of contractual with associational elements.[78] The 'overlapping concept' also applies in economic theories of networks, which view them as hybrid creatures with a middle position along a continuum between market and hierarchy, between exchange contracts and hierarchical organisation, a position that is determined by their transaction costs.[79] However, social science and network theory studies have reserved their greatest fury for the notion of a continuum, precisely because simple notions of 'mixed forms' of contract and organisation appear to obscure the more subtle characteristics of networks;[80] and these, as we have just seen, relate to the institutionalisation of contradictions that cannot be expressed through the notion of a continuum. Networks do not seek a compromise between contradictory expectations – between competition and co-operation, independence and hierarchy, individual and collective perspectives – within such reconciliatory mixed forms. Rather, they seek to retain the tension between distinct expectations, such that neither individual nor collective orientation is compromised, but rather mutually intensified. Networking is distinctive in many ways from more usual corporate forms: the contradictory dedication of transactions to profit maximisation both within the organisation and to the benefit of decentralised 'profit centres'; the peculiarly paradoxical reinvidualisation of the collective; the collision-filled double operational orientation towards collective and individual identity. These are the reasons why networks are not a half-way house between contract and organisation, but rather represent an intensified form of individualisation and collectivisation. Networks do not position themselves 'between' but rather 'beyond' contract and organisation. They must

[78] Ulmer in *Münchener Kommentar* (1997), on § 705, 89, rejects the concept of 'company-like' relationships, but nevertheless accepts that the preconditions of § 705 BGB could be trumped by the constitutive elements of exchange or trust contracts. Similarly, Zirkel (1990), 350*f*. Although, according to Ulmer, on § 705, 99, distribution systems and franchising should be characterised by the dominance of trustee interests.

[79] Williamson (1985), 180*ff*; (1991a), 281, 291.

[80] Above all, Powell (1990); but also Lars-Gunnar Johanson (1987), 'International Relations in Industrial Systems: A Network Approach Compared With the Transaction-cost Approach', *International Studies of Management and Organization* 17, 34*ff*; Sydow (1992), 145*ff*; Mark Ebers and Wilfried Gotsch (1993), 'Institutionenökonomische Theorie der Organisation' in Alfred Kieser (ed), *Organisationstheorien*. Stuttgart: Kohlhammer, 193*ff*; Hakanson and Johanson (1993), 35*ff*; Michael Hutter and Gunther Teubner (1993), 'The Parasitic Role of Hybrids', *Journal of Institutional and Theoretical Economics* 149, 706*ff*, 707*ff*; Mahnkopf (1994), 58*ff*; Roger Laufer (1995), *Networks, Legitimacy and Society: Neither Market Nor Hierarchy*. Paris: ESSEC Workshop: Action, Structure and Organization.

continuously conclude contradictory 'agreements, which suit their particular interests – that is, not simply as integral parts of the organisation, but also as contemporaneously autonomous "actors" within the value creation chain'.[81]

VI. POLYCORPORATE REGIME: NETWORKS AS CORPORATE GROUPS?

Currently, only one firmly established legal institution incorporates contradictions between individual and collective orientation, hierarchy and heterarchy, and co-operation and competition in much the same manner as networks: that is, the corporate group. The law governing corporate groups has also been marked by tension between concepts of individual relationships between single companies (buzzword: independent juridical persons) and unitary concepts of the complex organisation (buzzword: the corporate group as an autonomous business organisation). And there is one concept of the corporate group – the group as a polycorporate network – that deals explicitly with the contradictory unity/multiplicity of the group.[82] Thus, the law of corporate groups shows that legal doctrine has the potential to reflect productively upon and meet the challenges posed by the phenomena of networks. Indeed, parallels between contract networks and corporate groups are astounding. There are not only similar contradictions between unity and multiplicity, both in the internal structure and in the external relations, but also similar legal hazards are created by groups and by networks. The risks posed by business networks that we detailed in the first Chapter – trust-based risks, bilateralisation, power and information asymmetries, contractualisation, boundary-blurring, overlapping responsibilities and political manipulation – can be identified *mutatis mutandis*

[81] Oechsler (1997a), 475; Ensthaler and Gesmann-Nuissl (2000), 2268.

[82] On attempts to translate the paradox of *unitas multiplex* within the corporate group into doctrinal concepts, principles and norms, Ludwig Raiser (1964), 'Die Konzernbildung als Gegenstand rechts- und wirtschaftswissenschaftlicher Untersuchung' in Ludwig Raiser, Heinz Sauermann and Erich Schneider (eds), *Das Verhältnis der Wirtschaftswissenschaft zur Rechtswissenschaft, Soziologie und Statistik*. Berlin: Duncker & Humblot, 51*ff*; Ulrich Bälz (1974), 'Einheit und Vielheit im Konzern' in Fritz Baur (ed), *Funktionswandel der Privatrechtsinstitution: Festschrift für Ludwig Raiser*. Tübingen: Mohr Siebeck, 287*ff*, 324; Peter Hommelhoff (1982), *Die Konzernleitungspflicht: Zentrale Aspekte eines Konzernverfassungsrechts*. Cologne: Heymanns, 214*ff*; for an explicit use of network theory for the law of corporate groups, Gunther Teubner (1990b), 'Unitas Multiplex: Problems of Governance in Group Enterprises', in Gunther Teubner and David Sugarman (eds) *Regulating Corporate Groups in Europe*, Baden-Baden: Nomos, 67–104, 82*ff*; Marc Amstutz (1993), *Konzernorganisationsrecht: Ordnungsfunktion, Normstruktur, Rechtssystematik*. Bern: Stämpfli, 256*ff*; Kirchner (1993), 202*ff*; (1996), 228*ff*; (2000), 339*ff*; Ulrich Ehricke (1996), 'Gedanken zu einem allgemeinen Konzernorganisationsrecht zwischen Markt und Regulierung', *Zeitschrift für Unternehmens- und Gesellschaftsrecht* 25, 300*ff*, 308*ff*, 320*ff*.

in the case of corporate groups.[83] This has given rise to repeated demands that networks of contracts should be subordinated to the law of corporate groups – a highly complex regulatory structure. The legal consequences for just-in-time systems, franchising chains and virtual enterprises would be drastic. They range from intensified fiduciary duties between dominant and dominated firms, across the imposition of compensation rules for subsidiaries under § 311*ff* AktG (Stock Law), to include not only the creation of creditors' external liability, but also the imposition of co-decisional rights for corporate group work councils.[84]

To date, discussion has largely debated the questions of whether contractual networks fulfil factual concentration preconditions and whether the legal consequences would be appropriate.[85] In the meantime, case law has explicitly excluded the application of the law of corporate groups to contract networks, though the question remains highly controversial.[86] There is, however, the more fundamental question of whether one should not more carefully distinguish the logics of action in corporate groups from that of networks. This is due to the difference between 'market failure' and 'organisational failure'. In both cases, the choice of institutional arrangement depends upon the balance between

[83] See especially, for comparison of corporate groups and networks, the careful study by Bayreuther (2001), particularly its treatment of deficits in contract law, 149*ff*. In the social sciences, parallels have been drawn between business networks and corporate groups with reference to their structures and their risks: Thomas Hess (2000), 'Anwendungsmöglichkeiten des Konzerncontrolling in Unternehmensnetzwerken' in Jörg Sydow and Arnold Windeler (eds), *Steuerung von Netzwerken*. Opladen: Westdeutscher, 156*ff*, 158*ff*; Jörg Sydow (2001), 'Zum Verhältnis von Netzwerken und Konzernen' in Günther Ortmann and Jörg Sydow (eds), *Strategie und Strukturation*. Wiesbaden: Gabler, 271*ff*, 283*ff*; Windeler (2001), 234*ff*.

[84] Arguing for analogous application of corporate groups law to just-in-time systems, Däubler (1988), 834*f*; (1993), 1*ff*; Nagel (1988), 2292; Nagel, Riess and Theis (1989), 1508; Thomas Klebe and Siegfried Roth (1990), 'Technische und organisatorische Aspekte des Just-in-Time-Delivery', *Computer und Recht* 6, 677*ff*, 679; Lehmann (1990), 1851; Schlotke (1990), 269*ff*; Wagner (1992), 69*f*; Michael Martinek (1993b), *Moderne Vertragstypen. Band III: Computerverträge, Kreditkartenverträge sowie sonstige moderne Vertragstypen*. Munich: Beck, 304*ff*, 307; Ensthaler (1994), 817, 819; Kessen (1996), 185; Brunhilde Steckler (1996), *Die rechtlichen Risiken der Just-in-Time-Produktion*. Stuttgart: Boorberg, 139*f*; Wellenhofer-Klein (1997), 981; Bayreuther (2001), 560*ff*; only in exceptional circumstances, Steinmann (1992), 171; in the case of outsourcing, Heribert Hirte (1992), 'Gesellschaftsrechtliche Fragen des "Outsourcing"' *Computer und Recht* 2, 193*ff*, 193, 197. Sceptical, Dirk Uwer and Jörg Uwer (1997), 'Rechtsfragen der Regulierung von Hersteller-Zulieferer-Beziehungen in der Automobilindustrie', *Deutsche Zeitschrift für Wirtschaftsrecht* 7, 48*ff*, 53; Kulms (2000), 34. Arguing for the application of the law of corporate groups only in the case of highly organised franchising, Martinek (1987), 640; Brigitte Buschbeck-Bülow (1989), 'Betriebsverfassungsrechtliche Vertretung in Franchise-Systemen', *Betriebs Berater* 44, 352*ff*; (1990), 'Franchise-Systeme und Betriebsverfassung', *Betriebs Berater* 45, 1061*ff*; Oechsler (1997a), 476*f*; Pasderski (1998), 73*ff*; Bayreuther (2001), 363.

[85] A recent comprehensive analysis arguing for, with comprehensive notation, Bayreuther (2001), 40*ff*; 76*ff*; contra, Schimansky (2003), 137*ff*.

[86] Documentation of case law and academic opinion, Bayreuther (2001), 32*ff*, 34*ff*.

'variety' and 'redundancy' appropriate to prevailing environmental expectations.[87] The notion of variety denotes the multitude of and difference between the elements within a system; redundancy is deployed to measure the degree to which possession of knowledge of one element furnishes knowledge over other elements without recourse to additional information. Variety and redundancy are two different, though not necessarily opposing, measures of complexity.[88]

Pure market-driven contracts give rise to a relatively high degree of variety with a relatively low level of redundancy. Whilst they are extraordinarily flexible, correctable and innovative, they nonetheless are weaker at establishing long-term orientation, decisional power, coherence, and accumulated experience. The invention of the formal organisation contributed to solving the problem of the absence of redundancy, but nonetheless achieved this only at the cost of a loss of variety. Rigidity, bureaucracy, motivational problems, innovative weakness and high information costs are not problems that are restricted to governmental organisations, but also make themselves especially well felt within private businesses.[89]

'Missed opportunities' – this drives a new experimentalism in institutional arrangements, which has been described as the 're-entry' of the distinction into an already differentiated realm.[90] The decision on re-entry is not founded in rational choice decisions but rather in the unco-ordinated interaction of evolutionary mechanisms of variation (trial and error), selection (competition and power), and retention (institutionalisation).[91] This is the emergent moment of networks. Networks result from the re-entry of the distinction between market and hierarchy. In the words of the Japanese scholars Imai and Itami:

[87] Imai and Itami (1984), 298*ff*; Teubner (1993b), 48*ff*; Littmann and Jansen (2000), 69.

[88] Niklas Luhmann (1987), 'Die Differenzierung von Politik und Wirtschaft und ihre gesellschaftlichen Grundlagen' in N Luhmann, *Soziologische Aufklärung 4: Beiträge zur funktionalen Differenzierung der Gesellschaft*. Opladen: Westdeutscher, 32*ff*, 47*ff*; (1988), 'Organisation' in Willi Küpper and Günther Ortmann (eds), *Mikropolitik: Rationalität, Macht und Spiele in Organisationen*. Opladen: Westdeutscher, 165*ff*.

[89] Williamson (1991a), especially 277*ff*; (1991b), 'Strategizing, Economizing, and Economic Organization', *Strategic Management Journal* 12, 75*ff*, 81*ff*; (1993), 'Calculativeness, Trust, and Economic Organization', *Journal of Law and Economics* 36, 453*ff*. Correcting the economic one-sidedness of the transaction cost approach, Dirk Baecker (1993), *Die Form des Unternehmens*. Frankfurt: Suhrkamp, 103*ff*; (2002), 21*ff*.

[90] Generally on the concept of *re-entry*, George Spencer Brown (1972), *Laws of Form*. New York: Julian, 56*f*, 69*ff*; Elena Esposito (1993), 'Ein zweiwertiger nicht-selbständiger Kalkül' in Dirk Baecker (ed), *Kalkül der Form*. Frankfurt: Suhrkamp, 96*ff*, 97*ff*; Niklas Luhmann (1993), 'Observing Re-entries', *Graduate Faculty Philosophy Journal* 16, 485*ff*; (1997), 179*ff*. On re-entry in organisations, Luhman (2000), 462*ff*. On re-entry in networks, Teubner (1991), 117*ff*; (1993b), 48*ff*; (2002a), 316*ff*; Rölle and Blättel-Mink (1998), 74*ff*, 84; Littmann and Jansen (2000), 69*f*; Windeler (2001), 239*f*.

[91] Teubner (1991), 117*f*; (1993b), 43*ff*; (2002a), 321*ff*; Rölle and Blättel-Mink (1998), 74*ff*, 84; Littmann and Jansen (2000), 69*f*; Windeler (2001), 239*f*. For a evolutionary view of

> Market principles penetrate into the firm's resource allocation and organization principles creep into the market allocation. Interpenetration occurs to remedy the failure of pure principles either in the market or in the organization.[92]

The 'pure' contract and the 'pure' organisation are established by virtue of the market/hierarchy distinction. Organisations define their boundaries with reference to the market. Contractual arrangements in their turn define themselves in contrast to formal organisations. Difficulties within the mixed relationship between variety and redundancy, however, result in the assumption by contracts of organisational elements. In a similar manner, large organisations experiment with the incorporation of market-like elements. Networks are a particularly interesting case within this game of experiment with de-differentiation and fluid transition. Arrangements created by the institutional market/hierarchy distinction are made subject a second time to the market/hierarchy distinction. Contracts incorporate organisational elements within themselves, whilst organisations are injected with market-like elements.[93]

Further, contractual networks differ from corporate groups in their re-entry constellations. Two types – organisational and market networks – can be distinguished, which, depending upon which segment of the initial market/hierarchy distinction dominates, afford the residual segment only a secondary orientation position. 'Organisational networks', that is corporate groups, are created when formal organisations internally reproduce the distinction between an organised sphere and a spontaneous sphere. Decentralised and multidivisional groups are the most significant innovation within this area; their final highly decentralised form being characterised as 'network groups'.[94]

private legal institutions, see Amstutz (2001), 303*ff*; of just-in-time contracts, Gunther Teubner (2002b), 'Idiosyncratic Production Regimes: Co-evolution of Economic and Legal Institutions in the Varieties of Capitalism', in John Ziman (ed) *The Evolution of Cultural Entities: Proceedings of the British Academy*, Oxford: Oxford University Press, 161*ff*.

92 Imai and Itami (1984), 285.

93 The distinction to simple type mixing again becomes apparent here. Type mixing means that different structures within a system are combined with one another. Re-entry means that an autonomous system with its own structures and clear borders to its environment internally re-constructs various structures found within its environment by virtue of various irritations. These structures, however, are not imported from the environment, but are independent constructions of the system that remain distinct from environmental structures. On the peculiarities of re-entry, see notations in fn 90.

94 The business historian Giulio Sapelli (1990), 'A Historical Typology of Group Enterprises: The Debate on the Decline of "Popular Sovereignty"' in David Sugarman and Gunther Teubner (eds), *Regulating Corporate Groups in Europe*. Baden-Baden: Nomos 193*ff*, 195*ff* uses the following typology: 'Historically, from the prevalence of the "patrimonial group" we have passed to that of the "financial group", then to the "industrial" and, finally, to the "managerial" and "network group". It is the latter group which is functional in the context of present-day global competition.'

Large-scale groups react to their high level of redundancy by attempting to intensify variety through a threefold strategy:[95]

(1) Direct and centralised hierarchical command is replaced by indirect and contextual management of independent subsidiaries (general policy making, management-personnel policies, indirect profit management).
(2) Long hierarchy chains are broken up by internal markets: relations between the centre and the subsidiaries are subject to a simulated capital market, giving rise to group-internal markets for labour, management resources, and product.
(3) Functional differentiation within the whole group that results in an inadequate maximisation of particular functions is dispensed with in favour of segmented differentiation, in which autonomous profit centres are afforded a double orientation: their own profit and the profit of the entire organisation.

In contrast, 'market networks', that is co-operation contracts between individual firms, are founded within a contractually structured market sphere. Here the emergence of a network responds to the deficits of intense variety within market relationships, and seeks to increase redundancy through the incorporation of organisational elements. Franchising systems emerge when pure contractual arrangements cannot fulfil the co-ordination requirements demanded by a distribution system (centralised advertising, cross-regional image unity, decentralised distribution, strong local variations).[96] Contracts do not create sufficient incentives for franchisors to build and manage a unitary distribution system; neither do they possess sufficient mechanisms to control opportunistic franchisee behaviour. In addition, information asymmetries in relation to local customs cannot be overcome by the application of simple contractual mechanisms. Just-in-time systems exhibit a similar redundancy problem. In order to ensure quality and timely supply, suppliers must be subjected to narrow technical co-ordination, thus necessitating a high degree of redundancy within organisational regulation. In order to ensure precise command throughout the logistical chain, the producer must acquire comprehensive information, and indisputable management and control powers.[97] 'Contract failures' exert pressure to introduce hierarchical

[95] See Teubner (1993a), 75*ff*; Manuel Theisen (2000), *Der Konzern: Betriebswirtschaftliche und rechtliche Grundlagen der Konzernunternehmung*. Stuttgart: Schaeffer-Poeschel; Sydow (2001), 290*ff*.

[96] See Paul H Rubin (1978), 'The Theory of the Firm and the Structure of the Franchise Contract', *Journal of Law and Economics* 21, 223*ff*; Dnes (1991), 134*ff*; Schimansky (2003), 76*ff*.

[97] Lange (1998), 53*ff*; 77*ff*; Bayreuther (2001), 541*ff*, each with further notations.

elements within the contract – establishment of stronger internal incentives and controls and a reduction in information asymmetries.

These stark differences between organisational and contractual networks preclude the definition of contractual networks as corporate groups. This confirms case law, which deems that only corporate-law-founded concentrations, and not contractually based concentrations, fulfil the dependency requirements under § 17 AktG.[98] Contractual networks are distinguished from corporate groups in the manner of the re-entry of the market/hierarchy distinction. Contractual networks are forms of market co-ordination within which built-in hierarchies are afforded only a secondary position. Corporate groups are corporate law bodies, incorporating secondary market-like elements. This is the essential distinction in their logics of action. Market networks are primarily subject to market logic. The primary concern is with exchange, competition, individual interests and individual actor rents. In contrast, the corporate group is primarily governed by an organisational orientation: co-operation, hierarchy, collective purpose, corporate profit. In each case, the opposing (market/hierarchy) orientation is only a secondary one, and must be adapted to the demands of the dominant orientation. Similarly, differences arise with regard to directive instruments: within market networks, influence is primarily exercised by means of contract, bargaining, opposing power, market power and exchange position; whilst property, company law influences, management rights and organisational competences play the major controlling role within organisational networks.[99]

In terms of legal policy, the law of corporate groups is not adequate since it serves wholly different policy aims from the ones that typical networking risks would seem to necessitate. The German law of corporate groups, in particular, is in major part concerned with dependencies between members within the group, and not with constituting a novel, network-like, form of business organisation.[100] This is the one weakness in the otherwise excellent study by Bayreuther, which, with its preoccupation with the law of corporate groups, lays too strong an emphasis upon dependency phenomena, to the detriment of the appropriate overall regulatory framework. As a result, Bayreuther's conclusions are

[98] BGHZ 90, 381, 395*f*; BGHZ 121, 137, 145.

[99] Similarly, Kirchner's distinctions (2000), 351*ff*, between the primacy of success in corporate groups and the primacy of co-operation within contractual networks. Also, with similar thoughts, Erich Schanze and Karl Heinz Haunhorst (1993), 'Security of Tenure in Conventional and "Flexible" Employment Regimes: A Neo-Institutional Perspective', *European Journal of Law and Economics* 2, 179*ff*.

[100] In more detail, Gunther Teubner (1990), 'Die "Politik des Gesetzes" im Recht der Konzernhaftung: Plädoyer für einen sektoralen Konzerndurchgriff' in Fritz Baur (ed), *Festschrift für Ernst Steindorff*. Berlin: de Gruyter, 261*ff*, 265*ff*.

problematic: within a 'normal' constellation, neither franchising nor just-in-time systems are supposed to be comparable with the corporate group; the law of corporate groups should only be given analogous application to networks in cases of 'extreme', even 'pathological' dependency.[101] However, the appropriate rules for 'normal' networking are of major interest – pathological cases are only a residual issue. The law of contractual networks should not be distracted by dependency phenomena, but should instead dedicate itself from the outset to novel forms of network co-ordination, concentrating upon the particular problems that they pose.[102]

This does not, to be sure, preclude the careful analogous application of special rules of the law of corporate groups to networks, especially when a comparable position of dependency is created.[103] But, on closer analysis, neither the rules applying to 'contractual corporate groups' (*Vertragskonzern*), nor even liability schemes for 'qualified de facto corporate groups' (*qualifizierter faktischer Konzern*), would seem to be suitable in this case. At best, only an analogy to external liability rules is appropriate, and only then for those contractual networks that exhibit a comparable degree of extreme economic dependency. In short, the analogy to the corporate group should only be made in cases when networks are so centralised that, all formal independence notwithstanding, the organisation created is a de facto comprehensive business unit. However, such units are, to all intents and purposes, no longer networks, but rather centralised individual businesses, with only apparently independent network nodes.

VII. IDIOSYNCRATIC REGIME: 'NETWORK CONTRACT' AS A NEW LEGAL CONCEPT?

Given these considerations, all the various efforts to subsume networks under existing legal categories appear to have failed. Instead, networks seem to be legal phenomena *sui generis*; a form of organisation that has developed in step with the evolution of economic institutions and that now requires its own legal principles and legal norms.[104] In addition to all that we have learnt about the differences between the operational

[101] Bayreuther (2001), 527*ff*, 579*ff*.

[102] Lange (1998), 447*f*.

[103] See, more precisely, Chapter 5 (III); Chapter 6 (III).

[104] Deploying the concept of the 'symbiotic contract' in support of the independent institutionalisation of long-term relationships, Schanze (1991), 89*ff*; (1993), 691*ff*; Kirchner (1993), 202*ff*; (1996), 228*ff*; (2000), 339*ff*; Kai-Thorsten Zwecker (1999), 'Franchising als symbiotischer Vertrag: Beziehungen zwischen Gesellschaftsrecht und Franchising', *Juristische Arbeitsblätter* 31, 159*ff*, 164. This concept, however, does not place the multilateral character of networks that is of such interest to this study to the fore.

logics of networks and those of contractual exchange, partnerships, corporations, and corporate groups, they seem to lack any of the three well-known interest constellations found within private law. Could it be that the holy trinity of private law – 'exchange', 'trust' and 'common interest', as it was once so aesthetically expressed[105] – is incomplete, such that a fourth mode of private co-operation needs now to be established? Networks do not in any case fall within the adversarial interest constellation of exchange, in which each party retains their advantage and are liable only to the good faith stipulations of § 242 BGB (*mea res agitur*). However, the interest constellation present within fiduciary relations within which the interests of one party are subordinated to those of the other and which give rise to intense fiduciary regulations and duties (*tua res a me quasi mea agitur*), is equally inadequate for networks, because it emphasises the individual interests of the contractual partners and neglects collective ones. And finally, as demonstrated above, interest constellations that co-operatively bind individual interests together, direct them to a common goal within corporate law relationships and subject them to typically intensified 'corporate law' fiduciary duties (*nostra, ergo et mea res agitur*), are similarly ill-suited to networks. As we have seen, the network is a contradictory combination of conflicting individual and common interests (*et mea et nostra rea agitur*). Is the network in need – due to the paradoxes of contract/association co-operation/competition, and collective/individual – of its own legal regime?

To date, the most ambitious doctrinal response has been an independent notion of the 'network contract' as a genuinely multilateral agreement. The honour of 'juridical invention' is attributed to Möschel, that of doctrinal elaboration to his acolyte, Rohe. They discovered the network contract within Bank Gironets, and have also identified its presence within other instances of hierarchical and heterarchical networking.[106] According to Rohe, network contracts are concluded where a party external to the network who wishes to undertake business with it – be that in the guise of a client or of a new network member – need only make contact with one network participant. With this, not only is one contract directly created between the external actor and the individual network member, but also a contractual relation arises between the external party and all the other members of the network. The individual network member thus not only acts in his own name and his own interest, but is also implicitly acting as an agent for and in the

[105] Franz Beyerle (1932), *Die Treuhand im Grundriss des Deutschen Privatrechts*. Weimar: Böhlau, 16*ff*; Ulmer (1969), 265*ff*; Martinek (1987), 239*ff*.

[106] Möschel (1986), 223; Rohe (1998), 85*ff*; 356*ff*. In more detail, Karl Larenz and Manfred Wolf (1997), *Allgemeiner Teil des Bürgerlichen Rechts*. 8th edn, Munich: Beck, 470.

interest of other members of the network. By the same token, such members are supposed from the outset – although, of course, only by virtue of implicit agreement – to have afforded the individual network member a power of agency, such that the external contract was concluded in representation of other members of the network. These agency powers are implicitly created with the very first bipolar contract with a network member and are repeated in the other bilateral contracts within the network. From this instant on, then, although they can clearly not be positive performance duties by virtue of their implicit nature, limited (contractual) fiduciary duties are created between the external party and various members of the network.

This is obviously a grandiose fiction.[107] Implicit, mutual and multilateral representation of members of the network by one another and the creation of a large number of implied powers of agency for dealing with parties external to the net (in all their implicit delineation as secondary contractual claims) – this bears no relation to the real bargaining and agreement processes of networks with outsiders. Were powers of representation and agency be said to exist, they would simply be legal fictions set against the very different real-world operations of networks. The characterisation of 'network' contract on the basis of the implied representation of all the other members of the network, a status which is itself derived from a number of equally implicit powers of agency, is a total

[107] The reaction of legal scholars has been overwhelmingly critical: Uwe Hüffer (1987), 'Die Haftung gegenüber dem ersten Auftraggeber im mehrgliedrigen Zahlungsverkehr', *Zeitschrift für das gesamte Handelsrecht und Wirtschaftsrecht* 151, 93*ff*, 106*ff*; Ingo Koller (1987), 'Grundstrukturen des Bankhaftungsrechts unter besonderer Berücksichtigung des Zahlungsverkehrs' in Johannes Köndgen (ed), *Neue Entwicklungen im Bankhaftungsrecht*. Cologne: RWS Verlag Kommunikationsforum, 21*ff*, 25; Johannes Köndgen (1987), 'Bankhaftung: Strukturen und Tendenzen' in *ibid*, 133*ff*, 144*f*; Pikker (1987), 1057; Eberhard Schwark (1987), '100 Bände BGHZ: Bank und Wertpapierrecht', *Zeitschrift für das gesamte Handelsrecht und Wirtschaftsrecht* 151, 325*ff*, 339; Jürgen Schröter (1987), 'Bankenhaftung im mehrgliedrigen Zahlungsverkehr', *Zeitschrift für das gesamte Handelsrecht und Wirtschaftsrecht* 151, 118*ff*, 126*ff*; Claus-Wilhelm Canaris (1988), *Bankvertragsrecht*. 4th edn, Berlin: de Gruyter, para 393; Thomas Schürmann (1994), *Haftung im mehrgliedrigen bargeldlosen Zahlungsverkehr*. Berlin: Duncker & Humblot, 206*ff*; Alfons van Gelder (1995), 'Schutzpflichten zugunsten Dritter im bargeldlosen Zahlungsverkehr?' *Wertpapier Mitteilungen* 49, 1253*ff*; Dorothee Einsele (1999), 'Haftung der Kreditinstitute bei nationalen und grenzüberschreitenden Banküberweisungen', *Archiv für die civilistische Praxis* 199, 145*ff*, 172*ff*; (2000), 'Das neue Recht der Banküberweisung', *Juristenzeitung* 54, 9*ff*, 14*f*; Wellenhofer-Klein (1999), 177; Krebs (2000), 313*ff*; Ulrich Wackerbarth (2000), 'Die Haftung für zwischengeschaltete Banken im mehrgliedrigen Überweisungsverkehr', *Zeitschrift für Wirtschaftsrecht* 21, 1187*ff*, 1193; Katja Langenbucher (2001), *Die Risikozuordnung im bargeldlosen Zahlungsverkehr*. Munich: Beck, 101*ff*; Markus Stoffels (2001), *Gesetzlich nicht geregelte Schuldverträge: Rechtsfindung und Inhaltskontrolle*. Tübingen: Mohr Siebeck, 268*f*; Gottwald in *Münchener Kommentar* (2003), § 328, 144. A more balanced appreciation of the network contract in Jürgen Oechsler (1997b), *Gerechtigkeit im modernen Austauschvertrag: Die theoretischen Grundlagen der Vertragsgerechtigkeit und ihr praktischer Einfluss auf Auslegung, Ergänzung und Inhaltskontrolle des Vertrages*. Tübingen: Mohr Siebeck, 353*ff*, 384*ff*; K Schmidt (1999), 1018; Peter W Heermann (2003), *Geld und Geldgeschäfte*. Tübingen: Mohr Siebeck, 95*f*.

misunderstanding of network co-ordination. It is not founded upon the mutual contractual agreement of all participants. Instead, a bilateral transaction (mostly, but not always contractual) is concluded with only one network member – accompanied by the legitimate expectation that this network member is connected with other members of the network. With this, social expectations emerge that are binding upon participants.[108] Representation and agency powers are clearly the wrong legal categories to take account of those expectations. Were one to wish to make serious use of them, then the resulting legal construction, which would perforce require contractual agreement between all parties, would not only be at odds with reality, but would also be counterproductive for the parties to networked transactions:

> The construction of a transactional superstructure, under whose umbrella individual transactions would be placed, and their central direction by a common purpose as a mode of primary coordination, would make particularistic contacts, and with this, the founding of close multilateral contractual relationships, an absolute necessity.[109]

The construction finally topples to its doom when a valid contractual agreement is absent. Clearly, a network contract that derives its effectiveness from the notions of implied representation and implied agency relations established between all members of the network will be greatly endangered by a single transaction made within the network if the validity of that transaction could be impugned on such grounds as mistake, deceit or duress. Rohe is aware of this problem and tries to compensate for this flaw by a greater judicial recourse to the dark arts of interpretation – 'objective' interpretation of contractual will, protection of trust of the partner, and considerations of business efficacy.[110] Finally, in his efforts to deal with the case of void bipolar contracts within the whole net, Rohe himself falls back on those judicial fictions that he so strongly criticises, whereby network contracts are to be understood as 'contracts protecting third parties'. If Rohe is really committed to this double construction – that is, a 'network contract' in cases of valid bilateral contracts, and a third party protective contract in the event of a void contract – then it would surely make much more sense to favour imposed legislative solutions from the outset; a solution that would save much consternation in the face of the troublesome lack of contractual intent.

[108] Laying particular emphasis on the non-consensual character of duties within the network – not traceable to the will of the parties – Krebs in opposition to Rohe (2000), 314. In effect, also Möschel (1986), 211*ff*, 217*ff*, 222*ff* and K Schmidt (1999), 'Gesetzliches Schuldverhältnis'.

[109] Picker (1999), 429.

[110] Rohe (1998), 176*ff*.

The network contract fiction becomes similarly mired in a curious contradiction if its application is extended beyond heterarchical networks to include hierarchical networks. In the case of heterarchical networks (Bank Gironets, credit card systems, merchandise transport systems), external customers are supposed to be full members (!) of the network. However, this is supposed not to be the case in hierarchical networks.[111] This curious contradiction can only be explained with reference to the author's (secret) regulatory orientation: he seems to welcome the possibility of 'piercing liability' for members who are not directly contractually related to each other only in heterarchical networks, but not in the case of hierarchical networks.[112] Even more curiously, however, this rule, Rohe supposes, is also subject to its own exception. Should the network hierarchy be made up of more than two levels, 'piercing liability' would be appropriate within hierarchical networks.[113] In general, however, the notion of the network contract appears to be wholly diluted in its application to hierarchical networks; what remains of it is simply the idea of an overarching network purpose.[114]

The fictitious and contradictory nature of multilateral agency might discredit the entire notion of the network contract. This is a fate, however, that the network contract has not itself earned. Möschel's network contract concept is far more realistic than Rohe's and offers much broader perspectives for new legal constructions than simple recourse to implicit multilateral agency fictions.[115] Möschel's 'network contract' takes on a more metaphorical character and hints at its further extrapolation in the light of categories such as 'special relationship' and 'trust'. Notwithstanding the criticism that it deserves, even Rohe's suggested legal treatment of the consequences of the networking phenomenon offers up perspectives for future divergence from the model of the bipolar contract. Sadly, it suffers from the small disadvantage that its fictional legal categories bear no relationship to reality. Nonetheless, what we should retain from Rohe's vision is the idea that a simple bilateral contract can

[111] Rohe (1998), 84*f*, 169 for heterarchical networks, 430 for hierarchical networks. Wackerbarth (2000), 1193 correctly argues that an interest analysis would only justify to include credit institutes, and not clients, within the circle of members of the network.

[112] Rohe does not himself ask what the situation should be in hierarchically organised transport systems or heterarchically organised franchising. In the first case, should the client be a network member? In the second, are internal relationships created between franchisees? In any case, transport networks cannot be included within the 'mesh net' (Gitternetz) category; neither can franchising be deemed to fall under the 'stellar network' (Sternennetz) category, Rohe (1998), 356*f*.

[113] Rohe (1998) 463*ff* with reference to the *Fiat* Case, OLG Stuttgart NJW-RR 1990, 491, discussed above.

[114] Rohe (1998), 388*ff*, 412*ff*; strangely, the contractual idea is reborn in relation to contractual dealers with active sub-centres (465).

[115] Möschel (1986), 211*ff*, 217*ff*, 222*ff*. Also, K Schmidt (1999), 1018.

give rise to legal relationships with all the other partners within a network. This furnishes an independent parallel to the corporate law conception governing entry within a firm. Corporate law facilitates entry by means of the construction of a membership contract between the new party and a collective actor (collective organisation or legal person); this is not possible in the case of networks. An adequate legal construction for networks is therefore still to be identified.

3

Networks as Connected Contracts

I. GENERALISATION OF CONNECTED CONTRACTS AND THEIR RE-SPECIFICATION FOR NETWORKS

IN THE LIGHT of all of this doctrinal discussion, is the concept of connected contracts the appropriate legal characterisation for networks? As a provisional conclusion, three points should now have become clear. First, the classification of networks within corporate law, or the law applying to corporate groups, is wholly inappropriate.[1] Second, in the light of the radical individual orientation within networks, contract rather than corporate law is the correct order for systematic regulation of 'market networks'.[2] Third, an independent legal category of 'network contract', focused upon the rules of agency, fails to prove convincing.[3] If these are accepted as starting points, the following consequence flows: the comprehensive doctrinal treatment of networks can only be founded upon a 'law of contractual organisation' that incorporates 'organisational' elements, that is, relational and multilateral elements, within the category of contract law. A law of contractual organisation will be sharply distinguished from corporate law by virtue of the fact that the common purpose of the network will be given recognition equal to that afforded to the individual purposes of members of the network, such that neither purpose is relegated to the role of a simple economic goal. Furthermore, members of the system will not be exclusively regarded as 'organs' of the organisation, but will also be viewed as autonomous 'actors'. In short: the law of relational contracts will be infused with network logic. 'Relational contracts', 'company-like legal relationships',

[1] For the company law qualification, Chapter 2; for qualifications under the law of corporate groups, see Chapter 2 (VI).

[2] On this question, Chapter 2 (II and VI). The contractual tendency is also shared by lines of thought that feel an independent form of contract, 'the co-operative contract', is necessary in addition to existing Civil Code contracts: Hartmut Oetker (1994), *Das Dauerschuldverhältnis und seine Beendigung: Bestandsaufnahme und kritische Würdigung einer tradierten Figur der Schuldrechtsdogmatik*. Tübingen: Mohr, 232*f*; Kulms (2000) 23*ff*. See also Sprau in *Palandt* (2003), § 705, 37. For less strict forms of virtual business, see Lange (2001a) 147*f*.

[3] On the network contract, Chapter 2 (VII).

and 'connected contracts' comprise three doctrinal constructions that may serve as elements of an incipient law of contractual organisation, but they require further development.[4]

There should be little doubt that the notion of a relational contract is a category particularly well suited to capturing the long-term, co-operative and organisational elements within networking.[5] In this area, foundational studies by Joerges (on status-based relationships within the contract), by Schanze and Kirchner (on symbiotic contracts), and by Kulms (on co-operation contracts) have had a dynamic impact upon discussion.[6] Studies by Lange on co-operation contracts, and by Nicklisch on complex long-term contracts, focusing mostly on practical case law, are similarly productive.[7] Strangely, however, the category of relational contract furnishes us with a relatively narrow box of normative tools with which to tackle the particularly interesting issue of multilateralism in networks.[8] As noted above, the concept of 'company-like legal relationships' evolved by the Federal High Court must be rejected as inadequate.[9] The outstanding issue is then one of whether the concept of connected contracts should be further developed and made equally productive for networked businesses, and in particular, for their multilateral aspects:

> We apply the term 'connected contracts' to all mutually impacting contractual relations, whether of a bilateral or multilateral nature, whose interconnection gives direct rise to legal consequences (of a genetic, functional or conditional type), be it that one contractual relationship impacts upon another (or others), or be it that mutual impacts may be observed.[10]

[4] For a law of contractual organisation that builds upon long-term contracts and connected contracts, see Teubner (1991), 130; (1992), 231*ff*; (2002a), 316*ff*. Taking this further, Larenz and Wolf (1997), 120*f* not only highlight the commonalities between networks and connected contracts, but also accept similar consequences in relation to internal and external liability within the network. Likewise, Amstutz and Schluep (2003), 890*ff*; Schluep (2003), 290*ff*. For a positive reception of the programme, though with a certain degree of scepticism for various of its consequences, especially in relation to external network liability, see Heermann (1998), 75*ff*; (2003), 93*ff*; Lange (2001a), 179*f*, 184*f*; Zwecker (1999), 163; Schimansky (2003), 112*ff*.

[5] Gierke still remains the point of reference for the discussion (1914).

[6] Joerges (1991), 21*ff*; Schanze (1991), 89*ff*; (1993), 691*ff*; Kirchner (1993), 202*ff*; (1996), 228*ff*; (2000); Kulms (2000), 55*ff*.

[7] Lange (1998), 117*f*, 126*ff*, 201*ff*, 297*ff*, 334*ff*; (2001a), 92*ff*; (2001b), 169*ff*; (2001c), 1805*ff*; Fritz Nicklisch (ed) (1987), *Der komplexe Langzeitvertrag: Strukturen und internationale Schiedsgerichtsbarkeit*. Heidelberg: Müller.

[8] See also Bayreuther (2001), 539. But see further the characterisation of the relationship between multi-lateralism and relationality in Ian R Macneil (1974), 'The Many Futures of Contracts', *Southern California Law Review* 47, 691*ff*, 792: 'The presence of additional parties begins to create circumstances genetic of relational character.'

[9] Genetic. See also Chapter 2 (IV).

[10] Gernhuber (1989), 710. Similarly, Larenz and M Wolf (1997), 469*f*; Josef Esser and Eike Schmidt (1995), *Schuldrecht: Ein Lehrbuch. Allgemeiner Teil I*. 8th edn, Heidelberg: Müller, 214.

Where, as in franchising, just-in-time systems and virtual enterprises, all traditional doctrinal constructions fail to prove convincing, we should seek to treat these phenomena – 'unforeseen by the Civil Code (BGB)' – in a realistic 'legal category that is new, but which is also compatible with the overall normative system'.[11] The concept of a legal connection, established between the many bipolar contracts within a network, accordingly presents itself for application. This would transform the spontaneously constituted 'final nexus' that connects the bipolar contracts (since their individual substantive aims are mutually interconnected) into a 'legally constructed purpose structure'. The notion of the 'economic unity' of separate contracts is constitutive of connected contracts. This concept, however, entails a peculiar contradiction, one that is already familiar to us from business networks – a number of contracts are directed to a common economic goal, which can only be achieved if all contracts are fulfilled, but which is at the same time wholly dependent upon the independent nature of the individual contracts.[12]

The legal institution of 'connected contracts' – a range of independent contracts that create an economic unity, notwithstanding their separate nature – first made itself known within the realm of contractual arrangements for credit. The judiciary responded to business practices with long chains of precedents that imposed drastic regulation in favour of third parties, but without, however, being able to furnish a convincing doctrinal construction.[13] This was only to be supplied by legal scholars with the concept of 'connected contracts'. In the course of a long and heated controversy about its legal nature, the notion of connected contracts was slowly given conceptual precision as an independent institution of its own.[14] Finally, connected contracts were codified, first within the special

[11] In support of the legal characterisation of networks as connected contracts – though without detailed elaboration, Teubner (1991), 130; (1992), 231; (2002a), 318*ff*; Larenz and M Wolf (1997), 470; Amstutz and Schluep (2003), 890*ff*; Schluep (2003), 290*ff*. Schimansky (2003), 121*ff* sheds light on similar tendencies in Dutch law.

[12] Gernhuber (1989), 710.

[13] Comprehensive comments on the case law in Heermann (1998), 200*ff*; (2003), 426*ff*.

[14] Mostly Gernhuber (1973), 470*ff*; (1989), 710*ff*; this construction is positively received and in part further developed by Joerges (1977), 32 with drastic consequences for the co-ordination of performances 64*ff*; (1981), 66 *ff*; Joerges in *Alternativkommentar* (1984), § 812, 16, 21; Eberhard Schwark (1978), 'Zum Verhältnis von schuldrechtlichen Vertragstypen und Vertragswirklichkeit, insbesondere beim Werklieferungsvertrag', *Rechtstheorie* 9, 73*ff*, 73, 89; Carl Baudenbacher (1985), 'Einwendungsdurchgriff beim finanzierten Immobilienerwerb?' *Juristenzeitung* 40, 661*ff*, 664; Heermann (1998), 72*ff*; (2003), 90*ff*; Volker Löhr and Jürgen Simon (1985), 'Probleme einer Reform des finanzierten Abzahlungskaufs' in Georgios Magoulas and Jürgen Simon (eds), *Recht und Ökonomie beim Konsumentenschutz und Konsumentenkredit*. Baden-Baden: Nomos, 61*ff*, 75*f*; Rüdiger Sannwald (1982), *Der Finanzierungsleasingvertrag über bewegliche Sachen mit Nichtkaufleuten*. Berlin: Duncker & Humblot, 90*f*; Max Vollkommer (1992), 'Zum Rückforderungsdurchgriff bei "verbundenen Geschäften"' in Walter Gerhardt (ed), *Festschrift für Franz Merz*. Cologne: Kommunikationsforum, 595*ff*, 606; Oechsler (1997b), 371; Schluep (2003), 287, 291. Against this approach, Bernd

regulation of § 9 Consumer Credit Law, § 4 Distance Investment Law and § 6 Time Sharing Law, and then, following the modernisation of contractual relations, within § 358 Civil Code (BGB).[15]

The general notion of connected contracts evolved primarily with regard to the special case of 'financed purchase' and was then only cautiously applied to other credit financing contracts.[16] As an unfortunate consequence, the particular problems of purchases made on credit supplied by a third party have left their indelible and altogether too powerful mark upon the institution. This is true both for the preconditions that must be fulfilled before the concept is recognised in law, and for its legal consequences. The concept of a genetic, conditional and functional connection between contracts has been formulated in general terms, but it remains tailored to the peculiarities of purchases by credit finance. This gives rise to a certain distortion of the general category in order to serve the needs of a particular problem, and so unduly restricts the range of problems tackled. However, connected contracts do not only arise within credit financing contracts. A comprehensive typology of the various different forms of contractual interconnection may still only be a matter for the future. Nonetheless, various candidates may be identified: sponsorship contracts, liability for prospectuses, project-related consulting contracts, project contracts, engineering contracts, transport networks, Giro networks, credit card systems, and of particular interest to this study, franchising, just-in-time systems and other business networks.[17] The remaining question is whether the legal construction of connected contracts can be fruitfully applied to virtual enterprises, franchising and just-in-time systems. Which are the appropriate legal conditions for connected contracting? What are the appropriate legal consequences?

Gundlach (1979), *Konsumentenkredit und Einwendungsdurchgriff*. Berlin: Duncker & Humblot, 166*ff*; Michael Coester (1992), 'Verbraucherschutz bei drittfinanzierten Geschäften (§ 9 VerbrKrG)', *Jura* 14, 617*ff*.

[15] Gernhuber's teachings on connected contracts were thus codified; see Vollkommer (1992), 606*f* and fn 62; Oechsler (1997b), 371; Heermann (1998), 73.

[16] See Roth in *Münchener Kommentar* (2002), § 242, 365, with further references.

[17] Giving particular attention to the associational nature of expertise contracts, Picker (1999), 428*ff* and Gunther Teubner (2003), 'Expertise as Social Institution: Internalising Third Parties into the Contract' in David Campbell, Hugh Collins and John Wightman (eds), *Implicit Dimensions of Contract: Discrete, Relational and Network Contracts*. Oxford: Hart, 333*ff*. On the network character of project contracts, Larenz and M Wolf (1997), 470; Fritz Nicklisch (2000), 'Vernetzte Projektverträge und vernetzte Streitbeilegungsverfahren', *Betriebs Berater* 55, 2166*ff*, 2167; of engineering contracts, Schluep (2003); of Gironets and transport networks, Rohe (1998), 65*ff* and 323*ff*; of credit card contracts, Heermann (2003), 426*ff*. On the associational nature of prospect liability, Teubner (1992), 217; similarly, Hans-Dieter Assmann (1986), 'Prospekthaftung als unerlaubter Haftungsdurchgriff? Zur Problematik des Anlegerschutzes durch richterliche Rechtsfortbildung' in Juristische Fakultät Heidelberg (ed), *Richterliche Rechtsfortbildung*. Heidelberg: Müller, 299*ff*, 307, 319.

II. STRUCTURAL AND FUNCTIONAL EQUIVALENCES

A comparison between the typical structures of the business networks investigated here and those of purchases by means of financed credit reveals ambivalences. Initially, there are striking similarities in the legal conditions and legal consequences of both. Certain authors are wholly convinced by the similarity. Rohe seeks to treat financed purchasing contracts as 'small networks' within an overall network contract category.[18] Heermann demonstrates sympathy for the suggestion that financed purchasing and contractual networks should be integrated within one unitary law of contractual organisation.[19] The essential similarity is provided by the fact that both contracts create a legally effective 'association' between several participants, even though the participants have not concluded a genuine multilateral agreement. In each case, multilaterality is established by a number of simple bilateral agreements. In neither case is the association forced into existence by legislation or case law. Rather, both associations constitute themselves within self-organisational market processes, drawing the subsequent attention of law and the application of supplementary and compulsory legal norms. In common with financed purchasing, networks exhibit a private and autonomous process of the self-constitution of a 'final nexus' through bilateral contracts, which is then translated into a normative (legislative or judicial) associational 'purpose structure' and into legal norms that are binding on the network.[20]

At the same time, however, differences between the two constructs cannot be ignored. Such differences force us to re-specify the distinct types of contractual interconnection.[21] Although both financed purchasing and business networks confront clients with hybrid forms, differences nonetheless arise in relation to modes of interaction with clients. Within financed purchasing, contractual contacts are established between the client and all network participants (vendor, bank, leaser, and possibly a guarantor), closely co-ordinating the common project. Within networks, by contrast, the client's contractual contact with the net is made with only one network participant whose contractual performance is, in turn, closely co-ordinated with the independent performances of other members of the network. Accordingly, the contractual interconnection typology should be re-specified, taking note of the particular external contractual relationship, in line either with a 'star', 'mesh' or 'layered'

[18] Without, however, really applying his agency model to small networks, Rohe (1998), 56*ff*.

[19] Heermann (1998), 75*ff*; (2003), 95*ff*.

[20] Thus, Gernhuber (1973), 470*ff*; (1989), 710*ff*, on the connected contracts.

[21] Rohe (1998), 356*f* suggests a legal typology in line with hierarchical/horizontal criteria.

model.[22] As hierarchical networks, franchising and just-in-time systems are 'star-shaped'; their nodes are grouped around a network centre. Within franchising, client contact is established with network nodes; in just-in-time systems, by the network centre. In both cases, client relationships with other network nodes are only established indirectly by virtue of their internal relations. In contrast, financed purchasing, other credit transactions in combination with guarantees, as well as some investments, are instances of 'layered' networking: the client concludes separate bilateral contracts with each partner, who in turn is interconnected with all other partners. These distinct structures explain why different legal problems arise, notwithstanding all the other similarities. The problem within layered constellations is one of whether a legal connection can be made between the separate client contracts, such that bilateral contractual effects can be (selectively) attributed to the entire network. Star-like constellations are dogged by the problem of whether an intensive contractual, rather than simple tort, relationship can be established, even though there are neither contractual relationships between client and network centre, nor contractual relationships between the client and other non-contractually bound network nodes. Mesh-like constellations also give rise to the same problem in relation to other non-contractually bound members of the network.[23]

If this comparison of structures reveals that the generalisation of the category of connected contracts only makes sense if respecified for different types of association, how do networks and financing contracts differ in their function? The economic function is equivalent in both cases. Both secure the independence of elements of economic performance that are functionally closely interconnected: product development, supply, and production.[24] This becomes particularly clear in the case of outsourcing: core competences are reserved to the central business unit; other competences are outsourced to independent suppliers; their interrelations are not simply a matter for market forces, but are instead co-operatively co-ordinated. The franchising scenario is also one

22 See, for the social science view, Paul Windolf and Jürgen Beyer (1996), 'Cooperative Capitalism: Corporate Networks in Britain and Germany', *British Journal of Sociology* 47/2, 205*ff*, which differentiates the 'Clique', 'Star', 'inverse Star' forms; from the legal perspective, Rohe (1998), 356*f*, who speaks about 'Mesh nets', 'Star-like nets' and 'Web-like nets'.

23 Rohe (1998), 356*f*, works these questions out clearly.

24 For a precisely formulated functional analysis of financed purchase and its legal problems, see Joerges (1981), 59*ff*; Klaus Hopt and Peter Mülbert (1989), *Kreditrecht.* 12th edn, Berlin: de Gruyter, vor § 607, 429*ff*; Josef Esser and Hans-Leo Weyers (1998), *Schuldrecht: Ein Lehrbuch. Besonderer Teil I.* 8th edn, Heidelberg: Müller, 108; Heermann (1998), 10*ff*; (2003), 78*ff*; on franchising, see Martinek (1987), 107*ff*; (1997), 84*ff*; Schimansky (2003), 26*ff*, 104*ff*; on just-in-time systems, see Nagel, Riess and Theis (1989), 1505*ff*; Lange (1998), 41*ff*; on virtual businesses, see Lange (2001a) 25*ff*; (2001b), 169*ff*; (2001c), 1805*ff*, each with further references.

of independent local business units carrying their own risks, and a contemporaneous joint effort to build an association for marketing, image-building and performance.[25]

Given the structural and functional equivalences between networks and financing contracts, it would be wrong in either case to react from a legal point of view to this instance of 'economic unity' by designating it to be the consequence of a false appearance or misrepresentation.[26] The common argument deployed against the financing contract constellation – that it entails the 'artificial' division of an original and fundamental economic unity into various contracts[27] – is misleading in the case of both institutions. Networking advantages are not to be found in 'artificiality', the misuse of legal form or in the misrepresentation of a unity that does not exist in reality. Rather, the advantage for all members lies in the hybrid nature of relations between separate units. The specific hazards posed by networks therefore have little if anything to do with misrepresentation, but instead encompass the new co-ordination risks posed by hybrids.

In contrast to Joerges, however, it should be noted that network-specific risks are not simply a result of an intensified division of labour within the market, but rather derive from the exact opposite: the supplementary and novel quality of reconnection between differentiated units, in our terminology, the 're-entry' of organisational elements within market structures. Were outsourcing a simple transfer of competences to the market, the legal problem would be relatively easy to solve. The functional relationship between performances addressed by Joerges also exists within the market. Within the pure market, however, the establishment of a functional relationship, or the co-ordination of separate performances, is a risk borne by the market interlocutor. This is the exact opposite of what happens within networks, as well as within financing contracts. Networking itself promises co-ordination between separate performances as a part of its overall performance package. Mastering the extreme difficulties (especially in relation to knowledge-based products) of co-ordinating differentiated and specialised labour performances is exactly the achievement that the 'net', as a unity, secures. Further, it is an achievement to which a customer of the net can lay legal claim and for which financial consideration is given. This networking 'added value', that is, the co-ordination of performances, impacts upon risk distribution between the network and the client. External network liability for internal network co-ordination becomes relevant at this point. Given the

[25] The most incisive analysis is still to be found in Martinek (1987), 121*ff*.

[26] See, Joerges (1981), 59*ff* in clear disagreement with the usual case law and literature approaches.

[27] Heinrichs in *Palandt* (2003) § 358, 2.

quasi-internalisation of functions as part of the contractual promise, externalisation of risk would be a case of *venire contra factum proprium*. The critical threshold between market and network co-ordination of performance is established by the fact that outsourcing is not simply a matter of transference of business activity to the market, but is instead a contemporaneous re-internalisation of the market (but not within the formal organisation) within an association of formally autonomous business units.[28]

III. A PRODUCTIVE 'UNSUSTAINABLE' CONTRADICTION

Can the legal category of 'economic unity', evolved in case law and doctrine to treat financing contracts and then incorporated within various consumer protection measures, as well as within § 358 Civil Code (BGB), adequately capture this economic function? This scenario does indeed entail the creation of an 'economic entity', but not one that can be properly understood within traditional categories of a legal person, a corporation or a multilateral contract. The proper formula is not one of simple 'economic unity', but rather one of an 'economic unity of contracts with contemporaneous separation of contracts'. Which legal concept might properly address this internal contradiction?

In a provocative move, Ernst Wolf has unveiled the glaring contradiction inherent in the concept of economic unity in the midst of separation.[29] 'Doctrinally unsustainable' is the verdict. How can we speak of 'economic unity', when all efforts are likewise focused on separation? Legislation also reproduces the contradictory language of case law. Wolf correctly denounces this as an antinomy: 'A "unity" cannot be "separate"'.[30] Oechsler is also struck by the 'paradox'.[31] According to Wolf, the entire construction is frustrated in consequence. The 'illogical' recourse of the High Court (BGH) to an 'inconceivable juxtaposition' of separation and unity is, it is thus argued, facilitative of the legally unfounded assertion, either of 'this' or of the 'other', and thus of the imposition of false legal consequences.

With this, Wolf strikes at the nerve of hybrid networks. However, in sharp contrast to his destructive impulses, the real issue is surely to make

[28] On the relationship between externalisation and re-internalisation within organisational theory, see Sydow (1992).

[29] Ernst Wolf (1978), *Lehrbuch des Schuldrechts. Zweiter Band: Besonderer Teil.* Cologne: Heymanns, 62*f*.

[30] E Wolf (1978), 62.

[31] Oechsler (1997b), 344, 359*ff*. Also critical, Rohe (1998), 56*ff*; Heermann (2003), 82*ff*.

productive use of the unsustainable contradiction.[32] The incontrovertible contradiction found within the notion of 'an economic unity of separate contracts' is not a logical failure to be banished from legal doctrine, but rather an exact reproduction of the social reality of hybrids, the source of their productivity, and of risks, to which the law must respond appropriately.[33] The antinomies of the 'economic unity' of separate organisations are not only to be found in the case of financing contracts, but are also present within corporate groups – as well as within business networks. All three cases concern economic networks that simultaneously intensify both market and organisational operations. The issue is always one of how contradictory demands can be turned to the uses of profitability. But, how might the legal process of balance end? There is surely no room for contradiction within law. How might this legal imperative be weighed up against business profitability? This returns the analysis to the central issue of internal network contradictions. If previous chapters were 'negative' in rejecting corporate law qualifications due to the hybrid nature of networks, the issue now is a 'positive' one of ascertaining whether and how the network-typical process of internalisation of external contradictions can be translated into legal reality constructs and legal consequences.

As stated above, networks must translate contradictory external demands into internal structures, such that contradiction is sustainable.[34] Networks are best understood as business 'search and adaptation processes', searching for an organisational form to ensure that 'contemporary challenges are recognised and responded to, without, however, any compromise being made in relation to the determination of future strategies and structures'.[35] The decisive network innovation is their ability to transform external contradictions into an internal tense, but sustainable, '*dual orientation*'. This dual orientation finds its paradigmatic mirror within the official definition of franchising: franchising is 'a vertical, co-operatively organised supply system built amongst legally autonomous firms, and founded on long-term fiduciary relationships'.[36] Firms thus possess a dual response to contradictory demands. They must always reckon with 'firm and loose connections with one another and

[32] However, Wolf (1978) cannot himself avoid the contradiction. Although he attempts to side-step it by designating the unity to be an economic relationship and defining the separation as a matter of legal contracts (60), the contradiction nonetheless returns when he refuses to admit that the contractually constructed relationship between contractual substance is dissolved by a contractually created exclusion of applicability within the contractual clauses (61).

[33] See Chapter 2 (III).

[34] Semlinger (1993), 332.

[35] Hirsch-Kreinsen (2002), 120.

[36] Deutscher Franchiseverband, at www.dfv-franchise.de.

within an association'.[37] This typical combination of strong and loose connections in hybrids is achieved with the aid of a dual orientation. *One and the same operation is exposed both to individual orientations of the network member and to the collective orientation of the network as a whole, and is burdened by the demand that it must find a balance in each context.*[38] In order to avoid the paradoxes that thus arise, the business must be 'de-totalised'; that is, divorced from its character as a total unity or as a total diversity, and constituted *uno acto* as an operational unity and diversity of autonomous actors.[39] In contrast to contracts and to organisations that exhibit either exclusively individual or exclusively collective orientation, networks evolve as novel configurations, within which the dual orientation of actions is constituted:

> Their reactive capacities are predominantly fuelled in both operational contexts by simultaneous operational opportunities (and the limits to them). Their operations reflexively relate both contexts to their activities and contexts. Knowledge bases are interpreted in parallel in the dual operational contexts. The dual incorporation of activities and results is indispensable – and far beyond their simple interconnection with network overarching industrial and social contexts. Actors can only be considered to be operationally active within networks if they reflexively take note of both contexts.[40]

Each operation within the hybrid must contemporaneously meet the normative demands of the bilateral social relationship established between individual actors, as well as overall network demands. The result is a remarkable form of network self-regulation based upon the

[37] Luhmann (2000), 375.

[38] On the key concept of 'dual-attribution', see Teubner (1991), 119*ff*. The theoretical explanation for the relationship between external contradiction and internal dual attribution is found in Teubner (1993b), 48*f*; (2002a), 316*ff*. For a further examination of the concept of dual attribution from the social science perspective, see Scharpf (1991), 621*ff*; Rölle and Blättel-Mink (1998), 74*ff*, 84, 265*ff*; Littmann and Jansen (2000), 69*f*; Windeler (2001), 194*f*, 224. From the legal point of view, network-typical dual-attribution is adapted for project contracts by Collins (1999), 248*ff*; for connected contracts, Schluep (2003), 306; for labour law questions raised by networks, see Thomas Kreuder (2000), 'Netzwerkbeziehungen und Arbeitsrecht: Individualarbeits- und betriebsverfassungsrechtliche Aspekte bei Franchisesystemen' in Dieter Simon (ed), *Zur Autonomie des Individuums: liber amicorum Spiros Simitis.* Baden-Baden: Nomos, 171*ff*, 203*ff*; Alain Supiot (2000), 'Les nouveaux visages de la subordination', *Droit Social* 63, 131*ff*, 135; for symbiotic contracts, see Zwecker (1999), 163; for virtual business, see Ensthaler and Gesmann-Nuissl (2000), 2268; Lange (2001a), 179*f*, 185; Mendes (2002), 13*f*; for franchising, Pasderski (1998), 4. For a critique of dual attribution, see Bräutigam (1994), 47*ff*; Oechsler (1997b), 382*f*; Rohe (1998), 417*f*; Bayreuther (2001), 399. Generally, however, such critiques are based upon a misunderstanding of what collective attribution within the network entails. For greater detail, see Chapter 6 (VI.2).

[39] See, for a similar organisational approach, Neuberger (2000), 209. On de-paradoxifying the *unitas multiplex* of the organisation, Luhmann (2000), 30*ff*.

[40] Windeler (2001), 195.

dual orientation of each operation.[41] This furnishes a convincing explanation for the profit sharing that economists have noted between network and nodes; a form of profit sharing that is sharply distinguished from profit sharing within a company law context. Whilst company law first apportions profits to the corporation and then distributes them amongst corporate members according to rules of allocation of profits, the profits of networks are simultaneously apportioned to the network centre and to the network nodes. In the language of economics: all transactions are attributed both to network profit and to the profits of individual actors. This double orientation acts as a constraint, since all transactions must pass the double test. At the same time, it proves to be an incentive as network advantage is intimately entwined with individual advantage. Subtly constructed contractual incentives and sanctions also seek to ensure that this double orientation influences an actor's motivations in practice as well as in theory.[42] The pivotal feature that distinguishes networks both from 'unconnected' contracts and from corporations is to be found in the 'residual claim' possessed by network nodes.[43] This is generally a stronger incentive than comparable incentives found within integrated firms, due to savings made in the costs of monitoring.[44] Economists capture this dual orientation within concepts such as 'principal–agent incentives' and 'information incentives'.[45]

How should law now respond to this transformation of external contradictions into an internal orientation that is simultaneously individual and collective? The answer is as follows: *through the dual constitution of contract and association within the legal reality construct and through the (selective) dual attribution of legal consequences both to the contractual partners and to the association*. Two questions are now posed in relation to the legal construct that transforms a business network into a connected contract: which legal preconditions qualify the network as a connected contract? Where is the boundary to be drawn to non-networked contractual relations?

[41] On the dual orientation of networks in other contexts, Scharpf (1991), 621*ff*.

[42] Dnes (1991), 136*ff*.

[43] Norton (1988), 202*ff* furnishes a particularly informative study on the basis of empirical analysis.

[44] James A Brickley and Frederick H Dark (1987), 'The Choice of the Organizational Form: The Case of Franchising', *Journal of Financial Economics* 18, 401*ff*, 411 *ff*; Dnes (1991), 136*ff*.

[45] Norton (1988), 202*ff*; see also Benjamin Klein and Lester F Saft (1985), 'The Law and Economics of Franchise Tying Contracts', *Journal of Law and Economics* 28, 345*ff*, 349*ff*.

IV. THE LEGAL CONSTRUCT OF REALITY: THE DUAL CONSTITUTION AS CONTRACT AND ASSOCIATION

1. Legal Characteristics of the Association

Our introductory quotation is a good *aide memoire* to guide the construction of the legal conceptualisation of the business network: 'network is not a legal concept'. The law cannot simply adopt wholesale the preconditions of social networking, such as the individual preconditions for intensified co-operative relationships.[46] Equally, the law cannot simply translate social science definitions into the preconditions of a legal construct, such as the economic formula of a 'hybrid between market and hierarchy', or the sociological formula of a 'trust-based co-operative institution'. Rather, the law must reconstruct the constitutive preconditions out of its own evolutionary logic. This is the reason why the legal notion of 'connected contracts' (§ 358(3) BGB)[47] proves to be so attractive to our purposes. Despite its independent conceptual status, the concept nonetheless derived its characteristics from its close relationship to the logic of the synallagmatic contract.[48] The interconnection of performances within the synallagma of the exchange contract serves as a model for the interconnection of bilateral contracts within the network. As is well known, the synallagma does not merely entail agreement on performance obligations; rather, the reciprocity between performances forms a subsidiary part of the substantive content of the contract.[49] The dispositive and compulsory norms of contract law build not only upon stipulated obligations of performance, but also upon a final contractual nexus, 'the purpose of the exchange', in order to ascertain the exact legal consequences of the performance relationship, imposing rules even in the absence of explicit contractual agreement and sometimes even in contradiction of it. Drawing a clearer parallel, in addition to agreed duties to perform, the connected contracts must also encompass inter-contractual relationships that then form a supplementary part of the substance of the contract. Once again, in an even clearer parallel to the synallagma: the

[46] This distinction between social and legal system is particularly clear in Amstutz (2003), 164*ff*.

[47] A contract for the supply of goods or for the provision of some other performance and a consumer loan contract are linked, if the loan fully or partially serves to finance the other contract and both contracts constitute an economic unit. An economic unit is to be assumed in particular if the entrepreneur himself finances the consideration of the consumer or, in the case of financing by a third party, if the lender in preparation for or for entering into the consumer loan contract uses the services of the entrepreneur.

[48] Gernhuber (1973), 470*ff*; (1989), 710*ff*.

[49] For an overview of synallagma theories, see Emmerich in *Münchener Kommentar* (2003), vor § 320, 12*ff*.

dispositive and compulsory norms of a law of contractual interconnection build upon this dual legal construct of performance duties plus 'final nexus' (or associational purpose) without need for reference to the will of the parties, or even in contradiction of it.[50]

The dual constitution of contract and association within the legal reality construct thus determines that, in order for a substantive legal interconnection to be established between the individual contracts, simple performance obligations must contain a supplementary 'reference' to the associative nature of the network. The notion of 'reference' is consciously chosen in order to highlight the close contextual relationship with the incorporation of private orders within an individual contract, more specifically, standardised contracts, fiduciary duties and technical and social norms. The vital point is the fact that a single contract is not limited to explicit bilateral agreement, but instead, and by virtue of its purpose and structure, also refers to other 'private' orders. This makes itself felt in financing contracts. Many efforts have focused upon the task of the more precise specification of the legal preconditions for the 'economic unity' of separate contracts.[51] Case law first dabbled with an extensive range of criteria and indicators before at last a leading principle established itself: the question of whether a firm and a finance creditor 'made their appearance in a common manner as one contractual party' should be decided from the viewpoint of the other contractual partner.[52] Naturally, the decisive factor is not the subjective intentions of the parties; even less is it the explicit contractual language, which, in reaction to case law, and in an effort to avoid the legal consequences of being designated as an association, has increasingly tended to emphasise the separate nature of contracts.[53] The financing contract must always limit loan disposition, whereby the party taking up a loan is usually denied free use over it.[54] The financing contract must always make reference to the purchasing contract in order to create a unity.[55] In principle, there must also always be a close degree of co-operation between vendor and bank, such as an enduring business relationship, in order to attest to the

[50] Thus, with clarity, Gernhuber (1989), 731, in protest at the constant attempt of financial institutions to separate economically interdependent legal contracts from each other. Most revealing is his rejection of the obvious business interest in legally contradictory behaviour: 'One can make a decision in favour of isolated contracts or in favour of financed purchase, but not in favour of the *contradictio in adiecto* of a legal business association with separate contracts.'

[51] For comprehensive review of the latest situation, see Habersack in *Münchener Kommentar* (2003) § 358, 26*ff*, 36*ff*.

[52] OLG Cologne ZIP 1995, 21; Heinrichs in *Palandt* (2003), § 358, 15.

[53] Gernhuber (1989), 731.

[54] BGH NJW 1983, 2250; Heinrichs in *Palandt* (2003), § 358, 14.

[55] OLG Cologne ZIP 1995, 21; Heinrichs in *Palandt* (2003), § 358, 15.

'contribution' of the vendor to conclusion of the loan, or to the securing of the loan by means of shared debt, guarantee or security transference.[56]

These elements were then to become legislative preconditions as the legislator regulated the connected contracts in the special case of consumer credit contracts. According to § 358(3) Civil Code (BGB), the loan must 'serve' the purpose of the financing the other contract. This entails two elements: first, the loan must refer to the other contract and be directed to the plan to transfer property; second, the contracts must form an 'economic unity'. This final point is not the subject of a general definition, but is instead illustrated by the (non-exhaustive) example that the grantor of a loan must avail himself of the 'contribution' made by the vendor to the conclusion of the loan.[57]

Moving beyond the peculiarities of credit financing contracts in order to establish a general category of connected contracts, which would also encompass our business networks, three particular legal preconditions leap out of case law and legislation. These establish the 'added value' of the dual constitution of 'connected contracts' as opposed to a bundle of unconnected and independent contracts within the market. The leading principle here is likewise one that the networked firms must make their appearance as 'a common contractual party'. The preconditions are to be taken cumulatively, thus furnishing a threshold over which genuine networking might be distinguished from simple market co-ordinated performance. In order for legally recognised connected contracts to exist, the following characteristics must be present in addition to the usual characteristics that create a bilateral contract:

(1) Mutual references within the bilateral contracts to one another, either within the explicit promises or within implicit contractual practice ('multi-dimensionality').
(2) A substantive relationship with the connected contracts' common project ('network purpose').
(3) A legally effective and close co-operative relationship between associated members ('economic unity').

This dual contractual and associational constitution is also indispensable in the case of our business networks. The legal preconditions for a franchising system cannot be satisfied by a simple concentration of

[56] Habersack in *Münchener Kommentar* (2003), § 358, 38; Heinrichs in *Palandt* (2003), § 358, 15.

[57] Heinrichs in *Palandt* (2003), § 358, 15.

bilateral distribution agreements, if these agreements only impose isolated duties upon distributors and fail to establish central co-ordination.[58] A franchising system will only be given legal recognition as a connected contract when the bilateral contracts establish a binding reference to the entire distribution system, either by an explicit reference within the contract or by an implicit reference in contractual practice. A first indicator for the existence of connected contracts is the imposition by the franchisor of standard contract terms that force franchisees to standardise distribution (often in an extremely strict manner). The contractual interconnection is thus commonly established by contractual obligations ensuring unitary and prescribed sales techniques, outlet design and business behaviour across the entire system. At its core, this ensures that members of the network have restricted opportunities to utilise services performed for them and due to them. The imperative of the preservation of the unitary image determines that franchisees will be restricted in the use of their own resources and performances supplied to them in the service of the overall network image. An additional criterion indicating the presence of a network is furnished by contractual regulation of centrally designed competition modes for the association, whereby individual contracts refer to a common marketing practice. The degree of incorporation is only strengthened when franchising contracts impose unitary purchasing practices on franchisees. This list of possible contractual references to the overall distribution system is non-exhaustive. The presence of one or other of these indicators, however, suggests that the franchising system satisfies the legal construct for its dual constitution as both contract and association.

Similar rules apply to just-in-time systems and virtual enterprises. Simple bilateral co-operation contracts established with a number of partners do not of themselves suffice to establish a contractual interconnection.[59] Connected contracts will only be recognised in law if multilateral co-operation beyond the boundaries of an individual contract forms an integral part of the transaction, by explicit reference within the contract, or by reference to co-operative practice. One important indicator for the presence of connected contracts is the vertical and horizontal computerised networking of partial performances.[60] As is well known, individual actors have an interest in association by virtue of its effects in minimising co-ordination costs, maximising the speed of

[58] On the distinction between a simple supply system and true franchising systems, see Walther Skaupy (1995), *Franchising: Handbuch für die Betriebs- und Rechtspraxis*. 2nd edn, Munich: Vahlen, 13; Rohe (1998), 376*f*; Schimansky (2003), 35*ff*.

[59] Rohe (1998), 364*ff*, develops criteria to aid in the distinguishing of co-operative networks from simple parallel contracts. See also Schluep (2003), 290*ff*.

[60] See comprehensively Nagel, Riess and Theis (1989), 1505*ff*.

co-ordination, and improving co-ordination through the application of information technologies. Legally recognised connected contracts, however, only come into existence when the performance of an overall transaction is parcelled out amongst a series of independent firms. In addition, this division of labour must not simply be co-ordinated by the market, but must instead be effected in closely co-ordinated agreement (in part, contractual, in part, spontaneous). And finally, this unitary (non-market) co-ordination must also form a part of the total performance package offered by the association.

2. Distinguishing Connected Contracts from other Constructions

Having achieved this hard-won position detailing the legal conditions for connected contracts, it is worth casting a brief glance backwards at other legal constructions of network relations. One is to construe a network as a multilateral contract between the members of the network. A true multilateral contract would of course stipulate that each partner legally contracts – either contemporaneously or sequentially – with every other partner. This, for example, was Vollkommer's idea for credit financing contracts when he still conceived of them as tri-dimensional contracts.[61] Rohe does the same in his efforts to create a network contract by (implicit) means of the mutual agency and representation of all network participants.[62] However, we can now clearly see that the construction of a

[61] According to Max Vollkommer (1973), 'Der Schutz des Käufers beim B-Geschäft des "finanzierten Abzahlungskaufs"' in Gotthard Paulus (ed), *Festschrift für Karl Larenz.* Munich: Beck, 703*ff*, 711 (though different in Vollkommer (1992) 606*f*: connected contracts), financed purchasing represents a true trilateral contract, in which each of the three parties undertakes performance not simply with an eye to matching consideration, but also with an eye to the contractual performances of various other parties. In this form of *sui generis* contract, purchase and loan are only dependent parts of the overall legal relationship. Critique nonetheless recognises the fictive character: where can we find three declarations of obligation that are also visible to all others? A genuine trilateral contract demands a single agreement between the three parties. In practice, however, only two bilateral exchange contracts are concluded, sometimes even three, where the bank and the vendor conclude a framework contract. The construction also creates difficulties with regard to legal consequences, since each impairment of performance disturbance or each mistake, deceit or duress would impact upon the entire triadic relationship. This does not, however, properly reflect the risk structure within financed purchasing. See Hopt and Mülbert (1989), vor § 607, 405; Gernhuber (1989), 716; (1979), 166; Oechsler (1997b), 380*f*; Heermann (1998), 67; (2003), 97. This criticism would also hold true for a similar construction of networks. The multilateral contract is not suited to networks since no declaration of intent is present as between all participants. Equally, the legal consequences are not correct, since the far too narrow performance interrelationship envisaged is not a true reflection of the risk structure. The provisions of contractual reciprocity in §§ 320*ff* BGB are not even appropriate for interconnected financing contracts, much less for networking, since their mutual interdependency is different in nature from the synallagma of bilateral contracts.

[62] Rohe (1998), 176*ff*.

comprehensive multilateral contract asks too much of social reality. Either it does so for simple doctrinal reasons ('wishful thinking'[63]), or it tends even to disregard its own preconditions, compensating for deficits in social reality by drastically reducing its own determining characteristics ('fiction'). In comparison with such common agreements, drawing in all participants, the construction of connected contracts is certainly more sensitive to the social reality of networks. Connected contracts are commonly established by local, decentralised and bilateral attachments to the net. Connected contracts do not require a genuinely multidimensional agreement in order to be legally recognised. In a more realistic frame of mind, the construction is satisfied with a number of simple bilateral contracts. Nonetheless, the construction is also effectively founded upon multilaterality since it demands the supplementary 'reference' of contracts to one another and to the overarching associational purpose.

In contrast, Heermann's 'trilateral synallagma' construction seems to be far closer to the conception of the connected contracts. It needs no conclusion of a genuine multilateral contract and instead builds upon two or three bilateral contracts in order to establish a tri-dimensional relationship of performance along the lines of *ut des ut det*.[64] And indeed, this construction establishes effective interconnection between contracts via a simple reference within a bilateral contract to another contract. Nonetheless, the concept is too narrow to serve as a general model for connected contracts since it insists on strict synallagmatic connections between all individual performances: consideration must be given for each specific association performance by another, clearly identified, performance.[65] However, in social reality, networks dispose of a far looser interconnection of contracts, and of a 'general reciprocity', which does not match individual performance with matching counterparts, but which instead expects individual performance in favour of the net in the vague expectation of future advantage. The ambitious concept of a trilateral or multilateral synallagma cannot adequately capture such internal interdependency. In contrast, the general reciprocity found within the connected contracts offers us a generalisable principle, with

[63] Gernhuber (1989), 716 on Vollkommer.

[64] Bernhard Pfister (1971), 'Der mehrseitige Austauschvertrag', *Juristenzeitung* 26, 284*ff*, 285; for careful elaboration, Heermann (1998), 162*ff*; (2003), 107*ff*. Critical, Stoffels (2001), 267.

[65] Heermann (2003), 160*f* is himself aware of this narrow perspective within the trilateral synallagma. How might the law capture the undoubted interdependency of underlying bilateral contractual relations within large-scale networks? Heermann (2003), 214, appears to sympathise with the contractual network. He then, however, begins to work without a clear doctrinal base satisfying himself that the legislator also envisaged the application of piercing liability (§ 676b III 7 BGB) to this, until now 'unknown dissection of the principle of privity'.

the aid of which legal preconditions and consequences can be concretised. Strict trilateral synallagmas should then be regarded as a sub-group of the connected contracts.

Equally, however, connected contracts also avoid the sledgehammer effects of corporate law constructions that, as we have seen, eagerly offer themselves up for application both to business networks and to credit financing contracts.[66] Once again, the concept of connected contracts has a finer feeling for social reality, laying a greater stress upon the individualistic characteristics of networking, satisfying itself with the existence of bilateral contracts and rejecting the need for company-like legal institutions (articles of association, incorporation, common purpose, agency, common property, legal personality). By the same token, however, the concept is also sensitive to collective elements in networks. Founded on the precondition that individual contracts must make reference to other contracts and the associational purpose, it offers a means to demarcate the connected contracts from simple contractual concentrations exhibiting lesser degrees of interdependence.

3. The Proprium of Connected Contracts

Does this, then, mean that the business network simply dissolves into a multitude of bilateral contracts? Are these contracts in turn distinguished by their supplementary addition to the usual run of contractual agreements of 'coupling agreements' and 'associational agreements'.[67] In short, are business networks only a special case within the 'normal' range of legally effective relations? No: a closer analysis of the three additional preconditions for their legal recognition – reference to the other contracts, associational purpose and co-operative relationship – reveals that a far more complex reality lurks behind the dual preconditions of contract and association.[68]

[66] Financed purchase is sometimes constructed as a partnership between bank and vendor. The common purpose is the execution of the financed transaction, common profit maximisation and the supply of a product bundle: Volker Emmerich (1971), 'Der finanzierte Abzahlungskauf', *Juristische Schulung* 11, 273*ff*, 279*f*; Klaus Nöcker (1972), 'Finanzierter Abzahlungskauf und Betrugstatbestand', *Der Betrieb* 25, 370*ff*, 371*f*; Peter Otto (1988), *Stellung der Bank bei der Finanzierung von Immobilienanlagen*. Berlin: Duncker & Humblot, 112. This is a misleading reduction of the bilateral contract to a collective unit (bank–vendor). At the same time, however, it also entails an arbitrary and one-sided overemphasis of the significance of the bilateral relationship since all three contribute to success.

[67] Thus, the suggestion made by Schluep (2003), 285, 304.

[68] This is in essence the reason why Möschel (1986), 211*ff* does not construe the network contract with the aid of traditional doctrine, but instead locates it within the reality of trust and special relationships. Kulms also ((2000), 185) emphasises that it is not sufficient to restrict the analysis to the contractual declaration: 'Networks describe contractual systems

The primary point to note is that the dual constitution of connected contracts acts as a veil for a social reality of 'networking' that cannot be captured within legal categories.[69] 'Network is not a legal concept'. Divorced from their own grammar and semantics, lawyers thus approach the *proprium* of the association with exotic formulas: 'final nexus', 'functional association', 'unity in separation', 'economic unity', 'accessorial purpose', 'trilateral synallagma', '*causa consumendi*'.

From a sociological perspective, this can all be understood in terms of the structural coupling of autonomous law with autonomous social practice. The specificity of networks lies in the fact that a contract observes its environment in a particular manner. Under normal conditions, contracts observe prevailing market conditions, in particular pricing, and adapt their internal structures accordingly. Following Luhmann's analysis of organisational behaviour, the creation of networks can be understood to take place, in contrast to the 'normal' situation, when simple market observation no longer suffices and the contractual system observes another contractual system rather than the market, adapting its internal norms accordingly. Under conditions of environmental turbulence, systems seek symbiotic relations with other systems, in order to place their relevant environment in an observable context.[70] As has been explained elsewhere, however, bilateral contractual systems within the hybrid do not coalesce into one unity but instead remain autonomous, each reflecting upon their own function and performance.[71] Amstutz develops this further, establishing an 'interconnection' between contracts that functions as a mutually reflexive relationship between two contracts that are still dedicated to their own projects, but which contemporaneously adapt to one another in mutual observation.[72] Commonly, this process coalesces into denser co-operative relations. In the language of systems theory, the inter-contractual 'references' detailed above are perceived of as the mutual observation and reflexive relationship between contractual systems. This relationship cannot, however, register on the legal radar in the form of the reflexive relationship conceived in

that are related to one another.' A sociological approach places a similar emphasis upon the fact that the specificities of the relationship cannot be reduced to bipolar stipulations, Windeler (2001), 239*ff*.

[69] This is the point at which Gernhuber's endeavours smoothly to insert contractual interconnection within doctrine must recognise their limits. This is clear at two points within his own construction: in the suggestive 'final nexus' formula, which is only seemingly a simple matter of agreement between the parties, and in the 'special relationship' notion which he imputes to parties who are not contractually bound to one another: Gernhuber (1989), 728, 741. Similar problems arise in relation to the notion of an independent coupling agreement that is supported by Schluep (2003), 285*ff*.

[70] Luhmann (2000), 407*ff*.

[71] Castells (2000), 187; Teubner (2002a), 330.

[72] Amstutz (2003), 164*ff*.

sociology. Instead, the interconnection within law takes the form of the three elements that go to make up the legal reality construct of connected contracts: mutual 'referencing' between contracts, 'associational purpose' and the 'co-operative relationship'. The legal interconnection between contracts is dependent upon the fulfilment of these preconditions. With this, however, traditional perceptions of private law autonomy once again become the target for critique. Contractual networking, it is thus supposed, remoulds autonomous bilateral legal relationships into heteronomous processes of organisation building. The first precondition of mutual contractual referencing is, by this token, not simply a matter of paying attention to other private orders within the contract, but rather also entails sweeping acceptance of the 'foreign' logic of another order. Overall, individual contracts must seemingly submit themselves to a single coherent system, which is respected by each individual contract. Accordingly, contractual connection with the network is thus often reduced to the status of a simple decision to join one heteronomous corporate order.[73] As stated above, mutual contractual referencing is similar to 'referencing' to standard contracts, to fiduciary duties, or to social and technical norms. Within the bilateral agreements that characterise business co-operation, we can observe a 'reference' to the internal institutional logic of networks: entry via bilateral contact, trust-based interaction, decentralised co-ordination and direction of individual orientation to the uses of the network. The second precondition of 'associational purpose' exhibits a similar mixed relationship between autonomy and heteronomy. The common purpose is determined in an autonomous manner: members of the network freely choose to submit themselves to the project that underlies contractual interconnection. But the dynamic of purpose-creation and purpose-adaptation is nonetheless largely a spontaneous event arising out of the relationship between the association's environment and its internal network structures, such that it is no longer directed by bilateral legal agreements. The third precondition of 'cooperative associational relationship' is, in its turn, largely independent of individual bilateral agreements, and instead constitutes itself as a spontaneous organisational structure out of multilateral network relations.

All three preconditions thus establish a *legal relationship between the individual contract and a spontaneous and extra-contractual private ordering*. This is the *proprium* of connected contracts. The scenario stands, however, in strong contrast to a Hayekian conception of spontaneous order, whereby a discovery process gives rise to a competitive order. Neither the market nor competition has a role to play. Instead, networking and

[73] This reduction of contractual conclusion to a simple entry decision clearly only captures the associational element; the bilateral element follows all the usual effective legal rules.

co-operation are the purveyors of a spontaneous order.[74] Generalised reciprocity is the fundamental motor of spontaneous order within the network:

> The basic network resource appears to be that 'one knows someone who knows someone'; and that the general demand for reciprocal help is so widespread that, should one be in a position to help, one simply cannot refuse without shortly being excluded from the network of mutual services. The mutual service network establishes its own exclusion mechanism powerful enough to create 'non-persons', whom nobody knows, and who thus lose all access to the functional system, all formal entitlements notwithstanding.[75]

Within such spontaneous network orders 'a heightened significance attaches to the durability of relationships established between (legally independent, but directing their economic operations in tandem) firms beyond the demands of simple bipolar stipulations'.[76] 'Beyond' bipolar stipulations: this is the determining factor. Various social co-ordination mechanisms of an extra-contractual nature – mutual observation, anticipatory adaptation, co-operation, trust, self-obligation, trustworthiness, negotiations, enduring relations[77] – give form to the overall network order leaving their indelible mark on each bilateral contractual relationship. Any endeavour to translate these co-ordination mechanisms into an elaborate legal agreement would, however, be a betrayal of the *proprium* of connected contracts.

The heteronomous stipulation becomes especially clear when specific network effects are aimed at. That is, not when networking seeks to profit from simple scale or collectivisation advantages,[78] but rather when added value is sought by means of the facilitation of multilateral communicative connections between members of the network (information, co-operation, exchange). This results in a tangible reduction in private law autonomy within individual bilateral contracts, since the detailed

[74] On spontaneous order in the market and under competitive conditions, as well as its relationship with legal norm production, see Friedrich A Hayek (1973), *Law, Legislation and Liberty. Volume 1: Rules and Order.* London: Routledge and Paul, 72*ff*; Viktor Vanberg (1986), 'Spontaneous Market Order and Social Rules: A Critical Examination of FA Hayek's Theory of Cultural Evolution', *Economics and Philosophy* 2, 75*ff*, 79*ff*; Robert D Cooter (1994), 'Decentralised Law for a Complex Economy', *International Review of Law and Economics* 23, 443*ff*, 447*f*. On the important differences between different types of spontaneous order, especially in relation to markets and relational obligations, Robert Gordon (1994), 'Hayek and Cooter on Custom and Reason', *Southwestern University Law Review* 23, 453*ff*.

[75] Niklas Luhmann (1995b), *Soziologische Aufklärung.* Opladen: Westdeutscher, 251*f*.

[76] Windeler (2001), 240.

[77] For a discussion on the mechanisms and effects of such extra-legal spontaneous orders, see Gordon (1994), 459; Jörg Sydow and Arnold Windeler (2000), 'Steuerung von und in Netzwerken' in Sydow and Windeler (eds), *Steuerung von Netzwerken: Konzepte und Praktiken.* Opladen: Westdeutscher, 1*ff*, 12*ff*; Windeler (2001), 240*ff*.

[78] On the important distinction between scale, collective and network effects, see Chapter 1 (VI).

stipulations of each bilateral contract must be dedicated to the securing of desired network effects. Credit card systems, within which bilateral contracts largely serve the purpose of technological networking, are a particularly dramatic example:

> But the technological links and potential for positive returns to scale in the credit card industry cannot themselves create value without a sophisticated system of contracts, including agreement on the compensation they will receive and the rules governing their conduct relative to the network. Thus, merchants will have a contractual relationship with a bank, which will to some extent be subject to the bank's contractual relationship with the credit card entity. If the merchant's bank did not issue the consumer's credit card, it in turn will have a contractual relationship with the issuing bank pursuant to which transactions may be cleared. The issuing bank will of course have a contractual relationship with the customer. All of these contracts are as vital to the functioning of the credit card network as are the electronic links that facilitate transactions.[79]

Amongst our business networks, just-in-time systems, in particular, exhibit this characteristic. The goal of achieving specific network effects gives rise to an extremely detailed bilateral contractual style that largely subordinates itself to the 'system imperatives' of the supply network.[80] The metaphor once deployed to characterise standard contract terms, the notion of 'voluntary subordination to the demands of a pre- existing legal order', finds its contemporary equivalent in this area. Virtual businesses and franchising systems do also exhibit a limited degree of comprehensive subordination of bilateral contracts to the demands of the network as a whole.[81]

What follows from these specific network characteristics for their doctrinal characterisation? Private law generally gives (very vague) expression to the peculiarities of spontaneous orders within concepts such as fiduciary duties and good faith (§§ 157 and 242 BGB). Such conceptions are nonetheless themselves predicated upon the existence of a contract between those entitled to make use of these provisions and those obliged to abide by them. By contrast, doctrine has responded to the creation of spontaneous order outside contractual mechanisms with the notion of 'special relationships'. And in practice, the factual mesh of bilateral contracts within the net does share all the characteristics of a special relationship that is located somewhere midway between contract

[79] Lemley and McGowan (1998), 21.

[80] The legal aspects of 'system imperatives' within just-in-time systems are particularly clear in Nagel, Riess and Theis (1989), 1505*ff*.

[81] This dedication to narrow network effects impacts upon the fiduciary duties of members of the network, see Chapter 4 (III) and (IV).

and tort.[82] This is not only true for business networks in the narrow sense, but also obtains in relation to financing contracts, with regard to which Gernhuber has clearly identified a 'special relationship' between the financial creditor and the vendor.[83] Both cases concern spontaneous orders, which are neither established by the usual means of legal agreement, nor by virtue of legislative or judicial intervention, but which are instead a result of bilateral contractual 'entry' within an overarching multilateral system of behavioural co-ordination.[84] Nonetheless, Gernhuber does not do justice to the constitutive role played by extra-contractual self-organisation when he seeks to apportion connected contracts either to 'a will to enter into legal relations', or, indeed, to an 'act of the legislature' or to 'judicial precedent'.[85] *Tertium datur*! The alternative – either voluntary agreement or legally imposed obligations – fails to recognise its *tertium*: spontaneous extra-contractual order-building, which constitutes the network. The metaphor of a 'final nexus', which leaves the real nature of legal relations somewhat nebulous, permits us only to guess at it.

Contractual interconnection – in stark contrast to the manifold bilateral contractual relations in the net, which can easily be subsumed under the normal categories of private law – is nothing more than an 'organised non-contractual relationship', which makes the conclusion of a real multilateral contract between all participants as superfluous as the use of corporate law to ensure vertical or horizontal integration within the corporation'.[86] To this degree, contractual interconnections, or their dual legal constitution out of bilateral contracts and a multilateral connectivity, adequately reflect the hybrid nature of market networks that are characterised by their combination of bilateral exchange relationships and multilateral networking.

Business networks cannot be reduced to one or other of these two elements. They are neither simple bilaterally established frameworks for legal relations, nor do they merely encompass a process of spontaneous

[82] Generally, on the special relationship category in private law, see Paschke (1987), especially 81*ff*; (1988) 'Vertragsbindung ohne Konsens?', *Rechtstheorie* 19, 523*ff*; Jürgen Schmidt (1987), '"Sonderverbindungen": Eine Problemskizze' in Günther Jahr (ed), *Gedächtnisschrift für Dietrich Schultz*. Cologne: Heymanns, 341*ff*, 348*ff*; Gernhuber (1989), 180; Picker (1983), 460*ff*; (1987), 1053*ff*; (1999), 428*ff*; Krebs (2000), 632*ff*. For a categorisation of networks as special relationships, see, in favour, Möschel (1986), 224; Picker (1999), 428*ff*; Krebs (2000), 107*f*, 312*ff*.

[83] Gernhuber (1973), 493; (1989), 741*f*.

[84] In contrast to Rohe (1998), Möschel's original considerations tended to categorise the network contract as a 'special relationship of a specific character', or to locate them in the 'third lane' midway between contract and tort: Möschel (1986), 223*ff*.

[85] Gernhuber (1989), 710.

[86] Picker (1999), 429.

networking between social positions, which might then be legally characterised with the aid of the notion of 'special relations'. In this regard, a distinction must then be drawn between simple networks and hybrid networks. The former can be given legal recognition, either by means of the notion of extra-contractual special relations, or by imposition of mutual duties of good faith that extend beyond the usual tort obligations. The latter are either organisational networks (corporate groups) that entail a combination of organisation and connectivity, or, market networks (co-operative contracts) that entwine contractual characteristics with connectivity.[87] Therefore, whilst it is correct to characterise business networks as an instance of 'special relations', the appellation nonetheless remains inadequate. If their hybrid character is to be taken seriously, *the reality construct giving them legal effect must combine bilateral contractual elements with multilateral special relations elements in a very particular manner.* It is this combination that characterises the typical reality construct of contract and association.

V. LEGAL CONSEQUENCES: SELECTIVE ATTRIBUTION TO CONTRACTUAL PARTNERS AND TO THE NETWORK

What is true for the preconditions for networks as connected contracts is also true for their legal consequences. The double orientation of network operations in social and economic practice must also find 'resonance' in the law of remedies.[88] This proposition holds true both in internal relations and in the networks' external relations. The appropriate legal response is the selective (!) attribution of responsibility for acts of the network to the contracts and to the network as a whole.[89] Here, a choice must be made between three modes of apportionment of responsibility, each to be applied in the light of prevailing circumstances: a cumulative mode, which apportions responsibility amongst a number of different members of the network; an alternative mode, which restricts responsibility only to one network level; and a complementary mode, within which the partial apportionment of responsibility amongst various network levels makes a whole only when each partial apportionment is viewed in a cumulative whole.

In this case, comparisons can once again be drawn to the synallagma in a mutual contract. The genetic, conditional and functional synallagma

[87] For these distinctions, see Teubner (2001), 560*ff*, and above, Chapter 2 (I).

[88] 'Resonance' is not a simple metaphor in this case; it designates the structural coupling of operatively closed systems. On the resonance of the legal system on social problem constellations, see Luhmann (2004), 381*ff*; specifically on economic problems, 452*ff*.

[89] For social science and legal reaction to dual attribution concepts, see references in fn 38. A more detailed analysis is found in Chapter 4 (V), and, in particular, in Chapter 6 (II).

detailed in §§ 320*ff* Civil Code (BGB)[90] offers us a generalisable blueprint for the legal consequences of interconnected obligations. And indeed, Gernhuber systematically worked out the legal consequences of credit financing contracts with specific reference to the orienting principles of the 'genetic, conditional and functional connectivity'.[91] In practice, this blueprint has also given a far more convincing interpretation of judicial precedent on connected contracts than many a competing doctrinal approach would give it credit for—that is, the models of the multilateral contract, the trilateral synallagma, the partnership, '*causa consumendi*', or simple good faith.[92] These three leading principles of connectivity are thus far more sensitive to the institutional logic of financing contracts. They have also resulted in the piercing liability for risks posed by the network, notwithstanding all the efforts made in legal practice to use standard form contracts to insert clauses that separate liability.

Nonetheless, those legal consequences slowly distilled out of the specific case of credit financing contracts must now be carefully generalised for application to the connected contracts category, and re-specified for business networks. A burning question thus remains as to whether so close an analogy can be drawn between the mutual independency of interconnected contracts and the synallagmatic model as Gernhuber seeks to suggest in his parallel application of the genetic, conditional and functional synallagma. Even in the case of credit financing contracts, criticisms have already been aired, asking whether the consequences flowing from these three principles can really be considered adequate when compared with competing constructions.[93] Heermann, for example, considers the analogy to synallagmatic consequences to be far too inflexible, especially with regard to its strictly automatic approach to the creation and discontinuation of obligations. By the same token, he smiles upon the application of the connected contracts construction to credit financing contracts, since it offers a far more concrete means to identify interdependence between contractual obligations (or the final mutual relationship between performance obligations) than more traditional

[90] § 320 BGB: (1) A person who is a party to a reciprocal [synallagmatic] contract may refuse his part of the performance until the other party renders consideration [performs], unless he is obliged to perform in advance. If performance is to be made to more than one person, an individual person may be refused the part performance due to him until the full consideration has been rendered …
(2) If one party has performed in part, consideration [performance] may not be refused to the extent that refusal, in the circumstances, in particular because the part in arrears is relatively trivial, would be bad faith.

[91] Gernhuber (1989), 731*ff*.

[92] For a demanding discussion of the different constructions, see Heermann (1998), 65*ff*; (2003), 78*ff*.

[93] Joerges (1981), 67; Löhr and Simon (1985), 75*f*.

solutions achieve.[94] This argument can be used to support the suspicion aired here that whilst the current doctrinal position on contractual interconnection represents a very good legal attempt to grasp specific networking realities, clear corrections and explicit distinctions are required to and amongst legal consequences, which should instead be tailored to each particular institutional networking logic.

1. Genetic Connectivity

The specifics of the legal consequences will be more closely detailed in following Chapters. This Chapter seeks only to identify the leading principles of the apportionment of dual responsibility for internal and external network relations with the aid of the concepts of genetic, conditional and functional connectivity. Genetic connectivity gives expression to the temporal dynamics in which the interdependency of the contracts arises. Thus, in much the same manner that a matching performance requirement automatically arises in tandem with a performance obligation within a mutual contract, sharing all the latter's validity and invalidity criteria, the individual contracts within the network would likewise be linked to one another by identical conditions of validity. However, whilst this narrow coupling closely matches the risk structures of credit financing contracts, it must nonetheless be modified for other networks. Bipolar co-operative contracts in franchising, just-in-time systems and virtual enterprises are never so narrowly connected to each other that each individual contract must be considered an 'accessory' to the validity of the other contracts.[95] However, even in this case there is a threshold at which the notion of genetic connectivity becomes relevant. When the overall status of the network is itself in question, the mutual interdependencies between bilateral contracts must be investigated. Nonetheless, such interdependencies do not have an 'automatic' effect, but are far better thought of as being mediated through termination rights.

[94] Heermann (1998), 74; (2003), 91.

[95] This important difference in the degree of interconnection is the reason why Rohe (1998), 3, 56*ff* distinguishes between horizontal and vertical networks and between their different legal consequences. Is the client a part of the network? Horizontal: yes; vertical: no. Are legal relations established between non-contractually bound members of the network? Horizontal: yes; vertical: no. Are non-contractually bound members of the network externally liable? Horizontal: yes; vertical: no. This distinction, however, is far too broad to capture the variety of differences between the inner logic of networks.

A far more significant feature than the interdependency of contractual validity is the genetic connectivity that is established between the network as a whole and internal expectations within individual contracts.[96] In practice, the establishment of a network does generate implicit network obligations within the bilateral contracts. This reorientation of bipolar contracts to an overarching purpose is one of the most important impacts of networking and restructures obligations comprehensively. This should not cause controversy – aside from the question of the precise legal construction – amongst legal specialists in networks.[97]

However, what is highly controversial is the question of whether a 'genetic connectivity' exists between individual bilateral contracts, on the one hand, and the relations between non-contractually bound members of the network, on the other.[98] It should be clear from the foregoing analysis that once connected contracts are created via the conclusion of a number of bilateral contracts, *uno actu* legal relationships are established between members of the network who are not bound to one another by a bipolar contract. If the defining feature of networking is the fact that it gives rise to specific communicative relationships between all members of the network, and if this has, as its legal counterpart, closely detailed bilateral contracts binding individual net members to the goal of producing network effects, then the obligation must extend to encompass all net relations, including those established between members who do not stand in a bilateral contractual relationship with one another. This is an indispensable part of networking logic, and one which the law must respect. This noteworthy logic is likewise present within credit financing contracts, even though it has attracted far less attention due to the dramatic imposition of piercing liability. Technically speaking, there is usually no contractual relationship between bank and vendor. Rather, relations are based on factual co-operation, or the 'contribution' of the vendor to the conclusion of the loan, or even, simply, upon a long-term

[96] See in detail, Chapter 4 (III-VI), examining the impact of the network purpose under the titles of duties of care and review of standard contracts.

[97] For franchising, Schimansky (2003), 120*ff*; for just-in-time systems, Lange (1998), 425*f*; for virtual businesses, Lange (2001a), 180*f*; (2001b), 169*ff*; (2001c), 1805*ff*; for networks generally, Rohe (1998), 204*ff*, 397*ff*, 437*ff*, 466*ff*.

[98] Rohe, 356*f*, 388, 430*ff* vehemently rejects this for hierarchical nets. Vehemence, however, dissipates in the face of various hierarchical levels, 463*ff*. By contrast, non-contractually bound members within heterarchical nets are deemed subject to comprehensive binding duties on the basis of the multilateral network contract; similarly vehement in relation to franchising, (2003), 117*ff*. Larenz and Wolf, by contrast, are in favour of mutual binding obligations for non-contractually bound members throughout the general networking category, (1997), 470; Kulms (2000), 232*f* (with differentiation according to the degree of co-operation); Amstutz and Schluep (2003), 890*ff*; Schluep (2003), 290, 302; for just-in-time systems, Zirkel (1990), 349; Lange (1998), 195*ff*; for virtual businesses, Lange (2001a), 188*ff*, 192; for franchising, Baumgarten (1993), 169*ff*; Krebs (2000), 381*ff*.

business relationship. Gernhuber and Heermann have nonetheless established that bank and vendor are liable to each other in contract for failed or incomplete performance.[99]

What do these troublesome legal relationships constitute, however? Gernhuber's response, in all its clarity, is 'special relations', which are lent the legal character of *culpa in contrahendo* by analogy. To the degree that no explicit contract exists between the creditor and the vendor, 'a special legal relationship must be recognised between the parties, which they themselves establish when they conclude each contract with the purchaser, or, loan-taker. The fact that further obligations flow from this is a direct consequence of the final nexus of a duty of care that is structurally instigated for each party upon initiation of contractual dealings.'[100] The arbitrary termination of the contract of sale would entail a breach of the vendor's obligations to the bank even though they might not be explicitly contractually bound to one another. Heermann's response is: 'trilateral synallagma'. A trilateral legal relationship might be distilled from the *do ut des ut det* structure hinted at within the simple bipolar contracts, such that a legally effective performance relationship might also be established between bank and vendor, be it in the form of the interpretation of the loan as a contract to the benefit of a third part, or be it through any other legal construction.[101]

This genetic connectivity between bilateral contracts and legal relations between non-contractually bound members of the network is in fact constitutive of business networks.[102] Just as was the case in relation to its legal conditions, the same is true of the legal consequences: the business network is a combination of a number of bilateral contracts and a multilateral special relationship between all members of the network. As noted above, 'networking' is established by means of simple local net contacts, and is constantly reshaped in this same manner. Bilateral contacts instigate a structure of expectations with respect to the network, within which each network member is more intensively bound with all

[99] In contrast, Klaus Hörter (1969), *Der finanzierte Abzahlungskauf.* Bad Homburg: Gehlen, 244*ff*; Gundlach (1979), 283.

[100] Gernhuber (1973), 493; (1989), 741*f*. Here there is a clear connection to the concept of 'special relations', one which Picker (1999), 438*f* seeks to apply productively to extra-contractual internal net relations. Similarly, Larenz and M Wolf (1997), 470.

[101] Heermann (1998), 93, 96*ff*, 106, 192; Krebs (2000), 381*ff*.

[102] Rohe also draws this conclusion (1998), 195*ff*; only, however, on the basis of his fictional agency construction. In an extraordinary construction he seeks to allow all net clients participation within all net relations. Even less convincingly, this should not apply to vertical nets. Question: what is the case in horizontal franchising (eg, hotel franchising chains)? Similar to text for the genetic connectivity, Zirkel (1990), 349; Larenz and M Wolf (1997), 470; Lange (1998), 195*ff*; (2001a), 188*ff*, 192; Krebs (2000), 381*ff*.

other members.[103] In any case, Heermann's trilateral synallagma, which might be expanded to form a multilateral synallagma within a large net, is surely not sustainable. The particular *'do ut des ut det'* structure, which is only possible within circular exchange and, at a pinch, might just be applicable to credit financed purchases, rapidly meets its Waterloo within large-scale nets.[104] Here, synallagmatic interconnection of individual obligations is displaced by a generalised form of reciprocity: individual performance is not undertaken in expectation of specific consideration, but rather performed to the benefit of the 'net' with a vague expectation of future advantages.[105] The implications of this genetic connectivity will be more closely detailed in following chapter.[106]

2. Conditional and Functional Connectivity

In contrast to the idea of genetic connectivity that governs the emergence of connected contracts, 'conditional' and 'functional' connectivities govern the continuation of relationships established between connected contracts.[107] Disturbances within an individual contract selectively impact via the connectivity upon another contract. Within the conditional connectivity, discontinuance of obligation in one contract has its 'automatic' counterpart in discontinuance of obligation in another. In the case of functional connectivity, a right to terminate the other bilateral contract intervenes, which keeps the options open for third parties, but which at the same time allows contracts to evolve functionally. In this case, too, however, the structure of risks in a business network is far looser than is the case for credit financing contracts. There is an important reason why automatic interconnection is eschewed here in favour of a process of regular intervention on the basis of discontinuation rights: the heightened selectivity of interconnection must be emphasised. Even within the simple synallagmatic scenario of a bilateral contract, not every performance disturbance impacts upon its matching consideration. Rather the purpose of the exchange acts as a filter. Insignificant breaches of obligation that have no effect upon the exchange purpose are dealt with in isolation. Only those breaches that endanger or impugn the purpose of the exchange have a selective impact upon their matching obligations to

[103] On the relationship between individual contracts and the overall network structure responsible for the creation of network effects, Lemley and McGowan (1998), 21. Generally on the decentralised connections to nets, see sociological studies by Stichweh (2000), 220*ff*.

[104] Heermann corrects himself in his subsequent monograph (2003), 160*ff* on multilateral contractual relations. However, this makes the issue of their appropriate doctrinal construction even more urgent.

[105] Semlinger (1993) 333*f*, with further references; Mahnkopf (1994) 71*ff*; Powell (1990).

[106] See comprehensively, Chapter 5 (V–VIII).

[107] Gernhuber (1989), 735*ff*.

perform the contract. A similar degree of selectivity can be noted within connected contracts. Overarching and internal legal correction is only permissible when the network purpose is affected.

The most difficult and most controversial problems arise, however, in relation to external liability towards clients and creditors of the network.[108] Is the dual attribution principle – argued here to be an appropriate legal reaction to network operational logic – in a position to facilitate the 'piercing' of connected contracts by parties who are external to the network? Is liability to be apportioned to the network centre, various selected members of the network, or to the network itself? Case law on bank gironets has been pioneering in this field, constructively misapplying the institution of contract to the benefit of a third party in order to allow clients to 'pierce' the net and lay claims against intervening banks with whom they have no contractual relations.[109] The significance of this jurisprudence, and especially its indirect impact upon other networks, cannot be overstated. Taking a closer look, however, such jurisprudence on financed contracts could be construed as simply establishing 'external' net liability, rather than entailing a piercing intervention within internal net relations.[110] The triangular financing contract constellation furnishes a starting point for our consideration of more comprehensive forms of networks. Thus, even in relation to the scenario of the credit financed purchase triangle, a distinction might be drawn between networking in its narrow sense and external network contacts. The 'economic unity' established between vendor and credit institution is the genuine co-operative network that builds up external relations with clients. From this perspective, the claim made by a client takes the nature of an external claim against the economic entity of the network. The legal

108 See comprehensively, Chapter 6 (III–VI).

109 BGHZ 96, 9, 17; BGH WM 1988, 246, 247; BGHZ 108, 386, 390. Comprehensive analysis of case law in René-Alexander Hirth (1991), *Die Rechtsprechung zum Vertrag mit Schutzwirkung zugunsten Dritter in ihrer Bedeutung für den Ausgleich von Drittschäden im Zahlungsverkehr.* Berlin: Duncker & Humblot, 56*ff*, 148*ff*; Dorothee Einsele (1999), 'Haftung der Kreditinstitute bei nationalen und grenzüberschreitenden Banküberweisungen', *Archiv für die civilistische Praxis* 199, 145*ff*, 149*ff*. On recent legal developments following the legislative focusing of liability on the primary bank by means of the 'quasi liability' of an intervening bank under § 676c I 3 (BGB), Jochen Hoffmann (2001), 'Grundfragen des Überweisungsgesetzes', *Wertpapier Mitteilungen* 55, 881*ff*, 887; Jörg Risse and Nicola Lindner (1999), 'Haftung der Banken nach dem neuen Überweisungsrecht', *Betriebs Berater* 54, 2201*ff*, 2205. The new rules prove so interesting from the networking point of view since a legislative fiction of 'accessory action' had to be created in relation to intervening banks, since banking 'networks' cannot be adequately treated in traditional market or organisational categories. Legislation is therefore not a 'positive rejection' of network contracts, as argued by Hoffmann (2001), 887, but rather an 'application of the network model': see Uwe Schneider (1999), 'Pflichten und Haftung der erstbeauftragten Kreditinstitute bei grenzüberschreitenden Überweisungen: Auf dem Weg zu einem Sonderrecht für Kettenverträge' *Wertpapier Mitteilungen* 44, 2189*ff*, 2192.

110 Larenz and M Wolf (1997), 470.

construction of economic unity between the vendor and creditor bank facilitates the attribution of responsibility for the behaviour of the supplier to the creditor bank, such that claims by the external client against the supplier can also be enforced against the bank.

This selective claim afforded to third parties within credit financing contracts triangles can serve as a generalisable model for connected contracts.[111] Techniques for allocation of responsibility should be applied to combat the external transfer of risks by the network.[112] Such risks derive directly from negative network effects and cannot be overcome by market forces alone.[113] Rather, they are a corollary to positive network effects, likewise an integral part of a bilaterally founded multilateral communication structure. Law must internalise such negative externalities. A detailed analysis of the impact of network effects upon law, describes the role of law in relation to negative effects as follows:

> If the network effects are real, significant, and negative, and if they cannot be solved within the market, courts should then consider which legal doctrines offer the appropriate remedy. To the extent that precedent permits, they should seek remedies from within the field of law that best take into account both the nature of the conduct complained of and whatever level of network effects exist. Within that field, courts should seek to pursue the course that provides an adequate remedy with the least possible disruption to other legal doctrines.[114]

Doctrinal approaches cleaving exclusively to the notion of special relations come to the same conclusion. They agree that the additional layer of extra-contractual organisation above contractual co-operation has created a legal vacuum within a central area of economic life; a vacuum that could be filled if the fact of organisational co-operation were to be confronted with a matching responsibility framework.[115] At its core, this is 'a matter of the correction of the questionable transfer of risk by contractual networking by means of the relativisation of the principle of privity of contract, so that the goal is one of bringing individual "feeder" contracts within the reach of the law pertaining to contractual interconnection'.[116]

Such new external risks are particularly clear in the case of hierarchical networking, most particularly franchising. Should individual franchisees be solely liable, not only for errors they themselves make as autonomous

[111] Larenz and M Wolf (1997), 470.

[112] For risk transfer in general, and with particular reference to franchising, see Krebs (2000), 381*ff*.

[113] Implicitly, Rohe (1998), 418, who denies, however, the need for the legal regulation of such negative network effects within hierarchical nets.

[114] Lemley and McGowan (1998), 198.

[115] Picker (1999), 431*f*. Similarly, Krebs (2000), 381*ff*.

[116] Amstutz and Schluep (2003), 890*ff*.

market actors, but also for system errors that they are helpless to correct? The construction of franchising as a simple bundle of individual contracts frees franchisors (the peak of distribution organisation) from all contractual liability for portions of the overall package of services that they have effectively performed themselves. Here, piercing liability, establishing the liability of the system (centre) would seem to be an imperative. Similarly, individual actors within heterarchical networks are likewise exposed to system imperatives within their client contacts, whilst failures within the system remain unsanctioned. The issue here, then, is one of the evolution of forms of external liability that mirror internal structures of responsibility.[117]

VI. LEGAL PROBLEMS OF INSTITUTIONALISED NETWORKING

This discussion completes the picture of the underlying principles of the legal model of the business network. The idea of 'networks as connected contracts' rests upon a legal construct, founded in its dual constitution as a contract and as an association and further defined by a selective process of dual attribution in relation to legal remedies. But this is not enough. Legal characterisation is not exhausted by the general definition of legal conditions and of legal consequences that adequately mirror the social reality of network organisation, even in all its contradictory and ambivalent nature. The matter is always also one of the normative response of the law to the specific risks posed by networking. These reactions always form an integral part of the 'neutral' process of network characterisation. At the very latest, institutionalised judicial review of standard form contracts marked the time at which the supposedly simple question of their 'conceptual' classification within contract law became determinative for the application of binding law. Thus, classification is

[117] Krebs has recently begun to argue for piercing liability within business networks, in particular within franchising and contractual dealing systems, basing his arguments on risk transfer and damage prevention: Krebs (2000), 316*f*; similarly, for networks in general, Möschel (1986), 211*ff*, 223; Teubner (1991), 121*ff*; (1993b), 57*ff*; (1992), 232; (2002a), 325*ff*. In agreement, Manfred Wolf and Christina Ungeheuer (1994), 'Vertragsrechtliche Probleme des Franchising', *Betriebs Berater* 49, 1027*ff*, 1033; Norbert Reich (1995), 'Garantien unter Gemeinschaftsrecht', *Europäische Zeitschrift für Wirtschaftsrecht* 6, 71*ff*, 76; Larenz and M Wolf (1997), 470; Amstutz and Schluep (2003) 888, 890; Schluep (2003), 290, 302*f*. Likewise, for virtual businesses, Lange (2001a), 185. With analogous consideration of corporate groups, Ehricke (1996), 319*f*; Oechsler (1997a), 482*ff*; Pasderski (1998) 37*ff*; Bayreuther (2001), 295*ff*, 399*f*, 400, 530, also argue for external liability under certain conditions. Similar suggestions in Martinek (1992), 75; (1993a), 582. Zirkel (1990), 350 confirms external liability for non-contractually bound members. Arguing in favour of tort-based liability for the network centre by means of extensive interpretation of § 831 BGB, Roth (1989), 436; Bräutigam (1994), 138*ff*. From the economic viewpoint, Gulati, Klein and Zolt argue for external liability under certain conditions (2000), 807, 930; Noll (2002).

co-determinate with a particular 'justice conception', from which divergence is only possible under very complex circumstances.[118]

This is the point at which the complex risks posed by the 'network paradox' become fully apparent. Network risks detailed in the first Chapter should thus be recalled.[119] Networks might well be a successful response to contradictory demands on business. Nonetheless, the internal networking structure itself gives rise to new problems: 'On the one hand, business networks seek an expansion of and an intensification of economic efficiency within business activities; on the other hand, this very action endangers their own functionality and existence, being especially challenging for the primary pre-condition for relations between network actors, or stability.'[120] Networks thus contemporaneously reproduce the very problems that they are designed to solve. Just like other modern institutions, networks also exhibit self-destructive tendencies. They might well respond productively to contradictory environmental demands, creating a hybrid structure, which internally minimises contradictions, and establishes the trust and co-operation between partners upon which new technological and production potentialities might be built. Equally, they might translate incompatible environmental demands into tense, but sustainable and productive, internal expectations. At the same time, however, they create a self-destructive potential, at least to the degree that they strengthen the tensions that their hybrid form and internal conflicts opposed to trust give rise to. If external pressures, such as temporal demands, flexibility requirements and pressures arising from sunk costs, intensify the individual tendency to opportunistic behaviour, then, as noted above, network failure might also be considered to be pre-programmed.[121]

Likewise, as noted above, private law can seek to correct such forms of 'network failure' with a fairly strong hope of success. This is not, however, possible through the detailed steering of behaviour by means of general incentives and sanctions, or even by means of individual judicial decisions. Instead, this will occur where law continues with its on-going implicit mission to stabilise expectations within contract and corporate law.[122] The issue of legal characterisation is therefore not simply a matter of the coherent subordination of business networks to contractual or corporate law forms. Rather, the controversy as to whether networks

[118] On this relationship, see Theo Mayer-Maly (1999), 'Wiederkehr des schuldrechtlichen Typenzwangs?' in Volker Beuthien (ed), *Festschrift für Dieter Medicus*. Cologne: Heymanns, 383*ff*; Stoffels (2001), 93*ff*, 415*ff*.

[119] See above, Chapter 1 (VI).

[120] Hirsch-Kreinsen (2002), 118.

[121] On the 'organisational paradox' of contradictory conditions, Cameron and Quinn (1988); Funder (1999); Hirsch-Kreinsen (2002), 111*ff*.

[122] See above, Chapter 1 (VI).

should be classified as contracts, organisations or connected contracts, must be placed in an institutional context that seeks systematically to promote those particular expectations that work against network failure.

The following Chapters will concern themselves with the extrapolation of the general model of the network as connected contracts to include all of these risks and the legal means of their solution. Three distinct constellations will be distinguished, whereby hybrids respond to the problems of paradoxical communication with specific organisational models. The primary thesis is: *internal conflicts derive from the simultaneous challenges posed by external contradictions. These take very distinct forms: (1) contradictions between bilateral exchange and multilateral connectivity; (2) contradictions between competition and co-operation; (3) contradictions between collective and individual orientation.* If such contradictions are successfully internalised within the network, but then in turn tend to endanger internal network co-ordination, as well as the trustworthiness and responsibility displayed by the network,[123] a need for legal regulation arises – regulation that is occasioned by the clash between operational logics. This conflict typology entails concrete legal responses: *(1) the regulation of network obligations and standard contracts (Chapter 4); (2) piercing intervention within the net into relations between non-contractually bound members of the network (Chapter 5); overarching but simultaneously decentralised network liability (Chapter 6).* The question tackled by following Chapters is therefore one of which legal constructions are individually best suited to satisfying the following challenges:

- the need to normalise, legitimise and stabilise the hybrid nature of networks;
- the need to secure a generalised reciprocity, which is distinct from its contractual equivalent, and to institutionalise conditional trust;
- the need to attribute responsibility for defects in performance;
- the need to combat the misuse of power through the application of rules on liability and termination;
- the need for mediation between conflicts of orientation within the overall network.

[123] Comprehensively, Bieber (1997), 125*ff*.

4

The Effects of Networks on Bilateral Contracts

I. DIFFERENTIATED DISCOUNTS

THE OPTICAL BUSINESS, 'Optik', is run by the leading firm, 'Apollo', in the form of a so-called 'dual system'. Apollo distributes optical goods through a first channel made up of 150 of its own subsidiaries, and also through a second channel, comprising 90 franchisees. Apollo bundles the purchasing of both channels in order to gain higher discounts from suppliers. Suppliers guarantee – without any degree of differentiation – discounts to the Apollo system of up to 52%. Apollo, however, supplies its franchisees with an 'official' production discount list. This list only details production discounts of up to 38%. The difference is returned by suppliers, without the franchisees' knowledge, to Apollo in the form of a 'kick-back' (differentiated discount).

Apollo had conducted negotiations in two stages. First, Apollo deployed the purchasing power of the overall Apollo system in order to obtain a unitary discount for the entire system – inclusive of franchisees – from suppliers. Then, in a second step, they again negotiated with suppliers, securing the diversion of the differentiated discount to Apollo. When this differentiated discount practice was accidentally revealed, the franchisees commenced an action against Apollo for repayment of the differentiated discount.

This case was treated by a variety of Courts of Appeal with diametrically opposed results and has since been settled by the Federal High Court (BGH) in favour of the claimant franchisees.[1] Leaving aside competition law issues, the relevant contractual question for us is one of whether Apollo, in its guise as the central franchising node, is obliged to pass on various networking advantages to franchisees. The Federal High Court had already supplied a negative answer to this question in a

[1] OLG Bremen WRP 2002, 224; OLG Düsseldorf WRP 2002, 235, OLG Frankfurt 23 July 2002 – 11 U (Kart.) 55/00); OLG Frankfurt 23 July 2002 – 11 U (Kart.) 42/00. BGH Pressemitteilung No 64/2003.

similar case (Hertz).[2] This case had examined the issue of whether car-leasing franchisors would be obliged to pass on the benefits of marketing cost subsidies supplied by automobile manufacturers on the leasing of their models. The Court argued that the clause in the standard contract laying down a general duty of the franchisor to 'support' the franchisees in the supply of goods could not be used 'to found the obligation' to pass on the benefits. Accordingly, various Courts of Appeal reproduced this reasoning within the Apollo case, stating that the franchising contract laying down Apollo's duty to pass on networking advantages to individual franchisees could not be construed as giving rise to this concrete obligation.[3] The Federal High Court, however, seized upon one particular clause within the standard contract, laying down Apollo's obligation to pass on to franchisees all advantages that would enable the optimisation of business success, and held that this clause provided sufficient justification for the claim.

However, concentrating only upon the interpretation of standard contracts fails to take note of network effects.[4] The model of isolated contractual relationships between three independent business strata (suppliers – franchisors – franchisees) which some of the courts applied is no longer appropriate. According to this model, suppliers enter into isolated bilateral contracts with franchisors, whose isolated bilateral contracts with franchisees in turn give them factual purchasing power, which they deploy against suppliers in order to obtain purchasing advantages. Since this model wholly disregards vertical quasi-integration within the network, franchisors are naturally free to determine for themselves whether and to what degree they will pass on negotiated discounts to franchisees. Even should support obligations or duties for the passing on of advantages be read into the bilateral franchising contract, it remains difficult to establish the obligation of the franchisor to pass on advantages that it has negotiated for itself. These advantages thus do not stem from the bilateral legal relationship with the franchisees, but rather from the 'factual' purchasing power of the franchisor.

Multilateral connectivity within the franchising system, however, gives rise to network effects that may justify the obligation to pass on advantages to members of the network. This, at any rate, was the line of reasoning followed by the Federal High Court, which deemed Apollo to be obliged to pass on to franchisees all the various advantages (in

[2] BGH 17 July 2001 – VIII ZR 59/01; OLG Stuttgart 16 February 2001 – 2 U 218/99. In contrast, tending to answer yes to the claim, OLG Munich WiB 1997, 1109. See also Reinhard Böhner (1998), 'Werbekostenzuschüsse und sonstige Einkaufsvorteile in Franchisesystemen', *Neue Juristische Wochenschrift* 51, 109*ff*.

[3] OLG Düsseldorf WRP 2002, 238.

[4] On network effects, see above, Chapter 1 (III, VI) and Chapter 3 (IV). On their impact on various legal fields, Lemley and McGowan (1998), 31*ff*.

particular, price advantages) that it had negotiated with its franchisees' suppliers. Initially at least, this decision would seem to be only a matter of interpretation of clauses within the standard contracts. The Apollo contract contained the following formulation:

> Point 6.3: 'Apollo supports partners in business development and system-appropriate business conduct and passes on advantages, ideas and improvements facilitative of optimal business success to partners'.

Regardless of how eager the judiciary is to present the question as one of the simple interpretation of contractual clauses, the distinction between the judgments is nonetheless not a simple matter of the more or less vague formulation of 'support obligations' within general contractual conditions. Instead, practical reasons also dictate that it would be inappropriate to found the decision solely within the interpretation of a general contractual condition. Subsequent to the Federal High Court decision, such clauses detailing the passing on of advantages will be weakened or even deleted, so that the judiciary will be required to decide the issue anew, and this time the court will be required to deal with the very structures of the franchising network. The decisive factor is the degree of functional dependency within the contractual and organisational relationships. Even where, as was the case in both the Hertz and the Apollo cases, standard contracts contain such clauses, their correct interpretation needs to be made in the light of market and organisational relations.

If the contractual distribution system displays an intense degree of vertical integration, the correct solution is clearly imposition of a duty to pass on advantages. This becomes clear if one makes a comparison with corporate integration of firms. Even the most fluid form of corporate integration, a partnership for the purposes of a collective purchase, results in a duty to pass on all the purchasing advantages to each member of the purchasing group.[5] This rule is cemented in the case of more densely co-ordinated partnerships and of companies. Had the relationship between Apollo and individual dealers been of a corporate character, the purchasing advantages negotiated from suppliers by Apollo on the basis of its 'corporate' purchasing power would 'automatically' under law have accrued to the profits of the company and would then have been distributed to participants under rules allocating profits within the corporation. Had Apollo retained only a portion of the purchasing advantages for itself, or even worse, arranged for *ex post* payments from suppliers without the knowledge of the other partners,

[5] See, for comprehensive analysis of the agency and corporate law problems posed by collective purchase, Karsten Schmidt (1988), 'Zur "Außenhaftung der Innengesellschaft": LG Konstanz NJW 1987, 2521', *Juristische Schulung* 28, 444*ff*, 445*ff*.

this would have constituted a breach of the rules of the company. Indeed, as we have seen above, some scholars characterise franchising systems as 'partnerships'[6] with the consequence that franchisors would, under this approach, be obliged by fiduciary duties arising from the partnership to pass on all advantages.

The particular difficulty here, however, is that (as previous Chapters have shown) the franchising relationship can neither be characterised as an isolated exchange contract, nor be designated as a partnership. Instead, it inhabits a precarious position between the two.[7] Does the characterisation of franchising networks as 'connected contracts' prove useful here?[8] Does the contractual interconnection provide justification for imposition of an obligation on the network centre to pass on the advantages it derives from existing joint purchasing power to individual members?

II. STRUCTURAL CONTRADICTION: BILATERAL EXCHANGE VERSUS MULTILATERAL CONNECTIVITY

The Apollo case is emblematic for the first – and indeed most typical – constellation, in which the internal structure of the hybrid network responds to contradictory market challenges. Internal network decision-making is simultaneously subordinated to the contradictory demands of bilateral exchange and multilateral connectivity.[9] One important reason for the contradictory expectations is the uncertainty of market actors about future market evolution. Uncertainty forces parties to conclude long-term exchange contracts that bind them within closely co-ordinated hierarchical or heterarchical co-operative relations, their mutually antagonistic interests notwithstanding.[10] These contradictory requirements of embedding and autonomy[11] are mirrored within the concrete contractual obligations of participants. In line with the logic of exchange contract, normal good faith duties (under § 242 Civil Code) within an exchange contract would never extend so far as to impose an obligation upon one contractual party to pass on to the other any advantages that

[6] Generally, on franchising, Baumgarten (1993), 114*ff*; Kessal-Wulf (1995), 249*ff*; for specific franchising constellations, Martinek (1987), 231*ff*; (1992), 78*ff*; (1997), 94*ff*; (2001), 327*ff*; Müller-Graff (1988), 141.

[7] See above, Chapter 2 (I-III).

[8] See above, Chapter 3 (IV and V).

[9] For the contradictory nature of external challenges as instigator for networking, see Cameron and Quinn (1988), 1*ff*; Buxbaum (1993), 701; Messner (1997b); Reiß (1998), 224*ff*; Funder (1999); Köhler (1999), 36*ff*; Sauer and Lang (1999); Luhmann (2000), 375, 407*ff*; Sydow and Windeler (2000), 6*ff*; Hirsch-Kreinsen (2002), 107.

[10] Kulms (2000), 227*ff*.

[11] Böhner (1998), 109.

have been negotiated with a third party. Exactly the opposite would obtain within a genuine associational relationship. Which preconditions, however, should be fulfilled for this to take effect?

Traditionally, such clashes between different logics of action would be overcome by means of a forced 'either-or' decision. Those approaches within academic literature that characterise franchising either as an exchange contract or as a partnership fall four-square within this tradition.[12] As our case demonstrates, diametrically opposed judgments of Courts of Appeal reinforce the well-known strict division made between market and organisation, which in turn is reproduced within the similarly strict division between contract and company law. However, the forced market/organisation and contract/corporation dichotomies tend to suppress an appropriate solution. They force a choice in favour of one of the contradictory business orientations, consigning the other to the obscurity of informality.

The preceding Chapters made frequent reference to social science analyses that reveal and continuously stress that contradictions are constitutive of networks.[13] Here, we are confronted with a concrete example of the contradiction between the logics of exchange and multilateral connectivity. The various escape paths out of these conflicts, delineated above as 'morphogenesis', coalesce within the specific logic of networks.

> If designed to close the functional gap between 'market' and 'hierarchy', co-operation must closely combine the highly effective advantages of the market model – that is, the production and communication advantages of specific transactional investments – with the predictability of hierarchical transactions and the flexibility advantages of loosely coupled networks. This description of functions is at core nothing less than a squaring of the circle by means of the application of transaction theory. The primary impetus for this is the contradictory challenge of ensuring predictable coordination of different partial systems/actors within an interdependent corpus, whilst at the same time leaving them, or even creating for them, sufficient opportunity for independent decision-making – that is, sufficient room to accept uncertainty or even added risk.[14]

Organisational theory characterises this process as 'detotalisation'. In reaction to external paradoxes, networks must 'mirror external diversity within their own institutions and functions, in order to deal with them'. This notion underlines the fact that 'antagonistic relations (in this case: bilateral exchange and multilateral co-operation [author's addition]) are cultivated within one and the same system – a paradoxical process only if

12 For discussion on these approaches, see above, Chapter 2 (I and II).
13 Chapter 2 (III), Chapter 3 (I).
14 Semlinger (1993), 332.

sectoral and temporal differentiation is ignored and totalised'.[15] Empirical studies have demonstrated that such an internal distinction between and subsequent recombination of exchange and co-operation logics is achievable in practice. Within successful business networks, the same actors were able to maintain formal exchange logic within 'exchange sectors' such as logistics, quality, quantity and price, whilst simultaneously combining it with trust-based co-operation in 'interconnected sectors' such as R&D and common planning.[16] 'Detotalisation' strategies thus aim to institutionalise the contradiction-dogged 'totality' of the business with new internal distinctions. Networking as a detotalisation strategy internalises contradictions, legitimates them as simple tensions, and, finally, finds contextual solutions through internal differentiation.

III. THE PURPOSE OF THE NETWORK AS THE YARDSTICK FOR DUTIES OF LOYALTY

The concept of 'purpose' becomes relevant in the law of connected contracts. Purpose should not be understood as the simple instrumental subordination of obligations for the attainment of an agreed goal. Instead, purpose encompasses the process whereby internal logic is brought into line with external demands.[17] Networks, with all their difficult internal problems of co-ordination, are particularly dependent upon 'visions' interlinking the system with its environment.[18] The appropriate legal category within which to capture such network logic, to institutionalise them and to combat their negative effects, is surely that of 'network purpose'. An independent legal category in its own right, the purpose of a network differs markedly both from the 'contractual purpose' of the exchange relation and from the 'corporate purpose' of private associations. It is readily apparent here that the much-clamoured-for explicit differentiation between network purpose, on the one hand, and corporate purpose, on the other, is in fact of practical importance.[19] Nonetheless, as we have seen, the effort to distinguish a 'common'

[15] Neuberger (2000), 207*ff*.

[16] Bieber (1997), especially 124*f*.

[17] The purpose concept within contract and company law not only unveils implicit agreement between parties on the goal of their project, such that it can be used to concretise fiduciary duties; but rather, it reconstructs external demands from the internal perspective of the contractual relationship. See, for the general good faith clause (§ 242 BGB), Teubner (1980), 50*ff*; (1989), 140*ff*; Kulms (2000), 193*ff*, 227*ff*, deploys the purpose concept in order to make the relationship between external market risks and internal organisational risks within complex contractual relations explicit.

[18] See, for a detailed analysis of their integrative effects within networks, Abel (2000), 163*ff*.

[19] Larenz and M Wolf (1997), 470; Rohe (1998), 358*ff*, 407*ff*, 437*ff*; Krebs (2000), 315; Bayreuther (2001), 289; Lange (2001a), 81*ff*; Schimansky (2003), 113, 125, 167.

purpose from a simple 'unitary' purpose has little chance of success. Rather, the primary feature that distinguishes network purpose from corporate purpose is its dual orientation to both association and contract, a dual orientation expressed within one formula of its purpose. Binding internal co-operation to a legally institutionalised network purpose may prevent conflicts from being viewed from the one-sided perspective of an exchange; at the same time, it also precludes one-sided corporate 'totalisation'. 'Network purpose' is a legal category that explicitly encompasses the contradiction between the individual and collective elements of networking.

Network purpose translates the external and insoluble contradictions that confront business into an internal and sustainable confrontation between different levels – network nodes, network centre and the entire network.[20] It must specifically fulfil the following task: *Contradictory demands will be translated into stable expectations by means of internal differentiation between temporal, social or material sectors*. For our purposes, this means that sectors must be distinguished in the network, within which the concept of network purpose dictates the dominance either of individual or collective orientation. Importantly, however, this does not delineate rigidly either pure 'individualistic' contractual areas or pure 'collectivised' associational spheres. This would simply reproduce the combination theory results as applied to mixed contracts, which were rejected above as being inadequate.[21] Notwithstanding the decision to afford primacy to one orientation, the *re-entry* of the secondary orientation is still indispensable. Within individual areas, adequate secondary attention must also be paid to the collective sphere. By the same token, collective spheres must also be marked by their due regard for individual issues. More concretely, should contexts be identified, within which either the individual or collective orientation is dominant, actors should nonetheless be constrained not only to pursue individual interest, but also to give effect to the overall interests of the network within one and the same operation.

The legal formula is as follows: the network purpose distinguishes contexts within which intensified loyalty duties toward the network arise from situations within which only the usual good faith duties of contract law apply; nonetheless, each obligation must be exercised and modified with due regard to the other. The legal task is one of distinguishing between contractual good faith duties and intensified loyalty duties toward the whole network. On the other hand, however, it should be noted that loyalty duties toward the network are not simply to be

[20] Semlinger (1993), 332.
[21] Chapter 2 (IV).

regarded as being identical with loyalty duties toward the organisation present in corporate law. Instead, they exhibit their own 'decentralised' bias. The individual/collective differentiation within networks is related to, but not identical with the corporate law distinction between a sphere of collective orientation and a sphere of personal orientation.[22] Corporate law recognises only voting, information and termination rights as personal rights. Management and agency rights are never given this status. Within network law, however, the exact equivalent to notions of management and agency is the paradigm of self-interested behaviour of a network member. These differences clearly derive from the already much discussed distinction between networks and collectives: the all-pervading combination of individual and collective orientation. The pooling of resources within the corporation proves to be a less effective mechanism to capture the realities of this combination than networking, which furnishes a contextual mode of fine-tuning the individual/collective relationship.[23]

Network purpose then becomes the yardstick, according to which the intensified duties of loyalty that arise out of multilateral networking of bilateral contracts can be identified and constituted. Here again, however, two aspects must be clearly distinguished: long-term contracts and networks.[24] The doctrine of long-term contracts has already identified its own intensified duties of loyalty, which apply to contexts in which bilateral co-operation overlays antagonistic exchange relations. Largely uncontroversial, this doctrine need not be examined in detail here. Instead, the more controversial notion of multilateral networking grabs our attention. Which intensified duties of loyalty arise out of the network process whereby individual spheres are overlain by collective spheres? This is the exact point at which the legal category of the network purpose comes into play.[25]

IV. SELECTED DUTIES OF LOYALTY TOWARD THE NETWORK

In principle, the list of network duties of loyalty is non-exhaustive.[26] The following passages, however, deal with striking situations in which

[22] On this distinction, see Ulmer in *Münchener Kommentar* (1997), § 705, 161, 186, 190*ff*; OLG Frankfurt NJW-RR 1995, 421, 422.

[23] Kulms (2000), 231, 261 also follows this line of argument, pleading for equivalence between loyalty duties and genuine corporate organisational rules.

[24] Rohe (1998), 438*ff*, similarly distinguishes 'network effective' and 'bipolar' obligation constellations.

[25] Amstutz (2003), 174*ff* has furnished a clear theoretical clarification here, arguing for judicial translation of 'network functional criteria'.

[26] On intensified network loyalty duties, Bayreuther (2001), 176*ff*; Stoffels (2001), 262*ff*; see, in particular, for franchising relationships, the Franchising Code of Conduct of 1

networking qualitatively alters the usual duties of good faith found both within exchange contracts and long-term contracts. Particular attention will be paid to the troublesome profit transfer constellation already discussed in the Apollo case. In addition, however, the equally troublesome issue of internal risk transfer will be tackled in the context of judicial review of standard contracts.

Duties of the network centre to disclose information. Compared to the normal exchange contract, duties of the network centre to disclose information are intensified in the case of multilateral networking. Ensuring a higher level of exchange of information is the goal pursued in order to secure the functionality of the network. This is particularly true for franchising where the securing of a unified performance standard for the entire system, regardless of local specificities, is of central importance.[27] In contrast to its common depiction, this is not simply restricted to matters such as the advertising of a unitary image. Instead, standardisation is also a necessity should such positive network effects be aimed for as standardised conditions for network node accessibility.[28] This problem also arises *mutatis mutandis* in the case of just-in-time systems and virtual enterprises, at least to the degree that the provision of information to suppliers is a precondition for the division of labour between members of the network.[29] In this case, network effects of mutual communicative accessibility play a decisive role. They justify the imposition of an intensified duty to disclose information upon the network centre, to the benefit of members of the network. This will result in a more intense obligation for the centre to ensure the flow of information, should even only one network member not have sufficient information to facilitate the

January 1992, annexed to the Competition Exemption Order, Commission Regulation (EEC) No 4087/88 of 30 November 1988, superseded by Commission Regulation (EC) No 2790/1999 No L 336/21; Rohe (1998), 437*ff*; Cosima Möller (2003), 'Der Franchisevertrag im Bürgerlichen Recht: Ein Beitrag zur Diskussion über die Rechtsnatur des Franchisevertrages', *Archiv für die civilistische Praxis* 203, 319*ff*; for just-in-time contracts, Lange (1998), 126*ff*; Rohe (1998), 397*ff*; for virtual businesses, Lange (2001a), 163*ff*, 185*ff*.

27 On specific informational duties, see OLG Munich BB 1988, 865; OLG Munich NJW 1994, 776; OLG Hamm NJW-RR 1994, 243, 244. For a more general perspective, Martinek (1987), 314; (1992), 87; Reinhard Böhner (1994), 'Schadensersatzpflicht des Franchisegebers aus Verschulden bei Vertragsschluss', *Neue Juristische Wochenschrift* 47, 635*ff*; Frank Braun (1995), 'Aufklärungspflichten des Franchisegebers bei den Vertragsverhandlungen', *Neue Juristische Wochenschrift* 48, 504*ff*; Eberhard Vom Dorp (1995), 'Haftung des Franchisegebers aus c.i.c.: Tendenzwende zur Rentabilitätsgarantie?' *Wirtschaftsrechtliche Beratung* 15, 285*ff*; Volker Emmerich (1995), 'Franchising', *Juristische Schulung* 35, 761*ff*, 763; Rohe (1998), 424, 438*f*; Stoffels (2001), 264.

28 On the relationship between network effects and standardisation, see Lemley and McGowan (1998), 55*ff*.

29 On the central importance of information policy in just-in-time systems, see especially Westphalen and Bauer (1993), 55*ff*; Detlef Schmidt (1991), 'Qualitätssicherungsvereinbarungen und ihr rechtlicher Rahmen', *Neue Juristische Wochenschrift* 44, 144*ff*, 147; Lange (1998), 77*ff*; Rohe (1998), 405.

smooth operation of the network. The yardstick against which duties of disclosure must be measured is that of the unified performance standard, a standard that clearly intensifies the extent of networking disclosure obligations in comparison to simple bipolar long-term contracts.[30]

Confidentiality duties. The corollary of duties of disclosure is the duty to maintain confidentiality with regard to third parties.[31] One typical risk is created by the inevitable access of all parties to information, in the confidentiality of which one or other party has a strong interest. This risk is created by virtue of the many interfaces of network nodes and the network centre. In view of their closely interlinked information technology systems, just-in-time systems are particularly susceptible to the misuse of confidential information. Mutual access to a partner's know-how is typical of the contract. Examples exist of manufacturers passing on knowledge of their suppliers' models to competitors, in order to then conclude contracts with that competitor.[32] Strict duties of confidentiality also apply in this context, even in the absence of explicit agreement, and they extend far beyond the normal provisions of competition law (§§ 17*ff* UWG). These duties of confidentiality are not only valid during the term of the contract, but also apply in pre- and post-contractual stages, giving rise to claims for damages.[33]

Non-discrimination. When a group structure is created, private law – labour law and corporate law in particular – imposes duties against discrimination that extend beyond the prohibition contained in competition law.[34] This extended obligation must also be respected within the network centre/node relationship.[35] The range of situations in which the positive duty of equal treatment arises becomes more extensive, the greater the degree of integration within the collective sector.[36] Although the non-discrimination principle does not apply to simple commercial agents,[37] the situation changes once the producer establishes a tightly

[30] Rohe (1998), 438f.

[31] See Zirkel (1990), 349; Christina Steinmann (1993), 'Abdingbarkeit der Wareneingangskontrolle in Qualitätssicherungsvereinbarungen', *Betriebs Berater* 48, 873*ff*; Lange (1998), 104, 215, 378; Rohe (1998), 406; Wellenhofer-Klein (1999), 164*ff*, 183.

[32] Klebe and Roth (1990), 679; Wellenhofer-Klein (1999), 165.

[33] On post-contractual liability, see especially Saxinger (1993), 232*f*; Lange (1998), 589.

[34] See the classic work by Ludwig Raiser (1948), 'Der Gleichheitsgrundsatz im Privatrecht', *Zeitschrift für das gesamte Handels- und Wirtschaftsrecht* 111, 75*ff*; Götz Hueck (1958), *Der Grundsatz der gleichmäßigen Behandlung im Privatrecht*. Munich: Beck; on the contemporary situation, see Ulmer in *Münchener Kommentar* (1997), § 705, 199*ff*.

[35] On authorised dealers, see Ulmer (1969), 380*ff*, 437; Rohe (1998), 478*f*; on supply networks, see Lange (1998), 322, 612; Kulms (2000), 253; for franchising, see Rohe (1998), 441.

[36] Lange (1998), 322, for supply networks.

[37] BGH BB 1971, 584. The High Court of the Reich had recognised a 'proportional' obligation to pay due regard to orders placed by business agents in the case of restricted supply, RG JW 1914, 403, 404.

integrated distribution network.[38] The non-discrimination principle undeniably applies to franchising networks.[39] In such cases, networking itself changes the quality of the transaction: the standard of service offered by the entire network thus demands that all network nodes be treated equally. As a counterpart to the network centre's directive rights, the non-discrimination rule compensates for centrifugal tendencies occasioned by nodal autonomy. The rule has particular application to unforeseeable bottlenecks within the network centre's production processes. In such cases, all system participants must be afforded proportionate rights of access to commodities.[40] The equal treatment rule might even be applicable between distinct groups of subsidiaries and franchised distribution nodes, at least to the degree that its application is necessary in order to attain network effects in external client relationships.

Loyalty duties to the entire network. The usual contractual duties of good faith of members of the network to the network hub are similarly intensified to the extent that they are transformed under the impact of network effects into duties of loyalty owed to the entire network.[41] The result is a far-reaching degree of subordination to directions from the network centre that is difficult to reconcile with nodal autonomy, particularly in relation to property, risks of shortfalls and potential shortfalls in profits. Subordination is justified, however, in pursuit of network effects. Within franchising, this results in an extraordinarily intense degree of standardisation.[42] Even a minimal deviation from unified standards dictated by the network centre can, if repeated, result in termination of the franchising contract. The famous example is, of course, McDonald's and franchise termination in the case of four proven examples of a grill temperature that was too low.[43] Such rigidity could not be justified in normal exchange contracts, since they are not subject to such a multilateral standardisation requirement.

Termination rights. Network effects also impact upon the termination rights of nodes and centre.[44] Members of the network are not only

[38] Klaus Hopt (1996), 'Wettbewerbsfreiheit und Treuepflicht des Unternehmers bei parallelen Vertriebsformen', *Zeitschrift für Wirtschaftsrecht* 17, 1533*ff*, 1538*f*.

[39] See Martinek (1997), 99, who criticises the individualistic orientation within the law of commercial distribution.

[40] Thus, correctly, Rohe (1998), 441, 478, who otherwise argues for a (too) restrictive application of the non-discrimination principle to 'pathological cases'.

[41] On intensified fiduciary duties within co-operative contracts, Lange (1998), 425*f*; (2001a), 180*f*; Wiedemann and Schultz (1999), 1, 4; Kulms (2000), 231*ff*.

[42] Rohe (1998), 415, 444*f*; Bayreuther (2001), 378*ff*.

[43] BGH NJW 1985, 1894. In effect, the right to termination was valid. See Reinhard Böhner (1985), 'Recht zur außerordentlichen Kündigung des McDonald's Franchisevertrages', *Neue Juristische Wochenschrift* 38, 2811*ff*.

[44] See Peter Ulmer (1975), 'Kündigungsschranken im Handels- und Gesellschaftsrecht: Zum Einfluss der Treupflicht auf die einseitige Vertragsbeendigung' in Wolfgang Hefermehl (ed), *Festschrift für Philipp Möhring*. Munich: Beck, 295*ff*, 307; Oetker (1994), 314;

required to provide a longer than usual period of notice because, as is also the case in long-term contracts, the normal applicable notice period would place the contractual partner at an undue disadvantage. In addition, multilaterality also creates the need for a longer period of notice when the impact upon the entire network would otherwise be disproportional. The Civil Code provides the requisite legal basis (§§ 627(II),[45] 671(II),[46] 723(II)[47] BGB), by precluding the normal period of notice at inopportune times. In comparison to far more intrusive strictures against opportunistic franchisee behaviour (for example, a contractual stipulation of re-investment), the duty to give notice of termination is to be assessed in relation to the entire network from according to the standard of proportionality.[48] In particular, network centre rights to terminate are restricted where members have made irreversible investments; in other words, where economic goods cannot be immediately capitalised and amortisation is only possible if the contractual relationship is maintained.[49] The network purpose also acts as a limit on the loyalty duties owed to the network centre. The Benetton 'shock-advertising' case law demonstrates that, all extreme centralisation tendencies within franchising apart, franchisees need not tolerate centrally directed advertising strategies where these endanger the overall profitability of the network.[50]

Joachim Jickeli (1996), *Der langfristige Vertrag: Eine rechtswissenschaftliche Untersuchung auf institutionenökonomischer Grundlage*. Baden-Baden: Nomos, 320; Lange (1998), 600*f*; Kulms (2000), 243*f*; Schimansky (2003), 187*ff*.

[45] The person obliged to perform services may only give notice in such a manner that the person entitled to services can obtain the services elsewhere, unless there is a compelling reason for untimely notice of termination. If he should give notice in untimely fashion without such cause, then he must compensate the person entitled to services for damage arising from this.

[46] An agent may only give notice in such a manner that the principal can make other arrangements for the transaction to be carried out, unless there is a compelling reason for premature termination. If he gives premature notice of termination without such a compelling reason, then he must compensate the principal for the damage thus incurred.

[47] Notice of termination [of a partnership] may not be premature unless there is a compelling reason for the premature termination. If a partner gives premature notice of termination without such a reason, then he must compensate the remaining partners for the damage thus incurred.

[48] On prescribed reinvestment, see Klein and Saft (1985), 352.

[49] This question is not dealt with in depth here since it regards long-term contracts and not multilaterality. See, however, Kulms (2000), 243*f*; Schimansky (2003), 240*ff*.

[50] BGHZ 130, 196; BGH NJW 1995, 2490; BGH NJW 1995, 2492. Clearly, the causation problems here are almost impossible to solve.

V. PROFIT SHARING?

One of the most difficult issues of duties of loyalty in networks characterises the exemplary case with which this Chapter began: in the differentiated discount case, does the network purpose require the network centre to pass on its negotiated purchasing discounts to all franchisees? In more general terms: does the network purpose impose an obligation on the net centre to pass on all networking advantages to members of the network?

As stated above, the simple company law apportionment of advantages to the association does not work here, since there is one important feature that sharply distinguishes networking from corporate law. Networks are not characterised by the precedence of collective interest above individual interest. Instead, they are indelibly marked by the profit-sharing principle, which creates the specific characteristic of networking in comparison to both market transactions and organisations.[51] Whilst company law establishes an obligation to seek profit for the benefit of the corporation, networking, in exact contrast, entails a legal right of the members to utilise the combination of decentralised and centralised profit-seeking components. This principle is clearly institutionalised in decentralised networks and finds its legal mirror in their characterisation as connected contracts. In addition, the network purpose obliges the network centre in particular to maintain this combination of centralised and decentralised profit-seeking. Thus, an intense degree of central consideration for the interests of individual nodes is prescribed. There is a mentoring duty to the benefit of nodes that is not necessarily commensurate with the interest of the network centre, or indeed, the overall interest of the network. A precise description of this duty is to be found within the work of Hugh Collins, whose book *Regulating Contracts* stipulates that in:

> hybrids, the duty would require the dominant member of the organization to make decisions based upon rational business considerations aimed at maximizing the joint profit of all members of the organization.[52]

Such a duty to share profits is virulent not only in franchising, but also in virtual enterprises, and is particularly intense in the case of just-in-time systems. The entire institution would forgo its specific advantages in productivity, if it were simply to be understood as a pricing strategy whereby the focal firm minimises its own costs to the disadvantage of

[51] For an economic view on network typical profit-sharing, Brickley and Dark (1987), 411 *ff*; Norton (1988), 202*ff*; Dnes (1991), 134*ff*. See, more comprehensively, above, Chapter 2 (III) and Chapter 3 (III).

[52] Collins (1999), 253.

suppliers.[53] Just-in-time systems modelled on the Japanese example are founded within the *idée directrice* of profit-sharing between suppliers and producers: the focal firm directs the entire network process in all its material (R&D, construction, quality control, logistics) and value-oriented (supply conditions, pricing) facets. At the same time, it ensures a fair division of jointly maximised profits.[54] 'Suppliers within the system must retain sufficient operational autonomy to allow for the maximisation of their own organisational efficiency; at the same time, profit-sharing must be simply and "justly" organised.'[55] Organisational science literature emphasises 'just' cost and yield distribution and sees it as a functional precondition for the existence of just-in-time systems.[56] In the real world, however, power imbalances do affect the profit-sharing process. This is the reason why the productive power of co-operation must be maintained by means of carrots and sticks that intensify common productivity. As a consequence, the apportionment of profit deriving from jointly intensified productivity is a conflictual and antagonistic affair.[57] Legal institutions need to be established to facilitate mediation in the paradoxical situation of antagonistic co-operation and asymmetrical dependency. Social practices furnish us with models for the law, more particularly, within the practice of just-in-time systems, where ground rules for sharing profits are concluded and applied via standard practices.[58] System suppliers are legally entitled to be regarded as contractual partners for profit, rather than mere parties to an exchange.[59] Legal profit-sharing duties, which act as an equivalent to company profit distribution, contribute to the ability of just-in-time systems to maintain

[53] For a comprehensive institutional analysis, ranging from the issue of co-operative challenges within just-in-time systems to the question of profit sharing, Lange (1998), 43*ff*. See, for a good analysis of the juridification of co-operative relations from a sociological viewpoint, Casper (1995); (1996), 'German Industrial Associations and the Diffusion of Innovative Economic Organization', *WZB-Discussion Paper* FS I, 96*ff*; (2001) 397*ff*.

[54] Bieber (1997), 122*ff*.

[55] Lange (1998), 51.

[56] Jörg Sydow, Arnold Windeler, Michael Krebs, Achim Loose and Bennet von Well (1995), *Organisation von Netzwerken: Strukturationstheoretische Analysen der Vermittlungspraxis in Versicherungsnetzwerken*. Opladen: Westdeutscher, 80*ff*.

[57] Daniel Bieber and Dieter Sauer (1991), 'Kontrolle ist gut! Ist Vertrauen besser? "Autonomie" und "Beherrschung" in Abnehmer-Zuliefererbeziehungen' in Hans Gerhard Mendius and Ulrike Wendeling-Schröder (eds), *Zulieferer im Netz: Zwischen Abhängigkeit und Partnerschaft*. Cologne: Bund, 228*ff*; Daniel Bieber (1992), 'Systemische Rationalisierung und Produktionsnetzwerke' in Thomas Malsch and Ulrich Mill (eds), *ArBYTE: Modernisierung der Industriesoziologie?* Berlin: Edition Sigma, 271*ff*; (1997), 121*ff*; Markus Pohlmann, Maja Apelt, Karsten Buroh and Henning Martens (1995), *Industrielle Netzwerke: Antagonistische Kooperation an der Schnittstelle Beschaffung-Zulieferung*. Munich: Hampp.

[58] See Kulms (2000), 129, 248, with further references.

[59] Mack (1975), 143; Kulms (2000), 248.

the productivity of stable co-operation.[60] This ensures that producers cannot simply transfer their turnover risk to suppliers. At the same time, however, when market conditions are unfavourable, reductions of 'profit percentiles' to suppliers is also facilitated.[61]

Within franchising, by contrast, the profit-sharing issue becomes most apparent when the network centre deploys network power to gain better conditions for the entire network from an external contractual party. In common with the differentiated discount case, such advantages usually comprise favourable purchase conditions, as in the form of bulk purchasing discounts. Equally, however, franchising systems are also often afforded favourable credit terms by financial institutions by virtue of the overall financial status of the network.[62] Credit is also granted to suppliers on more favourable terms where the expectation is one that overall system success will be realised at the level of individual franchisees.[63] If a manufacturer's goods are successfully marketed by franchisees, marketing subsidies from manufacturers are often paid to the focal franchising firm. Should the network centre be obliged to pass on these subsidies to franchisees in their entirety?[64]

What impact does this network advantage have on the differentiated discount case? As noted above, the interpretation of the standard contracts used in franchising can only furnish an interim solution. At the very latest, case law will be required to identify a solution within the structures of distribution when, in response to recent Federal High Court jurisprudence, these standard clauses are 'modified' so that the duty to pass on benefits is weakened, struck out, or even explicitly excluded. As we have seen (above, section III), the network purpose imposes an intensified duty of loyalty upon the net centre, a duty to support the interests of the entire network. A purchasing order is not simply made to satisfy the needs of the network centre alone, but it also serves the needs of individual franchisees and the entire network. Whilst the network centre acts in the guise of a direct representative of the franchisees, the latter nonetheless independently conclude purchasing contracts with suppliers in their own name. By contrast, the net centre (in its own name) concludes a framework contract with suppliers 'for' the whole franchise

[60] This is not only a matter of wishful thinking, but is instead an observable trend within case law; see, especially, Casper (1995); (2001), 397*ff*, who observes judicial orientation towards productivity in innovative just-in-time systems.

[61] Kulms (2000), 249.

[62] According to information supplied by Reinhard Böhner, members of large franchising chains are in practice more usually granted favourable credit than individual dealers.

[63] Weber (1983), 349; Bayreuther (2001), 380.

[64] See OLG Munich WiB 1997, 1109; OLG Stuttgart 16 February 2001 – 2 U 218/99; BGH 17 July 2001 – VIII ZR 59/01. See, more generally, Böhner (1998), 109*ff*.

system. The notion of agency would seem to be appropriate in this case.[65] The franchisor concludes the framework contract in its own name, and, as representative of the franchisees, it also concludes it in their interests and at their expense.[66] Furthermore, the network centre avails itself of a joint purchasing power that only exists by virtue of networking between franchisees and subsidiaries of the net centre. In this context, the operations of the network centre, including prior stages of negotiation with suppliers, fall firmly within what we called the collective network realm. As a consequence (and with due regard to the agreement with the suppliers) the network centre in the Apollo case was acting, as most pungently formulated by the Frankfurt Court of Appeals, as a 'dependent trustee' of the franchisees.[67] Such dependency is by no means a contradiction of the more usual right of the centre to direct franchisees' operations. As the elaboration of 'symbiotic contracts' in particular demonstrated, networks habitually exhibit fluctuating asymmetrical constellations of interests, which can be utilised within specific realms to justify directive rights for one party or, alternatively, for the other.[68]

In principle, the franchisor's breach of duty is already apparent since the discount differentiation was not openly revealed to franchisees,[69] but was paid *ex post* and without the franchisees' knowledge to the franchisor in a dubious 'kick-back' practice. Operating within the collective realm, the network centre is here subject to greater duties of disclosure of information. The obligations established by the network purpose extend far beyond normal duties of disclosure in contracts.

In effect, the network purpose would here demand that all potential efficiency gains from networking should be shared in practice by the whole network. The reason for creating a franchising system, after all, is the fact that collective purchasing advantages will be enjoyed by franchisees when they actually purchase goods. The opportunities created by franchising are realised within exactly those forms of purchasing advantage that give franchisees competitive advantages over non-networked individual dealers. Overall network efficiency, however, can only be increased where individual franchisees also have the possibility of passing on the pricing advantages derived from bulk purchasing to clients. This precept finds further analogous support within the principles of

[65] In the Apollo case, the centre had reached explicit agreement with suppliers that franchisees would only receive a maximum discount of 38% rather than 52%.

[66] Generally, on trusteeship (*Treuhand*), see, Heinrichs in *Palandt* (2003), vor § 104, 25; vor § 164, 6.

[67] OLG Frankfurt 11 U (Kart.) 55/00, 24.

[68] Schanze (1991) 69; (1993), 691*ff*; Zwecker (1999), 164.

[69] In a similar case, dealing with marketing subsidies afforded to an automobile leasing franchise by a car manufacturer, the Munich Appeals Court (OLG Munich WiB 1997, 1109) deemed the franchise centre to be obliged to provide information on the subvention.

profit-sharing discussed above in relation to just-in-time systems: networking, it is thus indicated, entails a general obligation to ensure that all networking advantages are distributed amongst members of the network. The network centre that retains the major portion of discounts for itself is in breach of this obligation to ensure the efficiency of the entire network.

This rule realises 'double attribution' as a legal consequence of networking, as analysed in the previous Chapter.[70] To whom in the network are operations, risks, losses and profits to be apportioned: to individual members, to the network centre, or to the network as a whole? In contrast to corporate law, which generally prescribes collective attribution, franchising principally divides attribution between the network centre, on the one hand, and members of the network, on the other. Set against this, the network purpose acts as a regulatory principle for cases of 'contractual collision', altering the specifics of attribution when the contractual realm is superseded and the associational realm applies. As demonstrated above, bulk purchasing discounts fall squarely within the collective realm. With this, network-specific dual attribution comes into play. Thus, the discount should not automatically be apportioned to the network centre, but should initially be understood as taking the form of an advantage of networking that accrues to the entire network, and should then be distributed amongst members of the network according to the equal treatment principle, and to the network centre in the light of equitable considerations.

The final result is one that is distanced from the logic of exchange contracts, and one that appears clearly to resemble corporate law approaches. Nonetheless, specific differences for a network do exist that distinguish the law of networks from corporate law. In company law, profit is first apportioned to the corporation and only then distributed amongst corporate members under rules governing distribution of company profits. In contrast, the network is marked from the outset by a bias in favour of decentralisation, which is in turn corrected by co-operative obligations. The franchisor cannot only lay immediate claim to his 'corporate law' portion, but should be allowed to assert his right to a suitable portion of the discount in order to cover 'overhead costs'. This feature provides an exemplary instance of the distinction between profit-sharing in networks and the pooling of profits in corporations.

[70] See above, Chapter 3 (V).

VI. RISK DISTRIBUTION? NETWORK PURPOSE AND THE JUDICIAL REVIEW OF STANDARD FORM CONTRACTS

The network purpose – as distinct from the contractual exchange purpose and the common purpose in corporate law – is not only relevant for duties of loyalty, but also plays its part in the judicial review of standard form contracts applicable to business networks.[71] Nonetheless, the direct application of existing regulation of standard contract terms to novel networking forms is a highly unpalatable process, since such regulation is primarily tailored to bilateral contract logic and only embodies those equitable considerations that are specific to it. Network logic has created new contractual constellations, which are clearly different in their apportionment of risk from existing types of contract. Alternatively, network logic – more particularly, its one-sided transfer of risk to the other contractual party – can be corrected by means of existing equitable norms found within dispositive rules of contract law. The paradigmatic example is a clause within just-in-time contracts which excludes the buyer's duty to inspect the goods at the time of delivery. Does the logic of networks justify derogation from the legislatively imposed duties of inspection (§§ 377, 378 Commercial Code (*Handelsgesetzbuch, HGB*)) within just-in-time systems?

The introduction of lean production has resulted in a far-reaching restructuring of the German automobile industry. In particular, just-in-time agreements with suppliers now include total quality management provisions. This entails computer-based ordering and the supply of matching components at the exact time of assembly or of warehousing, as well as the technological and computerised integration of suppliers within the manufacturer's quality control system. Amongst others, standard form contracts contain the following clauses: 1) inspection duties of the commercial code are suspended; 2) 'suppliers bear full responsibility for the assured quality of their products'. In the course of supply relations, there occur, nevertheless, defective products that are neither recognised by suppliers during the exit control process nor during the manufacturer's assembly process. A minimal entry control process would have revealed their existence. Defects in final products may result in massive reductions in value and associated costs. What happens if the manufacturer asserts its guarantee by claiming damages against its suppliers?

The notion of network purpose is relevant to the process of judicial review of standard contracts (under §§ 305*ff* Civil Code (BGB)) in a variety of ways: first, for the applicability of standard contract terms

[71] See Lange (1998), 123*ff*, 334*ff*; Rohe (1998), 397*ff*, 437*ff*, 466*ff*; Bayreuther (2001), 166*ff*.

regulation; second, for the underlying justification for the suspension of inspection duties; and third, for the potential compensation by other standard clauses for the exclusion of the inspection duty.

The formal applicability of standard contract regulation to just-in-time contracting is based on § 310 Civil Code (BGB).[72] Judicial review cannot be circumvented with the argument that contractual networks are founded within 'individually fashioned negotiation' in the sense specified by the provisions of § 305(I) Civil Code (BGB):[73] in order to achieve the network purpose within just-in-time systems the manufacturer needs to conclude the same contract with a variety of suppliers. The unitary nature of contracts within a supply network must always be guaranteed in order to effectively bind a variety of suppliers to the manufacturer, and to thus ensure the desired network effects. In particular, no manufacturer would agree upon the 'real possibility' of entry control with one supplier, denying others this opportunity. Case law, however, has identified the notion of 'real possibility' as the threshold criterion for the existence of individually fashioned negotiation.[74] Equally, however, even should various critical points within the overall contract be modified via negotiation, the entire clausal framework would still not constitute an individual contract.[75] Thus, just-in-time contracts are regularly subject to judicial control under §§ 307, 310 Civil Code (BGB).

However, it seems that the 'network purpose' would justify suspension of the inspection duty imposed by §§ 377*ff* HGB. Admittedly, the 1991 Pizza-Salami decision of the Federal High Court held that a clause allowing derogation from the inspection duty would constitute an inappropriate disadvantage, both since it infringed the equitable purpose of dispositive law in ensuring the speed and transparency of business

[72] § 310 (1) BGB: § 305 (2) and (3) and §§ 308 and 309 do not apply to standard business terms which are used in contracts with an entrepreneur, a legal person under public law or a special fund under public law. § 307 (1) and (2) nevertheless apply to these cases in sentence 1 to the extent that this leads to the ineffectiveness of the contract provisions set out in §§ 308 and 309; reasonable account must be taken of the practices and customs that apply in business dealings.
§ 307 BGB: (1) Provisions in standard business terms are ineffective if, contrary to the requirement of good faith, they unreasonably disadvantage the other party to the contract with the user. An unreasonable disadvantage may also arise from the provision not being clear and comprehensible.
(2) An unreasonable disadvantage is, in case of doubt, to be assumed to exist if a provision is not compatible with essential principles of the statutory provision from which it deviates, or limits essential rights or duties inherent in the nature of the contract to such an extent that attainment of the purpose of the contract is jeopardised.

[73] On this question in just-in-time systems, see Bernhard Nagel (1991), 'Schuldrechtliche Probleme bei Just-in-time-Lieferbeziehungen', *Der Betrieb* 44, 319*ff*, 321; Martinek (1993b), 308*ff*; (1993c), 311*f*; Westphalen and Bauer (1993), 8*f*; Lange (1998), 123*ff*, 175.

[74] For example BGH ZIP 1983, 76; BGH BB 1987, 784; BGH ZIP 1987, 448.

[75] Ralph Schuhmann (1996), 'Die Verhandlung komplexer Vertragsverhältnisse unter dem Aspekt des AGB-Gesetzes', *Betriebs Berater* 51, 2473*ff*, 2475; Lange (1998), 123.

operations, and also since it paid insufficient regard to the primacy of the buyer's interest in the avoidance of losses.[76] Accordingly, portions of the literature do deem clauses that derogate from the duty inspect goods within just-in-time systems to be void.[77] Nonetheless, the question remains as to whether this decision can be analogously applied to just-in-time supply systems, since they embody an innovation beyond the more usual business of contractual exchange, to which the provisions of the good old Commercial Code (HGB) are not tailored.[78] The exacting nature and rapidity of the integrated quality assurance system determine that all quality controls should be transferred to the production sites of suppliers.

Any analogous application of the High Court's finding that the duty of inspection imposed by the German Commercial Code cannot be suspended would leave the law entrapped within an old-fashioned supply model based upon strict divisions between business organisations. Such a 'traditional ritual' would trumpet the law's inability to adapt to new forms of hybrid or symbiotic contracts.[79] Such an application by analogy from ordinary sales would also be far too paternalistic, since suspension of the duty of inspection does not concern consumer protection, but is instead a matter of risk distribution within business operations. Equally, it would increase transaction costs as entry control measures would have to be installed for formalistic legal reasons alone and not because production technology demanded them. In effect, this would entail the unnecessary duplication of quality control mechanisms. Finally, maintenance of the duty of inspection would be an obstacle to innovation, since innovative contractual regimes would necessarily be stifled by a stubborn blanket application of the burden of inspection.[80] Seen from the perspective of the network purpose, in this context it is therefore justifiable to suspend the duty of inspection and to substitute supplier exit control mechanisms for manufacturer entry control.

This does not mean, however, that the network purpose would justify derogation from the duty of inspection without any form of compensation. Rather, the network purpose suggests a distinction in this

[76] BGH NJW 1991, 2633, 2634.

[77] Westphalen and Bauer (1993), 28*ff*; Barbara Grunewald (1995), 'Just-in-time-Geschäfte: Qualitätssicherungsvereinbarungen und Rügelast', *Neue Juristische Wochenschrift* 48, 1777*ff*, 1780*ff*; Uwer and Uwer (1997), 51.

[78] Horst Wildemann (1990), *Das Just-in-Time-Konzept: Produktion und Zulieferung auf Abruf*. Munich: Transfer-Centrum, 267; Nagel (1991), 323; Steinmann (1993), 30; Ensthaler (1994), 818; Rohe (1998), 399.

[79] Ludger Michael Migge (1991), 'Deutschland: Praktische Überlegungen bei der Vorbereitung von Qualitätssicherungsvereinbarungen', *Produkthaftpflicht International* 10, Part 1: 186–96, Part 2: 198–203, 200.

[80] Lehmann (1990), 1852; Nagel (1991), 323; Martinek (1993b), 336; (1993c), 333; Stoffels (2001), 263.

case: the organisational regulation of the inspection by means of a duty to establish entry quality control (§ 377*ff* HGB) must be distinguished from the regulation of risk found within the same provisions.[81] Organisational reasons indeed justify a substitution of manufacturer's entry control by suppliers' exit control. Network purpose, however, does not justify at all the sole apportionment of the risks of liability arising out of the allocation of the burden of inspection onto suppliers.[82] This is also the stance adopted by the Federation of German Industry (*Bund der Deutschen Industrie* (BDI)). According to the BDI working group on supply issues, 'fair quality assurance agreements should avoid any stipulation that would unduly impact upon the compulsory insurance protection of a participant, for example, by means of the total suspension of the entry quality control of the ordering party'.[83]

The substantive degree of transfer of risk which stems from the suspension of the duty of inspection is in fact dramatic. Initially this concerns the contractual warranties given between manufacturer and supplier. The manufacturer's action against the supplier would be precluded by § 377 of the commercial code were no immediate complaint made about an apparent defect. However, where this obligation is suspended, the result is a transference of risk to suppliers. The supplier is now liable for defects under contract law warranty rules. Liability might equally be increased under the applicable standard business terms.

A transfer of risk also arises within product liability under § 1 of the Product Liability Law (*Produkthaftungsgesetz* (ProdHG)). Granted, both manufacturers and suppliers qualify as manufacturers under § 4 ProdHG and are thus jointly and severally liable under §§ 5 and 1 ProdHG, such that suspension of the duty of inspection does not transfer the risk to external parties. Equally, both would be liable under the tort law provisions of §§ 823*ff*[84] Civil Code (BGB). Nonetheless, the subsequent apportionment of the debt is decisively altered by the suspension of the inspection duty. § 5 ProdHG and § 426 BGB apportion internal liability according to the circumstances, the degree of causation and the degree of fault. Contractual provisions altering liability apportionment are, however, recognised as valid. The suspension of the duty of inspection thus impacts upon liability to third parties, with the effect that in the final

[81] See also Lange (1998), 180.

[82] This is the core of the argument presented by Friedrich von Westphalen (1993), 'Qualitätssicherungsvereinbarungen: Prüfstein für AGB-Klauseln und Versicherungsschutz', *Computer und Recht* 9, 65*ff* and Grunewald (1995), who consider the suspension of inspection duty invalid.

[83] 'Leitsätze des BDI für Zuliefererbeziehungen 1994', IV 2*f*, 11.

[84] (1) A person who, intentionally or negligently, unlawfully injures the life, body, health, freedom, property or another right of another person is liable to make compensation to the other party for the damage arising from this.

analysis suppliers are the party which is liable.[85] The nub of the problem is the attendant risk of product liability; this is particularly so, since the opportunities to insure against this risk are limited.[86]

Such a dramatic degree of transfer of risk from a manufacturer to a supplier is by no means justified by the network purpose. Exactly the opposite: the real aim of networking is the establishment of an unusually close degree of co-operation between suppliers and manufacturers in the transition from a typical business operation through exchange contracts to just-in-time systems. One-sided transference of risk would be counterproductive. In practice, it would even endanger the purpose of the just-in-time contract under the terms of § 307(II)2 BGB, which declares a contractual clause to be invalid if 'it threatens the achievement of the purpose of the contract'. Network purpose thus demands equivalents that will substitute for the risk distribution originally foreseen by § 377 HGB, especially if, for organisational reasons, entry quality control is dispensed with. The quest for equivalents is certainly possible within judicial review of standard contracts, since the law allows for the use of other clauses in order to compensate for the invalidity of unfair clauses.[87]

The decisive question is then as follows: which clauses will compensate for a derogation from the duty to inspect incoming goods? A large portion of the literature is happy simply to accept that the usual quality assurance systems furnish adequate compensation.[88] This position, however, could be criticised for lacking sufficient differentiation, because the case law is often confronted with the following dilemma: in practice, simple price strategies do exist, which have little to do with the innovative restructuring of exchange contracts into closely co-operative just-in-time systems, and are instead all about the transference of risks to suppliers under the veil of the 'just-in-time' label.[89] Furthermore, 'true' innovations are also constructed differently. Is the judiciary in a position to develop the descriptive and control criteria that these distinctions necessitate? This differentiation, however, should not simply work with

[85] See, for a detailed analysis, Martinek (1993c), 318*ff*; Maximilian Fuchs (1994), 'Arbeitsteilung und Haftung', *Juristenzeitung* 49, 533*ff*, 538; Bernhard Nagel (1995), 'Gewährleistung und Produkthaftung im internationalen Produktionsverbund', *Der Betrieb* 48, 2581*ff*, 2582; Wellenhofer-Klein (1999), 332*ff*.

[86] Friedrich von Westphalen (1997), 'Deutschland: Optimale Vertragsgestaltung im Verhältnis Endhersteller/Zulieferer bei grenzüberschreitenden Lieferbeziehungen', *Produkthaftpflicht International* 16, 2*ff*, 2, 5; for an in-depth analysis of risk insurability, see Wellenhofer-Klein (1999), 285*ff*.

[87] On compensation in standard contract terms regulation, see Heinrichs in *Palandt* (2003), § 307, 10, with further references.

[88] Wildemann (1990), 266*f*; Martinek (1993c), 330*ff*; Saxinger (1993), 216*f*; Steinmann (1993), 873; Rohe (1998), 400*ff*; Baumbach and Hopt (2000), § 377, 6; Stoffels (2001), 263. In contrast, Grunewald (1995), 1777, does not consider this to be adequate.

[89] See here, the revealing empirical studies based on game theory, Casper (1995); (1996); (2001).

sociological typologies, but should instead be evolved in line with due regard to differing degrees of 'organisational dominance' and 'risk co-ordination'.[90] In effect, the issue is not one of the precedence of supplier interests. Rather, the legal policy is to secure demanding technological co-ordination between different stages in the market through legal protection of autonomy and legal support for co-operation within complex contractual relations.

Such a normative perspective for review of standard contracts within business networks can be gleaned from recent Federal High Court jurisprudence on another type of network, that is, the credit card contract systems.[91] Here the Court has used the regulation of standard form contracts to justify a dual intervention into the distribution of risk between different network participants. The one-sided comprehensive transference of the risks of the misuse of credit cards from issuers of credit cards to their contractual business partners was deemed invalid, since risk arising within the institution of the credit card system was declared to be 'procedurally immanent'. At the same time, the Court gave notice that it would, 'in view of the mutual interest in increased profit', accept a clause 'that appropriately shares the risk of misuse amongst issuers of credit cards and contracting businesses'. Whilst it does not yet make the network a corporate entity, 'mutual interest in increased profit' is exactly the typical network constellation that does necessitate a proportionate distribution of risk between network participants.

Criteria for proportionate distribution are furnished, in particular, by the 'procedurally immanent' nature of the risks posed by partial performances within the network, which cannot be apportioned to individual net members. Equally, however, degrees of dominance and insurance issues also have their role to play.[92] The legal test is whether contractual risk distribution can be made compatible with the real room for manoeuvre that parties have in relation to the control of risk.[93] Redistribution of risk is then called for where judges identify a striking mismatch between the allocation of risks by the contract and the practical capacity for control of risk.

Generalising these considerations, Kulms has developed alternatives to individual risk apportionment within the network.[94] He criticises Rohe's network contract, since, whilst this apportions risks to individual

[90] On the legal relevance of both of these criteria in just-in-time systems, Wellenhofer-Klein (1999), 282*ff*, 308*ff*.

[91] BGH JZ 2002, 1167.

[92] Heermann (2002), 'Anmerkung zu BGH JZ 2002, 1167' *Juristenzeitung* 57, 1170*ff*, 1173, applies the trilateral synallagma to the relationship between credit card system participants to come to a similar result, ending in risk and liability sharing.

[93] Wellenhofer-Klein (1999), 164*f*.

[94] Kulms (2000), 186f.

parties according to 'network duties of conformity', it fails to tackle the question of how uncertainty about future market evolution can be coped with in institutional structures. The solution is risk sharing via arrangements within complex contracts that bear a strong resemblance to formal organisations. Intensified duties of loyalty would take on the role played by genuine internal corporate rules. Applying this idea to the problems of entry control of quality, the duty of inspection (§§ 377*ff* HGB) might only be suspended when the 'supplier is adequately insured against risks in a different manner – say, through corporate compensation mechanisms'.[95]

Building on this, the suggestion is made here that judicial review of standard form contracts should evolve a differentiated scheme of risk distribution that is suitably adapted to three different groups of just-in-time system that have evolved in practice.

1. Cost Strategies

The just-in-time systems that have often been developed within the automobile, electrical and chemical sectors entail simple transference of risk to suppliers, but they do not give rise to real innovations of co-operation and mutual support.[96] Such 'fake' just-in-time systems are simple veils for pricing strategies. Manufacturers are aiming purely to save inventory costs and to speed up supply without, however, having any interest in technical integration or rationalising co-operation with suppliers.

In such cases, there is little reason why the strict Federal High Court stance adopted in the Pizza-Salami case should not apply, such that suspension of the duty of inspection would also be declared inadmissible in the face of a sham 'just-in-time' system.[97] Such cost strategies do not actually transform the exchange contract into a hybrid business network, which might justifiably claim that the imperatives of co-operation demand derogation from the inspection duty. Suspension of the duty is simply inadmissible. Distribution of risk between supplier and manufacturer would continue to be regulated by the rules of the Commercial Code.

[95] Kulms (2000), 232, 249.

[96] Casper (1995); (2001), 397*ff*. On risk transference by means of purchasing provisions, Wellenhofer-Klein (1999), 201*ff*.

[97] To this degree correct, Westphalen (1993), 68; Westphalen and Bauer (1993), 28*ff*; Grunewald (1995), 1780*ff*; Uwer and Uwer (1997), 51.

2. Modular Strategy

A second business strategy, drawing heavily upon the North American model, continues to pay full respect to the boundaries between business organisations, by concluding just-in-time agreements in the form of 'modular contracts'. This strategy is designed to ensure that standard market relations are maintained between manufacturers and suppliers, which both facilitate competition between suppliers and enable speedy transference to new suppliers. Business boundaries between suppliers and manufacturer are clearly maintained by means of strict formalisation of rules, duties and technical arrangements (modules). These boundaries are thus not only secured but also explicitly delineated. In the absence of vertical agreements, contractual arrangements ensure that each side exhibits a relatively low degree of asset specificity.[98]

This has a particular result for the regulation of standard form contracts. Whilst the duty of inspection might, technically speaking at least, be derogated from, the same is not true for risk distribution. When, all other distinctions between spheres of responsibility notwithstanding, the manufacturer's control over quality on delivery is replaced by the supplier's exit control for quality, this is, in effect, a clear case of delegation of quality oversight to suppliers by the manufacturer, who can thus not rid himself of liability for risks. In this situation, the manufacturers should be obliged by a contractual clause to exercise oversight over the supplier's exit quality control mechanisms and therefore also continue to bear the risk of 'non-censured' defects. The mode of risk distribution indicated by case law, which is discussed above, impacts strongly here.[99] The manufacturer can only free itself from the impact of these rules through the creation of a functional equivalent to §§ 377*ff* HGB, such as through a contractual commitment to joint liability for products, and then only in those exact proportions suggested by the duties of inspection imposed under business law.[100]

3. Pooling Strategy

A third strategy aims at a high integration of suppliers within the manufacturer's production operations with the aid of informational strategies and informal co-operation. The boundaries between firms are

[98] Casper (1995); (2001), 397*ff*. On modular suppliers, see also Horst Wildemann (1993), *Entwicklungsstrategien für Zulieferunternehmen: Forschungsbericht*. Munich: Transfer-Centrum, 143; Jörg Freiling (1995), *Die Abhängigkeit der Zulieferer: Ein strategisches Problem*. Wiesbaden: Deutscher Universitätsverlag, 172, 221; Wellenhofer-Klein (1999), 73.

[99] BGH JZ 2002, 1167.

[100] Grunewald (1995), 1784; Wellenhofer-Klein (1999), 347.

blurred to form a hybrid network, within which not only the chances but also the risks of the rationalisation strategy are enjoyed and borne in equal measure, that is, they are pooled. Such just-in-time systems entail 'resource pooling'. Commonly, the relationship evolves in the direction of single sourcing for supplies. The degree of co-operation is so intense that learning externalities arise. With this, the asset specificity of each side is greatly increased. Accordingly, a strong pooling element is built into the exchange contracts, which has a particular impact on the governance mechanism. The pooling strategy relates to profits. An intensive degree of quality assurance co-operation is present beyond the boundaries of individual firms; a form of co-operation that plays host to the transference of entry quality control to supplier production sites.[101]

Within this context, judicial regulation of standard terms must recognise that a suspension of the duty of inspection is indeed a necessary consequence of pooling. A duty of inspection would not make organisational sense. Neither, however, would individual apportionment of risk tally with the process of resource risk pooling. This is thus another instance in which judicial pronouncements on risk distribution in networks have an impact.[102] Compensatory clauses of fair risk distribution must be activated, which extrapolate from the pooling character of the entire just-in-time framework. In this context, the primary criterion would again be the 'procedurally immanent' apportionment of risks to each participant in the network, backed up by the secondary criteria of the degree of dominance and the insurability of the risk. If the contracts envisage a proportional pooling of the costs of risk control and other risks, the rules about risk imposed by §§ 377*ff* HGB can be avoided, so that costs may be shared in direct proportion to the value of the component to the final product.[103] Finally, individual apportionment must take place under the application of a formula that encapsulates value relationships within pooling.

The solution proposed here for duties of inspection proves to be generally applicable to other legal problems posed by just-in-time systems. The underlying principle is one in which the criteria for regulation of standard terms should be differentiated in line with the real nature of the particular just-in-time system. If the operation is a simple fig leaf for a strategy for the reduction of costs, the Federal High Court case law can be applied without further ado to all standard contract

[101] Casper (1995); (2001), 397*ff*. The term 'system suppliers' is also deployed here in order to emphasise the high degree of integration: Wildemann (1993), 143; Freiling (1995), 170; Wellerhofer-Klein (1999), 73.

[102] BGH JZ 2002, 1167.

[103] Likewise, Kulms (2000), 232, 249; see also arguments on the value relationship in Wellenhofer-Klein (1999), 296*ff*.

terms that reek of misuse of power. With regard to modular strategies, in contrast, derogations from positive law are possible in the case of proportional risk distribution. In the case of true pooling strategies, individual apportionment of risk is difficult and the matter should be decided with regard to the community sharing the risk. These distinctions should apply to all regulation of standard business terms, from price reduction clauses to one-sided performance provisions, renegotiation duties and temporal clauses.[104]

In conclusion, immanent risk distribution under positive law can only be derogated from to the degree that the manufacturer establishes proportional risk distribution. With this, 'old-fashioned' duties of inspection contained in the Commercial Code and other similar norms, which have no practical organisational relevance within just-in-time systems, are afforded a new function within judicial regulation of contracts. Now they might instead be deployed as a lever by the judiciary in their efforts to ensure an appropriate contractual model for novel networks.

[104] On standard contract terms regulation of these clauses, see Lange (1998), 126*ff*.

5

Piercing Liability Within the Network

The Special Relationship between Members of the Network Who Are Not Contractual Partners

I. FREE RIDING IN THE NETWORK

A CAR LEASING business is organised as a franchising network. In contravention of the systems contract with the franchisor, one franchisee maintains its cars in a highly dilatory manner. Customers are often afflicted by breakdowns or complain about other problems with the vehicles. Following the appearance in the local press of an article detailing quality failures within the named car leasing business, profits fall for all franchisees within the region. Despite the article, the dilatory franchisee continues to tolerate failures in quality. This situation is discovered by a more conscientious franchisee and reported to the franchisor. The franchisor, however, takes no action. Can the conscientious franchisee directly enforce an action against its dilatory colleague, in order to ensure the maintenance of quality standards?

The economic analysis of franchising by Klein and Saft was the first firmly to place the challenging issue of 'free-riding' in networks on the regulatory agenda.[1] An individual network member can minimise his own costs by undercutting standards, whilst at the same time profiting from the reputation established by other members who maintain higher standards. Hierarchical regulation of free-riding is notoriously ineffective. As a direct result, heterarchical control mechanisms maintained by other members of the network against a free-rider are highly significant. However, private law is, conceptually speaking, remarkably ill-prepared to deal with horizontal network relations. According to standard opinion, vertical relationships within distribution contracts – be

[1] Klein and Saft (1985), 349*ff*, 'The Economics of Free Riding'; Rohe (1998), 444, 476*f*; Bayreuther (2001), 379; Stoffels (2001), 264*f*; Schimansky (2003), 117*ff*. The well known McDonald's Case addressed by the Federal High Court had clear free-riding elements, BGH NJW 1985, 1894 (failure of McDonald's franchisees to observe the prescribed grilling temperature). For a different constellation, see Martinek (1992), 173.

they related to earnings, price, distribution or quality – generally have no direct horizontal effect amongst system participants. The manufacturer, supplier or franchisor may possess contractual claims in such vertical relations, such as a claim for an injunction instructing a franchisee to desist from behaviour that constitutes a breach of contract. Other participants such as dealers, suppliers or franchisees, by contrast, possess no directly enforceable claims against one another.[2] Vertical relationships are not construed as contracts for the benefit of third parties in the sense of § 328 Civil Code (BGB).[3] Whilst the number of persons claiming protection with regard to franchising is, in stark comparison to the case of expert liability, clearly restricted to those who participate in the system, liability of a franchisee for damages to other franchisees in accordance with a contract with protective effects for a third party (§ 328 BGB) is rejected by virtue of the risk of the unforeseeable extent of liability.[4] Notwithstanding all the problems of centralised control, protection of the franchising system against damage caused by the undercutting of standards is deemed to be the exclusive concern of the franchisor, who might initially enforce claims for the fulfilment of quality standards, and who, in any case, also possesses various simple means to terminate the contracts of free-riders.[5] It seems that the franchisor's obligations of good faith and responsibility towards conscientious franchisees, together with his duty to promote the franchising system, oblige him to take action against free-riders. In the case of a culpable failure to do so, the conscientious franchisee might be able claim damages from the franchisor on the basis of a failure to perform the contract.

The weakness of centralised oversight is, however, obvious. The franchisor is not always interested in the maintenance of the system of standards. Opportunistic and collusive behaviour does arise: the system centre may be poorly organised; the franchisor may desist from action against free-riding on the grounds of *de minimus non curat praetor*; the franchisor may maintain a personal relationship with the free-rider; or, the franchisor may feel it would be inopportune to take action against a particularly profitable franchisee. Similarly, whilst cases of opportunistic

[2] Baumbach and Hefermehl (2001), § 1 UWG, 789*ff*, 800*f*; Habermeier in Martinek and Semler (1996), § 33, 51*ff*; Rohe (1998), 436*f*; Schimansky (2003), 117*ff*.

[3] § 328 BGB: (1) Performance to a third party may be agreed by contract with the effect that the third party acquires the right to demand the performance directly.
(2) In the absence of a specific provision it is to be inferred from the circumstances, in particular from the purpose of the contract, whether the third party is to acquire the right, whether the right of the third party is to come into existence immediately or only under certain conditions, and whether the power is to be reserved for the parties to the contract to terminate or alter the right of the third party without his approval.

[4] Rohe (1998), 436*f*: clearly 'not desirable … because of incalculable accumulation of damages'.

[5] Rohe (1998), 439, 444, with reference to BGH NJW 1985, 1894.

franchisor behaviour in relation to the undercutting of standards may be an exception, the network centre nonetheless has an explicit conflict of interests in instances of peer-to-peer encroachment.[6] Where franchisees increase profits at the cost of other franchisees, the network centre profits from such 'unfair' inter-brand competition, at least to the degree that the profitability of the overall system also increases. Similarly, the network centre has very little motivation to intervene should profits not actually fall.

Just-in-time systems and virtual enterprises are also marked by the problem of the undercutting of standards and its consequences for conscientious suppliers. Owing to multiple interconnections of business operations, relations between suppliers are far more intense than within an ordinary distribution system. Just-in-time production modes necessitate intense relations both between suppliers and the manufacturer and between suppliers themselves.[7] Despite the independence of individual relations of supply, individual contracts must also be constructed in a manner that is compatible with the entire system. In particular, they must contain interconnections with other contracts. Intense personal networking, founded in close informational and technological relations, demands a dovetailing of supply and performance. This gives rise to a multifaceted relational network that is dependent upon constant communication.[8]

However, in exactly this case, Rohe, for example, denies that such interconnectedness is legally relevant.[9] Lange, in contrast, is aware of the problem and chooses a different path, by seeking to apply the principles that underlie contracts with third party protective effects, in order to argue for liability between suppliers on the basis of the interdependencies of suppliers within just-in-time systems.[10] The situation is similar in relation to virtual enterprises. Arguments are likewise made here in favour of contracts with protective effects for third parties; regulation is deemed necessary by virtue of the intense co-operation and co-ordination of individual performances.[11]

[6] The circle of a franchisee's potential victims is increased in the case of its breach of the explicit or implicit contractual rules of the franchising contract, to the degree that it encroaches upon the sphere of operations or circle of customers of another franchisee and at that franchisee's cost. Such cases are particularly current among authorised dealers. They are also a general feature of other distribution systems, inclusive of franchising: Baumbach and Hefermehl (2001), vor § 1 UWG, 800*ff*; Habermeier in Martinek and Semler (1996), § 33, 51*ff*.

[7] Kulms (2000), 107.

[8] For just-in-time systems, Lange (1998), 425; for virtual businesses, Lange (2001a), 178*ff*; (2001b), 169*ff*; (2001c), 1805*ff*.

[9] Rohe (1998), 389.

[10] Lange (1998), 195*ff*, 200.

[11] Lange (2001a), 354*ff*.

Nonetheless, the whole notion of the contract with protective effects for third parties leads us systematically astray. Clearly, the issue of the undercutting of standards is not a problem of bilateral contracting that may have some third party effects, but rather a networking phenomenon, in which loss of quality through an undercutting of standards impacts upon the entire project. Undercutting of standards gives rise to a negative network effect, that is, a devaluation of the entire network, to which the network is prone by virtue of intense interaction between members of the network.[12] In contrast, the contract with protective effects for third parties was developed to manage the case of a contractually non-involved third party, who was adversely affected by the externalities of a bilateral contract. Accordingly, the notion of the contract with protective effects for third parties has required the development of criteria for the identification of a 'third party interest' (implied terms, performance proximity, fiduciary relationship with the third party), which seem to be irrelevant to the business networks at hand. There are perfectly valid reasons why the example of 'small-scale networks', that is, financed purchasing, has witnessed the choice of very different doctrinal constructions, which are far better suited to capturing the realities of comparable interconnections between non-contractually bound members of the network, or between vendor and the creditor.[13]

II. STRUCTURAL CONTRADICTION: COMPETITION VERSUS CO-OPERATION

If attention is paid to the underlying structural contradiction typical for networks, it is readily apparent that the issue is different from the externalities arising from individual contract to which law typically responds by the device of contracts with protective effects for third parties. Instead, this is a second typical constellation evolved by hybrid networks in response to contradictory market demands.[14] Knowledge-based production, in particular, is not only subject to the contradictory demands of bilateral exchange and multilateral organisation. This structural contradiction was the governing theme in the preceding Chapter where it was shown to overlay obligations maintained between the parties to a dominant exchange relationship.[15] Within the current context a further structural contradiction becomes apparent: the contradiction

[12] For negative network effects, Lemley and McGowan (1998), 198 and above, Chapter 6 (VI).

[13] Gernhuber (1973), 493; (1989), 741*f*: "special relation" (*Sonderverbindung*).

[14] See generally Chapter 2 (III).

[15] See Chapter 4 (II).

between competition and co-ordination.[16] Network participants are faced with contradictory instructions: 'Co-operate with each other!', but do not forget, 'Compete with each other!'. Evidently, this form of goal-conflict has little to do with the typical externality problems treated by the doctrine of contracts with protective effects for third parties and should thus be approached with very different doctrinal categories.

Knowledge-oriented production creates manifest contradictions between two underlying forms of social experience. In the competition model, individual goals can only be attained at the cost of another. In the co-operation model, the aims of the one coalesce with the aims of the other. However, whilst co-operation is predicated upon interaction, competition is almost free of interaction. Competitive behaviour is dependent neither upon negotiation nor upon consent, and is instead a result of the internal calculations made by one competitor about another's behaviour. Interactive encounters between competitors are not precluded, but are not a precondition for operations. Nonetheless, or to date at least, this particular model has only seemed possible where competitive behaviour is clearly separated from co-operation:

> From a social structural perspective, this requires a sufficient differentiation of competitive situations, which, in its turn, is only possible if competition can be adequately separated both from exchange and from co-operation. The individuals with whom one competes may not be identical with the individuals with whom one co-operates; and likewise, they may not be identical with those with whom one engages in exchange. The appropriate social models must be distinguished from one another and realised in isolation.[17]

In accordance with these insights, collisions between such logics of action have until now been solved by a forced 'either-or' decision. The result has been the well-known rigid division between market and hierarchy, reinforced by equally rigid competition, contract and company law provisions. Nonetheless, enforced dichotomies between market/hierarchy and contract/organisation obscure underlying paradoxes. They require that decisions be made in favour of one of the contradictory orientations, forcing the other into the penumbra of informality. They are only occasionally stumbled upon by subversive sociologists with an interest in the shadowy partners to formal institutions.

Recent management studies, however, suggest that alternatives to the strict competition–co-operation distinction are not only conceivable in

[16] Details on the co-operation/competition conflict, Sydow (1992), 98*ff*; (1999), 299*ff*; Jansen (2000), 13*ff*; Littmann and Jansen (2000), 64*ff*; Klaus Semlinger (2000), 'Kooperation und Konkurrenz in japanischen Netzwerkbeziehungen' in Jörg Sydow and Arnold Windeler (eds), *Steuerung von Netzwerken*. Opladen: Westdeutscher, 130*ff*, 141*ff*.

[17] Niklas Luhmann (1995a), *Social Systems*. Stanford: Stanford University, 522*f*.

theory, but also are wholly plausible in practice. The multiple appearances of hybrid networks are attributed to a refined reaction to contemporaneous and contradictory demands for competition and co-operation.[18] 'Co-opetition' is the new magic formula, denoting the advantages that may be gained from the combination of co-operation and competition within arrangements via networking elements.[19] Co-opetition not only allows, but rather demands that the individuals with whom one competes are identical to those individuals with whom one co-operates. If a network is to institutionalise this form of social model, it must, in reaction to paradoxes,

> [r]eflect external diversity within its own institutions and functions, in order to tackle it. One indication of this ability is the neologism, co-opetition, which seeks to capture the notion that antagonistic relations (co-operation and competition) might be maintained within one and the same system – a notion that is only a paradoxical one, if sectoral and temporal differentiations were to be ignored and totalised.[20]

Taking a certain distance from such pure 'combinatory' positions, attention should be paid to the potential for de-paradoxification through re-entry. Simple combinations of competitive and co-operative behaviours would not furnish a safe path out of paradoxical oscillation. The notion of 're-entry', in the technical sense ascribed to it by Spencer Brown, does not, by contrast, demand negation of the distinction between the two sides of one decision.[21] Exactly the opposite: the distinction between competition and co-operation must instead be rigorously maintained and legally institutionalised. At the same time, however, the distinction is drawn a second time. This time, however, it is re-introduced into one side of the institutional arrangement and then, for its part, rigorously institutionalised.

Under conditions of re-entry, mixed competition–co-operation forms might be said not to be regressive or ideological: otherwise they would simply represent the pursuit of one orientation, without regard for the other, under the semantic veil of 'combination'. Similarly, the notion of re-entry is preferred, because it does not simply squander the particular advantages in performance of each of the two social models that can only be realised through their strict institutional separation. Rather, under certain conditions, re-entry can create intensified advantages through internal differentiation, at least to the degree that its stable identity is secured. This is only possible, however, under three conditions:

[18] See especially Jarillo (1993); Neuberger (2000), 207*ff*.
[19] Littmann and Jansen (2000), 64*ff*.
[20] Neuberger (2000), 209.
[21] Spencer Brown (1972), 56*ff*; 69*ff*.

1) stable institutionalisation of market competition through the conclusion of parallel and distinct bilateral contracts (in contrast to the creation of a unitary organisation);
2) institutionalisation of the re-entry of the co-operation–competition distinction within the system of contracts, such that market competition is covered by a co-operative operational realm;
3) an internal distinction between operational realms according to defined contexts.

These conditions allow for competition and co-operation with identical individuals in circumstances in which each situation and each context is clear. This opportunistic change in the primary orientation is promoted by co-operation as a matter of imperative: on occasions, competition, on occasions, co-operation, each as the circumstances demand. The networking organisational form imbues this constant oscillation with legitimacy; it furnishes a stable institutional framework for constant vacillation between co-operative and competitive operational behaviour.

III. PIERCING WITHIN THE NETWORK?

Legal efforts to institutionalise the hybrid must take note of such complications. However, it is exactly this bundle of questions that fails to find potential answers within the Civil Code. Whilst the question posed by the previous Chapter – whether overarching net-specific viewpoints might be insinuated into individual bilateral contracts – finds potential interlocutors in applicable private law within notions such as extended contractual interpretation, duties of loyalty, and, of course within the general clause governing good faith (§ 242 BGB), here the question is a far trickier one: how can a contractual relationship be established between non-contractually bound members of the network? The question is one of whether sanctions arise as between members of the network who are not bound to one another in a bilateral contract for:

> [t]he injurious behaviour of a participant within a performance chain or a system of networked contracts. Such sanctions would be applicable to defects in performance within bundles of bilateral contracts organised in pursuit of a unitary common goal.[22]

As Picker has clearly demonstrated, mutual contractual liability of non-contractually bound partners within the network is a challenge to law that has grown ever more intense in pace with the increasing networking of services and goods markets. Not only the spontaneous demand for fair

[22] Picker (1987), 1057; similarly, the question posed by Möschel (1986), 187*ff*; Rohe (1998), 98.

treatment, but also the sober arguments for deterrence demand some form of legal liability, even though positive law apparently prevents such claims. Imposition of liability upon extra-contractual individuals is necessary within the network for cases of financial loss. By virtue of networking, such individuals are bound by multifarious co-operative relations. These relations represent novel relational phenomena: 'organised non-contractual performance relations'. They are to be identified within the network in the technical and/or organised practice of consensual co-ordination between actors who are not bound by a bilateral contract to each other. Consequently, such actors consciously choose not to enter into any form of legal relationship with one another. The connectivity of individual transactions and their co-ordination by an overall network purpose makes the conclusion of multilateral contracts between members of the network superfluous. Such modern forms of co-operation are distinguished from traditional contracting since they achieve the same 'contractual' effects through simple organisational planning, without seeking embodiment in explicit legal forms.[23]

Despite considerable opposition, as a result multiple demands are heard for piercing liability within the network, albeit based on very different constructions of the legal claim.[24] At the same time, however, such demands are fully in line with the case law of the Federal High Court on the operations of bank gironets, with their extension of the banks' liability to clients of other banks.[25] Similarly, in the case that prefaced the first Chapter, the Court threaded its way through a variety of hierarchical levels to impose piercing liability within the network.[26] A question nonetheless remains as to how such piercing liability within the network should be doctrinally constructed.

Academic literature, however, is highly critical of the idea that bilateral contracts should be afforded a legal 'external impact' upon other members of the network. The accusation is that attempts to introduce the notion of network as a legal concept are only motivated by efforts 'to postulate contractual relations for the sole purpose of founding liability obligations'.[27] Clearly, 'extra-contractual obligations' between partners of

[23] Picker (1999), 430, explicitly founding these thoughts in network theory, 433, fn 80. Similarly, Larenz and M Wolf (1997), 470.

[24] Generally arguing for piercing liability between members of the network who are not connected via a bilateral contract, Teubner (1993), 232; Larenz and M Wolf (1997), 470; Kulms (2000), 232 (with distinctions according to co-operation intensity, 233); Rohe (1998), 195*ff* (though only for heterarchical networks); Amstutz and Schluep (2003), 888*ff*; Schluep (2003), 302; for piercing liability in just-in-time systems, Zirkel (1990), 349; Lange (1998), 195*ff*; in virtual businesses, Lange (2001a), 188*ff*, 192; in franchising systems, Baumgarten (1993), 169*ff*; Krebs (2000) 381*ff*.

[25] Since BGHZ 96, 9, 17.

[26] OLG Stuttgart NJW-RR 1990, 491.

[27] Koller (1987), 25.

connected contracts are judged to contradict fundamental principles of private.[28] The question as to whether a legal relationship (performance obligations, duties of care, protective duties) exists between those participants in a network who are not directly bound to one another through a bilateral contract arises in a variety of forms. For example, within the heterarchical network, do legal relations exist between those members of the network who are not bound to one another through bilateral contracts? And, in the hierarchical network, do horizontal legal relationships exist between members of the network beyond their vertical contractual relationship with the centre?

IV. PIERCING LIABILITY WITHIN PARALLEL CONTRACTS

Whilst piercing liability is most pressing in relation to business networks, it is also present within other legal arenas, which exhibit comparable constellations of multiple contracts concluded in parallel. Thus, a brief glance at similar situations, in which 'extra-contractual loyalty duties' arise, proves useful here. Tenancy law is an appropriate comparator to franchising and other forms of business co-operation in the case that a landlord contracts with tenants within a residential or business complex in a series of parallel tenancy agreements, and thus creates an equivalent to vertical obligations.[29] Comparable with the situation in networks, the duties of good faith within an enduring tenancy relationship thus acquire a particular meaning.[30] Similar to business co-operation, the law imposes no comprehensive obligation upon the landlord to treat all tenants in the same manner. Just as a franchisor is free to conclude individual agreements on mutual obligations (geographical contractual reach, franchising rates, length of franchise etc) with franchisees, so too is the landlord fully within his rights to treat various tenants within one property in an unequal manner as regards rents or the length of the tenancy.[31] However, a duty of non-discrimination is imposed upon the landlord should the

[28] Vehement critique of the notion of network as a legal concept is mainly directed towards the legal consequences of extra-contractual obligations. See especially Hüffer (1987), 107; Koller (1987), 25; Schröter (1987), 127; Heermann (1998), 77; (2003), 95*f*. Decidedly contra piercing liability in subcontracting business, Günter Hager (1991), 'Die Verflechtung von Verträgen: Planung und Risikoverteilung bei Großprojekten' in Hans-Leo Weyers (ed), *Die Verflechtung von Verträgen: Planung und Risikoverteilung bei Großprojekten*. Baden-Baden: Nomos, 65*ff*, 110.

[29] See in detail Karl Riesenhuber (1997), *Die Rechtsbeziehungen zwischen Nebenparteien*. Berlin: Duncker & Humblot, 149*ff*, with further references.

[30] Voelskow in *Münchener Kommentar* (2003), §§ 535, 536, 5.

[31] Voelskow in *Münchener Kommentar* (2003), §§ 535, 536, 6.

contract for the tenancy encompass regulatory provisions with a 'collective character', such as, for example, the establishment of common rules for the rented complex (common house rules), or the regulation of the use of facilities used in common.[32]

The parallel question to quality standards within franchising is whether the common house rules can have legal effect as between tenants. This notion of a legally binding obligation is supported by the argument that the common house rules are generally established in the interests of all tenants, in order to ensure tranquil common use of the property.[33] Common house rules, which are effectively included within a contract, initially impose obligations upon the tenant towards the landlord, which the latter can either enforce under § 541 BGB,[34] or call upon in extreme cases to justify contractual termination under § 543 BGB.[35] Tenants, in contrast, only possess causes of action against other tenants under denial of proper usage regulation (§§ 862, 865 BGB),[36] with potential for attendant claims for damages (§ 823 BGB).[37] The landlord can, under certain circumstances, and in the interests of all tenants, be obliged by § 535 BGB to terminate the contract of a party disturbing common house rules without further notice.[38] To this degree at least, the law applying to tenancy agreements is comparable with that applying to franchising.

However, various concerns are expressed about this triangular solution. Focusing dispute resolution upon the landlord is criticised as

[32] Voelskow in *Münchener Kommentar* (2003), §§ 535, 536, 7.

[33] In principle, in agreement, Michael J Schmid (1987), 'Die Hausordnung in Miethäusern', *Wohnungswirtschaft und Mietrecht* 40, 71*ff*; Riesenhuber (1997), 149*ff*.

[34] If the lessee persists with use of the leased property in breach of contract despite a warning by the lessor, then the latter may seek a prohibitory injunction.

[35] Voelskow in *Münchener Kommentar* (2003), §§ 535, 536, 100. § 543(1) BGB: Each party to the contract may terminate the lease for cause without notice for a compelling reason. A compelling reason is deemed to exist if the party giving notice, taking into account all circumstances of the individual case, including without restrictions any fault of the parties to the contract, and after weighing the interests of the parties, cannot be reasonably expected to continue the lease until the end of the notice period or until the lease ends in another way.

[36] § 862(1) BGB: If the possessor of property is disturbed in his possession by an unlawful interference, he may require the disturber to remove the disturbance. If further disturbances are to be feared, the possessor may seek a prohibitory injunction. § 865 BGB: The provisions of §§ 858 to 864 above also apply in favour of a person who possesses only part of a thing, in particular separate residential space or other space.

[37] Weidenkaff in *Palandt* (2003), § 535, 28.

[38] A-G Bad Segeberg, *Wertpapiermitteilungen* 2000, 601. § 535(1)(1) BGB: A lease agreement imposes on the lessor a duty to grant the lessee use of the leased property for the lease period. The lessor must surrender the leased property to the lessee in a condition suitable for use in conformity with the contract and maintain it in this condition for the lease period. He must bear all costs to which the leased property is subject.

out-of-date, patriarchal, and an instance of private justice.[39] This, it is argued, distances those who are affected by a situation from its solution. As a consequence, many authors have suggested a departure from traditional triangular (tenant–landlord–tenant) treatment of such cases, in favour of piercing liability; they deploy common house rules to establish direct causes of action between tenants.[40] Case law has yet to establish a clear line in this respect.[41] However, the Munich High Court did on one occasion conclude that one tenant might not take legal action against another tenant under §§ 862 and 906 BGB[42] for practising a musical instrument, should that practice take place during times prescribed by common house rules. Importantly, the judgment implies that tenants do have the right to bring a claim against other tenants should the latter not be observing common house rules, and that they should not be obliged to follow the indirect route of requiring the landlord to take action. In the concrete case at hand, the right to maintenance of the house rules corresponded to an equal obligation to tolerate the practising of musical instruments during periods permitted by the house rules; an obligation that might also be enforced under § 862 BGB. Clearly, the judgment of the Munich High Court also found its alternative justification in the fact that the common house rules concretised 'normal behaviour' within the property in the sense of §§ 862 and 906 BGB.[43]

The real impetus for the creation of cross-cutting actions between tenants would seem to be the existence of common house rules or rules on the use of common facilities. In a more generalised formulation: parallel tenancy contracts must be covered by an overarching private order, which then creates a legal connection out of what are, in principle, distinct contracts. Piercing relations can only be established between

[39] Wüst (1958) 123; Adolf Arndt (1965), 'Umwelt und Recht', *Neue Juristische Wochenschrift* 18, 26*ff*; for the same issue in labour law, see Theo Mayer-Maly (1978), 'Das Rechtsverhältnis zwischen Arbeitnehmern (bei traditioneller Einzelarbeit)' in Theodor Tomandl (ed), *Innerbetriebliche Arbeitnehmerkonflikte aus rechtlicher Sicht.* Vienna: Braumüller, 59*ff*, 64*f*; Hermann Meissinger (1954), *Treupflicht im Arbeitsrecht I.* Wiesbaden: Forkel.

[40] Wüst (1958), 125; Friedhelm Weyer (1972), 'Mietvertrag und Schutzwirkungen zugunsten Dritter in der Rechtsprechung des Bundesgerichtshofs', *Betriebs Berater* 27, 339*ff*, 341*f*; Schmid (1987), 71*ff*; Marian Paschke (1991), *Das Dauerschuldverhältnis der Wohnraummiete: Grundfragen der privatautonomen Gestaltung des Wohnraummietverhältnisses.* Berlin: Duncker & Humblot, 128*ff*; Helmut Koziol (1994), 'Delikt, Verletzung von Schuldverhältnissen und Zwischenbereich', *Juristische Blätter* 116, 209*ff*, 220; Riesenhuber (1997), 149*ff*; Krebs (2000), 120, 305, each with different legal constructions.

[41] The Federal High Court judgment rejecting this approach (BGHZ 62, 243, 246*f*) only dealt with usage of a common lift and should thus not be taken as authority against the critical case of the creation of connectivity beyond a simple collection of parallel contracts.

[42] § 906 BGB establishes a law of private nuisance that permits reasonable use of property.

[43] OLG Munich NJW-RR 1992, 1097.

tenants in the concrete presence of such a connectivity of contracts. The simple existence of parallel contracts is not a sufficient precondition.

Connectivity is the decisive feature and founding principle of cross-cutting relations, which must be inferred from the particular circumstances in which 'neighbouring parties' conclude parallel contracts. Within labour law, any effort to establish mutual duties of loyalty between employees would, for example, be a step too far.[44] Rather, a concrete interconnectedness established amongst individual employees needs to overlay parallel individual performances. Neither the abstract notion of the 'collective of employees', nor simple spatial relations between employees, would be a sufficient precondition. Mutual loyalty duties amongst employees should only be recognised where performance of work is co-ordinated within consensual agreements and owed to employee groups established by the firm, or generated by employees themselves.[45]

The same is true when the instigator of a construction project concludes parallel works contracts. Case law is still very restrictive in the case of overarching relations:[46] in principle, parallel contractual performances remain separate, whilst the risks arising from co-ordination accrue exclusively to the project instigator, so that the various businesses involved owe no duties of loyalty to one another.[47] Nonetheless, the situation will be different if the project instigator were to create explicitly a connectivity between the parallel businesses by, for example, requiring one business to give support to the others. In addition, recent literature has argued in favour of a contract with protective effects for third parties between parallel businesses in cases of intense co-ordination, because the preconditions of proximity of performance and the existence of an interest on the part of the promise are deemed to be fulfilled, whilst the need for the protection of the third party is readily apparent.[48] Finally, relationships between contractor and subcontractors are generally governed by non-co-ordinated profit maximisation: in contrast, co-ordinated consensus is a prerequisite for co-operative behaviour.[49]

[44] Comprehensively, with further references, Riesenhuber (1997), 149*ff*.

[45] Bernd Rüthers (1977), 'Probleme der Organisation des Weisungsrechts und der Haftung bei Gruppenarbeit', *Zeitschrift für Arbeitsrecht* 8, 1*ff*, 31; Krebs (2000), 94, with further references.

[46] Critical toward this case law, Kulms (2000), 179*ff*.

[47] BGH NJW 1970, 38, 40.

[48] Rolf Kniffka (1999), 'Anmerkung zu OLG Düsseldorf' *Baurecht* 30, 1312*ff*, 1313: 'objektive Zweckgemeinschaft zwischen den am Bau Beteiligten'; Gisbert Kaiser (2000), 'Die konkurrierende Haftung von Vor- und Nachunternehmer' *Baurecht* 31, 177*ff*, 180*ff*.

[49] Kulms (2000), 179; this distinction appears in Hager (1991), 76*ff*, who argues in favour of strict separation within the contractual chain, but all too briefly.

V. EXTRA-CONTRACTUAL DUTIES OF LOYALTY

1. Unfair Competition Law

Our excursion through various other legal realms reveals that piercing liability is desirable when a concrete connectivity lies over the simple parallel contracts. But what is the legal basis for such liability between members of the network? An initial and fairly simple construction for direct causes of action amongst members of the network is one derived from competition law. One starting point is misuse of breach of contract with regard to competitors under § 1 of the Law Against Unfair Competition (*Gesetz gegen unlauteren Wettbewerb* (UWG)).[50] The hybrid nature of members of the network as 'co-opetitors' would initially seem to justify actions derived from unfair competition law. Nonetheless, given the particularly intense degree of incorporation of franchisees within a unitary franchising network, or of suppliers within just-in-time systems with a clearly delimited number of participants – a degree of intensity which is neither ordinarily present amongst parties to contracts nor established in cases of selective distribution – serious doubts might be raised. Is it really appropriate that causes of action be established between members of the network for the maintenance of standards, or for observance of duties to promote the network promotion, obligations that both establish the goodwill of the network and constitute the defining characteristic of the network, on the doctrinal basis of a law against unfair competition that is itself imbued with principles of tort law? Thus, the core of the wrong committed by a free-rider is not to be found in the fact that it injures rights that are effective between *all* competitors; nor does it derive from the fact that it infringes upon general duties of care imposed by normal market behaviour. Rather, the particular wrong of a breach of the duty of good faith alleged by the other members of the network arises out of the fact that the free-rider

[50] See Baumbach and Hefermehl (2001), § 1 UWG, 694*f*, 708, 718, 756*f*, 797, 806*ff*. Whether this principle can also be applied to free-riding remains an open question. An analogous application, however, might be argued for, because franchising systems also exhibit prescribed standards and similarly constructed vertical relationships, which create a competitive situation for franchisees as regards the quality of services: a competitive race to the bottom in terms of quality standards (outlet design, services presentation, quality of advice and service, number and education of employees) must be prevented at all costs. The franchisee who undercuts standards and who is in breach of contract is seeking an unearned profit (competitive performance failure) by taking undue advantage of the contractual conscientiousness of other members of the network and enters into competition over quality with those members, thus entering into the sphere of application of the Law Against Unfair Competition. [Editor's note: the German law on Unfair Competition was revised in 2004 (Gesetz gegen den unlauteren Wettbewerb vom 3. Juli 2004 (BGBl. I 2004 32/1414)), but the reform does not affect the points made here.]

freely commits himself to membership of the network, in order to benefit from the goodwill that this system establishes. In other words, he breaches the generalised reciprocity that is available to all members of the network. The free-rider consciously subordinates himself to duties which are immanent to the system and to the maintenance of specific standards, in the full knowledge that the purpose of these duties can only be achieved on the basis of mutuality between all members of the network.

2. Network Contract Claims

An elegant means of creating cross-cutting relations is apparently offered by the network contract. As the second chapter highlighted, Rohe argues for the creation of a network contract between all participants, on the basis that each member of the network implicitly affords each other member a power of agency to conclude a network contract with a third party, and on the presumption that each member of the network who concludes a bilateral network contract once again does so implicitly as an agent for all other members.[51] On this view, legal relations are established between all members of the network from the very outset, including members who played no part whatsoever in the conclusion of the bilateral contract. The agency solution gives rise to the same effects that are visible within a true multilateral contract where all members of the network contract explicitly with one another.[52] And this is the intended effect of the network contract: each individual participant within a social network should be bound by law to all other participants. As a result, relations within such a multilateral contract would no longer constitute 'extra-contractual duties of loyalty', but would rather entail the usual gamut of obligations to co-operate that are established within a comprehensive contractual relationship.[53]

The elegance of this solution is won, however, at the cost of a banal fiction, which shows a fatal disregard for the factual elements of a contract.[54] But this is not even the most serious error within Rohe's version of the network contract. For our purposes, a more grievous fault is the remarkable degree of inconsistency: the contra-factual construction is supposed to apply only to heterarchical and not to hierarchical networks. Rohe makes a stark distinction with respect to piercing liability between the two forms of networking. In decentralised networking, as

51 Rohe (1998), 141*ff*.
52 Thus, Vollkommer's original construction (1973), 711 (departed from in Vollkommer (1992), 606*f*: connected contracts) for financed purchase.
53 Rohe (1998), 86*ff*.
54 See, for critique of Rohe, but also for the elements within his arguments that are worthy of retention, Chapter 2 (VII).

for example in the transfers of funds between banks, the network contract is deemed to give rise to piercing liability between members of the network. In hierarchical networks such as franchising and just-in-time systems, however, this effect is deemed to be 'undesirable'. Instead, breach is, in principle, a matter to be treated solely by reference to the bilateral contracts, and is to be pursued through the triangular contractual relationship via the network centre.[55] Suddenly, in this instance, and despite the multifaceted legal effectiveness of the network contract, no 'piercing legal relations' should be established between members of the networks. To the extent that networks are co-ordinated hierarchically by the net centre, members who are not bound explicitly by contracts with each other should no longer be legally committed to mutual co-operation. Consequently, 'extra-contractual duties of loyalty' are deemed to be an impossibility. All forms of co-operation, it seems, must be co-ordinated centrally, and obligations are owed exclusively to the network centre. Equally, or so it is argued, all complaints about failures to co-operate must be directed towards the centre, with the result that breach of duties of co-operation can only be sanctioned by the network centre.

With this, the network contract construction loses all of its tenuous connection to the social reality of networking. Not only are its preconditions for existence fictional, but this disregard for reality also extends to its legal consequences. Social science analyses repeatedly emphasise that, whilst many networks are hierarchically co-ordinated by a 'hub firm', this never undermines characteristics that define networking, that is, decentralised co-ordination of network nodes, intensive informal contacts between nodes, and mutual provision of information and co-operation between nodes.[56] Quite the opposite: mutual intensification may arise. Hirsch-Kreinsen furnishes us with a summary of the empirical research that focuses upon the assumption of hierarchical co-ordination within strategic networks by focal firms. To his summary, he adds the following observation:

> However, co-ordination in networking is not exclusively dominated by focal firms. Rather, they give rise to mutual interdependencies, with regard to technology, for example, or in relation to the flexibility and manageability of

55 Rohe (1998), 494*ff*; Schimansky (2003), 117*ff*.

56 See, for automobile industry suppliers, Manfred Deiß and Volker Döhl (1992), *Vernetzte Produktion: Automobilzulieferer zwischen Kontrolle und Autonomie*. Frankfurt: Campus; for the computing industry, Klaus-Peter Buss and Volker Wittke (2000), 'Mikro-Chips für Massenmärkte: Innovationsstrategien der europäischen und amerikanischen Halbleiterhersteller in den 90er Jahren', *SOFI-Mitteilungen* 28, 7*ff*, and for commercial distribution networks, Christoph Dörrenbächer and Heinz R Meißner (1991), 'IKEA: "The Hollow Elk Corporation"', *Informationen über multinationale Konzerne* 14, 21*ff*. Generally, on hierarchical nets, Windeler (2001), 43*ff*.

> the highly independent systems, which opens up the potential for small partners to influence the co-ordination of the network.[57]

Thus, the real defining characteristic of hierarchical networks is the fact that they permit the combination of centralised co-ordination with intense mutual operational interconnections. As noted above, just-in-time systems are marked particularly by the degree of intensity of disclosure of information, mutual consensus, and close co-operation between individual suppliers. The same is true for virtual enterprises, as well as for franchising networks. Whilst the degree of intensity of horizontal co-operation does vary to a significant degree, Rohe's supposedly exemplary hierarchical network constellation, with its exclusively centralised co-ordination function and its total lack of mutual relationships between network nodes, is very much a borderline case. Such a constellation would, in fact, entail a total renunciation of the advantages of networking, which, as is well known, are more or less identical with the efficiency gains derived from intensive horizontal co-operation. In effect, Rohe's star-shaped instances of co-operation are little more than a series of parallel contracts concluded by a firm with suppliers or distributors and no longer exhibit characteristics of networking.

In addition, a question arises as to piercing liability within franchising networks that are constructed, not along hierarchical lines, but upon the basis of a partnership. Confronted by such constellations, where co-operation is predicated on non-hierarchical lines, Rohe is unwilling to apply rules of piercing liability.[58] In this case, however, the refusal to recognise horizontal legal relations appears absurd.

In the final analysis, the network contract is similarly unsustainable in this context of hierarchical networking. In particular, the exclusion of cross-cutting liability in hierarchically co-ordinated networks is inappropriate. Clearly, the distinction between hierarchical and heterarchical networks does impact upon the quality of co-operation, the intensity of obligations, and upon the procedures governing sanctions. This issue, however, will be dealt with elsewhere.[59]

3. Contracts with Protective Effects for Third Parties

Is, then, the contract with protective effects for third parties the long-sought-after construction for the legal expression of non-contractual duties of loyalty arising between members of a network? For example, Lange reaches this conclusion for just-in-time systems and virtual

57 Hirsch-Kreinsen (2002), 109*f*.
58 Rohe (1998), 419.
59 See below (IV).

enterprises.[60] The starting-point is a degree of disquiet within private law: the entire project is shot through with the mutual obligations of performance that are established between businesses throughout the entire chain of wealth creation; such obligations, however, cannot be adequately translated into the standard instruments of private law. He suggests that each individual bilateral agreement for supply between the manufacturer and suppliers may be qualified as a contract entailing protective effects for third parties. The other suppliers would then be regarded as 'third parties', to whom certain contractual effects extend. This construction would also be applicable to various other networks.

The contract with protective effects for third parties is sometimes applied to other forms of parallel contracting (co-tenants, fellow employees, and co-businesses within construction contracts), in order to facilitate cross-cutting liability.[61] The contract with protective effects for third parties is also invoked in the case of 'small-scale networks', that is, financed purchases, in order to establish obligations between the creditor institution and the supplier, should they not be contractually bound to one another.[62] The construction has antecedents, being firmly anchored within case law and constantly applied by the judiciary, in order to capture contractual failures of every type. In our context, the jurisprudence on chains of bank transfers of funds has a particularly strong impact, since it has elevated the contract with protective effects for third parties to become the main instrument governing such networks.[63]

This legal construction thus displays considerable legitimacy as a potential firm doctrinal basis to explain various instances of piercing liability within contractual networks. Similarly, if piercing liability proves to be necessary in future for networking, case law will, in all likelihood, make recourse to this construction. Nonetheless, the construction is not particularly plausible in this context. In the final analysis, the contract with protective effects for third parties is inadequate for networks.[64] The demand for extra-contractual duties of loyalty within the network cannot be identified with the situation of detrimental impacts on a third party by a bilateral contract. Instead, such duties are due to operational interconnections to which the shared nature of the project gives rise. Similarly, whilst case law generally desists from applying a specially crafted legal

[60] Lange (1998), 195*ff*; (2001a), 188*ff*. Similarly, Larenz and M Wolf (1997), 470.

[61] Riesenhuber (1997), 149*ff*, with further references.

[62] Heermann (1998), 95*ff*.

[63] Since BGHZ 96, 9, 17.

[64] See also Lange (1998), 200 himself, who considers this to be a unsatisfactory emergency solution at best. Seemingly, the third party protection contract can neither explain multiple mutual impacts within a contractual network, neither does it furnish us with an effective regulatory instrument. See, for similar critique of the application of the third party protection contract to networks, Rohe (1998), 104*ff* and K Schmidt (1999), 1019.

category of, say, 'associational relationship', to other parallel contracting cases and applies instead the contract with protective effects for third parties, it nevertheless concedes that the justification for an extension of obligations is furnished by the common pursuit of a project beyond the parallel contracts.[65] The decisive criterion is a private autonomous bundling of performances in pursuit of a common project, and not the external impact of an individual contract. It is doubtful whether the simple extension of the effects of a bilateral contract to a third person can adequately address the issue of the interconnection of interests and risks within the network.[66] In stark contrast, use could be made of the connected contracts construction, since it reveals the multilateral interdependencies within the network, reflects other interests of participants, including in particular the shared project, and, furthermore, facilitates the creation of rights to participation and imposes obligations requiring mutual co-operation.[67] In short, the contract with protective effects for third parties is the law's reaction to contractual externalities; the notion of connected contracts, by contrast, represents law's reaction to network effects.[68]

Is the distinction made between the contract with protective effects for third parties and the notion of connected contracts simply a flight of theoretical fancy? No, the distinction is also of practical relevance, specifically where individual bilateral contracts contain divergent obligations. Naturally, this is often the case within parallel contracting.[69] The more the performances of members of the network are heterogeneous, the more likely will 'contract collisions' occur. Thus, they are more common within just-in-time systems and virtual enterprises than within franchising.[70] In this context, the contract with protective effects for third parties, being a mere 'accidental' extrapolation from a single contract, exclusively determines the obligations owed to the third party. Such an individualised perspective on the protection of the third party cannot express the collisions between two or more contracts and precludes overarching criteria that might solve them. In stark contrast, connected contracts work explicitly from the perspective of an overarching purposive interrelationship between individual contracts, and thus decide upon colliding obligations from the viewpoint of the entire system – in

65 Riesenhuber (1997), 181.

66 Lange (1998), 200.

67 Thus, Wiethölter's request for legal networking constructions (1988), 21*ff*.

68 Möschel (1986), 225, explicitly relates legal issues of networking to the problem of externalities. This argument is expanded upon in the following with reference to the distinction drawn between external contractual effects and networking effects.

69 On such divergent obligations, Riesenhuber (1997), 189*ff*.

70 On the relationship between networks, connected contracts and contractual collisions, Amstutz (2003), 170*ff*; Schluep (2003), 290*ff*.

effect, with reference to the function of the network. The instrument which is better suited to coping with contractual collisions within networks is the overarching perspective, and not the contract with protective effects for third parties, because only the former derives its standards from the functional requirements of the network rather than from one single contract.[71]

4. Duties of Loyalty in Connected Contracts

Connected contracts should thus offer a superior legitimacy for cross-cutting liability within the network than the contract with protective effects for third parties. Gernhuber has already demonstrated this in relation to financed purchases, where failures in performance arise as between vendors and banks who have not concluded a contract with one another. In this case, the notion of connected contracts establishes a special legal relationship between non-contractually bound participants, along the lines of *culpa in contrahendo*.[72] In relation to cross-cutting liability, M Wolf, Amstutz and Schluep have drawn direct parallels between networks and connected contracts.[73] Their comparable nature is made clear, when Möschel characterises the network contract as a multilateral 'special relationship, which binds individual contracts within a system'.[74] The bindingness is not created through a declaration of the will of the parties, but rather arises out of network-related obligations within individual contracts that activate a system with a unitary purpose. Krebs deploys a detailed typology to demonstrate that networks do in fact entail a 'qualified special relationship' that necessitates cross-cutting liability.[75] Picker furnishes us with a generalisation, maintaining that the contractual analysis must be replaced by one of an 'extra-contractual organisation', in order to permit the recognition of networks as 'special relationships' and for the provision of suitable grounds for legal liability.[76]

Where a choice is made in favour of connected contracts, analogies might also be made to company law without fear of confusion between a contractual network and a corporation. Kulms, for example, makes a suggestion in this direction, fruitfully applying the company law model of duties of loyalty to extra-contractual duties within complex contracts:

71 Amstutz (2003), 173*ff*.
72 Gernhuber (1973), 493; (1989), 741*f*.
73 Larenz and M Wolf (1997), 470; Amstutz and Schluep (2003), 890*f*; Schluep (2003), 290*ff*.
74 Möschel (1986), 223*ff*.
75 Krebs (2000), 84*ff*, 107, 312*ff*, 440*ff*.
76 Picker (1999), 429.

'[U]nder certain circumstances, the duty to promote the purpose of co-operation will also apply to a "system participant" within a contractual network, with whom no direct contractual relationship is established.'[77] The clear distinction drawn above between network purpose and corporate purpose should guard against any inappropriate collapsing of the two forms, and should, at the same time, highlight the differences in the qualities of the duties of loyalty owed between the members of the network. As stated above, by virtue of the constant and continuing simultaneous presence of individualistic orientations, network obligations diverge from corporate obligations, since they are contemporaneously limited by the apportionment of residual profit to individual members of the network.[78]

In comparison with the contract with protective effects for third parties, connected contracts offer more contextually appropriate criteria for cross-cutting liability. For this purpose, networking that is facilitative of cross-cutting liability must be distinguished from simple instances of parallel contracting, which do not give rise to a common project and within which co-ordination is the sole responsibility of a vertical contractual partner who likewise bears all co-ordination risks. The same question has arisen, as we have seen, with regard to parallel contractual relationships within tenancy, the law of construction projects, and labour law.[79] The criteria established there – common usage regulation and common private legal orders – are justified by the constitutive purpose of connected contracts. Connected contracts thus only facilitate cross-cutting liability on the understanding that three conditions are fulfilled: mutual referencing of contracts; a concrete network purpose; and a co-operative relationship.[80] Parallel contracts only transmute into connected contracts when they fulfil these conditions. Individual contractual claims against one contractual partner are only then transformed into rights of participation and co-decision, which might be activated by other parties. Equally, the simple delineation of individual spheres is only superseded by a collective private order with common behavioural rules on fulfilment of these preconditions.

However, the concept of connected contracts also places limits upon cross-cutting liability. In contrast to the jurisdictional reach of the third party protection contract, which must either be determined with reference to the imputed will of the parties, or objectively established with

[77] Kulms (2000), 232; similarly, Lange (1998), 425; (2001a), 178*ff*.

[78] On the distinction between network purpose and corporate purpose, and on material differences between network and corporate obligations, Chapter 2 (III), and Chapter 4 (III).

[79] See Riesenhuber (1997), 149*ff*.

[80] See, on the legal reality construct (preconditions for) of connected contracts, above, Chapter 3 (IV).

regard to the performance proximity of the individual contract, the limit to imposition of additional duties is created in the light of the distinction made between the collective and the individual realm in the net.[81] Cross-cutting liability is not generally applicable within contractual networks. Rather, it should only arise should the collective realm be materially impacted upon. Outside this realm, the sole obligations arising are good faith duties commonly associated with bilateral contracts. It is this characteristic that distinguishes network from corporation, since such individual and collective relational duality is wholly foreign to the latter.

VI. PROTECTIVE OBLIGATIONS, PERFORMANCE OBLIGATIONS, PROMOTION OBLIGATIONS

A more detailed analysis of extra-contractual loyalty obligations reveals their independent nature. Such obligations are neither identical to simple duties of care current within tort law; nor are they commensurate with the contractual obligations that would be derived from a 'network contract' or from a genuine multilateral contract. In effect, certain network obligations are protective in nature, designed to defend the interests in integrity of participants in networks from mutual impairment. To this degree and in an echo of contracts with protective effects for third parties, one might denote such obligations a functional form of tort law and accordingly categorise them as general duties of care.[82] However, here the peculiarity in relation to tort law is once again apparent, since the real justification for protective obligations is the existence of specific risks arising in networks. Protective obligations within the network are applied in reaction to negative effects of networks, or to the risks inherent to the narrow intermeshing of operational spheres. Just-in-time systems are a very good example of the manner in which networking multiplies mutual contacts and simultaneously increases the risks of injury. In particular, computerised networking necessarily lays bare secret techniques of production, not only to the network centre, but also to other network participants. Even in the absence of a contractual relation, the imposition of intensified duties of confidentiality follows.[83]

81 For this distinction, Chapter 4 (III).

82 Comprehensively, from a private law theory perspective, Gert Brüggemeier (1986), *Deliktsrecht. Ein Hand- und Lehrbuch.* Baden-Baden: Nomos, 70*ff*, 73; (2004), *Common Principles of Tort Law: A Pre-Statement of Law.* London: British Institute of International and Comparative Law (BIICL), chap D II.

83 On confidentiality duties in networks, see Zirkel (1990), 349; Steinmann (1993), 56; Lange (1998), 104, 215, 378; Rohe (1998), 406; Wellenhofer-Klein (1999), 164*f*, 183.

The distinction between extra-contractual duties of loyalty and tort-based duties of care is, however, revealed where the former extend beyond protection of the interests in integrity of other participants. On the basis of generalised reciprocity, networking creates expectations for participants of a share in the positive benefits of contractual performances. In legal terms, such expectations are embodied in the right to benefit from obligations owed to other participants in the system, or by the right to benefit from obligations to promote the network owed to the system as a whole. Clearly, this is one area where tort law meets its limits, and one area where the justification of piercing liability in connected contracts would seem more closely to fit the material facts of networking.

The difference from genuine contract law is similarly clear. Even where connected contracts are deployed to justify rights to benefit from obligations to perform contracts and are not simply restricted to obligations designed to protect third parties, beneficial rights must nevertheless be understood simply as claims for damages, and not as primary actions for fulfilment of obligations to perform a contractual duty. The same limitation is present in contracts with protective effects for third parties, where duties might and do extend beyond simple protective obligations to impose duties to perform. In this case, the contract with protective effects for third parties similarly only extends a secondary remedy to third parties (damages), and does not found a primary cause of action (for performance).[84] Within networks, the same limitation derives directly from generalised reciprocity. This justifies general expectations that mutual performances will flow 'from the network', but it does not establish specialised claims for specific performance against individual members of the network.[85] As soon as transactions within the network are realised, however, members are protected by claims for damages. Rohe similarly dismisses the 'normal' actions for specific performance applicable within contract law and argues for the limitation of applicable claims in networks to simple secondary actions, since he also identifies clear structural differences between contracts and networks.[86] Predictably, however, the 'network contract' construction also causes him problems again in this regard. Where the law of agency elevates each network member to the status of contractual party in a fully fledged multilateral agreement, it logically follows that general contractual rules, inclusive of claims for specific performance, should also apply. Accordingly, Rohe

[84] Gernhuber (1989), 512, 518*ff*, 534*ff* draws this distinction in a particularly clear manner; similarly, Gottwald in *Münchener Kommentar* (2003), § 328, 108.

[85] On generalised reciprocity within networks, see Semlinger (1993), 333*f*, with further references; Powell (1990).

[86] Rohe (1998), 195.

sees himself forced to augment the silent provision of powers of agency and the equally silent act of the conclusion of contract through an agent, with a further secret: the silent limitation of contractual actions to claims for damages. Silence is sometimes eloquent.

VII. ANALOGIES TO COMPANY LAW: DERIVATIVE ACTION WITHIN THE CONTRACTUAL NETWORK?

The quality of individual extra-contractual obligations within the network is of course related to the distinction drawn between hierarchical and heterarchical organisation of networks, but care should be taken not to place too great an emphasis upon the distinction. Specifically, material effects of networking within hierarchical organisations should not be overlooked. This is the reason why the preceding pages took great pains to refute the assertion that hierarchical networks do not give rise to horizontal duties of co-operation, or that the sanctioning of failures in performance is the exclusive function of the network centre.[87] Even Kulms' distinction seems to be too narrow. Whilst he assumes that mutual obligations of co-operation arise within hierarchical networks, he nevertheless makes a distinction with regard to their legal effectiveness based upon the degree of intensity of co-operation. Accordingly, where 'company-like relations' are predominant, as is the case within confederal franchising, piercing liability is deemed unproblematic.[88] Below this threshold, however, only the 'system overlord' may enforce appropriate behaviour amongst members of the network. Members of the network would not enjoy claims as amongst themselves, or at best, might only call upon the tort provisions of § 1 UWG or § 826 BGB.[89] This assertion should nonetheless be resisted with the aid of the logic of networking: to the degree that the material structures of complex contractual relations require co-ordination between nodes of a network, the law must respond by the imposition of effective horizontal duties of loyalty.[90]

Nonetheless, hierarchical co-ordination should be constructed such that cross-cutting liability is only a secondary instrument, leaving the primary oversight function in the hands of the network centre. Loyalty conflicts amongst members of the network should first be brought to the attention of the centre. A claim against an offending party by an injured member should only be activated once the centre has failed or refused to

[87] Against Rohe (1998), 436*f*; Schimansky (2003), 119*f*.
[88] Kulms (2000), 232*f* with recourse to Martinek's typology (1987), 252.
[89] Baumbach and Hefermehl (2001), § 1 UWG, 708*ff*.
[90] Lange, in effect, also reaches this result (1998), 195*ff*; (2001a) 188*ff*.

take action. With this, the vital connection is made to a particular corporate law construction, which also appears to be appropriate for cases of connected contracts.

Coming back to our starting case of standards-undercutting in franchising, it is highly questionable whether the standards should immediately afford all franchisees a general cause of action: this might incite franchisees who are in competition with one another to misuse this right in an effort to disadvantage competitors. Equally, an abundance of claims and judicial rulings might also damage the constant and flexible evolution of the standards. The franchising contract clearly imposes a duty upon the franchisor to safeguard the interests of all members of the network through its oversight of the observance of the standards of the system. Accordingly, the franchisor must be accorded a degree of discretion. Triangular adjudication of conflicts between franchisees by the franchisor thus also serves a neutral balancing of interests.

It is therefore appropriate to require a franchisee who has been injured by standards-undercutting, primarily, and in the interests of the entire network, to direct his complaint to the franchisor. Interests of franchisees that are worthy of protection by means of according franchisees direct claims to enforce standards only arise in the case of opportunistic behaviour by the franchisor or collusion between the franchisor and the free-rider. And even then, the conscientious franchisee's cause of action against a free-rider must be restricted to cases of grievous breaches, which give rise to a perceptible danger of disadvantage to the network (such as the withdrawal of goodwill) and consequently of injury to the conscientious franchisee. Again, it is difficult to derive all these preconditions from the contract with protective effects for third parties. Instead, their rationale is meaningful only by reference to the functional conditions of franchising and to the corollary notion of connected contracts.

In one particular constellation, namely, exclusive injury to the purpose of the network, an analogy to corporate law might found a cause of action. As noted above, the characterisation of franchise contracts as company-like orders is rejected for very good reasons.[91] Nonetheless, this does not preclude the drawing of any analogy to company law in justifiable instances, which may occur, in particular, when multilateral relationships that are not expressed through bilateral contracts are relevant. Where the imposition of duties to promote the system leads us to conceive of the franchising contract as multilateral connected contracts entailing the harmonisation of the interests of multiple actors,[92] and where the purpose of the network might be systematically injured by

[91] See above, Chapter 2 (II and III).

[92] Rather than many others, Rohe (1998), 8, 78*ff*, 280*ff*, 438*ff*, and, indeed, often. For more detailed review of network purpose, see above, Chapter 4 (II).

opportunistic or collusive behaviour by a franchisor, parallels may be safely drawn to the situation of collusive behaviour between the management of a company and various corporate actors, at a cost to the entire company, and thus to the disadvantage of the remaining corporate actors. Franchisors are entrusted by franchisees with the task of maintaining and promoting the system (for example, its goodwill) in the interests of all franchisees. This gives rise to those types of problem that are much noted within company law and have been analysed from the economic perspective of principal–agent theory.

Within company law, a claim through which a single member enforces the claims of the entire corporation in his own name, is termed an *actio pro socio* or derivative action.[93] In doctrinal terms, the derivative action confers a cause of action upon an individual actor for enforcement of a right possessed by the company. In practice, such actions arise where the normal allocation of responsibility within a company no longer functions owing to massive internal conflicts. Specifically, such situations arise when a majority of members oppose enforcement of the right, or management fails to take appropriate action. Various constellations might be distinguished: in the case of partnership, the issue concerns enforcement of claims between members (for example, duties of disclosure), whereby the claim is limited to the fulfilment of the corporate purpose, but might, in any case, be demanded of each member. § 432 BGB authorises each actor to pursue derivative actions for all joint claims in their own name for the benefit of all creditors.[94] But § 432 BGB does not apply to corporations with a separate legal personality and with their own body of rules governing the organisation of the representation of the company. In principle, only the responsible organs of the company can enforce claims against the assets of the company. Nonetheless, the *actio pro socio* is recognised as a subsidiary means to permit the apportionment of responsibility. The *actio pro socio* is not a contractual cause of action possessed by an individual person, and is only applied as a subsidiary mechanism if the responsible corporate organs remain inactive. Whilst the *actio pro socio* plays a limited role within the law applicable to companies with limited liability, by apportioning supplementary responsibility to individual corporate actors, it is not generally established within the law applying to joint stock companies. Although § 147 Law Applying to Joint Stock Companies (*Aktiengesetz* (AktG)) allows, in this

[93] See on this and on the following, K Schmidt (2002), 629*ff*.

[94] 432(1) If more than one person is to demand indivisible performance, then to the extent that they are not joint and severable creditors, the obligor may only effect performance to all of them jointly and each obligee may only demand performance for all of them. Each obligee may demand that the obligor deposit the thing owed for all obligees or, if it is not suitable for deposit, that it be surrendered to a court-appointed depositary.

regard, a minority of shareholders to require the management of a listed company to fulfil certain demands, it does not provide a cause of action for shareholders. Instead, shareholders are afforded specific company law causes of action under §§ 309(IV), 17(IV), 318(IV) AktG. These concern cases of collusive behaviour by a parent company that prevents a subsidiary company from enforcing company law relief measures against its parent firm.

When the constellation of interests accompanying the *actio pro socio* is compared with that present in the case of franchisor inaction in the face of free-riding by the undercutting of standards, it is readily apparent that the subsidiary *actio pro socio* procedural mechanism serves to solve a very similar problem within companies. Whilst the *actio pro socio* is used to enforce contractual claims under § 423 BGB within partnerships,[95] it is limited at the very outset to collusive behaviour on the part of a representative organ. Were the goal to be one of interpreting the maintenance of each and every standard of the franchising system as an obligation owed to all the other franchisees, the parallel to § 432 BGB would readily suggest itself. Thus, the maintenance of standards should not be pursued in the interests of the individual claimant, but should rather be pursued in the interests of all members of the network. A free-rider who was judicially constrained to observe the standards of the system would then be required to fulfil duties to supply contractual performance in pursuit of the purpose of the network and to the benefit of all the members of the system. Reservations about the endowment of all franchisees with an immediate cause of action for the maintenance of standards that would be valid against all other franchisees might be met by limiting the *actio pro socio* to a subsidiary procedural mechanism. It should be applied only when the responsible franchisor fails to take action. The conscientious franchisee would then be authorised to take action against a free-rider for the maintenance of standards, whenever a franchisor remains inactive by reason of opportunistic or collusive behaviour. Equally, just as the *actio socio pro* is restricted in such cases to claims on behalf of the company, validity of actions within franchising systems might also be restricted to those designed to attain the common network purpose in the sense of requiring fulfilment of the franchisor's duties to promote the system. By the same token, the enforcement of those actions that clearly do not serve to attain the purpose of the network would be excluded.

[95] BGB 423 Forgiveness agreed between the obligee and a joint and several debtor is also effective for the other obligors if the parties to the contract intended to terminate the whole obligation.

VIII. HIERARCHICAL MULTILATERAL NETWORK

Finally, attention should again be directed to the introductory case detailed in the first Chapter.[96] This deals with the issue of extra-contractual duties of loyalty between distant positions maintained within a hierarchical multilateral network. In this case, a distribution hierarchy was created with the aid of bilateral contracts between the network centre and A-dealers, and bilateral contracts between A-dealers and B-dealers. In time, the network centre was (incorrectly) to force an A-dealer to terminate its contract with a B-dealer. The Court granted the B-dealer a piercing liability claim against the centre. Rohe argues that this judgment proves the existence of his network contract.[97] This is incorrect: neither the construction of the powers of agency of all the members of the network for all other members, nor the presumption of their powers of representation, are suited to this situation. In addition, Rohe finds himself trapped within a remarkable contradiction, when he argues that hierarchical networks should be precluded from the ambit of piercing liability, whilst he still seeks to facilitate piercing liability between a variety of heterarchical levels.

In stark contrast, the justificatory fragments deployed by the State High Court – 'incorporation' of distribution dealers, 'a trust relationship' between distribution system members, 'dominance' by the centre of the system, 'unitary nature' of the distribution system, 'enduring business relations' – approximate far more closely to reality than does the fictive agency-derived contractual construction, albeit that the Court failed to make clear its precise references to labour law, company law or commercial law. In effect, however, they do refer to the legal concept of connected contracts. Individual contracts within the various hierarchical levels are incorporated in an overarching system, which is dominated by the system centre and which binds individual contracts together in a highly detailed manner. The automobile distribution system substantially fulfils the three preconditions for connected contracts worked out above.[98]

(1) *Mutual referencing of contracts to one another.* This characteristic, which can often only be indirectly imputed with reference to the mutual positioning of contracts, is present here in an unusually explicit and elaborated form. A-contracts, in particular, contain provisions on the drawing up of B-contracts, on the detailed organisation of lower hierarchical levels and on the rights of control exercised over the second hierarchical level by the system centre. Indeed, without concluding a fully fledged multilateral contract amongst all hierarchical levels via an

[96] See above, Chapter 1 (I); OLG Stuttgart NJW-RR 1990, 491.
[97] Rohe (1998), 463*ff*.
[98] See above, Chapter 3 (IV).

agreement of all participants, this instance of contracting nonetheless entails legally effective mutual referencing between contracts, since a multitude of independent bilateral contracts explicitly refer to one another.

(2) *Association with system purpose.* The association of individual contracts with the network purpose of the creation of a hierarchical distribution system follows from each of the bilateral contacts – in particular from the clauses found within A-contracts.

(3) *Factual co-operation.* Intensive co-operation is present between the different levels, which on occasions even extends beyond bilateral relations to encompass direct contact between levels that are placed at a distance from one another in the hierarchy. The legal consequence of identifying some connected contracts is the imposition of 'extra-contractual loyalty duties', which are even, and specifically so, effective in relation to remote positions within the overall hierarchy. Equally, such duties instigate direct mutual obligations between the centre of the system and all levels in the hierarchy, justifying a cross-cutting action against the centre of the system in the case of unjust contractual termination.

6

External Liability of Networks

Expanding the Range of Responsibility

I. FRANCHISING IN SERVICES: 'ORGANISED IRRESPONSIBILITY'

A LARGE ORGANISATION within the financial services sector is established as a multilateral hierarchical network through bilateral franchising contracts. The network deploys the services of about 2,000 legally independent, but economically interdependent, financial advisors to address the needs of around 250,000 clients. Financial advisors are strictly co-ordinated by the network centre. Clients are, for the major part, doctors, dentists, technicians and economists. The network offers financial services, life assurance policies, and the provision of information. Independent advisors are bundled together in decentralised groups, which are subject to central direction. Significant one-off tasks, such as product and market development, are entrusted to inter-organisational regulatory committees or so-called working groups.[1]

The incorrect conduct of a long-term investment project by one independent advisor causes a large financial loss to a client. However, incorrect performance cannot in the final analysis be directly attributed to the financial advisor, because precise causes for the loss are to be found in a general directive given by the centre of the network to the financial advisor. In turn, the directive's content was the result of errors of co-ordination between the centre of the network and the working group responsible for that particular task.

This example sheds light on a particularly crass form of network failure: financially weak and economically dependent network nodes, bound to follow network directives, are nonetheless the sole parties liable for grievous organisational errors within highly organised networks, because they, alone, have a contractual relationship with the client by

[1] On the empirical background of service franchising, see Jörg Sydow and Martin Kloyer (1995), *Managementpraktiken in Franchisingnetzwerken. Arbeitspapiere Band 171.* Wuppertal: Fachbereich Wirtschaftswissenschaften; Bennet von Well (2001), *Standardisierung und Individualisierung von Dienstleistungen.* Wiesbaden: Gabler; Windeler (2001), 45*f*.

virtue of their legal independence. Since tort law does not impose a liability analogous to product liability on other members of the network within the services sector, the sole corrective in such cases is the contractual liability of the particular party to the contract.[2] The client that has suffered loss is unable to pursue a claim against the network centre, to whose directives advisors are subordinate. Neither can a claim be pursued against the members of the working group which was responsible for the error. Equally, there is no question of the imposition of liability upon the entire service-providing network, since the network has no corporate legal personality. The impasse is itself a result of network organisation. If members of the network are organised by means of individual bilateral contracts, rather than through a corporate organisation, the result is a remarkable degree of 'organised irresponsibility' within networks. Strong criticisms have been aired about these constellations since the early 1990s: bilateral contractual agreements to the detriment of third parties; collectivisation of operations in the absence of comparable collectivisation of responsibilities; intensification and transference of risk to external parties, without adequate arrangements for the absorption of risk.[3] Amongst lawyers, however, such criticisms have been rejected as inappropriate suspicions towards innovative and efficient forms of organisation.[4] Given the general euphoria about such new forms of economic organisation, their inherent risks have been understated or even wholly ignored.[5]

[2] Liability lacunae in services networking are regarded as particularly troublesome by Teubner (1991), 124; Bräutigam (1994), 190; Pasderski (1998), 162; Rohe (1998), 416; Krebs (2000), 382. For a fundamental critique of lack of legal attention for the problems posed by service networking, especially in view of its increasing significance, see Martinek (1997) 97*f*.

[3] On the lack of network responsibility, see Collins (1990a), 732*ff*; (1990b), 346*ff*; (1999), 248*ff*; Teubner (1991), 37*ff*; (1993b), 57*ff*; (1992), 213*ff*; Felstead (1991), 37*ff*; Joerges (1991), 17*ff*; Macaulay (1991), 215*ff*; Sciarra (1991), 251*ff*; Ott (1995), 214*f*. The discussion on 'organised irresponsibility' is particularly focused on formal organisations. However, the question is also raised in other social configurations: see James S Coleman (1982), *The Asymmetric Society*. Syracuse: Syracuse University, 79*ff*; (1990), *Foundations of Social Theory*. Cambridge, MA: Harvard University, 553*ff*; (1991), 'Natural Persons, Corporate Actors, and Constitutions' in J Rogers Hollingsworth and Robert Boyer (eds), *Contemporary Capitalism: The Embeddedness of Institutions* 2, 81*ff*; Ulrich Beck (1992), *Risk Society: Towards a New Modernity (Theory, Culture and Society Series)*. London: Sage; (1995), *Ecological Politics in an Age of Risk*. Cambridge: Polity; from the legal sociological perspective, Klaus Röhl (1987), 'Die strukturelle Differenz zwischen Individuum und Organisation oder Brauchen wir ein Sonderprivatrecht für Versicherungen und andere Organisationen?' in Marcus Lutter, Walter Oppenhoff, Otto Sandrock and Hanns Winkhaus (eds) *Festschrift für Ernst C Stiefel*. Munich: Beck, 574*ff*.

[4] Rohe (1998), 418; Bayreuther (2001), 399*ff*; Schimansky (2003), 125*ff*.

[5] Schanze (1991), 98 apodictically asserts that network liability is 'simply not needed looking at the variety of institutions that sensibly reach both the organizer or the main symbiotic partner and the dependent unit'. Within service providing networking, however, the institution of the net centre remains wholly impervious to liability claims. Nonetheless, Schanze does recognise the need for intensification of legal liability when discussion

Recently, however, a change of opinion is tangible. Management science and organisational theory, at least, have diagnosed many symptoms of failure in networks.[6] Legislation has been introduced in various segments of the market that imposes a specific form of network liability.[7] Meanwhile, using a variety of doctrinal constructions and preconditions, a striking number of legal authors have argued in favour of the imposition of piercing liability upon the centre of the network and its other members.[8] Even economists have asked for increased network liability, especially for virtual enterprises, which are active on the Internet, and they have developed extensive models for liability.[9] Particularly noteworthy is the evolution of forms of collective liability within the economic practice of networking itself. Large-scale creditors are increasingly

focuses on cases of liability evasion under the rubric of 'regime deception': see Schanze and Haunhorst (1995), 195. Rohe also admits of liability problems within the services sector, if somewhat reluctantly (Rohe (1998), 416), but then returns to his categorical doubts about the need for network liability.

[6] On the various dimensions of network failure, Messner (1994), 566*ff*; Johannes Weyer (ed) (2000), *Soziale Netzwerke: Konzepte und Methoden der sozialwissenschaftlichen Netzwerkforschung*. Munich: Oldenbourg, 25; Hirsch-Kreinsen (2002), 111*ff*. For empirical research on this question, see Grabher (1993); (1994); Messner (1994); (1997a); (1997b); Kern (1996); Hirsch-Kreinsen (1997); theoretical explanations in Bieber (1997), 119*ff*; Rölle and Blättel-Mink (1998), 76*ff*; Ortmann and Sydow (1999), 206; (1999), 305*ff*; Abel (2000), 166*f*; Heidenreich (2000), 98*ff*; Heidling (2000), 76*ff*.

[7] § 676b(III7) BGB and § 676e(V) BGB (Civil Code) impose piercing liability on intervening banks in favour of the client who has made a transfer. See, for exhaustive details, Heermann (2003), 214*ff*, 223. See also Chapter 4 (IV).

[8] For imposition of piercing liability on the net centre or other members of the network under existing liability rules, see Möschel (1986), 211*ff*, 223 (distribution systems: network contract); Roth (1989), 436 (automobile distribution: expanded vicarious liability); Zirkel (1990), 350 (just-in-time systems: risk pool as comprehensive relationship under the law of obligations); Teubner (1991), 129*ff*; (1993b), 57*ff*; (1992), 232; (2002a), 324*ff* (franchising: quasi-contractual network liability); Bräutigam (1994), 138*ff* (franchising: expanded vicarious liability); Wolf and Ungeheuer (1994), 1033 (franchising: apparent power of agency; third party protection contract); Reich (1995), 76 (franchising: expansion of tort law); Ehricke (1996), 319*f* (co-operation contracts: analogous application of company liability law); Larenz and M Wolf (1997), 470 (networks in general: external direct liability); Oechsler (1997), 482*ff* (franchising, just-in-time systems: analogous application of piercing liability of corporate groups); Pasderski (1998), 37*ff* (franchising: expansion of tort and contractual liability); Krebs (2000), 316*f*, 381*ff* (franchising and authorised dealer systems: direct liability within 'special relationships'); Bayreuther (2001), 399*f*, 530 (franchising: law of corporate groups); Lange (2001a), 185 (virtual businesses: law of contractual organisation); Amstutz and Schluep (2003), 888, 891 and Schluep (2003), 290, 302*f* (networks: piercing liablitiy). Sympathy is shown for the concept of network liability by Heermann (1998), 76. To date at least, Martinek ((1992), 75; (1993a), 582) has largely restrained himself from commenting on external network liability. Nonetheless, his preference for the application of company law to strictly directed franchising systems would seem to hint at rules of piercing liability in corporate groups. In any case, he criticises existing law, 'since the common conduct of business operations that is sought by contractual parties is not accompanied by the similarly collective exposure to liability risks', (1993a), 582. With a similarly cautious approach, K Schmidt (1999), 1019, on network liability within banking gironets, which in the meantime has attracted comprehensive legal regulation.

[9] Gulati, Klein and Zolt (2000), 807, 930; Noll (2002).

demanding the creation of collective liability funds within the franchising system, in order to minimise their exposure to the liability of individual franchises.[10]

The need for external network liability, which includes the network centre and/or other members of the network within the range of liability, is particularly apparent in the case of franchising since two particular characteristics converge here: strict hierarchy and decentralised external contacts. Notwithstanding their decentralised legal structure and system of bilateral contracts, franchising systems are hierarchically organised and strictly directed businesses. Nonetheless, external contacts are not made with the network centre, which is mainly responsible for decision making and the financial performance of the network. Instead, external contact is made only with 'interlocutory' franchisees, who are subject to management from the centre and enjoy only limited financial resources. As our starting case demonstrates, the problem is even more extreme in the case of the franchising of services, since, in contrast to franchising within the goods market, product liability regulation does not apply.

The situation is clearly different in the case of just-in-time systems. Here, the financially powerful network centres themselves establish contractual relations with external clients, such that they are exposed to rules of primary liability. By the same token, supply firms are commonly liable under the law of product liability. In such cases, the problem of responsibility is more one of the appropriate internal apportionment of risks of external liability between the supplier and the producer.[11] In contrast, virtual enterprises exhibit a median approach towards external liability. In general, external clients establish contractual relations with the network centre, which is mostly responsible for decision making and has large financial resources, such that the contractual liability of the network centre offers the client good potential for appropriate redress. Nevertheless, clients are likewise denied the opportunity of taking action against other members of the network, since the latter are only bound to one another by individual contracts. Here, a question arises as to whether, and under what conditions, other members of the network should be included within claims of liability.[12]

II. STRUCTURAL CONTRADICTION: *UNITAS MULTIPLEX*

The need for external parties to pursue claims against other members of the network arises with networking externalities, which in turn derive

[10] Information received from Reinhard Böhner.
[11] See, comprehensively, Wellenhofer-Klein (1999), 282*ff*.
[12] See Lange (2001a), 185.

from a third constellation of the underlying paradox of networking. As discussed above, the first constellation related to the contradiction between bilateral exchange and multilateral connectivity; the second, to the contradiction between competition and co-operation that enterprises respond to by choosing to organise themselves as hybrid networks.[13] In its third constellation the networking paradox relates to contradictions, ambivalences and paradoxes that appear within the ascription of action and of responsibility. To which actor in the network is economic action ascribed? Who are the winners of advantages derived from the network, who are the victims of network losses in economic terms? Which parties make a profit, and which are exposed to liability: individual or collective actors?

Networks themselves eschew a clear reaction to the problem of the ascription of responsibility. Exactly the opposite: the reaction is one of strategic ambivalence.[14] In contrast to contracts, whereby liability can only be apportioned to the individual parties, and differing also from corporate organisations, which apportion liability collectively to the legal person, networks consciously leave the apportionment question vague and unaddressed. The hidden paradox here is one of '*unitas multiplex*': the confusing multitude of independent actors present 'within' the unitary collective actor.[15] Is the network simply a trust-based relationship established between autonomous actors, with each being apportioned their share of success or failure on a wholly individual basis? Alternatively, is the network itself an independent collective actor, operating autonomously in particular environments, demanding its own share of loyalty from individual members of the network, and also acting as a focal point for liability?[16] Or is it both? And, if yes, how?

[13] For general discussion of network paradoxes, see Chapter 2 (III), Chapter 3 (III). On the first constellation, see Chapter 4 (II). On the second, see Chapter 5 (II).

[14] Scharpf (1991), 621*ff*; Rölle and Blättel-Mink (1998), 74*ff*, 84, 265*ff*; Littmann and Jansen (2000), 69*f*; Windeler (2001), 225*ff*.

[15] For a comparable problem in relation to corporate groups, see the edited volume focusing on such structural contradictions by David Sugarman and Gunther Teubner (1990), *Regulating Corporate Groups in Europe*. Baden-Baden: Nomos; Teubner (1990b), 85*ff*.

[16] It is perhaps telling that even social scientists feel that they must commit themselves either to collective unity or to simple inter-positional relationships, and are likewise unable to give a clear-cut answer. The chameleon-like tactic adopted by networks seems to be effective both in practice and in theory. Arguing strongly in favour of simple relationships and against collective identity, Wolf Heydebrand (1999), *The Network Metaphor as Key to the Analysis of Complex Production and Service Relation in a Global Economy*. Stuttgart: Akademie für Technikfolgenabschätzung in Baden-Württemberg; Kämper and Schmidt (2000), 219*ff*; Tacke (2000), 317. Clearly in favour of collectivity, but only under certain conditions, Teubner (1993b), 54*ff*; (1992), 226*ff*; Sydow and Windeler (1998), 265*ff*; Windeler (2001), 225*ff*; Castells (2000), 177*f*, 187, 209, 214. Luhmann (2000), 408, offers a judgment of Solomon: Networks '. . . can intensify themselves to establish their own social systems when they create clear borders and their own recursively applicable history, and likewise build network typical trust upon these foundations'.

The simultaneous instructions that are supplied by the paradox differ again in this context. Here, it is no longer exchange versus association, or co-operation versus competition. Instead, we find the contradictory imperatives: on the one hand, 'Obey, you are a part of a larger commonly pursued project'; on the other, 'Be autonomous, you are responsible for your own actions!' Once again, the stark distinction drawn between contract and organisation, so beloved both in social theory and in legal doctrine, furnishes us only with overly simplistic solutions, which fail adequately to capture reality. In the meantime, the practice of hybrid networking has identified its own solution: that of 'double attribution':

> Since network activities occur within a dual framework of reference, business networks always exhibit a process of simultaneous ascription to network businesses and to the network.[17]

This technique of social attribution is the most significant characteristic of hybrid networks. It distinguishes them from contracts and organisations, which rely instead upon a simple apportionment of liability, either to individual actors or to the collective actor. One and the same economic transaction is thus exposed to double attribution – to the individual actor in his guise as a network node, and to the overarching network itself.[18] The process of double attribution furnishes networks with the means to maintain far better relations with their environments. One and the same network is therefore in a position to make its appearance within one environment as a multitude of individual actors, and in another, as a unitary collective actor with a clearly defined identity. Thus armed with chameleon-like characteristics, networks can gain entry to environments that would otherwise be closed to them were they organised simply in the form of a contract or a collective. The 'positional gains in environmental relationships',[19] which already accrue in cases of clear-cut collectives, are once again intensified within hybrid networks.

[17] Windeler (2001), 227.

[18] Comprehensively, on network typical double attribution in social reality and in law, Teubner (1991), 119*ff*; (1993b), 50*ff*; (1992), 226*ff*; (2002a), 320*ff*. Taking the analysis further, Scharpf (1991), 621*ff*; Pasderski (1998), 4; Rölle and Blättel-Mink (1998), 74*ff*, 84, 265*ff*; Collins (1999), 248*ff*; Zwecker (1999), 163; Ensthaler and Gesmann-Nuissl (2000), 2268; Kreuder (2000), 203*ff*; Littmann and Jansen (2000), 69*f*; Supiot (2000), 135; Lange (2001a), 179*f*, 185; Windeler (2001), 194*f*, 227; Mendes (2002), 13*f*.

[19] See Luhmann (1995a), chap 5 VI; Gunther Teubner (1988), 'Enterprise Corporatism: New Industrial Policy and the "Essence" of the Legal Person', *American Journal of Comparative Law* 36, 130*ff*, 133*ff*.

III. EXTERNAL LIABILITY OF NETWORKS

Obviously, such new forms of social attribution also contemporaneously pose new risks for external parties. Their chameleon-like nature lends hybrid networks a superior degree of adaptability within a turbulent environment. Network unity, or alternatively, the autonomy of individual actors within the network, is stressed in turn, as context or opportunity dictates.[20] By the same token, however, permanent transition from collective to individual and back again, creates negative externalities, whereby the network is unduly relieved of responsibility towards third parties.[21]

1. Highly Centralised Networks

Once again, a distinction will be drawn between two contexts: centralised and decentralised networks.[22] At this stage, however, the issue is not that certain networks simultaneously display hierarchical characteristics. Rather, in certain 'pathological' cases, enterprises are institutionalised as simple contractual networks, but they are, in practice, highly centralised, with the consequence that they no longer benefit from typical networking gains in efficiency.[23] In particular, the double attribution that is typical for networks no longer plays a role in social practice: all transactions are apportioned to the unitary hierarchy. Given that such networks are so highly centralised and network node autonomy so greatly restricted, they should be treated simply as hierarchical organisations in contractual clothing. Such 'networks' are no more than strategic instruments for the evasion of mandatory law.[24] Empirical data appear to support the assertion that certain businesses do deploy a disaggregation strategy in order to avoid the external liability and labour law provisions

[20] Ortmann and Sydow (1999), 214.

[21] This critique is reproduced from the economic perspective by Noll (2002); from the sociological perspective by Ortmann and Sydow (1999), 214; Weyer (2000) 25; and from the legal perspective by Collins (1990a), 732*ff*; (1990b), 346*ff*; (1999), 248*ff*; Teubner (1991), 107*f*; (1993b), 57*ff*; (1992), 230*ff*; Zirkel (1990), 346; Bayreuther (2001), 399*f*; Lange (2001a), 179*f*, 185.

[22] This distinction appears in several variants: Martinek (1987), 231*ff*; (1992), 65*ff*, 78*ff*; (1997), 94*ff*; (2001), 327*ff*; Rohe (1998), 11*ff*, 356*ff*; Ensthaler and Gesmann-Nuissl (2000), 2267; Bayreuther (2001), 528*ff*, 580*ff*; Lange (2001a), 56*ff*; Teubner (2002a), 326*ff*.

[23] The 'pathological' network forms the focus for Bayreuther's work (2001).

[24] These arguments are also recognised by authors who stress networking efficiency gains: see Schanze (1993), 694; Ehricke (1996), 319*f*; Bayreuther (2001), 443.

that would otherwise attach to a unitary enterprise.[25] Notions of 'flexibility' and 'private deregulation' might well have a certain fashionable cachet. Translated into the sober language of the law applying to these cases, however, they denote no more than simple evasion of mandatory legal norms.[26]

In such extreme cases, where the economic reality underlying a contractual network is one of a unitary organisation with a highly centralised information, production, distribution and management structure,[27] problems of liability emerge when the choice of contractual form is made solely in order to evade the applicable law. Ideally speaking, mandatory rules should be applied analogously to those quasi-hybrids, which no longer exhibit the typical efficiency gains of networking between autonomous nodes. Since such centralised hybrids are functional economic units, they should also be treated as units for the purposes of liability. There is an imperative need for legal sanctions for 'regime deception'.[28] Should a chosen contractual form be revealed to mask organisational forms that are substantively comparable with corporations, the matter is one of misuse of legal form. Accordingly, liability law must prevent parties from evading the protective norms of the law of corporate groups through their choice of formal organisational form.[29] Highly centralised contractual networks would then be subject to piercing liability under the principles applicable to corporate groups, particularly, the rules applying to 'qualified factual corporate groups'.[30] In practice, this piercing liability is no longer applied with regard to the specific management structures and practices maintained within a corporate relationship. Instead, and in convergence with principles of tort law, this piercing liability is evolving into an independent concept applicable in all cases of extreme economic dependency, regardless of the legal form chosen.[31] By the same token, networks should not generally be subject to the strictures of corporate

[25] Henry Hansmann and Reinier Kraakman (1991), 'Toward Unlimited Shareholder Liability for Corporate Torts', *The Yale Law Journal* 100, 1879*ff*, 1881, 1913*ff*; Collins (1990b), 360*ff*; see also Felstead (1991), 53*f*; Schanze (1991), 100; Hirte (1992), 193*f*.

[26] Collins (1990a), 744.

[27] Martinek (1987), 123*ff*, 214*ff*; Dnes (1991), 133*ff*; Felstead (1991), 52; Bayreuther (2001), 394*ff*.

[28] Schanze and Haunhorst (1995), 195.

[29] Ehricke (1996), 319*f*; Bayreuther (2001), 443.

[30] Explicitly, Ehricke (1996), 320*ff*; Oechsler (1997), 482*ff*; Pasderski (1998), 37*ff*, 89; Bayreuther (2001), 295*ff*, 399*f*, 530. Martinek appears also to favour this form of external liability within his general conception, even if the issue is not explicitly addressed: Martinek (1987), 23*ff*, 633*ff*, 640; (1993b), 301*f*; Buschbeck-Bülow (1989), 352; (1990), 1061; Nagel (1988), 2292; Nagel, Riess and Theis (1989), 1508; Klebe and Roth (1990), 679; Lehmann (1990), 1851; Schlotke (1990), 269*ff*; Hirte (1992), 193, 197; Steinmann (1992), 171; Wagner (1992), 69*f*; Ensthaler (1994), 817, 819; Kessen (1996), 185; Steckler (1996), 139*f*; Wellenhofer-Klein (1997), 981.

[31] Oechsler (1997), 465, 484, 467*ff*.

law. Instead, piercing liability would only apply as a part of the effort to combat misuse of legal form.[32] Following this argument to a logical conclusion, this would then result in the extensive liability of the net centre. Inclusion of other members of the network in the circle of liability makes sense only in those cases in which franchising committees act as quasi-corporate organs of collective decision-making for the entire network.[33]

2. Decentralised Networks

By contrast, the issue of legal responsibility rises in complexity when it comes to decentralised networks. In this case, the matter is not one of the misuse of a legal form or the strategic deployment of highly centralised networks in an effort to circumvent mandatory law. Rather, decentralised networks exhibit all the typical negative externalities of networking, externalities that derive from intensified operational interconnections between network nodes.[34] Liability law must accordingly respond to the following four difficulties:

(1) *Diffusion of spheres of responsibility.* This issue is directly related to a structural deficit within networking – the lack of clear limits to a business (borders of the firm).[35] Whilst heterarchical networks do rely on a division of labour, services are nonetheless performed for a client in close co-operation such that the limits to individual areas of operation are systematically obscured. Accordingly, it is difficult or even impossible to identify individual spheres of responsibility.[36] Simple imposition of individual liability only upon the portion of the network that maintains relations with an external client would thus seem to be inadequate in principle. In addition, however, heterarchical networks often give rise to triadic performances, whereby only a portion of the performance is autonomously completed for the client by the network node, whilst the character of a second portion is dictated by the network centre, and a third portion is directly organised by that same centre. In such cases, it would accordingly seem to be appropriate to afford an external party a direct cause of action against the network centre, at least to the degree

[32] Oechsler (1997), 482*ff*; Pasderski (1998), 37*ff*, 89; Bayreuther (2001), 295*ff*, 399*f*, 530.

[33] On this problem, see Hirte (1992), 197*f*.

[34] Precise consideration in Amstutz and Schluep (2003), 888.

[35] The obscuring of boundaries within networks is comprehensively analysed by Badaracco (1991); Sabel (1991), 23*ff*; Picot and Wigand (1996); Ashkenas, Ulrich, Jick and Kern (1995); Krystek, Redel and Reppegather (1997); Ortmann and Sydow (1999), 207*ff*; Luhmann (2000), 235*ff*; Windeler (2001), 262 *ff*.

[36] On the dysfunctional effects of dissolution of boundaries within networking, Ortmann and Sydow (1999), 206. On consequential problems for legal apportionment of responsibility, see Zirkel (1990), 346; Wellenhofer-Klein (1999), 282*ff*.

that a failure in performance relates to those portions of conduct that are directly governed or organised by the network centre.

(2) *Compensation for deficits within tort liability.* Networks providing services have expanded drastically in recent years. This development has revealed severe deficits within tort liability.[37] A legislative scheme of liability for provision of services, comparable with that for product liability, and suitably sensitive to interconnections or hierarchies of independent service providers, does not exist. Equally, quite apart from their limited chances of success, European endeavours to establish a services liability directive fail properly to address this point. Draft proposals work with a fiction and result only in imposition of a poorly defined duty of substitute liability placed upon the franchisor for actions of the franchisee.[38] Case law on liability for services is likewise poorly developed in comparison with product liability, and struggles with the problem of division of labour.[39]

But it also is questionable whether simple tort liability is adequate for production and supply networks. It is surely not appropriate to focus all intensified obligations deriving from the relationship with the client upon the contracting network node, and to impose only tortious duties on all other members of the network. Equally, however, the imposition of vicarious liability for actions of a network node on the network centre does not properly reflect the connectivity of business networks.[40] Instead, principles resembling a piercing liability would seem to be necessary in order to capture the phenomenon of close operational co-ordination between the network centre and the network nodes. Network liability must impose intensified obligations in relation to third parties both upon the system centre and upon all members of the system involved, without, however, exposing them to the full range of obligations that derive from the contract.

(3) *A privileged position in comparison with corporate organisation.* It should now be clear that networks derive significant gains in efficiency and in legitimacy from their organisation via bilateral contracts, and that a blanket imposition of corporate legal form upon them would not

[37] See Krebs (2000), 382.

[38] Proposal for a directive on liability for service provision, COM/1990/482, OJ C/1991/12/8. Commission green paper on the creation of service provision liability, COM/1994/260 (23 June 1994). For an analysis of the proposed directive on external liability within franchising, see Bräutigam (1994), 149*ff*, 190*ff*. On the recent state of the debate, see Christopher Hodges (2000), *Position Paper: Safety of Services*. At: http://europa.eu.int/comm/consumers/cons_org/assembly/event32/event32_wrk3–1_en.pdf.

[39] See the concerns of Brüggemeier (2004), chap E I1e.

[40] Arguments in favour of the expanded application of vicarious liability (831 BGB) to independent businesses, Roth (1989), 436; Bräutigam (1994), 130*ff*, 138*ff*; Pasderski (1998), 168*ff*. However, given the notorious difficulties of application, § 831 BGB is not a particularly effective form of liability.

correspond to their real structure.[41] Nonetheless, where networks and organisations share various associational characteristics, a certain degree of convergent treatment will be necessary in relation to particular issues. Thus, for example, the law unduly privileges contractually organised franchising systems over either corporate groups that distribute goods and services through subsidiaries or unitary franchising businesses organised under company law, both of which are subject to stronger forms of corporate liability.[42] The same is true for virtual enterprises founded upon bilateral contracts for co-operation, which possess a degree of corporate character similar to that exhibited by genuine legal corporations.[43] This privileged position with regard to liability cannot be justified substantively and results in illegitimate gains in transaction costs. 'Piercing of the contractual veil' will be necessary under certain conditions, and in order fully to exclude negative external effects.[44]

(4) Network regulation. Taking into account that laws governing legal liability promote not only distributive policies, but also preventative and interventionist policies,[45] the potential for external intervention into networks is very limited. Networks cannot be steered by simply influencing the individual goals of the nodes. The concentration of efforts on imposing legal sanctions upon the network node in order to influence networking behaviour is wholly misplaced. Yet, this is exactly the scheme that is created through the imposition of individual exposure to the risk of liability upon members of the network who establish contractual relations with external parties. The result is a dramatic failure in intervention, since the addressees of intervention have been wrongly chosen. Interventionist signals sent out by the imposition of legal liability only reach one network node and are rarely, if ever, received by other network nodes or by the network centre responsible for internal management.[46] No direct connection is made with the cost–benefit calculations of those

[41] See above, Chapter 2 (II, VI).

[42] For comprehensive analysis of various franchising network forms and the distinctions between them, Martinek (1987), 33*ff*, 75*ff*; Bauder (1988), 42*ff*. Oechsler (1997), 482 and Bayreuther (2001), 443 criticise the fact that the legal form adopted within network organisations privileges them above corporations with regard to external liability. See also Kirchner (1993), 200 on institutional advantages when corporations are compared with contractual networks.

[43] For a comprehensive comparison of virtual businesses with legal corporations, Mayer, Kram and Patkos (1998), 45*ff*; Lange (2001a), 67*ff*.

[44] Lange (2001a), 185.

[45] Eg Mertens in *Münchener Kommentar* (1997), vor § 823, 44*ff*; Brüggemeier (2004), Chap A I, with further references; taking a more restrictive view, Karl Larenz (1987), *Lehrbuch des Schuldrechts. Band I. Allgemeiner Teil.* 14th edn, Munich: Beck, 421*ff*, 423; Josef Esser and Leo Weyers (2000), *Schuldrecht: Ein Lehrbuch. Besonderer Teil. II.* 8th edn, Heidelberg: Müller, 135*ff*.

[46] This, however, is the primary precondition for effective intervention within organisations: Brüggemeier (2004), chap A I.

members of the network who are involved in the transaction.[47] This, however, must be the goal of all intervention within networks.[48] Seen from the viewpoint of prevention, in the case of damaging instructions given by the network centre, giving a right of action to the member of who is externally liable against the network centre is also inadequate. Given their extreme economic dependence, members of the network will rarely risk an action for redress against the network centre. These problems are particularly notorious within just-in-time and franchising systems.[49] As a consequence, the law must evolve a form of external liability that directly impacts upon the cost–benefit calculations made by all central and significant decision makers within the network.

IV. DECENTRALISED NETWORK LIABILITY

These four difficulties speak in favour of external network liability. However, network liability must be constructed differently from the individual liability that attaches to natural persons and from the collective liability that is imposed on organisations. The thesis pursued here argues that a form of network liability must be developed within the doctrine of connected contracts that addresses these problems.[50] The external liability of networks extends beyond the individual liability imposed on single members of the network by virtue of their status as contractual partners, to encompass other members of the network within the circle of those liable for breach of obligation, to the exact degree that they participated within the particular transaction. Network liability, however, does not extend as far as corporate liability, since the network possesses no independent property to which a liability claim might attach. Instead, the network only enters the equation in order to permit a

[47] On interventionist potential within liability law, see Michael Adams (1985), *Ökonomische Analyse der Gefährdungs- und Verschuldenshaftung*. Heidelberg: Decker and Schenck, 88*ff*; Peter Behrens (1986), *Die ökonomischen Grundlagen des Rechts*. Tübingen: Mohr Siebeck, 174*ff*; Brüggemeier (1986), 47*ff*; (1988), 'Produkthaftung und Produktsicherheit', *Zeitschrift für das gesamte Handelsrecht und Wirtschaftsrecht* 152, 511*ff*, 512*ff*; (2004), chap AI; Schäfer and Ott (2000), 85*ff*.

[48] Picker (1999), 428 stresses prevention when he argues that special extra-contractual relationships should give rise to liability. With specific regard to functional networking preconditions, Amstutz and Schluep (2003), 888.

[49] On the lack of readiness of members of the network to pursue claims against the net centre within franchising, see Christine Windbichler (1998), 'Neue Vertriebsformen und ihr Einfluss auf das Kaufrecht', *Archiv für die civilistische Praxis* 198, 261*ff*, 281; Krebs (2000), 382; on the same problem in just-in-time systems, Wellenhofer-Klein (1999), 201.

[50] An argument already pursued by Teubner (1991), 129*ff*; (1993b), 57*ff*; (1992), 226*ff*; (2002a), 324*ff*. Showing a similar preference for the adoption of a solution founded within network liability, Wolf and Ungeheuer (1994), 1033; Reich (1995), 76; Krebs (2000), 316*f*, 381*ff*; Lange (2001a), 185. These general notions of network liability will be further developed here and integrated within doctrine applying to contractual relationships.

transfer of responsibility to other members involved in the particular activity of the network, whether centre or nodes. A form of network liability needs to be developed that not only combats problems posed by networking, but which also presents a conceptual framework that avoids the pitfalls into which the competing doctrinal constructions to be discussed in the following paragraphs have fallen.

1. Network Contract

The major service offered by Möschel's idea of a network contract is the manner in which it relates external network liability to the division of responsibility within the network. The innovative action taken by the Federal High Court when imposing piercing liability on banking networks is recognised as being correct in its effects, even if founded on an inadequate doctrinal base. The network contract, it is argued, will extend liability to other members within the banking network with suitable doctrinal foundations. When an external client is 'connected' by means of a 'network contract' with his own bank to a larger network of banks, the chain of numerous banks can be leapfrogged, in order to give the client a direct cause of action against the bank that has breached its obligations.[51]

By the same token, however, Rohe's supplementary efforts to relocate the network contract within traditional private law with the help of a Byzantine conception of all-encompassing, but unexpressed, powers of agency, as well as the silent conclusion of contracts in the name of all members of the network, have predictably fatal consequences for external networking liability. Once again, they lead to contradictions in the treatment of heterarchical and hierarchical networks. Within heterarchical networks, clients themselves are supposed to become members of the network, such that the conclusion of a contract affords them causes of action against all members of the network. With this move, external liability is transformed into a form of internal liability.[52] This rather remarkable transformation of a client into a member of the network not only defeats the economic function of networks. In addition, it also contradicts the original idea of a network contract, whereby a 'connection' of the client to the network denotes an external contact, without transforming the client into a member of the network. The degree of overkill is even recognised by Rohe himself, who subsequently seeks to

[51] Möschel (1986), 211*ff*.

[52] Rohe (1998), 169: 'Thus, we cannot talk about "third parties". Instead, all are members of the network (with different obligations).'

dilute its effects, by precluding clients from pursuing claims for specific performance against other banks, even though they are supposedly members of the network.[53]

In the case of hierarchical networks, Rohe then makes an even less plausible distinction. Clients never become members of the network within hierarchical networks. Consequently, they are never afforded causes of action against other members of the network or the network centre.[54] This differential treatment of external liability in relation to heterarchical and hierarchical networks operates with a rather exaggerated view of the significance of hierarchy, such that Rohe's hierarchical networks seem to be devoid of any networking structures whatsoever. Social science studies, by contrast, repeatedly emphasise that the success of networking depends on the intelligent combination of heterarchical and hierarchical features.[55] Why should subordination franchising be spared liability if co-ordinated and confederal franchising are recognised as horizontal networking forms and are thus subject to it? More commonly, arguments take exactly the opposite line: the greater the hierarchical degree of direction within an organisation, the greater the justification for piercing liability. In contrast, piercing liability is surely less justifiable in the case of the heterarchical co-ordination of equally empowered members of the network.[56]

In the final analysis, Rohe's network contract simultaneously affords external parties too great and too small a degree of protection. Equally, it supplies only partially satisfactory solutions to the four particular networking problems detailed above. It is only fully appropriate for dispersal of responsibility within heterarchical networks. For the case of hierarchical networking, it neither compensates properly for deficits within tort law, nor overcomes the privileged position against liability that is won for themselves by networks in comparison with corporate organisations, and even gives the wrong interventionist signals to members of the network, since it frees the network centre and other members of the network from the consequences of a breach in their obligations.

2. Apparent Agency

As some authors suggest, rules of 'apparent agency' may also be used to justify legal claims brought by external clients against the network centre

53 Rohe (1998), 195*ff*.
54 Rohe (1998), 356*f*, 389*ff* (just-in-time systems), 416*ff*, 430*ff* (franchising).
55 Heidling (2000), 65*ff*; Windeler (2001), 43.
56 Representative, Bayreuther (2001), 443.

on the basis of a contract.[57] The projection of a unitary image makes it difficult for clients to appreciate that franchisees are in fact independent enterprises. Thus, the franchisor's behaviour in encouraging franchisees to present a unitary image, as well as its corresponding lack of regard for the independent nature of franchisees, can be used to impute a will to the franchisor to give full powers of agency to each business unit. Thus, each franchisee takes on the appearance of a branch of the franchisor, such that a direct contract is concluded between the client and the franchisor under the rules of apparent agency. Result: 'The franchisor rather than the franchisee is bound by a contractual obligation.'[58]

Apparent agency, however, systematically fails to address the social reality of networking. Franchisees normally conclude contracts with clients in their own name, at their own risk, and with no intention to act as agents for the franchisor. Furthermore, were the judiciary to apply the rules of apparent agency, this would very quickly be undermined by publicity campaigns conducted by franchisors' associations and by a couple of well-placed statements of clarification on invoices and shop doorways.[59] The point is not misleading clients, misuse of legal form or creation of a false impression, which must then be corrected through rules on apparent agency. The connectivity of individual dealers is not a systematic denial of reality, to be combated with legal rules. Rather, networking is itself a new reality, which plays out according to its own rules.

However, even though neither doctrinal construction – network contract and apparent agency – seems to be fully appropriate, it should be noted that both do, at least in part, react with sensitivity to a new reality in distribution, applying suitable liability sanctions to a reality that is distinct from autonomous individual market dealers or an organisation of branches within a firm. It is once again readily apparent that networks dissect traditional concepts of contract law. Neither the rules on the formation of contracts in one's own name, nor those on formation in the name of another party, are in a position fully to capture the logic of networking. On the one hand, contractual responsibility is apportioned only to the franchisee, with the effect that the common operation of the

[57] Jens Ekkenga (1990), *Die Inhaltskontrolle von Franchiseverträgen: Eine Studie zu den zivilrechtlichen Grenzen der Vertragsgestaltung im Bereich des Franchising unter Einschluss des Vertragshändlerrechts*. Heidelberg: Recht und Wirtschaft, 97 and fn 331; Bräutigam (1994), 38*ff*; Wolf and Ungeheuer (1994), 1028*ff*; Pasderski (1998), 90*ff*; Heinrichs in *Palandt* (2003), § 164, 6; Weidenkaff in *Palandt* (2003), vor § 581, 22; Claus-Wilhelm Canaris (1995), *Handelsrecht*. 22nd edn, Munich: Beck, § 18 III 5a. Highly critical of the construction, Eike Ullmann (1994), 'Die Verwendung von Marke, Geschäftsbezeichnung und Firma im geschäftlichen Verkehr, insbesondere des Franchising', *Neue Juristische Wochenschrift* 47, 1255*ff*, 1256; Rohe (1998), 431*ff*.

[58] Wolf and Ungeheuer (1994), 1032.

[59] For greater details, see Ullmann (1994), 1259*ff*; Rohe (1998), 432*f*.

whole network is not subject to appropriate external liability. On the other hand, however, responsibility is solely placed on the franchisor, with the result that no value is placed on the autonomous action of the franchisee. The practice of contracting with franchising networks seems to be somewhere in between. Network logic apparently dictates that both franchisor and franchisee present themselves to the world 'in common'. The franchising system in its guise as an independent institution is 'representative' – and not just in its appearance – of franchisees. Even where the 'formal' bond is created by individual contracts concluded between clients and franchisees, the 'material' transaction is one conducted between client and the entire network as a unitary economic unit. Within this constellation, the close interrelationship between franchising systems and third party financing contracts is once again readily apparent. In the case of the latter, the vendor and creditor institution might be judged as 'taking on a common character as a single contractual interlocutor'.[60] This test should not be regarded as a simple test of whether the appearance of agency prevails. Instead, the test should be approached in an objective rather than subjective manner.

It is again apparent that the logic of networks will be captured by double attribution. Can the law also implement double attribution in this case? In practice, a rudimentary form of double attribution already exists at the moment of formation of a contract. Usually, contracts between clients and franchisees make more or less explicit reference to the existence of a franchising system, because the contractual partner clearly identifies himself with a brand name. The contract accordingly makes it clear that a client is not simply contracting with an individual dealer in the market, but is instead confronted with an integrated network of autonomous economic actors. By this token, the assumptions underlying network contracts and notions of apparent agency are not wholly false: the existence of a network already affords the act of concluding a contract a different substantive quality, such that contractual effects should not simply impact upon the network node as the concrete contract partner, but must also be apportioned to the network. The only problem is how to find more appropriate modes to give concrete expression to this assumption.

3. Contract with Protective Effects for Third Parties

What other legal institutions can adequately address networking in the context of external liability? Possible solutions are offered, on the one hand, by the contract for the protection of a third party, and, on the other, by *culpa in contrahendo* by a third party (*Sachwalterhaftung*). However, and

[60] OLG Cologne ZIP 1995, 21; Heinrichs in *Palandt* (2003), § 358, 15.

notwithstanding their close relationship to the particular problem posed, both solutions are subject to weighty objections about their compatibility with the logic of networking. First, both models of liability, each of which addresses the issue of effects of contracts upon third parties, relate exclusively to individual contracts and cannot adequately deal with the multilaterality in networks. Contracts with protective effects for third parties would exclusively address the agreements within networks. *Culpa in contrahendo* would relate exclusively to the external contract concluded with the client. Neither construction can address adequately the problems of network liability on their own. Second, even the combination of both models fails properly to capture the problems of multilaterality. Network obligations to a client should be distilled out of the interplay of all agreements made within the connected contracts. In the final analysis, they should be derived from a reconstruction of the overarching purpose of the network. As a consequence, it is proposed to combine the principles of contracts with protective effects for third parties with *culpa in contrahendo*, but only to the degree that both are prised out of their individualistic contractual straitjacket and inserted within a notion of multilateral contractual relationships.[61] Sacrificing any one of these three elements upon the altar of a 'neat' solution results only in a restricted understanding of the complex relations maintained between networks and their external clients.

The case law that applies the contract with protective effects for a third party to networks for transferring money for the purpose of permitting clients to make direct claims against intermediary banks has not simply plucked its justification out of the air.[62] Instead, judges used a construction that has often proven its value by selectively puncturing the boundaries of the bilateral contract, and, at the same time, maintaining privity of contract. An even more exact test than that of 'performance proximity' is the test of 'intended third party performance impact', which further inserts itself neatly within the construction of network liability.[63] This test

[61] In earlier publications, I left the question of whether network liability should build upon the principles of the third party protection contract, or, alternatively, required its own construction, open: Teubner (1990a), 309; (1992), 231*f*. It cannot be doubted that certain principles of the third party protection contract form adequate criteria for network liability, criteria highly preferable above other misleading constructions. Nonetheless, the third party protection contract is not really adequate, since it places no value either on the client's contract, or on the associational character of the transaction. Thus, the following pages argue for a combination. Similar considerations can be found in Larenz and M Wolf (1997), 470.

[62] Case law since BGHZ 96, 9, 17. See, for the third party protection contract and the new legislative regulation of liability for bank transfers, (§§ 676a BGB) Langenbucher (2001), 466*ff*.

[63] See for the differentiation between these two combinations within the third party protection contract, Gernhuber (1989), 512*ff*; Gottwald in *Münchener Kommentar* (2003), § 328, 107*f*.

reconstructs in law a structural characteristic of networking: a division of labour exists within networks, such that individual members of the network perform a series of individual operations that are also simultaneously integrated with one another and performed for the benefit of the client; however, performance is also undertaken in such a manner that only one member of the network, rather than the collective or a series of participants in the network, enters a contract with the client. At the same time, important distinctions between the internal and external relationships of the network become apparent. Whilst the contract with protective effects for a third party does not contain suitable criteria for the capturing of relations between members of the network who are not bound contractually with each other,[64] the notion of 'intended third party performance impact' is quite fruitful in relation to external network liability. Performances are completed within the net with the intention of favouring a third party.

However, some premises of the contract with protective effects for a third party are misleading for the liability of networks.[65] One premise is to found the whole construction on implied terms. This causes particular problems for networks, since members of a network often make explicit use of bilateral contracting in their efforts to avoid liability with respect to third parties. Nevertheless, case law has (correctly) managed to impose a form of expanded liability against the will of other members of the network.[66] But then, this liability can no longer be based upon implied terms. The second premise demands the existence of a fiduciary relationship between one partner of the contract and the third party, which does not fit at all within the network constellation. The judiciary was accordingly quick to dispense with this premise of a fiduciary relation in cases of liability of networks, and to substitute for it typical criteria of networks (mass business, unitary procedures, risks typical for the operation).[67] The same is true for principles relating to the transfer of defences against the third party (§ 334 BGB) and to a contractual

[64] See the argument presented in Chapter 5 (VI).

[65] See, for the different problem constellation in relation to internal liability within the network, Chapter 5 (VI).

[66] Rohe's attempt to relate network liability to the 'will' of network participants, such that a distinction can be made between hierarchical and heterarchical networks, is highly questionable (1998) 418*f*: within credit payment operations 'participants had, by contrast, at least approved the results of dominant case law'(!); within franchising systems they had not done so since 'participants clearly did not want them (such results), they could not be justified within the net contract', Highly critical of Rohe's efforts to establish network liability out of party will, Krebs (2000), 314: 'the particular interests of persons who control a network . . . clearly contradict such legal imputation. If direct obligations arise in this context, they do so only by virtue of the existence of objective law, and not since the parties wished it to be so.'

[67] BGHZ 69, 82, 86.

exclusion of liability. The greatest problems, however, arise out of the premise that the contract with protective effects for a third party only furnishes an asymmetrical perspective on networking. Obligations toward the third party are only perceived from the perspective of internal agreements made between participants in the network. There is no room for shaping these obligations from the perspective of an external client. It is therefore once again apparent that 'multilateral economic operations cannot, in the long term, be adequately captured and explained within a contractual model that is derived principally from bilateral relationships'.[68] In order to make it appropriate for network liability, the contract with protective effects for a third party would need to undergo drastic changes. But the one feature worth retaining is the concept of 'intended third party performance impacts'.

4. *Culpa in contrahendo* by Third Parties (*Sachwalterhaftung*)

In an effort to avoid the asymmetry, one might concentrate upon the client contract and justify liability of other members of the network or the network centre from this perspective. As already noted, a contract with the network entails from its very inception a connection between the external client and the network as such, because performance is dependent upon the operations of other members of the network. In such cases of expansion of a contract to include autonomous third party performance, recourse to, and appropriation of, the notion of *culpa in contrahendo* by third parties (*Sachwalterhaftung*), § 311(III)(1) BGB (Civil Code)[69] immediately suggests itself.[70] In addition to the contracting network node, the network centre and/or other members of the network are also responsible for the fulfilment of obligations to the client, and should be made responsible for any breach of obligations within their areas of operation.

Culpa in contrahendo by third parties does not offer as strong a purchase for doctrinal evolution as does the contract with protective effects for a third party. To date, the notion of the individual liability of independent

[68] See, K Schmidt (1999), 1019, for external liability of banking money transfer nets.

[69] § 311(3) BGB: An obligation with duties under § 241(2) may also come into existence in relation to persons who are not themselves intended to be parties to the contract. Such an obligation comes into existence in particular if the third party, by laying claim to being given a particularly high degree of trust, substantially influences the pre-contract negotiations or the entering into of the contract.

[70] 'A person who is neither a party to a contract nor a representative of one of the parties, but is still involved in the conclusion of a contract. The *Sachwalter* stands within the camp of one of the contracting parties and enjoys the other party's confidence due to his conduct. According to court rulings there is a personal liability *culpa in contrahendo*, the so-called *Sachwalter* liability.' Clara-Erika Dietl and Egon Lorenz (2005), *Dictionary of Legal, Commercial and Political Terms*. 5th edn, Munich: Beck, 637*f*.

third parties, with its origin in the individual liability imposed upon agents acting in their own economic interest and with the full confidence of contractual parties, has only been firmly established at the time of the conclusion of the contract.[71] If independent third parties have a significant impact upon contractual negotiations, act in their own economic interests, and are trusted by parties to a contract, they are liable under rules of *culpa in contrahendo*, even though they are not themselves parties to the contract.

This liability has witnessed a dramatic expansion in the realm of liability based upon a prospectus for investment in projects.[72] Parallels to networking are apparent.

> Investors confronted with the complex of partners that groups around an investment project are confronted with one contractual party, whose exact character is very difficult to determine. Initiators develop an investment project, which will be performed by a company, with the aid and advice of a variety of experts. They propose that individual contributions will be supplied by means of a more or less *independent distribution organisation*, such that an investor is confronted by a multitude of project declarations by the various different participants found within the differentiated distribution system, the reliability of each of which he must assess independently.[73]

Parallels to network liability are apparent if the individual members of a project are seen as participants within an independent distribution system. A network of bilateral contractual relationships identifies its own unity within the distribution 'project'. Typically, actors are both 'contractual partners' within and 'organs' of the distribution system. Which nodes within the distribution network establish a particular contractual external contact is often only a matter of coincidence: managers of the company, solicitors, accountants, financial advisors or investment advisors. Typically, trust is invested in the whole 'distribution system'. Is it really appropriate, in such a case, to permit haphazard forms of external contact to determine the question of liability? The problem within investment projects is then as follows: should 'civil law rules of liability, which are designed primarily to apply only to contractual operations, be used in the attempt to regulate the supply of the assets of a public corporation by a formal organisation that, for its part, cannot be properly categorised within company law typologies'.[74] Usually, the investment project is the common task of a network of solicitors, accountants, financial advisers and financing institutions. Case law has accordingly included all such

[71] On current developments and the state of debate, see Schramm in Münchener *Kommentar* (2001), § 164, 11; Emmerich in *Münchener Kommentar* (2003), § 311,195*ff*, in particular for applicable law following modernisation of the law of obligations.

[72] See Emmerich in *Münchener Kommentar* (2003), § 311, 162*ff*.

[73] Assmann (1986), 319 (emphasis by the authors).

[74] Assmann (1986), 307.

parties within the circle of liability, on account of their own impact upon and responsibility for the conclusion of the contract.

The particular problem of network liability tackled in this study is only occasionally confronted by instances of *culpa in contrahendo*, for which other members of a network must also be made liable. It is interesting to note that *culpa in contrahendo* furnishes us with a model for network liability, albeit that it does not give it this name. Although they are not themselves contractual parties, members of the network are liable for any breach of obligation traceable to them under contractual principles and at the moment of the conclusion of a contract. However, the vast majority of our problems of network liability arise only after formation of a contract. Accordingly, the question then arises as to whether the principles of third party liability can be extended beyond simple *culpa in contrahendo* to apply to cases of subsequent breach of contract. The comparable nature of the interest constellations before and after conclusion of the contract speaks in favour of such an extension.[75] In practice, various Federal High Court judgments and a portion of academic literature accept that third party liability also applies to cases of breach of contract.[76] According to this line of opinion, this liability attaches to actors in whom the other contractual party trusted for purposes of the performance of the contract, and who are, in fact, the parties whose economic interests are at stake.[77] Nonetheless, this line of opinion does not yet secure certain results. The new provisions found within § 311(III)(1) BGB certainly make it possible to pursue this line of doctrinal thought.[78] However, particular uncertainties remain, since practice has yet to throw up a sufficient number of cases where this reasoning could be applied explicitly. Networking is clearly the area within which this third party liability might prove itself. In any case, network centres would meet the relevant criteria: (1) reliance on trust; (2) influence on contractual performance; (3) interested economic party.

With a particular eye to the new provisions of § 311(III)(1) BGB, a distinction should be made between the status of 'parties' within bilateral contracts, negotiation systems, and networks. As a common rule, it is fair to assume that the parties to bilateral contracts remain constant throughout the various phases of contractual negotiation, contractual conclusion and

[75] BGHZ 70, 337, 341.

[76] BGHZ 14, 313; BGH NJW 1964, 2009; BGHZ 70, 337; BGH NJW-RR 1987, 335; Schilken in *Staudinger* (2001), § 164, 15; Schramm in *Münchener Kommentar* (2001), § 164, 12; Emmerich in *Münchener Kommentar* (2003), § 311, 222; sceptical, Gernhuber (1989), 565*f*.

[77] BGHZ 70, 337, 341; Schramm in *Münchener Kommentar* (2001), § 164, 12.

[78] Thus, Emmerich in *Münchener Kommentar* (2003), § 311, 204, even though with various doubts. BGB § 311: An obligation [to respect the rights and legal and other interests] of the other party comes into existence on (1) the commencement of negotiations for a contract, or (2) the initiation of negotiations where one party, in view of the prospective contract, gives the other party the opportunity to affect his rights and legal and other interests or entrusts them to him, or (3) similar contacts between businesses.

contractual performance. In contrast, this is not necessarily the case in relation to multi-polar relationships. The 'parties' in the negotiation phase may be different from those who conclude the contract. And again different 'parties' may act in the performance phase. Usually, complex and enduring contractual relationships exhibit the following constellation: a host of independent experts of all types commonly play a part in contractual negotiations; the contract, however, is only concluded by one enterprise, which then divides the labour of performance of the contract amongst a variety of independent actors. Within franchises involving services, the franchisor is not a party to the contract with a client, but is actively involved in the performance together with the other parties. The implicit assumption made within bipolar contracting that the two parties remain constant should thus be dispensed with. Instead, a systematic distinction should be made between 'negotiation parties', 'contractual conclusion parties' and 'contractual performance parties'.[79] Contract law has already firmly established this distinction in relation to the negotiation phase. *Culpa in contrahendo* by third parties recognises a plurality of 'negotiation parties' within the pre-contractual phase, who are not necessarily identical with the subsequent 'contractual conclusion parties', and makes the former liable for their own breaches of obligation. The claimant's circle of interlocutory partners is accordingly extended through a combined application of *culpa in contrahendo* and the contract with protective effects for a third party. The nature of the defendant's circle of co-respondents nonetheless remains highly controversial, and understandably so, given the ban on the conclusion of a contract that places a burden on a third party. Networks nonetheless seem incontrovertibly to demand an extension of liability for third parties.[80] They include additional economically independent actors within the whole transactional process, without, however, giving them formal legal recognition as 'contractual partners' within the contract. It is nonetheless true that they are included within the formation of a contract to the extent that the contract contains reference to the network and to the division of the burden of contractual performance amongst independent economic actors. Contract law should thus be required to recognise 'performance parties' regardless of whether they were originally acting as 'contractual conclusion parties' or as 'negotiation parties'. The new provisions of § 311(III)(1) BGB, which extend contractual liability in the case of reliance on third parties, might facilitate this approach.

[79] On these concepts, but with scepticism about the notion of the performance party, Gernhuber (1989), 566.

[80] The need for this extension is particularly stressed by Möschel (1986), 222*ff*; Picker (1999), 428*ff*; Krebs (2000), 23*ff* from the viewpoint of the special relationship, and by Rohe (1998), 195*ff* from the viewpoint of the network contract, albeit only for heterarchical networks.

A brief excursion through law applicable to banking gironets should bring further clarification to the argument. New liability rules imposed by the law governing transfers of funds (§ 676 BGB) offer us sufficient glimpses of a special 'network liability' or 'special law applicable to contractual chains',[81] which indeed combines aspects of the contract with protective effects for a third party with *Sachwalterhaftung*.[82] At first glance, the new regulation on money transfers seems to preclude networking liability, since it concentrates liability for all errors within the transfer network upon the client's bank. Nonetheless, doubts arise: why does the law not simply apply § 278 BGB,[83] rather than work with the fiction of liability for vicarious agents? The reason lies within the network logic governing transfer operations. Autonomous 'transporters' are not vicarious agents. The gironet is not organised by the client's bank.[84] Consequently, the gironet cannot simply be made subject to classical principles of liability under § 278 BGB. Instead, the law is forced to create independent channels of liability for cases of a breach of obligation by independent actors within the network, which whilst not named network liability as such, are justified through the above-mentioned fiction.

The particular network problems become even clearer under § 676(b)(III) (sentence 6)[85] and § 676(e)(V)[86] BGB liability regulation.

[81] See, the formulations of Schneider (1999), 2192, which make it clear that networks require special rules. Similarly, at core, Langenbucher (2001), 466*ff*. See also Wackerbarth (2000), 1187*ff*.

[82] Hoffmann (2001), 887.

[83] § 278 BGB: The obligor is responsible for fault on the part of his legal representative, and of persons whom he uses to perform his obligation, to the same extent as for fault on his own part.

[84] For critique of the § 278 BGB solution, Rohe (1998), 120*ff*; K Schmidt (1999), 1017.

[85] § 676(b)(3) BGB: The transferor may demand the return of the transfer amount up to an amount of 12,500 euros (guarantee amount) plus fees and expenses already paid for the transfer if the transfer has been executed neither by the end of the transaction period nor within an additional period of time of fourteen banking days from the demand of the transferor for return on. The transfer amount is in this case to bear interest from the commencement of the transaction period up to crediting of the guarantee amount to the account of the transferor at the rate of interest specified in subsection (1) sentence 2. Upon demand for return by the transferor and the end of the additional period of time the bank transfer contract is deemed to be terminated. The banking institution is entitled to terminate the contract if the banking institution cannot reasonably be expected to continue the contract, weighing the interests of both parties, provided it has paid the guarantee amount or pays it simultaneously. The transferor need not, in the cases cited in sentences 3 and 4, pay the agreed fees and expenses. Claims under this subsection do not exist if the bank transfer has not been executed because the transferor has given the transferring banking institution erroneous or incomplete instructions or if an intermediate bank expressly specified by the transferor has failed to execute the bank transfer. In the second case of sentence 6, the banking institution expressly specified by the transferor is liable to the transferor in the place of the transferring banking institution.

[86] § 676 (e) BGB: (5) Where claims fail because the transferor specified the banking institution commissioned with forwarding, then the banking institution must put the transferor in the same position he would be in if § 676b (3) applied. Apart from this, § 676b (4) applies with the necessary modifications.

Should a bank client explicitly require that a specific intermediary bank be included within the transfer operation, the client's bank is relieved of all liability for transfer errors made by the intermediary bank. Nevertheless, the doctrinal construction is doubtful.[87] Is it a contract with protective effects for a third party? A liquidation of third party damages? A legislatively imposed transfer? Or even: 'liquidation of a third party cause of action'?[88] Doctrinal clarity only arises where the liability of the intermediate bank is justified by a recourse to the structure of the network. The contract between the instructing and intervening bank contains an 'intended third party performance impact' in the form of the performance of a transfer of funds, which would justify liability under the standards of the contract with protective effects for a third party. However, this does not yet fully capture the entire operation. As legislation prescribes, reference must be made to the transfer contract between client and instructing bank in order to make obligations concrete. Yet, in line with its purpose, the contract contains reference to the gironet: performance should be divided between autonomous economic actors. Further intermediate banks are not vicarious agents under § 278 BGB, but rather the above-mentioned independent 'performance parties' to the contract for the transfer of funds. As members of the network they satisfy the criteria for imposition of *Sachwalterhaftung*: (1) 'personal direct economic interest in'; (2) 'personal effort to awaken trust for'; and (3) 'contractual sovereignty' over their part of the performance. In the final analysis, however, the simple combination of a single transfer contract and a single payment contract does not adequately describe the obligations imposed upon an intervening bank. Instead, the contracts must be viewed within the context of the overarching gironet system, in order to give rise to a properly apportioned distribution of risk between the participants. In summary: this legislative regulation of complex network liability dispenses with the usual doctrinal categories, and instead selectively apportions liability to individual members of the network.

5. Network Liability

As the banking gironet demonstrates, however, *Sachwalterhaftung* also has certain deficits if applied to connected contracts. Once again an asymmetry is apparent. For its part, this liability is largely one-sided, attaching only to an individual contract. Whilst the particular problem posed by the contract with protective effects for a third party was its

[87] Heermann (2003), 214*f*, with further references, 230.

[88] Empathy must be expressed for despair felt by Hoffmann (2001), 886*ff*, in his efforts to identify a traditional doctrinal solution.

overemphasis upon internal networking relationships, *culpa in contrahendo* suffers from the defect that it refers only to the external client contract, such that its criteria for 'third party obligations' are exclusively derived from this contact. Accordingly, the doctrines of a contract with protective effects for a third party and *culpa in contrahendo* have a complementary relationship with one another. Whilst the latter places obligations on other parties who have a relationship with the client, the contract with protective effects affords the client the status of a creditor of other members of the network. At first glance, the two constructions might be thought to be easily substituted for one another. This, however, is not the case, since their criteria for imposition of obligations are constructed differently. The contract with protective effects for a third party defines its criteria with reference to agreements that are internal to the network, and attaches its protection to the client. *Culpa in contrahendo* defines its criteria with reference to the client's contract and reaches out from this position to impose obligations on other members of the network. 'Contractual collision', or divergence between the obligations deriving from the internal network agreement and from the client contract is a constant danger within the entire constellation.[89] Contractual collision cannot be combated from the sole perspective of either one or other contracts. The suitable solution is combination of both perspectives and of the criteria for obligations owed to third parties established by each.

In turn, however, a combination of both contracts is a necessary but not a sufficient precondition for combating contractual collision. Neither the contract with protective effects for a third party, nor the external network agreement, nor even a combination of the two, are able to identify sufficient suitable criteria. Instead, criteria should be distilled from the network as a whole. The problems created by forced bipolarisation of social relationships make themselves readily felt in this area.[90] The reduction of complex economic relationships into chains of bilateral contractual relations gives rise to a discrepancy between legally recognised bilateral relationships on the one hand and economic technological, social, medical and other forms of multilateral relationship on the other. Case law has responded to this discrepancy, first with the doctrinal notion of 'intended third party performance impact' within the doctrine of contracts with protective effects for third parties protection, and second, through *culpa in contrahendo* by third parties. Each legal institution is deployed to reintegrate simple extra-contractual performance relationships within bilateral contracts. However, both notions are still

[89] On the relationship between networking, connected contracts and contractual collision, see Amstutz (2003), 170*ff*.

[90] On bilateralisation problems, see Chapter 1 (VI).

far too dependent upon the individual bilateral contract. Case law merely expands the individual contract in line with the dimension of third party impact. It has not yet, however, directed its explicit attention to the multilateral aspects. Here, further clear distinctions must be drawn between 'market-mediated' division of labour and 'network-mediated' division of labour. Whilst a market-mediated division of labour clearly justifies a sharp separation of bipolar contracts, a networked division of labour gives rise to connected contracts, which differ substantively from the contextual relationships envisaged by the contract with protective effects for a third party or the notion of culpa in contrahendo. The particular obligations of participants in a network can only be properly assessed from the perspective of the overarching network purpose – *ex definitione*: from environmental relationships. At core, network liability entails combination of the 'third party performance impact' criteria established within the contract with protective effects for a third party with the preconditions for *Sachwalterhaftung* – 'personal direct economic interest', 'personal awakening of trust', 'contractual sovereignty' – and their assessment with reference to the entire network.

In practice, this form of network liability gives rise to similar results to those envisaged by Picker and Krebs for imposition of piercing liability within so-called 'special relationships' (*Sonderverbindungen*). Picker argues that special relationships should give rise to liability, since modern economic networking establishes 'extra-contractual performance relationships', which private law cannot capture within its traditional forms.[91] His characterisation of novel performance relationships as the technical and organisational connectivity of legally isolated relations is based on empirical observation of networking phenomena and emphasises that actors which are external to the overall transaction are 'responsible for performance' only in relation to a portion of that overall transaction. This is the exact role played by the network centre within distribution systems with regard to client relationships. Characteristically, each party that is responsible for performance completes his portion of performance within the realm of a foreign contractual relationship and therefore never establishes legal relationships with the beneficiary of this performance. According to Picker, completion of individual portions of performance under the umbrella of an overall network makes the establishment of a fully fledged multilateral contractual relationship superfluous. He argues in favour of network liability from this perspective. Krebs takes a similar line, including franchising within his typology of special relationships and arguing in favour of piercing liability of the franchisor to the client within a perspective of a policy of

[91] Picker (1999), 428*ff*.

prevention.[92] Networks should be regarded as a particular form of 'special relationship'. However, as connected contracts, they are subject to a particular form of liability, which differs from the general rules on piercing liability within special relationships, since network liability should be justified by reference to the above noted combined constellation of three contexts: internal network agreement (agreed third party performance impacts), external client contracts (*culpa in contrahendo* criteria) and overarching association (network purpose).[93]

V. SELECTED CONSTELLATIONS OF LIABILITY

1. Franchising in Services

Our introductory case poses the following question: should liability for breaches of performance obligations within franchising of services only apply to the local outlet, that is, the single network node which is actually contracting with the client, even though he is bound to follow instructions from the net centre, and when breaches can be traced to mistakes made by the network centre and by network working groups? Network liability would expand the circle of liability when the combination of three elements is realised: (1) elements derived from the contract with protective effects for a third party; (2) preconditions for the imposition of *culpa in contrahendo* by third parties; and (3) criteria for the existence of an overarching network. In this case, the interplay of elements would lead to imposition of network liability upon the franchisor in the following manner.

(1) 'Third party protection': standard franchising contracts ensure that internal contracts make reference to external client contracts. They determine that the transaction with external clients is the final objective of the franchising system. Further, external contracts are concluded in close accordance with internal rules of the franchise operation. In this case, the notion of 'third party performance impact', which forms the criteria of the doctrine of contracts with protective effects for a third party, has legal implications. Internal network agreements reflect the fact that performances of network obligations within franchises are completed for the benefit of a third party, the client. Accordingly, the client does fall neatly into the position provided for by a contract with protective effects for a third party: that is, there are no claims for specific performance of

[92] Krebs (2000), 381*f*.

[93] For similar arguments, see Larenz and M Wolf (1997), 470.

contractual obligations, but rather there are claims for liability in damages in the event of a breach of obligations.

(2) In reverse, the client's contract refers to the franchising system. In other words, it refers to a set of connected contracts, which not only permits but expects division of the work of performing the contractual obligation. Performance is not undertaken by mere branches of the defendant organised within a unitary business under corporate law. Neither is performance a matter of a pure market's division of labour where the client is responsible for its co-ordination. Instead, the client has the reasonable expectation that partial performances are closely co-ordinated by the franchise system itself, that is, by a contractually defined co-operative relationship between the network centre and network nodes. Within franchising for the provision of a service, a 'client-distanced' network centre prepares the services offered, whilst a 'client-proximate' service outlet passes on concrete services to clients.[94] Therefore, the franchisor as the 'client-distant' participant does not become a contractual party with the client. Neither is the franchisor subject to claims for specific performance under the contract. Nonetheless, as a 'performance party', the franchisor is 'included' within the contract at the moment of the formation of the contract. In accordance with the structure of distribution within the network, performance is not completed solely by the franchisee, and is instead divided between franchisee and franchisor and completed in a process of co-operation between the two. By the same token, the franchisor is not a simple vicarious agent of the franchisee. Instead, the franchisor possesses its own special position as an autonomous economic actor, autonomously completing its own portion of contractual performance and, at the same time, exercising rights of instruction over those portions of performance completed by the franchisee. With this, the franchisor satisfies the criteria for recognition as a 'performance party' – criteria developed in relation to *Sachwalter* liability, first for cases of *culpa in contrahendo* and later also in cases of breach of contract. Accordingly, these criteria are fulfilled in regard to franchising liability if:

1) the franchisor has its 'own direct economic interest' within the contract (not simply provision, etc);
2) the franchisor has its own mode of 'awakening trust in itself'. This is indeed the major function of the net centre within franchising systems; that is, creating trust in the system's product or performance by creating trust in the brand name of the franchisor;
3) the franchisor possesses 'contractual sovereignty'.

[94] Kulms (2000), 114. See also Benjamin Klein (1995), 'The Economics of Franchise Contracts', *Journal of Corporate Finance* 2, 9*ff*, 11.

In this latter area, a policy of prevention plays a role. Restriction of external liability to the franchisee fails to address the constellations of interests within the network. Interventionist signals sent to a franchisee have a relatively limited impact by virtue of the latter's economic dependency and dependency upon instruction. In this case, no interventionist signals whatsoever reach the franchisor.[95] The franchisor not only determines the conditions of internal network agreements. At the same time, the franchisor also exercises detailed control over client contracts. The franchisor owns the business concept, which he subsequently protects with contracts during its operationalisation, and oversees its performance in individual detail. The franchisor prescribes the technological and service apparatus, as well as the mode within which services are carried out. Even offices must be outfitted according to instructions given by the franchisor.

(3) 'Connectivity': in contracting with a network of connected contracts a typical disjunction emerges between the contractual debtor (franchisee) and the independent (partial) performance actor (franchisor). Causes of action which the client may have against the franchisor cannot be ascertained simply by reference to the client contract or to the internal franchising contract. Instead, they can only be ascertained by reference to the entire franchising system and its external relations – in the final analysis, with reference to the networking purpose. The special position that the franchisor possesses as central co-ordinator within the network justifies direct imposition upon it of a variety of contractual obligations: whilst the franchisor is not liable to the client for performance of the contract, he is liable for breach of contractual obligations once they are carried out. Equally, the franchisor's liability does not extend to liability for the full variety of contractual failings that might take place in the course of a transaction. Instead, it is restricted to the franchisor's own breach of obligations in relation to his portion within the overall performance for the benefit of the client. With this, franchisor liability is limited to errors in the system for which the franchisor is responsible: errors within the technical business concept (know-how and procedures), further development of the concept, support for the concept and for education of franchisees. Franchisees, by contrast, are liable for execution of the concept in practice.[96]

The same is also true for inclusion of other members of the network within the potential circle of liability. In principle, franchisees should not be called upon to be responsible for breach of obligations committed by other franchisees. And the franchisor should only be liable when he is a

[95] For prevention policy considerations of franchising and other constellations with similarly dependent external nodes, see Krebs (2000), 381*ff*.

[96] Bräutigam (1994), 52*f*.

directly involved 'performance party' for his own breach of obligations. In our starting case, a working group was responsible for the system's errors that occurred. Indeed, internal working groups, advisory committees and representative organs of members of the network are quite common in franchising.[97] In practice, the regular establishment of quasi-corporate elements within contractual networks is a great challenge posed to any individualistic contract-oriented interpretation of networks. This is especially true when questions of external liability arise.[98] The network liability argued for within these pages would pay adequate regard to the co-responsibility of such working parties. Nonetheless, the result is not one of apportionment of liability to them as collective units. Instead, liability is extended to individual members of those quasi-corporate organs. Within our opening case, therefore, the potential circle of liability is extended to encompass individual members of the working group in their guise as 'performance parties'.

2. Intersecting Liability

One further remarkable extension of liability within networks is the notion of intersecting liability. The problem can be traced back to the permeable nature of organisational boundaries within networking. The blurring of boundaries between individual enterprises and the network gives rise to a 'Moebius strip organisation', within which boundaries between internal and external organisation become so difficult to identify that apportionment of operations to individual members of the network is unclear.[99] Quasi-internalisation of market functions within the network, together with quasi-externalisation of network organisation, makes it difficult to determine internal boundaries of the organisation.[100] Internal intersection between network nodes, network centre, working groups, divisions and branches within the network thus gives rise to difficult problems of co-ordination, direction and management.[101] In the transition from hierarchy to network, intersections between nodes that were once co-ordinated from above need to be reconfigured in order to secure the contractual liability of the organisation. On the other hand, the

[97] On internal committees within franchising nets, see Heinz Dingfelder (1992), 'Richtige Betreuung von Franchise-Nehmern: Die Betreuungsphilosophie von NBB', *Jahrbuch Franchising* 103*ff*, 114*f*; Sydow and Kloyer (1995), 32*f*; Martinek (1997), 100; Bayreuther (2001), 382*f*.

[98] Martinek (1997), 100, offers sharp critique of the avoidance of the problem through individualistic contract law.

[99] Sabel (1991), 23*ff*; Windeler (2001), 262*ff*.

[100] Sydow (1992), 105*ff*; Hirsch-Kreinsen (2002), 114.

[101] On the management problem, Brockhoff and Hauschildt (1993), 396*ff*; Specht (1995), 2265*ff*.

new constellation differs from a market-based division of labour within a complex transaction.[102] In this latter case, clients bear the risk of solving intersection problems between individual products and services. Networks, by contrast, offer to perform the entire complex operation. At the same time, their decentralised structure intensifies the risks caused by intersection. Empirical studies have revealed that decentralised constellations within which decision-making power rests with satellite firms give rise to particular problems in relation to product safety, or to 'particularly subtle risks, created by interaction between subsystems within a technically complex project'. The division of labour and decentralised control that is typical of hybrid networks creates risks since '. . . an easy assumption is created that the entire product will be safe if each individual sub-system is safe'.[103] All efficiency gains of hybrids notwithstanding, external risks are intensified by typical co-ordination errors between network nodes.

Within network practice itself, and by virtue of these problems, new management techniques of 'intersection management' have emerged, with their own tasks involving optimising procedures and control techniques.[104] At the level of legal responsibility, liability for intersectional errors is becoming a hot issue. Who is responsible and liable for co-ordination in a network of independent economic actors? Within a unitary organisation, collective liability would apply since it is the organisational duty of management to co-ordinate intersections of departments. Pure market-based relationships see the risk of liability transferred to the client who is responsible for co-ordination of partial performances. Within networks, however, there is only apparent clarity about responsibilities: the network centre is responsible in cases of hierarchical networking; within heterarchical organisations, each individual firm bears responsibility. However, problems do arise in such cases, which demand collective network liability, especially where attribution of causal responsibility to the network centre or to the network nodes fails to prove convincing. Networking gives rise to a constellation

[102] This is the important distinction between externalisation of functions (market) and quasi-externalisation (network). See Sydow (1992), 105*ff*.

[103] Eads and Reuter (1983), 95; on intensified safety risks in distribution networks which are due to an extensive division of labour, Egon Endres and Theo Wehner (1996), 'Zwischenbetriebliche Kooperation aus prozessualer Perspektive' in Dieter Sauer and Hartmut Hirsch-Kreinsen (eds), *Zwischenbetriebliche Arbeitsteilung und Kooperation*. Frankfurt: Campus, 81*ff*, 95*ff*.

[104] On intersection management, see Kremer (1984), 7*ff*; Brockhoff and Hauschildt (1993), 396*ff*; Specht (1995), 2265*ff*; Ortmann and Sydow (1999), 207*f*, 213*ff*; Windeler (2001), 264*f*. On intersection optimalisation, see Deiß and Döhl (1992), 5, 9; Richard Vahrenkamp (1994), *Produktions- und Logistikmanagement*. Munich: Oldenbourg, 215. Zum 'Schnittstellen-Controlling', Peter Horváth (ed) (1991), *Synergien durch Schnittstellen-Controlling*. Stuttgart: Poeschel.

within which it is often impossible to identify which operations should be apportioned to network nodes or to the network centre. Thus, it is understandable that there should be a demand that the law should clearly distinguish spheres of competences in an effort to end defects in the apportionment of responsibility.[105] Nonetheless, this solution is illusory 'where internal planning and direction of a network node can rarely be distinguished from necessarily simultaneous overall network planning'.[106] Individual apportionment of legal responsibility in such cases is merely arbitrary and wrong, especially where it ignores a structurally determined diffusion of responsibility within co-operative networking, or even seeks to reverse it.

The alternative is a collective attribution of responsibility to the network, or to the narrower factual co-operative relationship between those network participants within which incriminating operations arise. This is an exact parallel to the imposition of collective liability upon various actors, should causal attribution to individual actors no longer be possible.[107] This should not, however, equate with a collectivisation of liability in the sense of a concentration of liability upon pooled property (a legal corporation or corporate body). Instead, liability should be imposed upon the concrete 'responsibility focus' of the network. This will result in the joint and several liability of (concretely involved) members of the network without getting bogged down in the impossible task of a legal reconstruction of individual causal relationships. This procedure is again an expression of double attribution, now within external network liability. Individual apportionment of responsibility to members of the network or to the network centre is no longer appropriate since apportionment of causal responsibility to individual actors is empirically defeated by the diffusion of responsibility within networked operations. In its place, responsibility must first be apportioned to the network as a whole or the concrete project within the network, then making it possible to extend liability to individual actors who have been involved in the project.

[105] Eg, Di Fabio (1997), 245, 264 argues in favour of a legal separation of operational spheres within networks.

[106] Hirsch-Kreinsen (2002), 114. Sceptical about the law's ability to identify effective boundaries within networks, Windeler (2001), 262, fn 169.

[107] On the undermining of traditional causal attribution of liability to collective actors under conditions of intense interdependency, Gunther Teubner (1994), 'The Invisible Cupola: From Causal to Collective Attribution in Ecological Liability' in Gunther Teubner, Lindsay Farmer and Declan Murphy (eds), *Environmental Law and Ecological Responsibility: The Concept and Practice of Ecological Self-Organization.* Chichester: Wiley, 17*ff*; Brüggemeier (2004), chap F.

This form of 'collective' liability is often criticised by the argument that it is not compatible with the individualistic contractual structure established by the network.[108] However, the critics fail to understand properly the nature of the notion of collectivisation that is applied. Generally speaking, 'collectivisation' entails two scenarios. In the first scenario, liability is extended to another person, who is made responsible for damage, which the person has not caused. Extension of liability is justified in this case by joint membership within a single collective.[109] In the second scenario, liability is extended to the collective itself; that is, the corporate unit, whose pooled resources justify establishment of a new focus for liability. Critics of network liability generally point to the second scenario, thus missing the real point.[110] To make the counter-argument clear: networks created through bipolar contracts can only attract the first form of collective liability. Other members of the network are liable even though they are not contractual partners. The justification for this is their membership in the collective. An independent pool of resources does not exist. Nonetheless, initial apportionment of liability to the network as such is not meaningless (this is the major source of the misunderstanding). Instead, the ascription of liability to the network takes on the role of transferring apportionment of responsibility, through which the external contractual liability of one network node is first transferred to the network as such and then further apportioned amongst the net centre and other (involved) individual members of the network.[111] Although this procedure will give a legal guarantee that the entire network and not simply a single network node will be liable, it does not constitute a collective liability in the terms of the second scenario, but instead aims to ensure an appropriate decentralised, multiple and selective apportionment of liability between the network centre and the network nodes. In contrast to collective liability applicable to formal organisations, this liability re-individualises collective network liability, and attributes it amongst the individual units that are involved.[112]

Drawing an analogy to the well-known notion of market share liability, one could talk here of 'network share liability', which is significant when the cause of damage can no longer be traced to individual network

[108] Critical of the 'collective' character of network liability, Bräutigam (1994), 40*ff*, 47*ff*; Rohe (1998), 417*ff*; Bayreuther (2001), 399*f*; Schimansky (2003), 125*ff*.

[109] See, comprehensively, Teubner (1994), 95*ff*.

[110] Especially Bräutigam (1994), 48*f*; Rohe (1998), 417*f*.

[111] This transfer of responsibility apportionment is realised in the EU directive.

[112] At this point there is convergence between these suggested solutions and the tort law solution proposed by Bräutigam (1994), 79*ff*, although the latter is unable to overcome the structural problems inherent to vicarious liability of § 831 BGB. Similar also the notion of network liability developed by Zirkel (1990), 349f.

nodes, but is instead traceable to the act of networking itself.[113] There is no collective actor present, whose pool of resources might justify the imposition of liability. The network, however, can serve as an initial attractor for an attribution of liability, and then as a point of reference for a re-individualisation of liability of network nodes. Re-individualisation is suitable in cases where no individual causal relationship can be established between network nodes and the damage that has arisen, but where an imposition of common liability, however, would be an exaggerated solution. Instead, individual nodes should be made liable on a *pro rata* basis in line with their concrete involvement. This is similar to the liability model imposed by § 128 HGB (Commercial Code) in cases where no common property exists. It exactly mirrors networking structures, which recognise simultaneous individual and collective action, but do not pool resources. As a result, re-individualisation of responsibility occurs in line with the 'network share' of various actors, rather than by an analysis of their 'causal contributions', which may even be wholly impossible to effect.

113 Teubner (1994), 91*ff*.

Bibliography

ABEL, JÖRG (2000) 'Netzwerke und Leitbilder: Die Bedeutung von Leitbildern für die Funktionsfähigkeit von Forschungs- und Entwicklungsnetzwerken' in Johannes Weyer (ed) *Soziale Netzwerke: Konzepte und Methoden der sozialwissenschaftlichen Netzwerkforschung*. Munich: Oldenbourg, 161–85.

ACKERMANN, MARKUS (1998) 'Rechtliche Aspekte von virtuellen Unternehmen' *Handbuch der modernen Datenverarbeitung* 200, 40–53.

ADAMS, MICHAEL (1985) *Ökonomische Analyse der Gefährdungs- und Verschuldenshaftung*. Heidelberg: Decker & Schenck.

ALTERNATIVKOMMENTAR: WASSERMANN, RUDOLF (ed) *Alternativkommentar zum Bürgerlichen Gesetzbuch*.

(1980) *Band 2. Allgemeines Schuldrecht*. Neuwied: Luchterhand.

(1984) *Band 3. Besonderes Schuldrecht*. 2nd edn, Neuwied: Luchterhand.

ALTVATER, ELMAR, BRUNNENGRÄBER, ACHIM, HAAKE, MARKUS and WALK, HEIKE (eds) (1997) *Vernetzt und Verstrickt: Nicht-Regierungs-Organisationen als gesellschaftliche Produktivkraft*. Münster: Westfälisches Dampfboot.

AMSTUTZ, MARC (1993) *Konzernorganisationsrecht: Ordnungsfunktion, Normstruktur, Rechtssystematik*. Bern: Stämpfli.

—— (2001) *Evolutorisches Wirtschaftsrecht: Vorstudien zum Recht und seiner Methode in den Diskurskollisionen der Marktgesellschaft*. Baden-Baden: Nomos.

—— (2003) 'Vertragskollisionen: Fragmente für eine Lehre von der Vertragsverbindung' in Heinrich Honsell (ed) *Aktuelle Aspekte des Schuld- und Sachenrechts: Festschrift für Heinz Rey*. Zürich: Schulthess, 161–76.

—— and Schluep, Walter R (2003) *Innominatverträge: Allgemeine Lehren und Besonderer Teil*. 3rd edn, Basel: Helbing & Lichtenhahn.

ARNDT, ADOLF (1965) 'Umwelt und Recht' *Neue Juristische Wochenschrift* 18, 26–28.

ASHKENAS, RON, ULRICH, DAVE, JICK, TODD and KERN, STEVE (1995) *The Boundaryless Organization*. San Francisco: Jossey-Bass.

ASSMANN, HANS-DIETER (1986) 'Prospekthaftung als unerlaubter Haftungsdurchgriff? Zur Problematik des Anlegerschutzes durch richterliche Rechtsfortbildung' in Juristische Fakultät Heidelberg (ed) *Richterliche Rechtsfortbildung*. Heidelberg: Müller, 299–322.

BACHMANN, REINHARD (ed) (2000) *Die Koordination und Steuerung interorganisationaler Netzwerkbeziehungen über Vertrauen und Macht*. Opladen: Westdeutscher Verlag.

BADARACCO, JOSEPH L (1991) *The Knowledge Link: How Firms Compete Through Strategic Alliances*. Boston: Harvard Business School Press.

BAECKER, DIRK (1993) *Die Form des Unternehmens*. Frankfurt: Suhrkamp.

—— (2002) *Organisation und Gesellschaft*. Witten-Herdecke: Universität.

BALLERSTEDT, KURT (1963) 'Der gemeinsame Zweck als Grundbegriff des Rechts der Personengesellschaften' *Juristische Schulung* 3, 253–63.

BÄLZ, ULRICH (1974) 'Einheit und Vielheit im Konzern' in Fritz Baur (ed) *Funktionswandel der Privatrechtsinstitutionnen: Festschrift für Ludwig Raiser.* Tübingen: Mohr Siebeck, 287–338.

BATESON, GREGORY (1987) *Steps to an Ecology of Mind: Collected Essays in Anthropology, Psychiatry, Evolution, and Epistemology.* Northvale, NJ: Aronson.

BAUDENBACHER, CARL (1985) 'Einwendungsdurchgriff beim finanzierten Immobilienerwerb?' *Juristenzeitung* 40, 661–68.

BAUDER, WOLFGANG (1988) *Der Franchise-Vertrag: Eine systematische Darstellung von Rechtstatsachen.* Tübingen: Universität.

BAUMBACH, ADOLF and HEFERMEHL, WOLFGANG (2001) *Wettbewerbsrecht.* 22nd edn, Munich: Beck.

——, Duden, Konrad and Hopt, Klaus (2000) *Handelsgesetzbuch.* 30th edn, Munich: Beck.

BAUMGARTEN, ANDREAS K (1993) *Das Franchising als Gesellschaftsverhältnis: Eine Studie zur spezifischen zivilrechtlichen Qualität des Rechtsverhältnisses zwischen Franchise-Geber und Franchise-Nehmer.* Göttingen: Universität.

BAYREUTHER, FRANK (2001) *Wirtschaftlich-existentiell abhängige Unternehmen im Konzern-, Kartell- und Arbeitsrecht.* Berlin: Duncker & Humblot.

BECK, ULRICH (1992) *Risk Society: Towards a New Modernity.* London: Sage.

—— (1995) *Ecological Politics in an Age of Risk.* Cambridge: Polity.

BEHRENS, PETER (1986) *Die ökonomischen Grundlagen des Rechts.* Tübingen: Mohr Siebeck.

BENZ, ARTHUR (1996) 'Regionalpolitik zwischen Netzwerkbildung und Institutionalisierung: Zur Funktionalität paradoxer Strukturen' *Staatswissenschaften und Staatspraxis* 1, 23–43.

BERNHARD-ECKEL, STEFAN (1997) *Der Just-In-Time-Vertrag.* Baden-Baden: Nomos.

BERWANGER, ELIZABETH (2000) *Der Gesellschaftsvertrag eines virtuellen Unternehmens.* Münster: Universität.

BEYERLE, FRANZ (1932) *Die Treuhand im Grundriss des Deutschen Privatrechts.* Weimar: Böhlau.

BIEBER, DANIEL (1992) 'Systemische Rationalisierung und Produktionsnetzwerke' in Thomas Malsch and Ulrich Mill (eds) *ArBYTE: Modernisierung der Industriesoziologie?* Berlin: edition sigma, 271–93.

—— (1997) 'Probleme unternehmensübergreifender Organisation von Innovationsprozessen' in Daniel Bieber (ed) *Technikentwicklung und Industriearbeit: Industrielle Produktionstechnik zwischen Eigendynamik und Nutzerinteressen.* Frankfurt: Campus, 111–40.

—— and Sauer, Dieter (1991) 'Kontrolle ist gut! Ist Vertrauen besser? "Autonomie" und "Beherrschung" in Abnehmer-Zuliefererbeziehungen' in Hans Gerhard Mendius and Ulrike Wendeling-Schröder (eds) *Zulieferer im Netz: Zwischen Abhängigkeit und Partnerschaft.* Cologne: Bund, 228–54.

BÖHNER, REINHARD (1985) 'Recht zur außerordentlichen Kündigung des McDonald's Franchisevertrages' *Neue Juristische Wochenschrift* 38, 2811–12.

—— (1994) 'Schadensersatzpflicht des Franchisegebers aus Verschulden bei Vertragsschluß' *Neue Juristische Wochenschrift* 47, 635–36.

—— (1998) 'Werbekostenzuschüsse und sonstige Einkaufsvorteile in Franchisesystemen' *Neue Juristische Wochenschrift* 51,109–12.

BOISSEVAIN, JEREMY (1974) *Friends of Friends: Networks, Manipulators and Coalitions*. Oxford: Oxford University Press.

BOSWORTH, BRIAN and ROSENFELD, STUART A (1993) *Significant Others: Exploring the Potential of Manufacturing Networks*. Chapel Hill: Regional Technology Strategies.

BRAUN, FRANK (1995) 'Aufklärungspflichten des Franchisegebers bei den Vertragsverhandlungen' *Neue Juristische Wochenschrift* 48, 504–05.

BRÄUTIGAM, PETER (1994) *Deliktische Außenhaftung im Franchising: Eine Untersuchung zur außervertraglichen Schadensersatzhaftung der Mitglieder von Franchisesystemen*. Baden-Baden: Nomos.

BRICKLEY, JAMES A and DARK, FREDERICK H (1987) 'The Choice of the Organizational Form: The Case of Franchising' *Journal of Financial Economics* 18, 401–20.

BROCKHOFF, KLAUS and HAUSCHILDT, JÜRGEN (1993) 'Schnittstellen-Management: Koordination ohne Hierarchie' *Zeitschrift Führung und Organisation 62*, 396–403.

BRODOCZ, ANDRÉ (1996) 'Strukturelle Kopplung durch Verbände' *Soziale Systeme* 2, 361–87.

BRÜGGEMEIER, GERT (1986) *Deliktsrecht. Ein Hand- und Lehrbuch*. Baden-Baden: Nomos.

—— (1988) 'Produkthaftung und Produktsicherheit' *Zeitschrift für das gesamte Handelsrecht und Wirtschaftsrecht* 152, 511–36.

—— (2004) *Common Principles of Tort Law: A Pre-Statement of Law*. London: British Institute of International and Comparative Law (BIICL).

BRUNKHORST, HAUKE (1999) 'Heterarchie und Demokratie' in Hauke Brunkhorst and Peter Niesen (eds) *Das Recht der Republik*. Frankfurt: Suhrkamp, 373–85.

BUSCHBECK-BÜLOW, BRIGITTE (1989) 'Betriebsverfassungsrechtliche Vertretung in Franchise-Systemen' *Betriebs Berater* 44, 352–54.

—— (1990) 'Franchise-Systeme und Betriebsverfassung' *Betriebs Berater* 45, 1061–62.

BUSS, KLAUS-PETER and WITTKE, VOLKER (2000) 'Mikro-Chips für Massenmärkte: Innovationsstrategien der europäischen und amerikanischen Halbleiterhersteller in den 90er Jahren' *SOFI-Mitteilungen* 28, 7–32.

BUXBAUM, RICHARD M (1993) 'Is "Network" a Legal Concept?' *Journal of Institutional and Theoretical Economics* 149, 698–705.

CAMERON, KIM S and QUINN, ROBERT E (1988) 'Organizational Paradox and Transformation' in Robert E Quinn and Kim S Cameron (eds) *Paradox and Transformation: Towards a Theory of Change in Organization and Management*. Cambridge, MA: Ballinger, 1–18.

CANARIS, CLAUS-WILHELM (1971) *Die Vertrauenshaftung im deutschen Privatrecht*. Munich: Beck.

—— (1988) *Bankvertragsrecht*. 4th edn, Berlin: de Gruyter.

—— (1995) *Handelsrecht*. 22nd edn, Munich: Beck.

CASPER, STEVEN (1995) 'How Public Law Influences Decentralized Supplier Network Organization: The Case of BMW and Audi' *WZB-Discussion Paper FS I*, 95–314.

—— (1996) 'German Industrial Associations and the Diffusion of Innovative Economic Organization' *WZB-Discussion Paper FS I*, 96–306.

—— (2001) 'The Legal Framework for Corporate Governance: Explaining the Development of Contract Law in Germany and the United States' in Peter A Hall and David Soskice (eds) *Varieties of Capitalism:The Institutional Foundations of Comparative Advantage*. Oxford: Oxford University Press, 387–416.

CASTELLS, MANUEL (2000) *The Rise of the Network Society*. Oxford: Basil Blackwell.

COESTER, MICHAEL (1992) 'Verbraucherschutz bei drittfinanzierten Geschäften (§ 9 VerbrKrG)' *Jura* 14, 617–24.

COLEMAN, JAMES S (1982) *The Asymmetric Society*. Syracuse: Syracuse University Press.

—— (1990) *Foundations of Social Theory*. Cambridge, MA: Harvard University Press.

—— (1991) 'Natural Persons, Corporate Actors, and Constitutions' in Rogers Hollingsworth and Robert Boyer (eds) *Contemporary Capitalism: The Embeddedness of Institutions* 2, 81–102.

COLLINS, HUGH (1990a) 'Ascription of Legal Responsibility to Groups in Complex Patterns of Economic Interaction' *MLR* 53, 731–44.

—— (1990b) 'Independent Contractors and the Challenge of Vertical Disintegration to Employment Protection Laws' *OJLS* 10, 353–80.

—— (1999) *Regulating Contracts*. Oxford: Oxford University Press.

COOTER, ROBERT D (1994) 'Decentralized Law for a Complex Economy' *International Review of Law and Economics* 23, 443–51.

DÄUBLER, WOLFGANG (1988) 'Informationstechnische Unternehmensverkettung und Arbeitsrecht' *Computer und Recht* 4, 834–41.

DÄUBLER, WOLFGANG (1993) 'Mitbestimmung und logistische Kette' in Wolfgang H Staehle and Jörg Sydow (eds) *Managementforschung 3*. Berlin: de Gruyter, 1–17.

DAVIDOW, WILLIAM H and MALONE, MICHAEL S (1992) *The Virtual Corporation: Structuring and Revitalizing the Corporation for the 21st Century*. New York: Harper.

DEAKIN, SIMON, CHRISTEL LANE and WILKINSON, FRANK (1994) '"Trust" or Law? Towards an Integrated Theory of Contractual Relations Between Firms' *Rechtstheorie* 21, 329–49.

DEIß, MANFRED and DÖHL, VOLKER (1992) *Vernetzte Produktion: Automobilzulieferer zwischen Kontrolle und Autonomie*. Frankfurt: Campus.

DI FABIO, UDO (1997) 'Verwaltung und Verwaltungsrecht zwischen gesellschaftlicher Selbstregulierung und staatlicher Steuerung' *Veröffentlichungen der Vereinigung der deutschen Staatsrechtslehrer* 56, 235–77.

DINGFELDER, HEINZ (1992) 'Richtige Betreuung von Franchise-Nehmern: Die Betreuungsphilosophie von NBB' *Jahrbuch Franchising*, 103–16.

DNES, ANTONY W (1991) 'The Economic Analysis of Franchising and its Regulation' in Christian Joerges (ed) *Franchising and the Law: Theoretical and Comparative Approaches in Europe and the United States*. Baden Baden: Nomos, 133–42.

DÖRRENBÄCHER, CHRISTOPH and MEIßNER, HEINZ R (1991) 'IKEA: "The Hollow Elk Corporation"' *Informationen über multinationale Konzerne* 14, 21–27.

DUBIEL, HELMUT (1990) 'Die Ökologie der gesellschaftlichen Moral' in Stefan Müller-Doohm (ed) *Jenseits der Utopie*. Frankfurt: Suhrkamp, 123–37.

DUSCHEK, STEPHAN (1998) 'Kooperative Kernkompetenzen: Zum Management einzigartiger Netzwerkressourcen' *Zeitschrift Führung und Organisation* 67, 230–36.

EADS, GEORGE and REUTER, PETER (1983) *Designing Safer Products: Corporate Responses to Product Liability Law and Regulation*. Santa Monica: Rand.

EBENROTH, CARSTEN-THOMAS (1980) *Absatzmittlungsverträge im Spannungsverhältnis von Kartell- und Zivilrecht*. Konstanz: Universitätsverlag.

—— and Strittmatter, Marc (1993) 'Fremdbestimmte Investitionen in der Umstrukturierung von Absatzmittlungsverhältnissen auf dem Automobilsektor' *Betriebs Berater* 48, 1521–35.

EBERS, MARK and GOTSCH, WILFRIED (1993) 'Institutionenökonomische Theorie der Organisation' in Alfred Kieser (ed) *Organisationstheorien*. Stuttgart: Kohlhammer, 193–242.

EHRICKE, ULRICH (1996) 'Gedanken zu einem allgemeinen Konzernorganisationsrecht zwischen Markt und Regulierung' *Zeitschrift für Unternehmens- und Gesellschaftsrecht* 25, 300–25.

EINSELE, DOROTHEE (1999) 'Haftung der Kreditinstitute bei nationalen und grenzüberschreitenden Banküberweisungen' *Archiv für die civilistische Praxis* 199, 145–89.

—— (2000) 'Das neue Recht der Banküberweisung' *Juristenzeitung* 54, 9–19.

EISENHARDT, KATHLEEN and WESTCOTT, BRIAN (1988) 'Paradoxical Demands and the Creation of Excellence: The Case of Just-in-Time Manufacturing' in Robert E Quinn and Kim S Cameron (eds) *Paradox and Transformation*. Cambridge, MA: Ballinger, 169–93.

EKKENGA, JENS (1990) *Die Inhaltskontrolle von Franchiseverträgen: Eine Studie zu den zivilrechtlichen Grenzen der Vertragsgestaltung im Bereich des Franchising unter Einschluss des Vertragshändlerrechts*. Heidelberg: Recht und Wirtschaft.

EMMERICH, VOLKER (1971) 'Der finanzierte Abzahlungskauf' *Juristische Schulung* 11, 273–81.

—— (1995) 'Franchising' *Juristische Schulung* 35, 761–64.

ENDRES, EGON and WEHNER, THEO (1996) 'Zwischenbetriebliche Kooperation aus prozessualer Perspektive' in Dieter Sauer and Hartmut Hirsch-Kreinsen (eds) *Zwischenbetriebliche Arbeitsteilung und Kooperation*. Frankfurt: Campus, 81–120.

ENGEL, CHRISTOPH (1993) 'Rezension: Oliver E Williamson: Die ökonomischen Institutionen des Kapitalismus' *Rabels Zeitschrift für ausländisches und internationales Privatrecht* 57, 556–65.

—— (2001) *Vertrauen: Ein Versuch*. Bonn: Max-Planck-Projektgruppe Recht der Gemeinschaftsgüter.

ENSTHALER, JÜRGEN (1994) 'Haftungsrechtliche Bedeutung von Qualitätssicherungsvereinbarungen' *Neue Juristische Wochenschrift* 47, 817–23.

—— and Gesmann-Nuissl, Dagmar (2000) 'Virtuelle Unternehmen in der Praxis: Eine Herausforderung für das Zivil-, Gesellschafts- und Kartellrecht' *Betriebs Berater* 55, 2265–71.

ERNST, DIETER (1994) *Inter-firms Networks and Market Structure: Driving Forces, Barriers and Patterns of Control*. Berkeley: University of California.

ESPOSITO, ELENA (1993) 'Ein zweiwertiger nicht-selbständiger Kalkül' in Dirk Baecker (ed) *Kalkül der Form*. Frankfurt: Suhrkamp, 96–111.

ESSER, JOHN P (1996) 'Institutionalizing Industry: The Changing Forms of Contract' *Law and Social Inquiry* 21, 593–629.

ESSER, JOSEF and SCHMIDT, EIKE (1995) *Schuldrecht: Ein Lehrbuch. Allgemeiner Teil I 1*. 8th edn, Heidelberg: Müller.

—— and WEYERS, HANS-LEO (1998) *Schuldrecht: Ein Lehrbuch. Besonderer Teil I*. 8th edn, Heidelberg: Müller.

—— and —— (2000) *Schuldrecht: Ein Lehrbuch. Besonderer Teil. II*. 8th edn, Heidelberg: Müller.

FELSTEAD, ALAN (1991) 'The Social Organization of the Franchise: A Case of "Control-led Self-Employment"' *Work, Employment & Society* 5, 37–57.

FIKENTSCHER, WOLFGANG (1974) 'Zu Begriff und Funktion des "gemeinsamen Zwecks" im Gesellschafts- und Kartellrecht' in Wolfgang Hefermehl, Rudolf Gmür and Hans Brox (eds) *Festschrift für Harry Westermann*. Karlsruhe: Müller, 87–117.

FLETCHER, GEORGE P (1985) 'Paradoxes in Legal Thought' *Columbia Law Review* 85, 1263–92.

FLORENZ, PETER (1992) *Das Konzept des vertikalen Marketing: Entwicklung und Darstellung am Beispiel der deutschen Automobilwirtschaft*. Bergisch Gladbach: Eul.

FLUME, WERNER (1977) *Die Personengesellschaft. Allgemeiner Teil des bürgerlichen Rechts*. Vol 1. Berlin: Springer.

FREILING, JÖRG (1995) *Die Abhängigkeit der Zulieferer: Ein strategisches Problem*. Wiesbaden: Deutscher Universitätsverlag.

FUCHS, MAXIMILIAN (1994) 'Arbeitsteilung und Haftung' *Juristenzeitung* 49, 533–40.

FUCHS, STEPHAN (2001) 'Networks' *Soziale Systeme* 7, 125–55.

FUNDER, MARIA (1999) *Paradoxien der Reorganisation*. Munich: Hampp.

GEBHARDT, HANS-PETER (1994) *Der Zuliefervertrag*. Cologne: Heymanns.

GEISER, GORDON (2001) 'Virtuelle Unternehmen und reale Unternehmensträger' *Multimedia und Recht* 4, 715–21.

GELDER, ALFONS VAN (1995) 'Schutzpflichten zugunsten Dritter im bargeldlosen Zahlungsverkehr?' *Wertpapier Mitteilungen* 49, 1253–62.

GERNHUBER, JOACHIM (1973) 'Austausch und Kredit im rechtsgeschäftlichen Verbund: Zur Lehre von den Vertragsverbindungen' in Gotthard Paulus, Uwe Diederichsen and Claus-Wilhelm Canaris (eds) *Festschrift für Karl Larenz*. Munich: Beck, 455–94.

—— (1989) *Das Schuldverhältnis: Begründung und Änderung, Pflichten und Strukturen, Drittwirkungen*. Tübingen: Mohr Siebeck.

GERUM, ELMAR, ACHENBACH, WIELAND and OPELT, FRANK (1998) 'Zur Regulierung der Binnenbeziehungen von Unternehmensnetzwerken: Ein Problemaufriss' *Zeitschrift Führung und Organisation* 67, 266–70.

GIERKE, OTTO VON (1914) 'Die Wurzeln des Dienstvertrags' in Juristenfakultät der Universität Berlin (ed) *Festschrift für Heinrich Brunner*. Munich: Duncker & Humblot, 37–68.

GOFFMAN, ERVING (1961) *Asylums: Essays on the Social Situation of Mental Patients and Other Inmates*. Garden City: Anchor Books.

GORDON, ROBERT (1994) 'Hayek and Cooter on Custom and Reason' *Southwestern University Law Review* 23, 453–60.

GRABHER, GERNOT (1993) 'The Weakness of Strong Ties: The Lock-in of Regional Development in the Ruhr Area' in Gernot Grabher (ed) *The Embedded Firm: On the Socio-Economics of Industrial Network*. London: Routledge.

—— (1994) *Lob der Verschwendung*. Berlin: Sigma.

GRUNEWALD, BARBARA (1995) 'Just-in-time-Geschäfte: Qualitätssicherungsvereinbarungen und Rügelast' *Neue Juristische Wochenschrift* 48, 1777–84.

GULATI, MITU G, Klein, William A and Zolt, Eric M (2000) 'Connected Contracts' *University of California Los Angeles Law Review* 47, 887–948.

GUMBRECHT, HANS ULRICH and PFEIFFER, LUDWIG K (eds) (1994) *Materialities of Communication (Writing Science)*. Stanford, California: Stanford University Press.

GUNDLACH, BERND (1979) *Konsumentenkredit und Einwendungsdurchgriff*. Berlin: Duncker & Humblot.

HAGE, JERALD and ALTER, CATHERINE (1997) 'A Typology of Interorganizational Relationships and Networks' in J Rogers Hollingsworth and Robert Boyer (eds) *Contemporary Capitalism*. Cambridge: Cambridge University Press, 94–126.

HAGER, GÜNTER (1991) 'Die Verflechtung von Verträgen: Planung und Risikoverteilung bei Großprojekten' in Hans-Leo Weyers (ed) *Die Verflechtung von Verträgen: Planung und Risikoverteilung bei Großprojekten*. Baden-Baden: Nomos, 65–113.

HAKANSSON, HAKAN (1997) 'Organization Networks' in Arndt Sorge and Malcolm Warner (eds) *The Handbook of Organizational Behaviour*. London: Thomson, 232–40.

—— and Johanson, Jan (1993) 'The Network as a Governance Structure: Interfirm Co-operation Beyond Market and Hierarchies' in Gernot Grabher (ed) *The Embedded Firm*. London: Routledge, 35–51.

HALFMANN, JOST (1997) 'Die Implementation von Innovationen als Prozeß sozialer Einbettung' in Daniel Bieber (ed) *Technikentwicklung und Industriearbeit: Industrielle Produktionstechnik zwischen Eigendynamik und Nutzerinteresse*. Frankfurt: Campus, 87–110.

HANSMANN, HENRY and KRAAKMAN, REINIER (1991) 'Toward Unlimited Shareholder Liability for Corporate Torts' *The Yale Law Journal* 100, 1879–1934.

HARDT, MICHAEL and NEGRI, ANTONIO (2000) *Empire*. Cambridge, MA: Harvard University Press.

HARRISON, BENNETT (1994) *Lean and Mean: The Changing Landscape of Corporate Power in an Age of Flexibility*. New York: Basic Books.

HAYEK, FRIEDRICH A (1973) *Law, Legislation and Liberty. Volume 1: Rules and Order*. London: Routledge & Paul.

HEDBERG, BO, DAHLGREN, GÖRAN, HANSSON, JÖRGEN and OLVE, NILS-GÖRAN (1992) *Virtual Organizations and Beyond: Discover Imaginary Systems*. Chichester: Wiley.

HEERMANN, PETER W (1998) *Drittfinanzierte Erwerbsgeschäfte: Entwicklung der Rechtsfigur des trilateralen Synallagmas auf der Grundlage deutscher und U.S.-amerikanischer Rechtsentwicklungen*. Tübingen: Mohr Siebeck.

HEERMANN, PETER W (2002) 'Anmerkung zu BGH' *Juristenzeitung* 56, 1173–75.

—— (2003) *Geld und Geldgeschäfte*. Tübingen: Mohr Siebeck.

HEIDENREICH, MARTIN (2000) 'Regionale Netzwerke in der globalen Wissensgesellschaft' in Johannes Weyer (ed) *Soziale Netzwerke: Konzepte und Methoden der sozialwissenschaftlichen Netzwerkforschung*. Munich: Oldenbourg, 87–110.

HEIDLING, ECKHARD (2000) 'Strategische Netzwerke' in Johannes Weyer (ed) *Soziale Netzwerke*. Munich: Oldenbourg, 63–86.

HESS, THOMAS (2000) 'Anwendungsmöglichkeiten des Konzerncontrolling in Unternehmensnetzwerken' in Jörg Sydow and Arnold Windeler (ed) *Steuerung von Netzwerken*. Opladen: Westdeutscher Verlag, 156–77.

HESSINGER, PHILIPP, EICHHORN, FRIEDHELM, FELDHOFF, JÜRGEN and SCHMIDT, GERT (2000) *Fokus und Balance: Aufbau und Wachstum industrieller Netzwerke*. Opladen: Westdeutscher Verlag.

HEYDEBRAND, WOLF (1999) *The Network Metaphor as Key to the Analysis of Complex Production and Service Relation in a Global Economy*. Stuttgart: Akademie für Technikfolgenabschätzung in Baden-Württemberg.

HIRSCH-KREINSEN, HARTMUT (1995) 'Dezentralisierung: Unternehmen zwischen Stabilität und Desintegration' *Zeitschrift für Soziologie* 24, 422–35.

—— (1997) 'Innovationsschwächen der deutschen Industrie: Wandel und Probleme von Innovationsprozessen' in Gotthard Bechmann (ed) *Technik und Gesellschaft. Jahrbuch 9: Innovation: Prozesse, Produkte, Politik*. Frankfurt: Campus, 153–74.

—— (2002) 'Unternehmensnetzwerke – revisited' *Zeitschrift für Soziologie* 31, 106–24.

HIRTE, HERIBERT (1992) 'Gesellschaftsrechtliche Fragen des "Outsourcing"' *Computer und Recht* 2, 193–98.

HIRTH, RENÉ-ALEXANDER (1991) *Die Rechtsprechung zum Vertrag mit Schutzwirkung zugunsten Dritter in ihrer Bedeutung für den Ausgleich von Drittschäden im Zahlungsverkehr*. Berlin: Duncker & Humblot.

HODGES, CHRISTOPHER (2000) *Position Paper: Safety of Services*. http://europa.eu.int/comm/consumers/cons_org/assembly/event32/event32_wrk3–1_en.pdf.

HOFFMANN, JOCHEN (2001) 'Grundfragen des Überweisungsgesetzes' *Wertpapier Mitteilungen* 55, 881–88.

HOLLINGSWORTH, J ROGERS and BOYER, ROBERT (1997) 'Coordination of Economic Actors and Social Systems of Production' in J Rogers Hollingsworth and Robert Boyer (eds) *Contemporary Capitalism*. Cambridge: Cambridge University Press, 1–48.

HOMMELHOFF, PETER (1982) *Die Konzernleitungspflicht: Zentrale Aspekte eines Konzernverfassungsrechts*. Cologne: Heymanns.

HOPT, KLAUS (1996) 'Wettbewerbsfreiheit und Treuepflicht des Unternehmers bei parallelen Vertriebsformen' *Zeitschrift für Wirtschaftsrecht* 17, 1533–39.

HOPT, KLAUS and MÜLBERT, PETER (1989) *Kreditrecht*. 12th edn, Berlin: de Gruyter.

HÖRTER, KLAUS (1969) *Der finanzierte Abzahlungskauf*. Bad Homburg: Gehlen.

HORVÁTH, PETER (ed) (1991) *Synergien durch Schnittstellen-Controlling*. Stuttgart: Poeschel.

HUECK, GÖTZ (1958) *Der Grundsatz der gleichmäßigen Behandlung im Privatrecht*. Munich: Beck.

HÜFFER, UWE (1987) 'Die Haftung gegenüber dem ersten Auftraggeber im mehrgliedrigen Zahlungsverkehr' *Zeitschrift für das gesamte Handelsrecht und Wirtschaftsrecht* 151, 93–117.

HUTTER, MICHAEL and TEUBNER, GUNTHER (1993) 'The Parasitic Role of Hybrids' *Journal of Institutional and Theoretical Economics* 149, 706–15.

IMAI, KEN-ICHI and ITAMI, HIROYUKI (1984) 'Interpenetration of Organization and Market: Japan's Firm and Market in Comparison with the U.S.' *International Journal of Industrial Organization* 2, 285–310.

JANSEN, DOROTHEA (2003) 'Soziologie, Rechtssoziologie und Rechtswissenschaft' in Stefan Machura and Stefan Ulbrich (eds) *Recht, Gesellschaft, Kommunikation: Festschrift für Klaus Röhl*. Baden-Baden: Nomos, 24–39.

JANSEN, STEPHAN (2000) 'Konkurrenz der Konkurrenz: Co-opetition als Form der Konkurrenz – Typen, Funktionen und Voraussetzungen von paradoxen Koordinationsformen' in Stephan A Jansen and Stephan Schleissing (eds) *Konkurrenz und Kooperation*. Marburg: Metropolis, 13–63.

JARILLO, J CARLOS (1993) *Strategic Networks: Creating the Borderless Organization*. Oxford: Oxford University Press.

JHERING, RUDOLPH VON (1871) 'Die Reflexwirkungen oder die Rückwirkung rechtlicher Thatsachen auf dritte Personen' *Jherings Jahrbücher* 10, 245–354.

—— (1884) *Der Zweck im Recht*. 2nd edn, Leipzig: Breitkopf & Haertel.

JICKELI, JOACHIM (1996) *Der langfristige Vertrag: Eine rechtswissenschaftliche Untersuchung auf institutionen-ökonomischer Grundlage*. Baden-Baden: Nomos.

JOERGES, CHRISTIAN (1977) *Bereicherungsrecht als Wirtschaftsrecht: Eine Untersuchung zur Entwicklung von Leistungs- und Eingriffskondiktion*. Cologne: Otto Schmidt.

—— (1981) *Verbraucherschutz als Rechtsproblem: Eine Untersuchung zum Stand der Theorie und zu den Entwicklungsperspektiven des Verbraucherrechts*. Heidelberg: Recht und Wirtschaft.

—— (1991) 'Status and Contract in Franchising Law' in Christian Joerges (ed) *Franchising and the Law: Theoretical and Comparative Approaches in Europe and the United States*. Baden-Baden: Nomos, 11–66.

—— and Teubner, Gunther (eds) (2003) *Rechtsverfassungsrecht: Recht-Fertigungen zwischen Sozialtheorie und Privatrechtsdogmatik*. Baden-Baden: Nomos.

JOHANSON, LARS-GUNNAR (1987) 'International Relations in Industrial Systems: A Network Approach Compared with the Transaction-cost Approach' *International Studies of Management and Organization* 17, 34–48.

KÄMPER, ECKARD and SCHMIDT, JOHANNES FK (2000) 'Netzwerke als strukturelle Kopplung: Systemtheoretische Überlegungen zum Netzwerkbegriff' in Johannes Weyer (ed) *Soziale Netzwerke: Konzepte und Methoden der sozialwissenschaftlichen Netzwerkforschung*. Munich: Oldenbourg, 211–35.

KAISER, GISBERT (2000) 'Die konkurrierende Haftung von Vor- und Nachunternehmer' *Baurecht* 31, 177–83.

KAPPELHOFF, PETER (2000a) 'Komplexitätstheorie und Steuerung von Netzwerken' in Jörg Sydow and Arnold Windeler (eds) *Steuerung von Netzwerken: Konzepte und Praktiken*. Opladen: Westdeutscher Verlag, 347–89.

—— (2000b) 'Der Netzwerkansatz als konzeptueller Rahmen für eine Theorie interorganisationaler Netzwerke' in Jörg Sydow and Arnold Windeler (eds) *Steuerung von Netzwerken: Konzepte und Praktiken*. Opladen: Westdeutscher Verlag, 25–57.

KATZ, MICHAEL and SHAPIRO, CARL (1985) 'Network Externalities, Competition, and Compatibility' *American Economic Review* 75, 424–40.

KENIS, PATRICK S and SCHNEIDER, VOLKER (eds) (1996) *Organisation und Netzwerk: Institutionelle Steuerung in Wirtschaft und Politik*. Frankfurt: Campus.

KERN, HORST (1996) 'Vertrauensverlust und blindes Vertrauen: Integrationsprobleme im ökonomischen Handeln' in Stefan Hradil (ed) *Differenz und Integration: Die Zukunft moderner Gesellschaften – Verhandlungen des 28. Kongresses der Deutschen Gesellschaft für Soziologie in Dresden 1996*. Frankfurt: Campus 1997, 171–82.

KESSAL-WULF, SIBYLLE (1995) *Die Innenverbände: Am Beispiel Publikumsgesellschaft, Franchising, Mitarbeiterbeteiligung und Betriebsverband*. Frankfurt: Lang.

KESSEN, HOLGER (1996) *Nachfragemacht der Automobilindustrie: Eine Analyse unter den Gesichtspunkten Kartellrecht, AGB-Recht und Konzernrecht*. Frankfurt: Lang.

KIRCHNER, CHRISTIAN (1993) 'Unternehmensorganisation und Vertragsnetz: Überlegungen zu den rechtlichen Bedingungen zwischen Unternehmensorganisation und Vertragsnetz' in Claus Ott and Hans-Bernd Schäfer (eds) *Ökonomische Analyse des Unternehmensrechts*. Heidelberg: Physica, 196–215.

—— (1996) 'Symbiotic Arrangements as a Challenge to Antitrust' *Zeitschrift für die gesamte Staatsrechtswissenschaft/Journal of Institutional and Theoretical Economics* 152, 226–43.

—— (2000) 'Horizontale japanische Unternehmensgruppen (keiretsu) im deutschen Konzernrecht' in Theodor Baums, Klaus J Hopt and Norbert Horn (eds) *Corporations, Capital Markets and Business in the Law: Liber Amicorum Richard M. Buxbaum*. London: Kluwer Law International, 339–62.

KLEBE, THOMAS and ROTH, SIEGFRIED (1990) 'Technische und organisatorische Aspekte des Just-in-Time-Delivery' *Computer und Recht* 6, 677–82.

KLEIN, BENJAMIN (1995) 'The Economics of Franchise Contracts' *Journal of Corporate Finance* 2, 9–37.

—— and Saft, Lester F (1985) 'The Law and Economics of Franchise Tying Contracts' *Journal of Law and Economics* 28, 345–61.

KNIFFKA, ROLF (1999) 'Anmerkung zu OLG Düsseldorf' *Baurecht* 30, 1312–14.

KÖHLER, HEINZ-DIETER (1974) *Über die Anwendbarkeit von Gesellschaftsrecht auf die sogenannten gesellschaftsähnlichen Rechtsverhältnisse*. Munich: Universität.

KÖHLER, HOLM-DETLEV (1999) 'Auf dem Weg zum Netzwerkunternehmen? Anmerkungen zu einem problematischen Konzept am Beispiel der deutschen Automobilkonzerne' *Industrielle Beziehungen* 6, 36–51.

KOLLER, INGO (1987) 'Grundstrukturen des Bankhaftungsrechts unter besonderer Berücksichtigung des Zahlungsverkehrs' in Johannes Köndgen (ed) *Neue Entwicklungen im Bankhaftungsrecht*. Cologne: RWS Verlag Kommunikationsforum, 21–34.

KÖNDGEN, JOHANNES (1981) *Selbstbindung ohne Vertrag: Zur Haftung aus geschäftsbezogenem Handeln*. Tübingen: Mohr Siebeck.

—— (1987) 'Bankhaftung: Strukturen und Tendenzen' in Johannes Köndgen (ed) *Neue Entwicklungen im Bankhaftungsrecht*. Cologne: RWS Verlag Kommunikationsforum, 133–58.

KOWOL, ULI and KROHN, WOLFGANG (1995) 'Innovationsnetzwerke: Ein Modell der Technikgenese' in Jost Halfman (ed) *Theoriebausteine der Techniksoziologie: Jahrbuch 'Technik und Gesellschaft'*. Frankfurt: Campus, 749–60.

—— and —— (1997) 'Modernisierungsdynamik und Innovationslethargie' in Birgit Blättel-Mink and Ortwin Renn (eds) *Zwischen Akteur und System: Die Organisierung von Innovation*. Opladen: Westdeutscher Verlag, 39–65.

KOZIOL, HELMUT (1994) 'Delikt, Verletzung von Schuldverhältnissen und Zwischenbereich' *Juristische Blätter* 116, 209–23.

KRAMER, RODERICK M (1999) 'Trust and Distrust in Organizations: Emerging Perspectives, Enduring Questions' *Annual Review of Psychology* 50, 569–98.

KREBS, PETER (2000) *Sonderverbindung und außerdeliktische Schutzpflichten*. Munich: Beck.

KREMER, GOTTFRIED (1984) 'Risiken bei Anlagenverträgen aus technischer Sicht' in Fritz Nicklisch (ed) *Bau- und Anlagenverträge: Risiken, Haftung, Streitbeilegung*. Heidelberg: Müller, 7–20.

KREUDER, THOMAS (2000) 'Netzwerkbeziehungen und Arbeitsrecht: Individualarbeits- und betriebsverfassungsrechtliche Aspekte bei Franchisesystemen' in Dieter Simon (ed) *Zur Autonomie des Individuums: liber amicorum Spiros Simitis*. Baden-Baden: Nomos, 171–208.

KRIPPENDORFF, KLAUS (1984) 'Paradox and Information' in Brenda Dervin and Melvin J Voigt (eds) *Progress in Communication Sciences 5*. Norwood: Ablex, 45–71.

KRYSTEK, ULRICH, REDEL, WOLFGANG and REPPEGATHER, SEBASTIAN (1997) *Grundzüge virtueller Organisationen: Elemente und Erfolgsfaktoren, Chancen und Risiken*. Wiesbaden: Gabler.

KULMS, RAINER (2000) *Schuldrechtliche Organisationsverträge in der Unternehmenskooperation*. Baden-Baden: Nomos.

LADEUR, KARL-HEINZ (1992) *Postmoderne Rechtstheorie: Selbstreferenz – Selbstorganisation – Prozeduralisierung*. Berlin: Duncker & Humblot.

—— (2000) *Negative Freiheitsrechte und gesellschaftliche Selbstorganisation*. Tübingen: Mohr Siebeck.

—— (2001) 'Die Regulierung von Selbstregulierung und die Herausbildung einer "Logik der Netzwerke"' *Die Verwaltung. Beiheft* 4, 59–77.

LAMERE, SHEENA, SMYER, TISH and GRAGERT, MARCIA D (1996) 'The Ageing Inmate' *Journal of Psychosocial Nursing and Mental Services* 34, 25–9.

LANE, CHRISTEL and BACHMANN, REINHARD (1996) 'The Social Construction of Trust: Supplier Relations in Britain and Germany' *Organization Studies* 17, 365–95.

LANGE, KNUT WERNER (1998) *Das Recht der Netzwerke*. Heidelberg: Recht und Wirtschaft.

—— (2001a) *Virtuelle Unternehmen. Neue Unternehmenskoordinationen in Recht und Praxis*. Heidelberg: Recht und Wirtschaft.

—— (2001b) 'Virtuelle Unternehmen' in Ulrich Noack and Gerald Spindler (eds) *Unternehmensrecht und Internet: Neue Medien im Aktien-, Börsen-, Steuer- und Arbeitsrecht*. Munich: Beck, 169–97.

—— (2001c) 'Virtuelle Unternehmen für Finanzdienstleistungen' *Betriebs Berater* 56, 1801–05.

LANGENBUCHER, KATJA (2001) *Die Risikozuordnung im bargeldlosen Zahlungsverkehr*. Munich: Beck.

LARENZ, KARL (1933) 'Zur Lehre von der Rechtsgemeinschaft' *Jherings Jahrbücher* 83, 108–77.

—— (1987) *Lehrbuch des Schuldrechts. Band I. Allgemeiner Teil.* 14th edn, Munich: Beck.

—— and Canaris, Claus-Wilhelm (1994) *Lehrbuch des Schuldrechts. Band II. Besonderer Teil. Halbband 2.* 13th edn, Munich: Beck.

—— and Wolf, Manfred (1997) *Allgemeiner Teil des Bürgerlichen Rechts.* 8th edn, Munich: Beck.

LAUFER, ROGER (1995) *Networks, Legitimacy and Society: Neither Market Nor Hierarchy.* Paris: ESSEC Workshop: Action, Structure and Organization.

LEHMANN, MICHAEL (1990) 'Just in time: Handels- und AGB-rechtliche Probleme' *Betriebs Berater* 45, 1849–55.

LEMLEY, MARK A and MCGOWAN, DAVID (1998) 'Legal Implications of Network Economic Effects' *California Law Review* 86, 479–611.

LESSIG, LAWRENCE (1999) *Code and Other Laws of Cyberspace.* New York: Basic Books.

LIEBOWITZ, STAN J and MARGOLIS, STEPHEN E (1994) 'Network Externality: An Uncommon Tragedy' *Journal of Economic Perspectives* 8, 133–50.

LIPPERT, INGE (1998) *Zwischen Pfadabhängigkeit und radikalem Wandel: Neuordnung von Prozeßketten im internationalen Maschinenbau.* Berlin: edition sigma.

LITTMANN, PETER and JANSEN, STEPHAN A (2000) *Oszillodox: Virtualisierung – die permanente Neuerfindung der Organisation.* Stuttgart: Klett.

LÖHR, VOLKER and SIMON, JÜRGEN (1985) 'Probleme einer Reform des finanzierten Abzahlungskaufs' in Georgios Magoulas and Jürgen Simon (eds) *Recht und Ökonomie beim Konsumentenschutz und Konsumentenkredit.* Baden-Baden: Nomos, 61–114.

LUBBERGER, ANDREAS (2000) 'Die neue Rechtsprechung des Bundesgerichtshofs zum Vertriebsbindungsschutz: Praktische Konsequenzen' *Wettbewerb in Recht und Praxis* 46, 139–48.

LUHMANN, NIKLAS (1965) *Grundrechte als Institution: Ein Beitrag zur politischen Soziologie.* Berlin: Duncker & Humblot.

—— (1974) *Rechtssystem und Rechtsdogmatik.* Stuttgart: Kohlhammer.

—— (1982) *Trust and Power.* New York: Wiley.

—— (1987) 'Die Differenzierung von Politik und Wirtschaft und ihre gesellschaftlichen Grundlagen' in Niklas Luhmann, *Soziologische Aufklärung 4: Beiträge zur funktionalen Differenzierung der Gesellschaft.* Opladen: Westdeutscher Verlag, 32–48.

—— (1988) 'Organisation' in Wolfgang Küpper und Günther Ortmann (eds) *Mikropolitik: Rationalität, Macht und Spiele in Organisationen.* Opladen: Westdeutscher Verlag, 165–85.

—— (1990) 'Sthenography' *Stanford Law Review* 7, 133–37.

—— (1993) 'Observing Re-entries' *Graduate Faculty Philosophy Journal* 16, 485–98.

—— (1995a) *Social Systems.* Stanford: Stanford University Press.

—— (1995b) *Soziologische Aufklärung.* Opladen: Westdeutscher Verlag.

—— (1997) *Die Gesellschaft der Gesellschaft.* Frankfurt: Suhrkamp.

—— (2000) *Organisation und Entscheidung.* Opladen: Westdeutscher Verlag.

—— (2004) *Law as a Social System.* Oxford: Oxford University Press.

MACAULAY, STEWART (1991) 'Long-Term Continuing Relations: The American Experience Regulating Dealerships and Franchises' in Christian Joerges (ed)

Franchising and the Law: Theoretical and Comparative Approaches in Europe and the United States. Baden Baden: Nomos, 179–238.

MACK, MANFRED (1975) *Neuere Vertragssysteme in der Bundesrepublik Deutschland: Eine Studie zum Franchising*. Bielefeld: Gieseking.

MACNEIL, IAN R (1974) 'The Many Futures of Contracts' *Southern California Law Review* 47, 691–816.

MAHNKOPF, BIRGIT (1994) 'Markt, Hierarchie und soziale Beziehungen: Zur Bedeutung reziproker Marktgesellschaften' in Niels Beckenbach and Werner van Treeck (eds) *Umbrüche gesellschaftlicher Arbeit: Soziale Welt. Sonderband 9*. Göttingen: Schwartz, 65–84.

MARTINEK, MICHAEL (1987) *Franchising: Grundlagen der zivil- und wettbewerbsrechtichen Behandlung der vertraglichen Gruppenkooperation beim Absatz von Waren und Dienstleistungen*. Heidelberg: Decker & Schenck.

—— (1992) *Moderne Vertragstypen Band II: Franchising, Know-How-Verträge, Management- und Consultingverträge*. Munich: Beck.

—— (1993a) 'Buchbesprechung: Christian Joerges, Franchising and the Law' *Rabels Zeitschrift* 57, 577–88.

—— (1993b) *Moderne Vertragstypen. Band III: Computerverträge, Kreditkartenverträge sowie sonstige moderne Vertragstypen*. Munich: Beck.

—— (1993c) 'Sind Rügeverzichtsklauseln in Just-in-time-Verträgen AGB-rechtlich wirksam?' in Michael Martinek, Günther Jahr and Elmar Wadle (eds) *Festschrift für Günther Jahr: Vestigia Juris*. Tübingen: Mohr Siebeck, 305–38.

—— (1997) 'Vom Handelsvertreterrecht zum Recht der Vertriebssysteme' *Zeitschrift für das gesamte Handelsrecht und Wirtschaftsrecht* 161, 67–101.

—— (2001) 'Franchising 2000: Standortbestimmung und Zukunftsperspektiven des Franchisevertriebs' in Dieter Ahlert (ed) *Handbuch Franchising und Co-operation: Das Management kooperativer Unternehmensnetzwerke* Neuwied: Luchterhand, 327–38.

—— and Semler, Franz-Jörg (eds) (1996) *Handbuch des Vertriebsrechts*. Munich: Beck.

MAYER, HORST, KRAM, ANGELO and PATKOS, BIANCA (1998) *Das virtuelle Unternehmen: Eine neue Rechtsform?* Dresden: Dresdner Forum für Revision und Steuerlehre.

MAYER-MALY, THEO (1978) 'Das Rechtsverhältnis zwischen Arbeitnehmern (bei traditioneller Einzelarbeit)' in Theodor Tomandl (ed) *Innerbetriebliche Arbeitnehmerkonflikte aus rechtlicher Sicht*. Vienna: Braumüller, 59–73.

—— (1999) 'Wiederkehr des schuldrechtlichen Typenzwangs?' in Volker Beuthien, Maximilian Fuchs and Herbert Roth (eds) *Festschrift für Dieter Medicus*. Cologne: Heymanns, 383–85.

MAYNTZ, RENATE (1993) 'Modernization and the Logic of Interorganizational Networks' in John Child, Michel Crozier and Renate Mayntz (eds) *Societal Change Between Market and Organization*. Aldershot: Ashgate, 3–18.

MEISSINGER, HERMANN (1954) *Treupflicht im Arbeitsrecht I*. Wiesbaden: Forkel.

MENDES, RODRIGO (2002) *'In medio stat virtus': Außenhaftung von virtuellen Unternehmen*. Magisterthesis. Frankfurt: Fachbereich Rechtswissenschaft.

MERZ, AXEL (1992) *Qualitätssicherungsvereinbarungen: Zulieferverträge, Vertragstypologie, Risikoverteilung, AGB-Kontrolle*. Cologne: Heymanns.

MESSNER, DIRK (1994) 'Fallstricke und Grenzen der Netzwerksteuerung' *Zeitschrift für kritische Sozialwissenschaft* 24, 563–96.

—— (1997a) 'Netzwerktheorien: Die Suche nach Ursachen und Auswegen aus der Krise staatlicher Steuerungsfähigkeit' in Elmar Altvater, Achim Brunnengräber, Markus Haake and Heike Walk (eds) *Vernetzt und Verstrickt: Nicht-Regierungs-Organisationen als gesellschaftliche Produktivkraft*. Münster: Westfälisches Dampfboot, 26–64.

—— (1997b) *The Network Society: Economic Development and International Competitiveness as Problems of Social Governance*. London: Frank Cass.

MIGGE, LUDGER MICHAEL (1991) 'Deutschland: Praktische Überlegungen bei der Vorbereitung von Qualitätssicherungsvereinbarungen' *Produkthaftpflicht International* 10, Part 1: 186–96, Part 2: 198–203.

MILES, RAYMOND E, Snow, Charles C and Miles, Grant (2000) 'The future.org' *Long Range Planning* 33, 300–21.

MÖLLER, COSIMA (2003) 'Der Franchisevertrag im Bürgerlichen Recht: Ein Beitrag zur Diskussion über die Rechtsnatur des Franchisevertrages' *Archiv für die civilistische Praxis* 203, 319–47.

MÖSCHEL, WERNHARD (1986) 'Dogmatische Strukturen des bargeldlosen Zahlungsverkehrs' *Archiv für die civilistische Praxis* 186, 211–36.

MÜLLER-GRAFF, PETER-CHRISTIAN (1988) 'Franchising: A Case of Long-Term Contracts' *Journal of Institutional and Theoretical Economics* 144, 122–44.

MÜNCHENER KOMMENTAR: KURT REBMANN, FRANZ JÜRGEN SÄCKER and ROLAND RIXECKER (ed) *Münchener Kommentar zum Bürgerlichen Gesetzbuch:*

(2001) *Allgemeiner Teil: §§ 1–240*. Vol 1. 4th edn, Munich: Beck.

(2003) *Schuldrecht Allgemeiner Teil. §§ 241–432*. Vol 2a. 4th edn, Munich: Beck.

(1997) *Schuldrecht. Besonderer Teil III. §§ 705–853*. Vol 5. 3rd edn, Munich: Beck.

MÜTHLEIN, THOMAS (1995) 'Virtuelle Unternehmen: Unternehmen mit einem rechtssicheren Rückgrat' *HMD – Praxis der Wirtschaftsinformatik* 185, 68–77.

NAGEL, BERNHARD (1988) 'Der Lieferant On Line: Unternehmensrechtliche Probleme der Just-in-time-Produktion am Beispiel der Automobilindustrie' *Der Betrieb* 41, 2291–94.

—— (1991) 'Schuldrechtliche Probleme bei Just-in-Time-Lieferbeziehungen' *Der Betrieb* 44, 319–27.

—— (1995) 'Gewährleistung und Produkthaftung im internationalen Produktionsverbund' *Der Betrieb* 48, 2581–90.

——, Riess, Birgit and Theis, Gisela (1989) 'Der faktische Just-in-Time-Konzern: Unternehmensübergreifende Rationalisierungskonzepte und Konzernrecht am Beispiel der Automobilindustrie' *Der Betrieb* 42, 1505–11.

—— (1990) *Just-in-Time-Strategien: Arbeitsbeziehungen, Gestaltungspotentiale, Mitbestimmung*. Düsseldorf: Hans-Böckler-Stiftung.

NEUBERGER, OSWALD (2000) 'Dilemmata und Paradoxa im Managementprozess' in Georg Schreyögg (ed) *Funktionswandel im Management: Wege jenseits der Ordnung*. Berlin: Duncker & Humblot, 173–219.

NICKLISCH, FRITZ (2000) 'Vernetzte Projektverträge und vernetzte Streitbeilegungsverfahren' *Betriebs Berater* 55, 2166–69.

—— (ed) (1987) *Der komplexe Langzeitvertrag: Strukturen und internationale Schiedsgerichtsbarkeit*. Heidelberg: Müller.

NIEBLING, JÜRGEN (1995) 'Simultaneous Engineering aus Sicht des beratenden Juristen' *Wirtschaftsrechtliche Beratung* 15, 505–06.

NÖCKER, KLAUS (1972) 'Finanzierter Abzahlungskauf und Betrugstatbestand' *Der Betrieb* 25, 370–73.

NOHRIA, NITIN and ECCLES, ROBERT (1992) *Networks and Organizations: Structure, Form, and Action*. Boston: Harvard Business School Press.

NOLL, JÜRGEN (2002) *Who Should Be Liable in a Virtual Enterprise Network*. www.pages.ssrn.com.

NORTON, SETH W (1988) 'An Empirical Look at Franchising as an Organizational Form' *The Journal of Business* 61, 197–218.

OECHSLER, JÜRGEN (1997a) 'Die Anwendung des Konzernrechts auf Austauschverträge mit organisationsrechtlichem Bezug' *Zeitschrift für Gesellschafts- und Unternehmensrecht* 26, 464–92.

—— (1997b) *Gerechtigkeit im modernen Austauschvertrag: Die theoretischen Grundlagen der Vertragsgerechtigkeit und ihr praktischer Einfluss auf Auslegung, Ergänzung und Inhaltskontrolle des Vertrages*. Tübingen: Mohr Siebeck.

OETKER, HARTMUT (1994) *Das Dauerschuldverhältnis und seine Beendigung: Bestandsaufnahme und kritische Würdigung einer tradierten Figur der Schuldrechtsdogmatik*. Tübingen: Mohr Siebeck.

OLBRICH, THOMAS J. (1994) 'Das Modell der "Virtuellen Unternehmen"' *Information Management* 4, 28–36.

ORTMANN, GÜNTHER (1999) 'Innovation als Paradoxieentfaltung: Eine Schlußbemerkung' in Dieter Sauer and Christa Lang (eds) *Paradoxien der Innovation: Perspektiven sozialwissenschaftlicher Innovationsforschung*. Frankfurt: Campus, 249–59.

—— (2003) *Organisation und Welterschließung*. Opladen: Westdeutscher Verlag.

—— and Sydow, Jörg (1999) 'Grenzmanagement in Unternehmensnetzwerken: Theoretische Zugänge' *Academy of Management Review* 59, 205–20.

OTT, CLAUS (1995) 'Contract Network in Distribution Systems' *Journal of Institutional and Theoretical Economics* 151, 212–17.

OTTO, PETER (1988) *Stellung der Bank bei der Finanzierung von Immobilienanlagen*. Berlin: Duncker & Humblot.

PALANDT, OTTO (2003) *Bürgerliches Gesetzbuch*. 62nd edn, Munich: Beck.

PASCHKE, MARIAN (1987) 'Außervertragliche Sozialbeziehungen: Eine Herausforderung der zivilrechtlichen Dogmatik' *Archiv für die civilistische Praxis* 187, 60–90.

—— (1988) 'Vertragsbindung ohne Konsens?' *Rechtstheorie* 19, 523–40.

—— (1991) *Das Dauerschuldverhältnis der Wohnraummiete: Grundfragen der privatautonomen Gestaltung des Wohnraummietverhältnisses*. Berlin: Duncker & Humblot.

PASDERSKI, EDGAR PAUL (1998) *Die Außenhaftung des Franchisegebers*. Aachen: Mainz.

PATERSON, JOHN and TEUBNER, GUNTHER (1998) 'Changing Maps: Empirical Legal Autopoiesis' *Social and Legal Studies* 7, 451–86.

PERROW, CHARLES (1986) *Complex Organizations*. 3rd edn, New York: Random House.

—— (1992) 'Small-firm Networks' in Nitin Nohria and Robert G Eccles (eds) *Networks and Organizations: Structure, Form and Action*. Boston: Harvard Business School Press, 445–70.

PFISTER, BERNHARD (1971) 'Der mehrseitige Austauschvertrag' *Juristenzeitung* 26, 284–86.

PICKER, EDUARD (1983) 'Positive Forderungsverletzungen und culpa in contrahendo: Zur Problematik der Haftungen "zwischen" Vertrag und Delikt' *Archiv für die civilistische Praxis* 183, 369–520.

—— (1987) 'Vertragliche und deliktische Schadenshaftung: Überlegungen zu einer Neustrukturierung der Haftungssysteme' *Juristenzeitung* 42, 1041–58.

—— (1999) 'Gutachterhaftung: Außervertragliche Einstandspflichten als innergesetzliche Rechtsfortbildung' in Volker Beuthien, Maximilian Fuchs and Herbert Roth (eds) *Festschrift für Dieter Medicus*. Cologne: Heymanns, 397–447.

PICOT, ARNOLD and REICHWALD, RALF (1994) 'Auflösung der Unternehmung? Vom Einfluß der Informations- und Kommunikationstechnik auf Organisationsstrukturen und Kooperationsformen' *Zeitschrift für Betriebswirtschaft* 56, 547–70.

——, —— and Wigand, Rolf T (1996) *Die grenzenlose Unternehmung: Information, Organisation und Management*. 4th edn, Wiesbaden: Gabler.

POHLMANN, MARKUS, APELT, MAJA, BUROH, KARSTEN and MARTENS, HENNING (1995) *Industrielle Netzwerke: Antagonistische Kooperation an der Schnittstelle Beschaffung-Zulieferung*. Munich: Hampp.

POWELL, WALTER (1990) 'Neither Market nor Hierarchy: Network Forms of Organization' *Research in Organizational Behavior* 12, 295–336.

PROVAN, KEITH G (2001) *Conceptualizing and Assessing Network Effectiveness: The Evaluation Perspective*. Lyon: European Group for Organizational Studies.

—— and Milward, H Brinton (1995) 'A Preliminary Theory of Interorganizational Network Effectiveness' *Administrative Science Quarterly* 40, 1–33.

RAISER, LUDWIG (1948) 'Der Gleichheitsgrundsatz im Privatrecht' *Zeitschrift für das gesamte Handels- und Wirtschaftsrecht* 111, 75–101.

—— (1964) 'Die Konzernbildung als Gegenstand rechts- und wirtschaftswissenschaftlicher Untersuchung' in Ludwig Raiser, Heinz Sauermann and Erich Schneider (eds) *Das Verhältnis der Wirtschaftswissenschaft zur Rechtswissenschaft, Soziologie und Statistik*. Berlin: Duncker & Humblot, 51–56.

RAISER, THOMAS (1999) *Das lebende Recht: Rechtssoziologie in Deutschland*. 3rd edn, Baden-Baden: Nomos.

RAMMERT, WERNER (1997) 'Innovation im Netz: Neue Zeiten für technische Innovationen' *Soziale Welt* 48, 397–416.

REHBINDER, ECKARD (1969) *Konzernaußenrecht und allgemeines Privatrecht: Eine rechtsvergleichende Untersuchung nach deutschem und amerikanischem Recht*. Bad Homburg: Gehlen.

—— (1997) 'Neues zum Durchgriff unter besonderer Berücksichtigung der höchstrichterlichen Rechtsprechung' in Heinz-Dieter Assmann (ed) *Wirtschafts- und Medienrecht in der offenen Demokratie: Freundesgabe für Friedrich Kübler*. Heidelberg: Müller, 493–514.

REICH, NORBERT (1995) 'Garantien unter Gemeinschaftsrecht' *Europäische Zeitschrift für Wirtschaftsrecht* 6, 71–77.

REIß, MICHAEL (1998) 'Mythos Netzwerkorganisation' *Zeitschrift Führung und Organisation* 4, 224–29.
RIESENHUBER, KARL (1997) *Die Rechtsbeziehungen zwischen Nebenparteien*. Berlin: Duncker & Humblot.
RISSE, JÖRG and LINDNER, NICOLA (1999) 'Haftung der Banken nach dem neuen Überweisungsrecht' *Betriebs Berater* 54, 2201–07.
ROHE, MATHIAS (1998) *Netzverträge: Rechtsprobleme komplexer Vertragsverbindungen*. Tübingen: Mohr Siebeck.
RÖHL, KLAUS (1987) 'Die strukturelle Differenz zwischen Individuum und Organisation oder Brauchen wir ein Sonderprivatrecht für Versicherungen und andere Organisationen?' in Marcus Lutter, Walter Oppenhoff, Otto Sandrock and Hanns Winkhaus (eds) *Festschrift für Ernst C. Stiefel*. Munich: Beck, 574–605.
RÖLLE, DANIEL and BLÄTTEL-MINK, BIRGIT (1998) 'Netzwerke in der Organisationssoziologie: Neuer Schlauch für alten Wein?' *Österreichische Zeitschrift für Soziologie* 23, 66–87.
ROTH, HERBERT (1989) 'Anmerkung zu OLG Karlsruhe' *Neue Zeitschrift für Verkehrsrecht* 2, 435–36.
RUBIN, PAUL H (1978) 'The Theory of the Firm and the Structure of the Franchise Contract' *Journal of Law and Economics* 21, 223–33.
RÜTHERS, BERND (1977) 'Probleme der Organisation des Weisungsrechts und der Haftung bei Gruppenarbeit' *Zeitschrift für Arbeitsrecht* 8, 1–46.
SABEL, CHARLES (1991) 'Moebius-Strip Organizations and Open Labor Markets: Some Consequences of the Reintegration of Conception and Execution in a Volatile Economy' in Pierre Bourdieu and James Coleman (eds) *Social Theory for a Changing Society*. Boulder: Westview Press, 23–54.
SANNWALD, RÜDIGER (1982) *Der Finanzierungsleasingvertrag über bewegliche Sachen mit Nichtkaufleuten*. Berlin: Duncker & Humblot.
SAPELLI, GIULIO (1990) 'A Historical Typology of Group Enterprises: The Debate on the Decline of "Popular Sovereignty"' in David Sugarman and Gunther Teubner (eds) *Regulating Corporate Groups in Europe*. Baden-Baden: Nomos, 193–216.
SAUER, DIETER and DÖHL, VOLKER (1994) *Kontrolle durch Autonomie*. Opladen: Westdeutscher Verlag.
—— and —— (1997) 'Die Auflösung des Unternehmens?' *Jahrbuch sozialwissenschaftliche Technikberichterstattung* 6, 19–76.
—— and Lang, Christa (eds) (1999) *Paradoxien der Innovation: Perspektiven sozialwissenschaftlicher Innovationsforschung*. Frankfurt: Campus.
SAXINGER, ANDREAS (1993) *Zulieferverträge im deutschen Recht: Zugleich eine Abhandlung zu den Besonderheiten langfristiger Schuldverhältnisse*. Baden-Baden: Nomos.
SCHÄFER, HANS-BERND and OTT, CLAUS (2000) *Lehrbuch der ökonomischen Analyse des Zivilrechts*. 3rd edn, Berlin: Springer.
SCHANZE, ERICH (1991) 'Symbiotic Contracts: Exploring Long-Term Agency Structures Between Contract and Corporation' in Christian Joerges (eds) *Franchising and the Law: Theoretical and Comparative Approaches in Europe and the United States*. Baden-Baden: Nomos, 67–103.

—— (1993) 'Symbiotic Arrangements' *Journal of Institutional and Theoretical Economics* 149, 691–97.

—— and Haunhorst, Karl Heinz (1995) 'Security of Tenure in Conventional and "Flexible" Employment Regimes: A Neo-Institutional Perspective' *European Journal of Law and Economics* 2, 179–97.

SCHARPF, FRITZ W (1991) 'Die Handlungsfähigkeit des Staates am Ende des Zwanzigsten Jahrhunderts' *Politische Vierteljahresschrift* 32, 621–34.

SCHIMANSKY, ANNIKA (2003) *Der Franchisevertrag nach deutschem und niederländischem Recht unter besonderer Berücksichtigung seines Netzcharakters und der Ansprüche bei Vertragsbeendigung*. Tübingen: Mohr Siebeck.

SCHLOTKE, HELMUT (1990) 'Vertikale Verknüpfungen von Unternehmen verschiedener Produktionsstufen durch Qualitätssicherungssysteme und Just-in-Time Lieferungen: Komplexe Langzeitverträge besonderer Art?' in Fritz Nicklisch (ed) *Verträge über Computertechnik in Forschung, Verwaltung, Wirtschaft und Technik*. Heidelberg: Müller, 267–77.

SCHLUEP, WALTER (2003) 'Zusammengesetzte Verträge: Vertragsverbindung oder Vertragsverwirrung' in Heinrich Honsell (ed) *Aktuelle Aspekte des Schuld- und Sachenrechts: Festschrift für Heinz Rey*. Schulthess: Zürich, 285–306.

SCHMID, MICHAEL J (1987) 'Die Hausordnung in Miethäusern' *Wohnungswirtschaft und Mietrecht* 40, 71–75.

SCHMIDT, DETLEF (1991) 'Qualitätssicherungsvereinbarungen und ihr rechtlicher Rahmen' *Neue Juristische Wochenschrift* 44, 144–52.

SCHMIDT, JÜRGEN (1987) '"Sonderverbindungen": Eine Problemskizze' in Günther Jahr (ed) *Gedächtnisschrift für Dietrich Schultz*. Cologne: Heymanns, 341–75.

SCHMIDT, KARSTEN (1988) 'Zur "Außenhaftung der Innengesellschaft": LG Konstanz, NJW 1987, 2521' *Juristische Schulung* 28, 444–47.

—— (1999) *Handelsrecht*. 5th edn, Cologne: Heymanns.

—— (2002) *Gesellschaftsrecht*. 4th edn, Cologne: Heymanns.

SCHNEIDER, UWE (1999) 'Pflichten und Haftung der erstbeauftragten Kreditinstitute bei grenzüberschreitenden Überweisungen: Auf dem Weg zu einem Sonderrecht für Kettenverträge' *Wertpapier Mitteilungen* 44, 2189–236.

SCHOLZ, CHRISTIAN (1994) 'Virtuelle Unternehmen: Faszination mit (rechtlichen) Folgen' *Jur-PC*, 2927–36.

SCHRÖTER, JÜRGEN (1987) 'Bankenhaftung im mehrgliedrigen Zahlungsverkehr' *Zeitschrift für das gesamte Handelsrecht und Wirtschaftsrecht* 151, 118–45.

SCHUHMANN, RALPH (1996) 'Die Verhandlung komplexer Vertragsverhältnisse unter dem Aspekt des AGB-Gesetzes' *Betriebs Berater* 51, 2473–76.

SCHULZE-OSTERLOH, JOACHIM (1972) *Das Prinzip der gesamthänderischen Bindung*. Munich: Beck.

SCHULZ-SCHAEFFER, INGO, JONAS, MICHAEL and MALSCH, THOMAS (1997) 'Innovation reziprok' *Jahrbuch Technik und Gesellschaft* 9, 91–127.

SCHÜRMANN, THOMAS (1994) *Haftung im mehrgliedrigen bargeldlosen Zahlungsverkehr*. Berlin: Duncker & Humblot.

SCHWARK, EBERHARD (1978) 'Zum Verhältnis von schuldrechtlichen Vertragstypen und Vertragswirklichkeit, insbesondere beim Werklieferungsvertrag' *Rechtstheorie* 9, 73–106.

—— (1987) '100 Bände BGHZ: Bank und Wertpapierrecht' *Zeitschrift für das gesamte Handelsrecht und Wirtschaftsrecht* 151, 325–54.

SCIARRA, SILVANA (1991) 'Franchising and Contract of Employment: Notes on a Still Impossible Assimilation' in Christian Joerges (ed) *Franchising and the Law: Theoretical and Comparative Approaches in Europe and the United States*. Baden-Baden: Nomos, 239–66.

SELZNICK, PHILIP (1969) *Law, Society and Industrial Justice*. New York: Russell Sage.

—— (1992) *The Moral Commonwealth: Social Theory and the Promise of Community*. Berkeley: University of California Press.

SEMLINGER, KLAUS (1993) 'Effizienz und Autonomie in Zulieferungsnetzwerken: Zum strategischen Gehalt von Kooperation' in Wolfgang H Staehle and Jörg Sydow (eds) *Managementforschung 3*. Berlin: de Gruyter, 309–54.

—— (2000) 'Kooperation und Konkurrenz in japanischen Netzwerkbeziehungen' in Jörg Sydow and Arnold Windeler (eds) *Steuerung von Netzwerken*. Opladen: Westdeutscher Verlag, 126–55.

SIEBERT, WOLFGANG (1935) *Das Arbeitsverhältnis in der Ordnung der nationalen Arbeit*. Hamburg: Hanseatische Verlagsanstalt

SIMON, FRITZ B (1997) *Die Kunst, nicht zu lernen: Und andere Paradoxien in Psychotherapie, Management, Politik*. Heidelberg: Carl-Auer-Systeme.

SKAUPY, WALTHER (1995) *Franchising: Handbuch für die Betriebs- und Rechtspraxis*. 2nd edn, Munich: Vahlen.

SMELSER, NEIL J and SWEDBERG, RICHARD (eds) (1994) *The Handbook of Economic Sociology*. Princeton: Princeton University Press.

SNOW, CHARLES C, MILES, RAYMOND E AND COLEMAN, HJ (1992) 'Managing 21st Century Network Organizations' *Organizational Dynamics* 21, 5–20.

SOERGEL, HANS TH (1991) *Bürgerliches Gesetzbuch mit Einführungsgesetzen und Nebengesetzen: Kohlhammer-Kommentar*. 12th edn, Stuttgart: Kohlhammer.

SPECHT, DIETER and KAHLMANN, JOACHIM (2000) 'Regelung kooperativer Tätigkeit im virtuellen Unternehmen' *Zeitschrift für Betriebswirtschaft* 70. *Ergänzungsheft* 2, 55–73.

SPECHT, GÜNTER (1995) 'Schnittstellenmanagement' in Bruno Tietz, Richard Köhler and Joachim Zentes (eds) *Handwörterbuch des Marketing*. Stuttgart: Schaeffer-Poeschel, 2265–75.

SPENCER BROWN, GEORGE (1972) *Laws of Form*. New York: Julian Press.

STAUDINGER, JULIUS VON (1995) *Kommentar zum Bürgerlichen Gesetzbuch: Mit Einführungsgesetz und Nebengesetzen. §§ 652–704*. 13th edn, Berlin: de Gruyter.

—— (2001) *Kommentar zum Bürgerlichen Gesetzbuch: Mit Einführungsgesetz und Nebengesetzen. §§ 164–240*. 13th edn, Berlin: de Gruyter.

STECKLER, BRUNHILDE (1996) *Die rechtlichen Risiken der Just-in-Time-Produktion*. Stuttgart: Boorberg.

STEINDORFF, ERNST (1973) 'Politik des Gesetzes als Auslegungsmaßstab im Wirtschaftsrecht' in Gotthard Paulus, Uwe Diederichsen and Claus-Wilhelm Canaris (eds) *Festschrift für Karl Larenz*. Munich: Beck, 217–44.

STEINMANN, CHRISTINA (1992) *Qualitätssicherungsvereinbarungen zwischen Endproduktherstellern und Zulieferern*. Heidelberg: Decker.

—— (1993) 'Abdingbarkeit der Wareneingangskontrolle in Qualitätssicherungsvereinbarungen' *Betriebs Berater* 48, 873–79.

STICHWEH, RUDOLF (2000) 'Adresse und Lokalisierung in einem globalen Kommunikationssystem' in Rudolf Stichweh *Die Weltgesellschaft: Soziologische Analysen*. Frankfurt: Suhrkamp, 220–31.

—— (2001) 'Strukturen der Weltgesellschaft' *Frankfurter Rundschau 13.3.2000.*

STOFFELS, MARKUS (2001) *Gesetzlich nicht geregelte Schuldverträge: Rechtsfindung und Inhaltskontrolle*. Tübingen: Mohr Siebeck.

STUMPF, HERBERT and JALETZKE, MATTHIAS (1997) *Der Vertragshändlervertrag*. 3rd edn, Heidelberg: Recht und Wirtschaft.

SUBER, PETER (1990) *The Paradox of Self-Amendment: A Study of Logic, Law, Omnipotence and Change*. New York: Lang. http://www.earlham.edu/~peters/writing/psa/index.htm.

SUGARMAN, DAVID and TEUBNER, GUNTHER (1990) *Regulating Corporate Groups in Europe*. Baden-Baden: Nomos.

SUPIOT, ALAIN (2000) 'Les nouveaux visages de la subordination' *Droit Social* 63, 131–45.

—— (2001) *Beyond Employment: Changes in Work and the Future of Labour Law in Europe*. New York: Oxford University Press.

SYDOW, JÖRG (1992) *Strategische Netzwerke: Evolution und Organisation*. Wiesbaden: Gabler.

—— (1999) 'Management von Netzwerkorganisationen: Zum Stand der Forschung' in Jörg Sydow (ed) *Management von Netzwerkorganisationen*. Wiesbaden: Westdeutscher Verlag, 293–314.

—— (2001) 'Zum Verhältnis von Netzwerken und Konzernen' in Günther Ortmann and Jörg Sydow (eds) *Strategie und Strukturation*. Wiesbaden: Gabler, 271–98.

—— and Kloyer, Martin (1995) 'Managementpraktiken in Franchisingnetzwerken' *Arbeitspapiere Band 171*. Wuppertal: Fachbereich Wirtschaftswissenschaften Universität Wuppertal.

—— and Windeler, Arnold (1998) 'Organizing and Evaluating Interfirm Networks' *Organization Science 9. Special Issue: Managing Partnership and Strategic Alliances*, 265–84.

—— and —— (2000) 'Steuerung von und in Netzwerken' in Jörg Sydow and Arnold Windeler (eds) *Steuerung von Netzwerken: Konzepte und Praktiken*. Opladen: Westdeutscher Verlag, 1–24.

——, ——, Krebs, Michael, Loose, Achim and Well, Bennet von (1995) *Organisation von Netzwerken: Strukturationstheoretische Analysen der Vermittlungspraxis in Versicherungsnetzwerken*. Opladen: Westdeutscher Verlag.

TACKE, VERONIKA (2000) 'Netzwerk und Adresse' *Soziale Systeme* 6, 291–320.

TEUBNER, GUNTHER (1980) 'Die Generalklausel von "Treu und Glauben"' in Rudolf Wassermann (ed) *Alternativkommentar zum Bürgerlichen Gesetzbuch. Band 2. Allgemeines Schuldrecht*. Neuwied: Luchterhand, 32–91.

—— (1988) 'Enterprise Corporatism: New Industrial Policy and the "Essence" of the Legal Person' *American Journal of Comparative Law* 36, 401–26.

—— (1990a) 'Die "Politik des Gesetzes" im Recht der Konzernhaftung: Plädoyer für einen sektoralen Konzerndurchgriff' in Jürgen F Baur, Klaus J Hopt and K P Mailänder (eds) *Festschrift für Ernst Steindorff*. Berlin: de Gruyter, 261–79.

—— (1990b) 'Unitas Multiplex: Problems of Governance in Group Enterprises' in Gunther Teubner and David Sugarman (eds) *Regulating Corporate Groups in Europe*. Baden-Baden: Nomos, 67–104.

—— (1991) 'Beyond Contract and Organization? External Liability of Franchising Systems in German Law' in Christian Joerges (ed) *Franchising and the Law: Theoretical and Comparative Approaches in Europe and the United States*, Baden-Baden: Nomos, 105–32.

—— (1992) 'Piercing the Contractual Veil? The Social Responsibility of Contractual Networks' in Thomas Wilhelmsson (ed) *Perspectives of Critical Contract*. London: Dartsmouth, 211–38.

—— (1993a) *Law as an Autopoietic System*. London: Blackwells.

—— (1993b) 'The Many-Headed Hydra:Networks as Higher-Order Collective Actors' in Joseph McCahery, Sol Picciotto and Colin Scott (eds) *Corporate Control and Accountability: Changing Structures and the Dynamics of Regulation*, Oxford: Oxford University Press, 41–60.

—— (1994) 'The Invisible Cupola: From Causal to Collective Attribution in Ecological Liability' in Gunther Teubner, Lindsay Farmer and Declan Murphy (eds) *Environmental Law and Ecological Responsibility: The Concept and Practice of Ecological Self-Organization*. Chichester: Wiley, 17–47.

—— (2002a) 'Hybrid Laws: Constitutionalizing Private Governance Networks' in Robert Kagan and Kenneth Winston (eds) *Legality and Community: On the Intellectual Legacy of Philip Selznick*. Berkeley: Berkeley Public Policy Press, 311–31.

—— (2002b) 'Idiosyncratic Production Regimes: Co-evolution of Economic and Legal Institutions in the Varieties of Capitalism' in John Ziman (ed) *The Evolution of Cultural Entities: Proceedings of the British Academy*. Oxford: Oxford University Press, 161–82.

—— (2003) 'Expertise as Social Institution: Internalising Third Parties into the Contract' in David Campbell, Hugh Collins and John Wightman (eds) *Implicit Dimensions of Contract: Discrete, Relational and Network Contracts*. Oxford: Hart, 333–64.

THEISEN, MANUEL RENÉ (2000) *Der Konzern: Betriebswirtschaftliche und rechtliche Grundlagen der Konzernunternehmung*. Stuttgart: Schaeffer-Poeschel.

ULLMANN, EIKE (1994) 'Die Verwendung von Marke, Geschäftsbezeichnung und Firma im geschäftlichen Verkehr, insbesondere des Franchising' *Neue Juristische Wochenschrift* 47, 1255–62.

ULMER, PETER (1969) *Der Vertragshändler: Tatsachen und Rechtsfragen kaufmännischer Geschäftsbesorgung beim Absatz von Marktwaren*. Munich: Beck.

—— (1975) 'Kündigungsschranken im Handels- und Gesellschaftsrecht: Zum Einfluß der Treupflicht auf die einseitige Vertragsbeendigung' in Wolfgang Hefermehl and Hans Carl Nipperdey (eds) *Festschrift für Philip Möhring*. Munich: Beck, 295–317.

UWER, DIRK and UWER, JÖRG (1997) 'Rechtsfragen der Regulierung von Hersteller-Zulieferer-Beziehungen in der Automobilindustrie' *Deutsche Zeitschrift für Wirtschaftsrecht* 7, 48–55.

VAHRENKAMP, RICHARD (1994) *Produktions- und Logistikmanagement*. Munich: Oldenbourg.

VANBERG, VIKTOR (1986) 'Spontaneous Market Order and Social Rules: A Critical Examination of FA Hayek's Theory of Cultural Evolution' *Economics and Philosophy* 2, 75–100.

VOLLKOMMER, MAX (1973) 'Der Schutz des Käufers beim B-Geschäft des "finanzierten Abzahlungskaufs"' in Gotthard Paulus, Uwe Diederichsen and Claus-Wilhelm Canaris (eds) *Festschrift für Karl Larenz*. Munich: Beck, 703–16.

—— (1992) 'Zum Rückforderungsdurchgriff bei "verbundenen Geschäften"' in Walter Gerhardt (ed) *Festschrift für Franz Merz*. Cologne: Verlag Kommunikationsforum, 595–610.

VOM DORP, EBERHARD (1995) 'Haftung des Franchisegebers aus c.i.c.: Tendenzwende zur Rentabilitätsgarantie?' *Wirtschaftsrechtliche Beratung* 15, 285–86.

VRIES, MICHAEL DE (1998) 'Das virtuelle Unternehmen: Formentheoretische Überlegungen zu Grenzen eines grenzenlosen Konzepts' in Andreas Brill and Michael de Vries (eds) *Virtuelle Wirtschaft*. Opladen: Westdeutscher Verlag, 54–86.

WACKERBARTH, ULRICH (2000) 'Die Haftung für zwischengeschaltete Banken im mehrgliedrigen Überweisungsverkehr' *Zeitschrift für Wirtschaftsrecht* 21, 1187–96.

WAGNER, JOACHIM (1992) '"Just-in-Time"-Produktion und betriebsverfassungsrechtliche Mitbestimmmung: Miteinander vereinbar oder "inkompatibel"?' *Demokratie und Recht* 19, 63–75.

WALZ, RAINER (ed) (1983) *Sozialwissenschaften im Zivilrecht*. Neuwied: Luchterhand.

WATZLAWICK, PAUL, BEAVIN, JANET H and JACKSON, DON D (1967) *Menschliche Kommunikation: Formen, Störungen, Paradoxien*. Bern: Huber.

WEBER, HANSJÖRG (1983) '"Franchising": Ein neuer Vertragstyp im Handelsrecht' *Juristische Arbeitsblätter* 15, 347–53.

WEBER, MAX (1978) *Economy and Society*. Berkeley: University of California Press.

WEICK, KARL E (1985) *Der Prozeß des Organisierens*. Frankfurt: Suhrkamp.

WELL, BENNET VON (2001) *Standardisierung und Individualisierung von Dienstleistungen*. Wiesbaden: Gabler.

WELLENHOFER-KLEIN, MARINA (1997) 'Just-in-time Production und betriebsverfassungsrechtliche Mitbestimmung' *Der Betrieb* 50, 978–82.

—— (1999) *Zulieferverträge im Privat- und Wirtschaftsrecht*. Munich: Beck.

WESTPHALEN, FRIEDRICH GRAF VON (1993) 'Qualitätssicherungsvereinbarungen: Prüfstein für AGB-Klauseln und Versicherungsschutz' *Computer und Recht* 9, 65–73.

—— (1997) 'Deutschland: Optimale Vertragsgestaltung im Verhältnis Endhersteller/Zulieferer bei grenzüberschreitenden Lieferbeziehungen' *Produkthaftpflicht International* 16, 2–9.

—— and Bauer, Carl-Otto (1993) *Just-in-Time-Lieferungen und Qualitätssicherungsvereinbarungen*. Cologne: Kommunikationsforum Recht, Wirtschaft, Steuern.

WEYER, FRIEDHELM (1972) 'Mietvertrag und Schutzwirkungen zugunsten Dritter in der Rechtsprechung des Bundesgerichtshofs' *Betriebs Berater* 27, 339–42.

WEYER, JOHANNES (2000) 'Zum Stand der Netzwerkforschung in den Sozialwissenschaften' in Johannes Weyer (ed) *Soziale Netzwerke: Konzepte und Methoden der sozialwissenschaftlichen Netzwerkforschung*. Munich: Oldenbourg, 1–34.

—— (ed) (2000) *Soziale Netzwerke: Konzepte und Methoden der sozialwissenschaftlichen Netzwerkforschung*. Munich: Oldenbourg.

WHITE, HARRISON C (1993) 'Markets, Networks and Control' in Siegwart M Lindenberg and Hein Schreuder (eds) *Interdisciplinary Perspectives on Organization Studies*. Oxford: Pergamon, 223–39.

WIEDEMANN, HERBERT and SCHULTZ, OLIVER (1999) 'Grenzen der Bindung bei langfristigen Kooperationen' *Zeitschrift für Wirtschaftsrecht* 20, 1–12.

WIELSCH, DAN (2000) *Freiheit und Funktion: Zur Struktur- und Theoriegeschichte des Rechts der Wirtschaftsgesellschaft*. Baden-Baden: Nomos.

WIETHÖLTER, RUDOLF (1988) 'Zum Fortbildungsrecht der (richterlichen) Rechtsfortbildung: Fragen eines lesenden Recht-Fertigungslehrers' *Kritische Vierteljahreszeitschrift für Gesetzgebung und Rechtswissenschaft* 3, 1–28.

WILDEMANN, HORST (1990) *Das Just-in-Time-Konzept: Produktion und Zulieferung auf Abruf*. Munich: Transfer-Centrum-Verlag.

—— (1993) *Entwicklungsstrategien für Zulieferunternehmen: Forschungsbericht*. Munich: Transfer-Centrum.

WILLIAMSON, OLIVER (1985) *The Economic Institutions of Capitalism: Firms, Markets, Relational Contracting*. New York: Free Press.

—— (1991a) 'Comparative Economic Organization: The Analysis of Discrete Structural Alternatives' *Administrative Science Quarterly* 36, 269–96.

—— (1991b) 'Strategizing, Economizing, and Economic Organization' *Strategic Management Journal* 12, 75–94.

—— (1993) 'Calculativeness, Trust, and Economic Organization' *Journal of Law and Economics* 36, 453–86.

—— (1996) *The Mechanisms of Governance*. Oxford: Oxford University Press.

WILLKE, HELMUT (1992) *Ironie des Staates: Grundlinien einer Staatstheorie polyzentrischer Gesellschaften*. Frankfurt: Suhrkamp.

—— (1997) *Supervision des Staates*. Frankfurt: Suhrkamp.

WINDBICHLER, CHRISTINE (1998) 'Neue Vertriebsformen und ihr Einfluss auf das Kaufrecht' *Archiv für die civilistische Praxis* 198, 261–86.

WINDELER, ARNOLD (2001) *Unternehmungsnetzwerke: Konstitution und Strukturation*. Wiesbaden: Westdeutscher Verlag.

WINDOLF, PAUL and BEYER, JÜRGEN (1996) 'Cooperative Capitalism: Corporate Networks in Britain and Germany' *British Journal of Sociology* 47/2, 205–31.

WOLF, ERNST (1973) 'Grundlagen des Gemeinschaftsrechts' *Archiv für die civilistische Praxis* 173, 97–123.

—— (1978) *Lehrbuch des Schuldrechts*. Cologne: Heymanns.

WOLF, MANFRED and UNGEHEUER, CHRISTINA (1994) 'Vertragsrechtliche Probleme des Franchising' *Betriebs Berater* 49, 1027–33.

WÜRDINGER, HANS (1934) *Theorie der schlichten Interessengemeinschaften*. Stuttgart: Enke.

WÜST, GÜNTHER (1958) *Die Interessengemeinschaft: Ein Ordnungsprinzip des Privatrechts*. Frankfurt: Metzner.

—— (1985) 'Die Gemeinsamkeit der Interessen' *Juristenzeitung* 23, 1077–81.

ZIRKEL, HERBERT (1990) 'Das Verhältnis zwischen Zulieferer und Assembler: Eine Vertragsart sui generis?' *Neue Juristische Wochenschrift* 43, 345–51.

ZUMBANSEN, PEER (2000) *Ordnungsmuster im modernen Wohlfahrtsstaat: Lernerfahrungen zwischen Staat, Gesellschaft und Vertrag*. Baden-Baden: Nomos.

ZWECKER, KAI-THORSTEN (1999) 'Franchising als symbiotischer Vertrag: Beziehungen zwischen Gesellschaftsrecht und Franchising' *Juristische Arbeitsblätter* 31, 159–64.

Index

www.ingramcontent.com/pod-product-compliance
Ingram Content Group UK Ltd.
Pitfield, Milton Keynes, MK11 3LW, UK
UKHW020242290926
15470UKWH00002B/680

9 781849 461740